...of architecture, environment, and visual culture. The series looks at thematics in our age of globalization that are shaping the built environment in unexpected yet radically significant ways.

—at extremes

Ulrich Beck, in "Risk Society's Cosmopolitan Moment" suggests that being at risk is the human condition at the beginning of the twenty-first century. While risk produces inequality and destabilization, he argues, it can be the catalyst for the construction of new institutions. The term extreme is defined as outermost, utmost, farthest, last or frontier. *Bracket [at Extremes]* seeks to understand what new spatial orders emerge in this liminal space of risks and extremes. How might it be leveraged as an opportunity for invention? What are the limits of wilderness and control, of the natural and artificial, the real and the virtual? What new landscapes, networks, and urban models might emerge in the wake of destabilized economic, social and environmental conditions?

bracket — at extremes — almanac 3

editors —
Maya Przybylski
Lola Sheppard

editorial board —
Julien de Smedt
Keller Easterling
Michael Hensel
Alessandra Ponte
François Roche
Mark Wigley

collaborators —
InfraNet Lab
www.infranetlab.org
Archinect
www.archinect.com

sponsor —
Graham Foundation
for Advanced Studies
in the Fine Arts
www.grahamfoundation.org

designer —
Thumb with Celine Gordon
and Camille Sacha Salvador
www.thumbprojects.com

published by —
Actar
Barcelona — New York
info@actar.com
www.actar.com

distributed by —
ActarD
Barcelona — New York
www.actar-d.com

Roca i Batlle 2
E-08023 Barcelona
T +34 93 417 49 93
F +34 93 418 67 07
salesbarcelona@actar.com

151 Grand Street, 5th floor
New York, NY 10013, USA
T +1 212 966 2207
F +1 212 966 2214
salesnewyork@actar.com

isbn —
978-0-9893317-6-0

Cataloging-in-Publication for this book is available from the Library of Congress, Washington D.C., USA.

Printed and bound in China.

Bracket At Extremes is set in AG Old Face, Dolly, and Whiteout, a typeface made for this publication.

Bracket
1. An overhanging member that projects from a structure and is usually designed to support a vertical load or to strengthen an angle
2. A fixture (as for holding a lamp) projecting from a wall or column
3. A. One of a pair of marks [ ] used in writing and printing to enclose matter or in mathematics and logic as signs of aggregation; B. One of the pair of marks < > used to enclose matter; C. Parenthesis
4. A section of a continuously numbered or graded series (as age ranges or income levels)
5. A pairing of opponents in an elimination tournament
[from Merriam-Webster]

We would like to acknowledge the contributions,
energy, dialogue and support of the following
people and institutions in the sphere of Archinect
and InfraNet Lab: Paul Petrunia, Geoff Manaugh,
David Gissen, Neeraj Bhatia, Mason White,
Callifornia College of Art, University of Waterloo,
University of Toronto, and Rice University. At the
Graham Foundation we would like to thank Sarah
Herda, Carolyn Kelly, and Stephanie Whitlock.
At Actar, we would like to thank Ramon Prat and
Ricardo Devesa for their continued support of
Bracket. At Thumb, we would like to thank Jessica
Young and Luke Bulman for their vision and
ongoing commitment in shaping the identity
of Bracket.

bracket — at extremes — almanac 3

IMBALANCE AND UNPREDICTABILITY AS A PRODUCTIVE PRACTICE

Maya Przybylski + Lola Sheppard

Examining the notion of extremes takes one away from a centre point, characterized by its predictability, balance and familiarity, and, instead, moves one towards a condition where unpredictability, disequilibrium and strangeness become the new normal. The way in which we define the familiar centre and its complimentary, capricious extreme and their respective potentials for design intervention and innovation is the primary investigation presented in this volume.

The condition of extremes suggests a tipping point; a moment in which a system shifts from one state to another, often unpredictable state. In many cases, the condition of extreme arises from a singular force exerting its impact on a region, to the detriment of other modes of inhabitation. As such, the conditions of extremes demands new tropes: new models of practice, new typologies of buildings, infrastructure and landscapes, and new pairings of program or infrastructure. The question remains: what is the role of architecture or infrastructure in such contexts? to redress? to mitigate? to capitalize on new opportunities?

Key to the understanding the implications of extremes is the relationship that it has to risk: the further we move away from a state of equilibrium, the more volatile the situation becomes, the more exposure we have to danger and loss, the more risk we take on. Do the risk and reward models familiar on the trading floors of global financial markets and real estate speculation projects hold up in design disciplines? How can risk and extreme circumstances be leveraged as a new, productive model for architecture; a model emphasizing speculation as a way to test scenarios, outcomes and tools?

Ulrich Beck, in *Risk Society*, argues that: "being at risk is the way of being and ruling in the world of modernity... global risk is the human condition at the beginning of the twenty-first century."[1] Until now, the developed world has largely been able to successfully displace the economic, environmental and political impact of its development to other nations and peoples, or other groups and stakeholders within their own nations, rendering the risk invisible. However with the financial crisis of 2008, and the increasingly tangible impacts of climate change, complete displacement of risk is no longer possible. The distant other is becoming inclusive not through mobility, but through shared risks, Beck argues. For one group or region to achieve seeming stability, another will likely lose it, given the voracious nature of the capitalist system, and its environmental costs. Beck thus asks: "is there an enlightenment function and a cosmopolitan moment of world risk society? What are the opportunities of climate change and the financial crisis and what form do they take?"

The projects presented in [*at Extremes*] pose questions, offer alternative narratives and new realities in which people, culture and ecologies adapt to conditions of imbalance, unpredictability and strangeness. These speculations tend to reject the generic strategies of risk mitigation, and rather, leverage the specificities of their context into unique and particular proposals.

In 'Pushing Frontiers,' a series of projects examines environmental extremes—whether outer space, the Arctic, sub-Saharan Africa, or the North American wilderness. These projects ask how architecture and design might grapple with vast territories in tactical and strategic ways, and what is architecture's role in occupying such frontiers? What tools and spatial typologies might enable a widened presence at such frontiers, and what are the impacts of this expanded presence? 'Tapping Resources' presents a suite of projects exploring environments and infrastructures just after a tipping point has been reached. As familiar spatial equations start to fail, what new opportunities are exposed and how can they be seized through design intervention? 'Advancing Tools and Materials' brings together a set of projects

---

1. Ulrich Beck, "Risk Society's Cosmopolitan Moment,"
Lecture presented at Harvard University, November 12th, 2008

Angels, 2006, by Gerry Judah. Mixed media and acrylic gesso on canvas.
Image courtesy of the artist.

speculating on how to make our widened presence more effective, through the introduction of new tools and technology, whether we look to colonize, revitalize, or, in some cases, simply record or document.

Two chapters in particular, 'Edging Demographics' and 'Stretching Frameworks,' look not to the environment, but towards shifts in population, policy, politics and economics as instigators of changed social and spatial orders. In speculating on new building and programmatic typologies, and in challenging traditional economic models, some of these projects might be read as projective archaeologies of current and future cities, and ways of life. Another version of extreme confronts not *where* we do things, but *how* we do things. 'Expanding Processes' highlights a collection of work that speculates on how operations and procedures may change in confronting limit states. Digital technologies, with focus on their processing and connective power, are key to some of this discussion. 'Hacking Ecologies' presents a series of projects examining how infrastructure and urbanism might enable life on increasingly unstable landscapes by affecting the very systems that create them. These projects are less about redressing landscapes to previous conditions, but rather, enabling more inclusive models of inhabitation in places previously or currently occupied.

Why the contemporary fascination with extremes? On the one hand, we are flooded, through the media, with a daily series of economic, environmental and social disasters. These situations test our sense of order, and in relation to design, challenge the question of what is the fine line between fiction and possible futures?

These scenarios challenge the viewer to revisit our contemporary biases and expectations. Extreme environments and conditions become a test of design's ability and ingenuity, begging the question: are there limits to the degree that we can reasonably engineer our environments in the future? And as our physical environments continue to change at ever faster rates, will notions of 'before' and 'after' states cease to be meaningful, but instead suggest that our environment is in a continuous, unfolding and ungraspable state of perpetual transformation?

Ulrich Beck suggests that our contemporary conditions of risk might initiate alternative models of governance by encouraging new networks of actors, and might give those typically marginalized a greater voice, by rendering material the impacts of our risk society. The collection of investigations in *Bracket [at Extremes]* similarly argues that a set of alternative spatial logics, actors, agents and networks are possible in our contemporary environments. By venturing away from a comfort of the known, new roles, territories and agencies for architecture and design are suggested. Not a lament for what has changed or been lost, the projects and essays collected here look lucidly but optimistically to these new conditions of risk and imbalance, and envision opportunities for invention.

pushing frontiers

ZERO ATMOSPHERE ARCHITECTURE

Jordan Geiger

Architects have in the past few years become understandably preoccupied with the condition of our planet. After all, Earth hosts us and our buildings; and it's getting less hospitable as our atmosphere heats up. We have asked deep questions concerning conceptions of nature, the roles technology plays in producing it, the way we think about atmosphere and how we construct, inhabit, acclimatize, archive, recreate, spatialize and otherwise process it. In theory, in material science, in the adoption of new parametric modeling software, architects have sought to rethink our formal, tectonic, and ontological relations to the air that buildings mediate and condition; to the atmosphere that imbues buildings and that buildings in turn produce. At its best, these efforts identify air itself as a commons, a public space that crosses from interior to exterior and in which architecture and its inhabitants volley between positions as subject and object. Environment now refers not merely to air or water, but to dynamic and synthetic relations between atmosphere, architecture and humans. Yet underlying most current work is an essential architectural focus on the sustenance and remediation of terrestrial air quality as produced, indoor and outdoor. Here is a formidable response to perceptions that the Earth's atmosphere is in imminent danger due to the last century's rapid production of greenhouse gases and its resultant warming of the globe.

But what about the other side of this coin: planning for loss, a life and an architecture in which Earth's atmosphere collapses? What comes of "zero atmosphere architecture"? Design for outer space has a short but intense history in its building culture and a long one in its philosophical and scientific roots, often predicated on speculations of Earth's eventual uninhabitability. That history entangles numerous strands of thought playing out on Earth today, including recurrent notions of cosmopolitanism and of a commons[1], as both public *space* and a public *discourse*. As space ships are a total integration of architecture with computer systems, constructions for outer space have been developed also as environments to test new fusions of architecture with human-computer interaction (HCI), literally in a vacuum. Free of any fixed context, inherent scale, or even orientation in a weightless environment, space ships are an evolving hybrid of architecture and HCI. These can be seen as portraits of interaction in high contrast, abstracted from so many earthly conditions that their every detail reveals what has been added as a reflection of cultural, social or ecological events back on the home planet. Spacecraft promote new ideas of shared space, of interface and human agency in the control of systems, of communications and digital media.

Ultimately, zero atmosphere architecture is an indicator of increasingly complex and converging dynamics at the global scale, and offers hints at how they can be engaged today as a field for design. To study zero atmosphere architecture is to reflect on its terrestrial counterpart in an era of large organizations that affect the built environment through planetary-scale technological, spatial and ecological reach; and to confront complex global changes with new working methods that involve writing missions, transferring technologies, and scaling to the body.

---

1. On how Garrett Hardin's seminal essay "The Tragedy of the Commons" has been variously used and abused since 1968, see David Harvey, "The Future of the Commons," *Radical History Review*, Winter 2011, p. 101-107. Harvey points out, for example, distinctions that have been overlooked between material/spatial commons versus discursive commons: "Cultural and intellectual commons are often not subject to the logic of scarcity and exclusionary uses of the sort that apply to most natural resources... We can all listen to the same radio broadcast or television program at the same time."

The Blue Marble, astronaut photograph, 1972. Courtesy of NASA Johnson Space Center.

1. Missions: Cosmopolitanisms versus an Atmospheric Commons

AS17-148-22727 or "The Blue Marble," the most commonly viewed image of Earth to date, was taken on December 7, 1972 by *Apollo 17* astronauts on their way to the moon. Noteworthy as much for its composition as for its history, the photograph captures one of the first mechanical images of the planet ever made, and does so with full illumination as the sun was behind Apollo at the time of the image's capture.

Apollo images poignantly epitomize both the ecological and scientific motives that accompanied the nationalist and territorial agendas of early space programs; as well as the shifts away from such motives in the NASA mission statement over the past ten years. In these shifts, a fraught global commons emerges in discourse and in the articulation of a public space, with the telematic relations between Mission Control and an airtight cabin literally constructing the space from the troposphere to the thermosphere, some 250,000 miles above us. Here is the formation and framing of an *atmospheric commons,* extending from the Earth's crust into orbit, an alternative social and spatial model to notions of cosmopolitanism that otherwise mark discussions of space as a global concern.[2]

Cosmopolitanism and the cosmopolitical appear today as recurrent yet equivocal and contested terms that variably join or break from polemics for a link between citizenship and the cosmos, a social paradigm for solidarity and notions of post-nationalism in Earth's lonely path as a single planet hosting intelligent life in space travel.[3] The word "cosmopolitanism" can be found in philosophy as far back as 412 B.C. with Diogenes of Sinope in ancient Greece. It is frequently understood in these roots and

2. Termed a "cosmopolitan turn" in Beck, Sznaider. "Unpacking cosmopolitanism for the social sciences: a research agenda" in *The British Journal of Sociology* Volume 57, Issue 1, (/doi/10.1111/bjos.2006.57.issue-1/issuetoc) pages 1–23 (March 2006), 1–23.
Within architectural discourse, see Jazairy, El Hadi. *New Geographies 4: Scales of the Earth* (Cambridge: Harvard University Press, 2011). This runs tandem to a

burgeoning new wave of publications in architectural theory speculating on a history of space travel as well. Most spectacular amongst these has been Nicholas de Monchaux. *Spacesuit: Fashioning Apollo* (Cambridge: The MIT Press, 2011)
3. Fuller, R. Buckminster. *Operating Manual for Spaceship Earth* (New York: E.P. Dutton & Co., 1963)

leading through Kant, most recently to Sociology in the work of Ulrich Beck. A recent genealogy for the "cosmopolitan" and the contrasting proposal for a "cosmopolitical" has been summarized as follows:

> A Stoic or a Kantian will call cosmopolitan anyone who is a "citizen of the cosmos" rather than (or before he or she is) a citizen of a particular state, an adherent of a particular religion, a member of a particular guild, profession, or family. Stengers intends her use of cosmopolitics to alter what it means "to belong" or "to pertain." She has reinvented the word by representing it as a composite of the strongest meaning of cosmos and the strongest meaning of politics precisely because the usual meaning of the word cosmopolite supposed a certain theory of science that is now disputed. For her, the strength of one element checks any dulling in the strength of the other. The presence of cosmos in cosmopolitics resists the tendency of politics to mean the give-and-take in an exclusive human club. The presence of politics in cosmopolitics resists the tendency of cosmos to mean a finite list of entities that must be taken into account. Cosmos protects against the premature closure of politics, and politics against the premature closure of cosmos.[4]

In these and other definitions, the cosmopolitical and the cosmopolitan are framed as expanded political and social statuses, extra-terrestrial or, as Stenger would have it, inter-spatial: citizenship mapped either to a limitlessly inclusive set of living beings or to the universe. Both of these, the public as *bodies* and as *spaces*, are intrinsically infinite and borderless in their externality. Yet that ambiguous spatiality already suggests what we may call an expanded, more *atmospheric* conception of space and society. Stengers' work in Science and Technology Studies may share some interests with Beck's efforts at describing risk society, but it reveals divergent presumptions — perhaps aspirations — about the feasibility and even desirability of a world society. In one text, Beck asks what are the opportunities to be found in climate change and in the global financial crisis,[5] a sort of silver lining for clouds of greenhouse gas. To objections that this represents a "mononaturalism," I would add that this and many other discussions remain defiantly planimetric — superficial — in their conception of citizenship's augmented space. As the following examples show, ours is now a *sectionally expanded notion of Earth*; while Beck contrasts globalization with cosmopolitanism, he nevertheless takes the globe to be the Earth's surface.[6]

Cosmopolitanism figures strongly in the language of state space programs, within the extensive work of Carl Sagan at NASA. Sagan was the astronomer who during the '70s popularized a discussion of Earth ecology and the responsibility of the sciences as the host of his own television series, *Cosmos*.[7] For the show's final episode, Sagan piloted an imaginary spaceship to an allegorical Earth-like planet, and used remote hand gestures at a computer console to query that world's ecological implosion. These scenes brought together all three concerns at hand with space architecture: the language of missions with words like cosmopolitanism; the back-and-forth exchanges between real and fictitious architectures for space, and the indicators for how human-computer interactions can move to engage the whole body within architecture now.

Sagan's invocations of cosmopolitanism correspond with a Kantian, or Beckian, framing of the word as described above. For Sagan, space architecture embodied cosmopolitanism as a vehicle for both global eco-consciousness and risk. And yet its presumptions of unity in such a consciousness and in its reference to human events extending far beyond the surface of the planet, his work foreshadows social and spatial thinking to come. Since the time of Sagan's work, NASA has seen a struggle over how inhabitation of space is conceived relative to a public concern. That struggle is visible in the agency's missions and in its very mission statement, both of which show a shift from the cosmopolitan to thinking in terms of an atmospheric commons.

4. Latour, Bruno. "Whose Cosmos, Whose Cosmopolitics? Comments on the Peace Terms of Ulrich Beck." In *Common Knowledge*, Vol. 10 Issue 3 (Fall 2004) 450-462 Stengers herself writes, "The prefix "cosmo-" indicates the impossibility of appropriating or representing "what is human in man" and should not be confused with what we call the universal. The universal is a question within the tradition that has invented it as a requirement and also as a way of disqualifying those who do not refer to it. The cosmos has nothing to do with this universal or with the universe as an object of science. But neither should the "cosmo" of cosmopolitical be confused with a speculative definition of the cosmos, capable of establishing

a "cosmopolitics." The prefix makes present, helps resonate, the unknown affecting our questions that our political tradition is at significant risk of disqualifying. I would say, then, that as an ingredient of the term "cosmopolitics," the cosmos corresponds to no condition, establishes no requirement." Stengers, Isabelle. *Cosmopolitics II* (Minneapolis: University of Minnesota Press, 2011), 355.
5. "In one word, it is risk—or, to be more precise, the perception of risk—that creates a public sphere across all boundaries." In Ulrich Beck. "Risk Society's Cosmopolitan Moment" lecture at Harvard University, November 12th, 2008.

6. More recently, a related and compelling notion of sectionally-expanded thinking can be found in work by Benjamin H. Bratton, under the rubric of the "Stack." See *The Stack: On Software and Sovereignty*, forthcoming from The MIT Press.
7. Cosmos' final episode, "Who Speaks for Earth?" is also its most polemical. In it, Sagan travels through space and a history of its human exploration; the building up and repeated collapses of human knowledge (dwelling at length on the Alexandrian Library, from within a simulation of its reading rooms created at Jet PropulsionLabs); and always in contrast with our era's confrontation with looming nuclear disaster. "Alexandria was the greatest

Amy Balkin, Public Smog, 2006.

This shift is practically embodied in the figure and work of James Hansen, the longtime director of NASA's Goddard Institute for Space Studies located at Columbia University. Arguably since his statements to Congress in 1988, Hansen was NASA's and the nation's most present and persistent voice in the scientific community calling attention to evidence of global warming and its origin in "anthropogenic changes of the atmospheric composition." This he attributes to evidence collected from meteorological equipment onboard manned and unmanned NASA craft; and its analysis in the global scientific community. While early work found its way into scientific journals, Hansen has chosen to address broader publics[8] since his claims of censorship during the administration of George W. Bush.[9] Since 2009, Hansen writes to explain his climate research for a lay reader, and to explain his view on the urgency for a global response.

Accusations by Hansen and his colleagues of state censorship are now well reflected on public record, as was the unannounced change of NASA's very mission statement in 2006. The agency's previous mission statement, "To understand and protect our home planet; to explore the universe and search for life; to inspire the next generation of explorers ... as only NASA can" was altered to "pioneer the future in space exploration, scientific discovery, and aeronautics research." The quiet elimination of the phrase regarding the home planet was met with national newspaper headlines and outcries from the scientific community at an obvious gesture to remove support for climatological research from the space agency's work. In essence, the administration used the language of the mission statement to decouple terrestrial and outer space atmospheres; and to unlink the decision-making about the agency's work from both NASA's own workers and from the citizenry funding it. The conditions for such a shift were ostensibly political, as so much other policy of the administration denied climate change and showed flat contempt for science.

Indicators of a larger awareness around an atmospheric commons can be read not only in NASA's activities since, but also has corollaries in other work, including art practices that now use Earth atmosphere, and air pollution itself, as a medium.

One example is the project "Public Smog,"[10] by Amy Balkin. Initiated in 2006 and ongoing since, the project is many things—a website, book, park, legislative action and more. As Balkin puts it:

> Public Smog is a park in the atmosphere that fluctuates in location and scale... Activities to create Public
> Smog have included purchasing and retiring emission offsets in regulated emissions markets, making them
> inaccessible to polluting industries... When Public Smog is built through this process, it exists in the unfixed

city the Western world had ever seen," Sagan states. "It is probably here that the word *cosmopolitan* (his emphasis) realized its true meaning—citizen, not just of a nation, but of the Cosmos."

8. Hansen updates his data and lists television appearances on his website at Columbia University, http://www.columbia.edu/~jeh1/

9. Bowen, Mark. *Censoring Science: Inside the Political Attack On Dr. James Hansen and the Truth of Global Warming.*

(New York, N.Y.: Dutton, 2008) See also: Juliet Eilperin (January 18, 2005). *"Putting Some Heat on Bush". Washington Post.* and Andrew Revkin (January 29, 2006). *"Climate Expert Says NASA Tried to Silence Him". The New York Times.*

10. http://publicsmog.org/—The project website is a vast collection of information that both explains and accretes to form the substance of the project. It includes information on a number of efforts to list "extra-state spaces" as UNESCO World Heritage sites, including the Moon itself,

at http://www.space4peace.org/moon/heritagesite.html The work is online and has been exhibited in galleries as well, including within the *Vapor* exhibition that I co-organized with Ali Sant in San Francisco in 2008, and in the 2012 *Documenta* in Kassel, Germany.

public airspace above the region where offsets are purchased and withheld from use.... Other activities to create Public Smog impact the size, location, and duration of the park. These activities include an attempt to submit Earth's atmosphere for inscription on UNESCO 's World Heritage List.

This work refers to the atmosphere between domains, what we might consider the respective purviews of designers and of space engineers; and it contains a few key conceptions of earth atmosphere as a commons. These are shared by figures at the heart of important state space programs like Sagan and Hansen at NASA. Balkin uses the project as a means of exposing inequities within industrial emissions trading and of asserting a way to subvert emissions trading for the creation of an atmospheric commons above Earth. Much of the artwork is expository, explaining its process, its legal, economic and scientific underpinnings for a general public. It also contains various accounts of its making, including Balkin's efforts to purchase offsets through the clandestine help of brokers who were not permitted to sell to individuals.

Balkin has pursued Public Smog in several different countries, each with their own emissions trading markets and legal structures in place to ensure the exclusive participation of large commercial concerns. A departure from this practice has been her advocacy to place Earth's atmosphere on UNESCO's World Heritage List. Not unproblematic itself, the artist writes:

> I think we need to protect the air as a commons, but phrasing it as 'international' brings up a whole raft of problems around state-based solutions. Any international agreement is an agreement between powerful states who are competing with each other and attempting to subjugate less powerful states into signing inequitable treaties (i.e., a contract between unequal subjects)...I am looking to UNESCO World Heritage as a framework and an institutional channel with a highly structured set of criteria/guidelines for the kind of atmospheric protection needed... The UN is weak in its ability to protect the atmosphere, because the organization represent states with unequal power, and lacks enforcement capabilities to protect the places on the list. That said, some UN treaties do have a positive impact, i.e. the 1976 Weather Weapons Treaty. So In that context, I'm continuing to pursue the effort to nominate the atmosphere to the World Heritage List, with the hope of success in this effort.[11]

Like Hansen's, Balkin's work understands Earth atmosphere first and foremost as a commons, both spatially and discursively; it therefore pits this understanding directly against its potential commodification. The atmospheric commons, we learn, is a space conditioned technologically, ecologically, but also politically and legally. Work on the atmospheric commons, for Balkin as for Hansen, challenges the sovereignty of nations within the strictures even of international organizations.

Many of these ideas of the atmospheric commons have philosophical origins in the Deep Ecology movement's primary author, Arne Naess—and, in turn, as far back as Baruch Spinoza's *Ethics*. Naess' 1973 article "The Shallow and the Deep, Long-Range Ecology Movement"[12] first proposed the phrase "deep ecology;" its tenets would be later elaborated[13] in homage to Spinoza's "Deus, sive Natura." "God, or Nature." the unity of *substances* as Spinoza describes them in his axiomatic and highly controversial *Ethics* (1677), philosophically positions a moral ground for humanity's relation to that which it might consider external to the natural world: *It is impossible that man should not be apart of Nature, or that he should be capable of undergoing no changes, save such as can be understood through his nature only as their adequate cause.*[14]

Naess wrote extensively at the boundaries of philosophy and ecological activism, and was even at one point named a candidate for Norway's Green Party. While he never appears to have written directly about Earth ecology from an external perspective or a discussion of space programs, his conception of monism in the unity of humanity with other natural and spiritual systems was also an inspiration to Sagan.[15]

The Blue Marble, Public Smog, and work of figures such as Sagan and Naess that lead between them all typify a common strand of language as well, one that contrasts with the so-called "cosmopolitan turn," and frames the physical and discursive spaces, and conceptions of human agency, located

11. my email exchange with the artist.
12. *Inquiry* 16: 95-100
13. Arne Naess, "Spinoza and Ecology," in *Philosophia*, Vol. 7, Num. 1, (March 1977) pp. 45-54
14. Baruch Spinoza, *Ethics* (trans. Julien Gautier 2010), Pars IV: De Servitude Humana, seu de Affectuum Viribus (Of Human Bondage, or the Power of the Affects)

Propositio 4.
15. Sagan mentions Spinoza by name only on a few occasions in his writings, though his descriptions of science and society evoke ideas found in the *Ethics* fairly clearly. See Carl Sagan, "Chapter 23: A Sunday Sermon" in *Broca's Brain: Reflections on the Romance of Science*. "Some people think God is an outsized, light-skinned male with

a long white beard, sitting on a throne somewhere up there in the sky, busily tallying the fall of every sparrow. Others—for example *Baruch Spinoza* and *Albert Einstein*—considered God to be essentially the sum total of the physical laws which describe the universe."

Tandem development: Von Braun develops schemes for the S-1 Space Station with Disney and NASA simultaneously.

instead in an atmospheric commons. They also contain a logic for approaches to work between large organizations: the populations and administrations needed to mobilize projects of global concern and on a planetary scale.

2. Technology Transfer: Facts and Fictions

If discourse around inhabiting outer space reflects terrestrial ideas of the public realm and atmosphere, then planning for space corresponds to composite efforts at projection: using renderings and engineering drawings, broadcast and telematic controls, to both sell and problem-solve an undertaking of unprecedented magnitude. Spatial, social and technological constructs volley or transfer between works of fact and fiction. These transfers offer a suggestion for design around similarly complex problems on the ground, in which the driver of change is not so much a narrative as a composite scenario.[16]

Engineer Wernher von Braun's career is illustrious as much for its inarguable contributions to rocket science as for its early career at the service of German national socialism. After the Allied victory, von Braun was brought to the United States under *Operations Paperclip* and *Overcast*. His postwar labors in the United States were crowned with his work as chief designer of the Saturn V launch vehicle, which was the key component in lifting the Apollo spacecraft to the moon. With that work, von Braun realized his longterm desire to support the achievement of a lunar landing. He would later be named director of NASA's Marshall Space Flight Center.

In tandem with his real development for space travel and inhabitation, though, von Braun pursued the mediatization of space travel through the design of numerous spacecrafts for the exclusive use of filmmaking. Throughout the '50s, von Braun collaborated with the Walt Disney Company, drawing and speaking about ways that livable environments would be staged to bring humanity to space. This work was best known to American audiences by the three television shows that von Braun and Disney aired on ABC: *Man in Space* (1955), *Man and the Moon*, (1955), and *Mars and Beyond* (1957).

These efforts are remarkable not only for the ease with which the rocket engineer could turn illustrator, public relations speaker and children's story-teller. These films were also the narrative proving ground for von Braun's true intentions as an aerospace engineer. A classic example, now on display at the Smithsonian museum's National Air and Space Museum, is the "Disney Space Station S-1" model. The S-1 was designed for the Disney-ABC TV productions, but reflected plans underway in von Braun's work at the space agency and finding dissemination elsewhere as well.[17] Details of the station's workings were prepared within the context of the "educational" programming for Disney, but had been worked out to great technical specifications with the hopes of promoting such a project at NASA.[18] The transfer of technologies between the two efforts had no conception of the station as public space per se, but rested on a partnership between the federal and private bodies founded in their shared interests.

16. See importantly Prelinger, Megan Shaw. *Another Science Fiction: Advertising the Space Race 1957 — 1962.* (Blast Books, 2010.) and Anker, Peder' The closed world of ecological architecture', *The Journal of Architecture*, 10: 5, 527 — 552.17. Collier's Weekly published his

manned space station in 1952.
18. Woodfill, Jerry. "Gallery of Wernher von Braun Moonship Sketches". The Space Educator's Handbook. NASA Johnson Space Center.

Film still from Stanley Kubrick's *2001: A Space Odyssey*, **1968.**

The particular case of the S-1 grows more interesting ten years later as it becomes the explicit model for the orbiting space station in Stanley Kubrick's film, *2001: A Space Odyssey*. The form, duties, internal space and even scale all match von Braun's model from the '50s. In Kubrick's vision of the station, the wheel performs two novel jobs as the setting for adapting Arthur C. Clarke's story. First, it provides the backdrop for an endless—endlessly *inescapable*—ship, on which the artificially intelligent HAL 9000 computer has gone out of control and become an enemy of the people it should be serving. The toroid is the same everywhere, closed and pockmarked at every step with HAL's haunting red eye. Here, the ubiquity of the human-computer interface is inseparable from its televeillance. HAL's omniscience is only supported by the donut-shaped pathway that forms the architecture. The terrestrial analogue for this centripetally controlled prison is not so much Jeremy Bentham's Panopticon[19] as it is a human Habitrail and a scenario for suffocation.

Other examples of disciplinary "technology transfer" in outer space abound, such as Douglas Trumbull's 1972 film *Silent Running* and the influence of its closed metabolic systems and tensegrity enclosure on the construction of "Biosphere 2" in Oracle, Arizona thirteen years later (not to mention

19. See Foucault, Michel. *Discipline and Punish: the Birth of the Prison* (New York: Random House, 1975). Here, the dispersion of HAL's eyes and other metabolic sensing systems is fundamentally different from the performance of the panopticon's centrally located guard's tower and its radiating arms of cells.

20. Star Trek has been analyzed exhaustively for its models of public space, race relations, technology and more; its role here is as an architectural and HCI (human-computer interaction) foil in considering the ISS. Both the ISS and the USS Enterprise act as litmus tests for their original and complex premises—technological, ecological, political and social. The ISS's service to a frail union of investing partner nations and the Enterprise's service to a United Federation of Planets in fact reemerge as valuable to what Stengers has termed a cosmopolitics

of "no requirement." The unity of architecture with embedded computing in outer space, an unwieldy and perhaps unavoidable future in which spatial routines set up social relations through the organization of working and living spaces, can be quickly undone by failed communications, navigational and information systems—and therein lies potential for new atmospheres, social and otherwise.

the inspiration it offered, in turn, for the film *Wall-E*). By contrast, one might consider the disjunctions between Star Trek's "Enterprise"—its process of design, and resulting social and spatial models—in all its distinctions from what has become the International Space Station.[20]

In each of these transfers between facts and fictions, questions are relocated and clarify their formulation on Earth: how do new models of society form in space? How do we replicate old ones? If the last century saw new architectural paradigms for understanding space (plan libre, Raumplan, and so on), how might atmosphere be a radically conceived paradigm for space in our century? Yet more importantly, these projects of our recent past suggest a productive method for addressing global scale problems. These lie in a disciplinary exchange that can rely on critical fictions to enable invention, suspend disbelief, and even finance a way through emergent problems in the built environment that are marked by multiple stakeholders and a scale that would otherwise forestall a breakthrough.

Planning for zero atmosphere architecture seems a tacit collaboration of fact and fiction, in which a complex routine is planned out that involves the collaboration of countless builders; the adaptation of industry, the reinvention of material assemblies, and so on. Its results are frequently intended as a custom construction with a terrestrial architectural analogue: the home-office, the commuter shuttle, the city. The gaps between fact and fiction are slim: speculations on the forms that such inhabitation might take and their execution—whether originating in the funded plans of a space program or in the pages of a Stanislaw Lem novel—are, importantly, nearly synchronous.

3. Scaling: HCI and the body

To transport and maintain the human organism off the earth and outside its sustaining envelopes requires a duplication of the earth itself—a protective enclosure and complex life support system that is, in effect, a rudimentary earth in miniature. The developed space vehicle—with its protective shields and energy collectors and converters; with its sensors and communicating devices—is a microminiaturized version of the earth itself a simulated planetary vehicle for the larger human community... The "closed ecology" of life support systems... is a systems model for the redesign of many of our large-scale industrial undertakings whose ecological malfunction degrades the quality of our environment... A similar model may also be applied to the refashioning of the metabolic support systems of many of our other human conveniences in the city, the private dwelling, transportation, communications, and similar services.
—John McHale, "Outer Space" [21]

This 1969 text on "futurology" suggests that the spaceship become a miniature, a replica; and McHale's interest in closed systems corresponds to the kind of thinking that gave rise to experiments like Biosphere 2. But the development of globally-networked human-computer interaction (HCI) since its writing suggest a different locus of the miniature, in the human body itself. Space architecture has itself promoted this change, as it first hosted telematic communications and now launches the thousands of satellites that enable the "internet of things" at the core of pervasive computing. This current paradigm of HCI relates global interactions in which individual agency in the environment is registered between the scale of a body with the extra-planetary scale of orbiting satellite networks and subsea cables that communicate with locative media of different kinds.

Let us return to the *Apollo 17* crew. More than any exposure of our own planet's surface, their "Blue Marble" image reveals the values that attended space missions and also the shifting identities for their astronauts. As documents of early spaceflight attest, astronauts and flight commanders on the ground frequently wrangled over whether an astronaut's work was essentially that of a pilot, a scientist or of a passive passenger.[22] Much of this bore a direct relation to the haphazard and largely untrusted relation between humans and computers that would condition the very survival of a crew, and it resulted in physical postures for the crew onboard. Just as the very material assembly, internal space configurations, mechanical performance and tectonics of the structure—the architecture—were without precedent, so were the protocols for digitally mediated interaction and collaboration. It revealed a social relation that was unleashed by remote communications in the "telecommute" of an astronaut. To the astronaut's list of job descriptions—pilot, scientist, passenger, he could now add photographer and even (upon landing) cinematographer.

21. McHale, John. *The Future of the Future* (George Braziller, New York 1969), 177-178.
22. David Mindell, "Programs and People," in *Digital*

Apollo: Human and Machine in Spaceflight (Cambridge: MIT Press, 2008)

Film poster advertising the 1972 film *Silent Running*.
The movie, later a model for *Wall-E*, depicts lonely space-
horticulturalists shuttling plants around space within
Fulleresque geodesic domes while awaiting word that
Earth atmosphere is safe for return.

This unsurprising task of representation has always been a familiar chore of frontierism, and certainly attended America's westward expansion, but it had multiple scales and publics in the case of the . missions. There was the need of representing the mission to US citizens, of representing the United States to the Soviet Union, and of representing humanity itself to any extraterrestrial life forms to be discovered.[23] Further, the *Apollo 11* mission's lunar landing on July 16, 1969 produced one real "movie," directed, filmed by and starring its own crew. The crew's bodies and body language even serve as media themselves, for understanding differences from our own terrain and atmosphere. Yet all of their work was enabled by onboard computer interfaces that preceded the embedded sensing and wireless networks that now underlie the so-called "internet of things" in our cities. Life onboard was at the behest of the "DSKY" or Display and Keyboard Unit, and its complex "verb-noun" syntax that asked crew to learn complex new languages and keyboard input routines to operate their ship.[24] The crew members' controls were limited to their hands, while the entire vessel itself was imbued with sensors that communicated internal metabolics and external readings back to terrestrial staff. In the DSKY as in Sagan's console, the cabin architecture mediates our bodies between minute interactions and the political, ecological, and technological systems that converge at the scale of an entire world.

Back on Earth today, the body senses and is registered across these extreme shifts in scale, within a built environment that is literally in the middle. Architecture and landscape are now the environments that condition human-computer interactions, as much as HCI conditions our architecture. Yet we still most consciously engage such interactions with a handheld device and through hand gestures. These sorts of interactions radically reform how we inhabit our buildings and cities already, whether adjusting a thermostat, communicating with a friend or navigating to an unknown destination. But the design of gesture can now open to the whole body, to the haptic, to the larger experience that we inhabit with our bodies at the scale of architecture and the city. With zero atmosphere architecture, we can today recognize the body itself as a medium for experience across the extremest of scales that we now inhabit. Rather than the hand gesture, the *body* gesture becomes a design area for transfer across scales. In an era of global telecommunications networks and a fraught global environment, the body is not merely a subject to be tracked across our cities; it is a sensor and an actuator in the built environment, a medium for registering and making atmosphere as an emerging commons.

Jordan Geiger is an architect and educator whose work crosses architecture and interaction design, considering implications of human computer interaction for social and environmental issues. He is Assistant Professor of Architecture at the University at Buffalo (SUNY).

23. This task takes on an ever expanding role today at the Visible Earth area of NASA's website. http://visibleearth.nasa.gov

24. Mindell, 166-167

LIQUID
HIGHWAYS

Miles Gertler + Karan Manchanda

SHIP TRAFFIC [1 YEAR PERIOD*]

NUMBER OF TRIPS

11-20   51-100   200+

1-10   21-50   101-200

EXCLUSIVE ECONOMIC ZONE BOUNDARIES

- - - - - - - - - - -

NORTHWEST PASSAGE ROUTES

———————— PRIMARY ROUTE
———————— DEEP DRAFT ROUTE
·················· PROJECTED ROUTES

NORDREG ZONE

//////////////

CHART + SURVEY STATUS

BASIC COVERAGE

ADEQUATE COVERAGE

OIL AND GAS SITES

······· PROVEN OIL DEPOSIT

◎ NATURAL GAS PRODUCTION SITE

◉ OIL PRODUCTION SITE

The circumpolar region: The current political framework, digital network coverage, industrial activity, and
ship traffic in the Arctic.

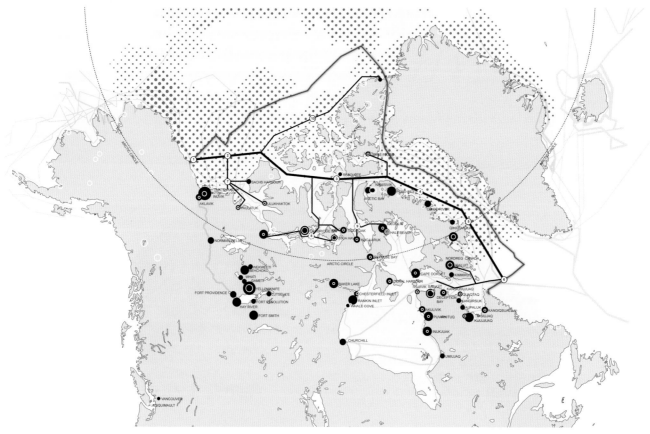

1. NORTHERN LANE STATION
2. DOCKING LANE
3. POLYMER LIPID MESH EXTENDED OVER WATER SURFACE TO SPEED UP FREEZING OF ICE ON "LAND SIDE" OF STATION
4. SALT BATTERY GUIDE LIGHTS
5. ICE GATHERING TROUGH, FOR COLLECTING LOOSE FLOES
6. SOUTHERN LANE STATION
7. CLUSTER OF AMPHIBIOUS ADVENTURE HUTS

The Liquid Highways network: An infrastructural spine ploughed by icebreaker through the Northwest Passage's deep-draft straits facilitates year-round shipping.

Canada's Northern frontier is one of the globe's geographic extremities. Populations dwindle as one approaches the polar region, an area defined by the remote, and by extreme climatic conditions. Winter temperatures are bitterly low, daylight and darkness ignore the laws of more temperate regions, and sheets of ice cover land and sea alike. Largely undeveloped, Canada's Arctic is one of the last pristine environments on the surface of the Earth.[1] The forces that make it inhospitable have in fact granted it a kind of ecological robustness. The archipelago region that surrounds the strategically important Northwest Passage (NWP) is home to a variety of native animal species that migrate through it in age-old patterns. Natural year-round freezing of the Passage has, until now, protected the delicate ecosystem from destructive industrial forces. But how will it survive once the arctic waters are navigable in an ice-free season, given the anticipated diversion of shipping traffic from the Panama Canal?

Shipping traffic is not the only threat, nor the most grave, to the arctic environment. The region as a whole is estimated to hold 25 percent of the world's remaining oil and gas resources, buried deep within our arctic territory.[2] The vast resource wealth of the polar region is impossible to ignore as pressure mounts to tap every available source. And as ice coverage melts, exposing routes to remote extraction sites, so too are mineral deposits revealed, further compounding the lucrative aura of the North.[3] Even with a minimum of infrastructure, serious mining efforts have existed in the region since the commissioning of the North Rankin nickel mine in 1955.[4]

With heightened economic stakes, the potential for political conflict increases in parallel, yet Canada, lacks an adequate constabulary presence to enforce its contested border claims. Canada's government has long made the claim that the Arctic waters, including the North West Passage, are sovereign territory. Other sea-going states dispute this claim, citing the UN Charter of the Laws of the Sea, which asserts that many straits between islands are too large to be considered internal waters. Since the archipelago can be navigated entirely through these channels as international routes, provided that it is not frozen over, these states are well positioned to dispute

1. Ellis, B., Brigham, L., eds. *Arctic Marine Shipping Assessment 2009 Report.* (Arctic Council, 2009, second printing), 8.
2. The Mariport Group Ltd. *Canadian Arctic Shipping Assessment: Main Report.* (Digby, Nova Scotia: The Mariport Group Ltd, 2007), 72. Canada's estimated oil reserves, some 180 billion barrels, place second only to those of Saudi Arabia, and 25 percent of this remaining recoverable light crude oil lies beneath the arctic ice.
3. ibid.
4. ibid., 70.

CURRENT PANAMA CANAL-ROUTED TRAFFIC   ROUTES SHORTER THROUGH NWP   RE-ROUTED TRAFFIC WITH LIQUID HIGHWAYS

	SHARE OF GLOBAL TRAFFIC	PROJECTED SHARE IN 2050
SUEZ	4%	3%
PANAMA	8%	4%
ARCTIC	<1%	5% (3% NORTHERN SEA ROUTE, 2%NORTHWEST PASSAGE)

Panama traffic diversion: By redirecting those routes which are more efficiently travelled through the Northwest Passage than through the Panama Canal, the Liquid Highways divert a sizable share of global shipping traffic, the revenues from which will help fund its operations and development.

Canada's claim to sovereignty over these waters. Canada's traditional response is that that these waters should be treated more as land, as they are used by the indigenous Inuit people when frozen for most of the year. However, this argument melts away with the effects of global warming. In the summer of 2007 the ice covering the North West Passage melted completely. Given the predicted expansion of navigable territory, how does Canada, a country with a small navy and extensive coastline, protect its ecological heritage, access its resource wealth, and assert its sovereignty?

The region will likely remain frozen in the winter for at least the next hundred years, but the passage will open up in summer months, and the absence of a concerted strategy will limit the country's ability to monitor resource exploration and extraction. The Canadian government has an opportunity to leverage the difficulty of the Northwest Passage's year-round navigation in a way that protects the region's natural environment, asserts Canada's sovereignty, and generates economic benefits as well. To this end, an infrastructural spine is proposed: a 'Liquid Highway,' ploughed by icebreakers through the Northwest Passage's deep-draft straits, facilitating year-round shipping. As a new institution, the network allows Canada to serve in its role as environmental steward and lends legitimacy to its claims of sovereignty in the North. In this proposal, the Passage is opened artificially and thus entry is unquestionably regulated by Canadian authorities. The extreme conditions of the site in fact offer a means for its control, while also preserving environmental conditions and enabling economic development through an increase in regulated tourism and the introduction of spin-off industries.

The two categories of problems affecting architecture that Doxiadis outlines in *Architecture in Transition* in 1963 are ever-present in Canada's contemporary Arctic context: "The first comprises the problems which require an understanding of local environmental situations and the role of architecture as the consolidating and coordinating discipline. The second category consists of the problems which are not connected with the environment and require action at a much higher level. The problems here are those which architecture faces in relation to industry, art, government, and the other forces of modern expanding society." [5] *Liquid Highways* suggests that a new proposed institution manage both the environmental and the anthropogenic challenges for the shared benefit of all stakeholders.

Carved by a fleet of icebreakers, the route allows the government to control shipping traffic in the NORDREG region[6] Levying tolls on trade ships that operate within it, the route becomes economically productive and enables the deployment of a series of environmentally sensitive "soft" interventions to preserve the region's ecological heritage and assist in the Passage's operation. These interventions are capable of responding to changes in their environment and managing an unpredictable flow of inputs to sustain basic functions. That is, contextual variability is an expected—and essential—design condition. The operation of the *Liquid Highways* depends on the reality of Arctic freeze cycles and a regional diversity that lends cultural and economic definition to a vast domain. The network's operation assumes a demand for access to the territory from a multitude of stakeholders, including government, industry, indigenous populations, and with increasing frequency, tourists "The stability of the system is rooted in its dynamics, in its capacity to handle and process movement, change, difference…" [7]

A variety of station types activate the route along its course by offering a new set of programmatic opportunities for prospective users. Each station is conceived of as a camp. A rotating staff and a constant flow of travelers, researchers, hunters, and ship crews populate these stations. The

---

5. Doxiadis, Constantinos A. "New Solutions for New Problems," in *Architecture in Transition* (New York: Oxford University Press, 1963), 88.

6. The NORDREG region demarcates the zone of surveillance extending over Canada's Arctic waters and maritime Exclusive Economic Zone in which the government has decreed it compulsory for all ships over a certain tonnage, foreign or otherwise, to declare their entry.

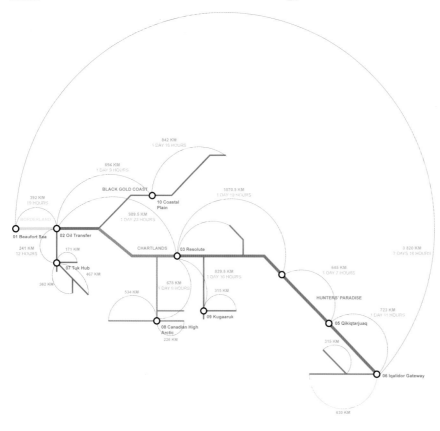

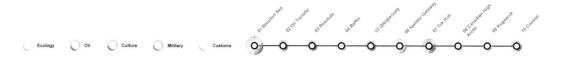

Route analysis: Traces of regionalism appear along each segment of the Liquid Highways: Borderland, near the American maritime frontier, the Black Gold Coast, along a resource-rich coastal plain, the Chartlands, the centre of bathymetric charting and other research stemming from the nearby Canadian High Arctic Research Station, and Hunter's Paradise, the rich ecological zone along the Baffin Island coast.

assemblage of users inhabits the various building elements that combine to form the stations. These components join together in a chain, creating a linked strip of program of various scales at points along the route's wayside.

Wayside stations can act as a portal from the navigation channel to the ice field surface beyond. Whereas the water-oriented staging deck is geared towards shipping operations (deliveries, disembarking, refueling, maintenance), the ice-side deck adopts a character specific to a station's programmatic identity. In Canada's maritime border regions, the terminuses of the *Highway*, the ice-side staging area is a base of operations for constabulary training and monitoring exercises.

On the Black Gold Coast, the station Northwest of Ellef Ringnes Island serves as a hub for oil and gas prospecting and extraction. The ice field allows staff and station operators to engage a range of multimodal transportation between scattered infrastructural nodes that tap into vast resource deposits. A rig operator might travel by snowmobile or by watercraft, depending on season and mission objective. In the ecologically rich Hunter's Paradise strait along Baffin Island's north coast, the "land" is well-traveled by Inuit, researchers, and tourists in search of traditional foods, observational data, and frontier vistas.

Just as a camp might develop from the scattered shelters of groups of explorers, so too do these arctic stations come into being gradually. Floating huts are deployed as brief rest-stops for researchers travelling remotely. In the winter they spread out and each hut informally claims the 'land' around it. As more charting is conducted, and as global warming makes the area easier to reach, the liquid highway becomes busier, demanding a more permanent life support system. The open ice field is now marked by the huts, equipment, vehicles, and eventually, station components, that link one by one to expand the network's reach.

7. Kwinter, Sanford. "Soft Systems," in *Culture Lab*, ed. Brian Boigon (Princeton: Princeton Architecture Press, 1993), 210.

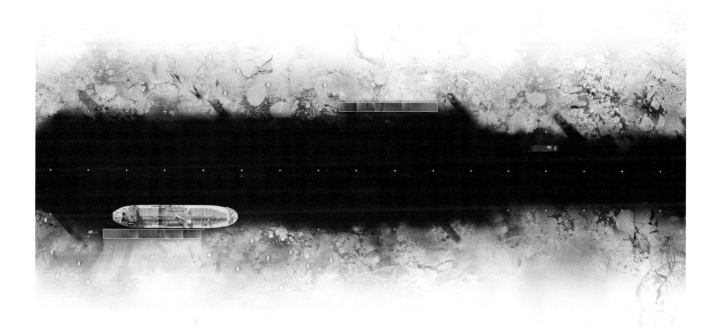

Beaufort Sea border region: Site plan of the Beaufort Station.

Spin-off industries, like cruises and guided tourism, IT support, and maintenance of the stations might flourish and grow local economies. In the case of the *Liquid Highways*, every intervention is the means to an ecological end and "piggybacks" off of a hard infrastructure that serves the economic or political dimension. For instance, the lights that mark the route's course and guide ships at night and in bad weather are powered by a salt-battery that not only makes the ice easier to break up, but also helps to re-establish the salinity of an ecosystem diluted by glacial melting. Icebreakers that plough the route also drag plastic polymer nets to attract trace elements of oil left over from industrial activity. An array of rods below each station component generates clean energy from the slow currents of the ocean while also acting as an artificial reef for small local species. The same polymer nets are buoyed with the salt-batteries at moments along the route's course. Thus, the water-filtration network expands and creates permanent clearings in the ice. These serve as ecological hubs, providing fish habitats and allowing whales and seals open access to air, and economic micro-sites, securing the stability of regional hunting and ecologically dependent tourism. The open route can be naturally refrozen within the space of fourteen days to accommodate migratory herd migration. This accommodates traditional hunting activities and the brief pause in shipping traffic increases the use of stations as sites for exchange, rest and anchorage.

In an extreme environment where the only permanence is a condition of flux, the *Liquid Highways* network seeks to reconcile and leverage environmental, economic and political dynamics that might otherwise compete, at the scale of a nation.

Miles Gertler graduated with Honours from the University of Waterloo School of Architecture and is pursuing his Masters of Architecture at Princeton University. He has worked in Den Haag, Paris, Rotterdam, and Toronto.

Karan Manchanda graduated from the University of Waterloo School of Architecture where he is now pursuing graduate studies. He has worked in studios in India, the United States, and Canada.

ADVENTURE HUTS

Amphibious short term on-site residences for researchers, rangers, and northern adventurers. Dispersed in winter ice to maximize usable surrounding surface, aggregated in summer to share watercraft.

AIR BUBBLER

Forces encroaching ice away using mechanized air propulsion system at station's waterline.

VORTEX ARRAY

Rigid vortex rod array harnesses ocean currents for power generation. Doubles as artificial reef environment for small fish.

CULTURE MODULE

Module for hunting, traditional foods, tourism, and arts. Equipped with smoking chambers, fish drying racks, storage, and small watercraft mooring berth. Run by Arctic Rangers.

VESSEL MOORING

Mooring enclave for small vessels such as fishing and hunting boats as well as personal watercraft.

STAGING DECK

Exterior deck area of Port and Military Modules connect to form flexible preparation, storage, and port zone. Equipped with a cargo elevator, stairs lead to the lower staging area on the ice-side of the station.

CARGO STORAGE

Storage holds liquid petroleum products, dry bulk goods, and special items for commercial users and for the maintenance of the route.

MILITARY MODULE

A remote base for training in harsh conditions, arctic operations, amphibious combat, and northern monitoring. Equipped with land and sea-based vehicles and a helicopter landing pad.

HOME MODULE II

Residential module, accommodates station crew, military personnel, and visiting researchers with shared recreational program at staging deck level. Sleeps 36.

HANGAR MODULE

An enclosable shelter for tug boats and other small water craft. Also facilitates the detention of small vessels.

HOME MODULE I

Residential module, accommodates station crew, military personnel, and visiting researchers with shared recreational program at staging deck level. Sleeps 36.

ARMOURED SHELL

Perforated blast armour. Scale of perforation relates to interior program demands for visibility and access to light. Prow is angled for maneuverability; provides mounting for ice teeth and vortex array.

PORT CRANE

In tandem with ship-mounted cranes assists in the maneuvering of cargo on deck.

CUSTOMS MODULE

Base of operations for customs, immigration, port, port security, and labour inspectorate. Serves as remote customs bureau and port in the Beaufort Sea US border region.

CONTROL ROOM

Bridge command for port and border operations. Direct satellite connection to all other stations, NORDREG Control in Iqaluit, and Central Command in Ottawa.

SALT BATTERY

Salt-releasing dual diode light and lane guide slows the re-freeze of ice surface by increasing salinity along Liquid Highway lanes. Re-salinization helps restore balance to water diluted by glacial melting.

CLEARING TUG

Tug boats trail ice breakers after route clearing to sweep loose ice into tributary collection troughs.

LIPID MESH

Polymer-embedded lipid mesh attracts trace oil residue left over from industrial processes and ship discharge. The mesh is trawled along the highway and lines its edges underwater.

OIL SOURCE

Privately-funded oil exploration and extraction points. Oil storage station modules likely situated nearby or along Liquid Highway.

NATIVE SPECIES

Drawn to the open strip of water and high levels of dissolved oxygen, native species like Arctic Char and mammals requiring access to air for breathing populate the Liquid Highways.

Kit of parts: Beaufort Station components fulfill military and monitoring roles, research functions, ecological remediation and accommodation.

Beaufort Station: Seen from liquid highway forged by ice breaking.

Settlement: Begins with the anchoring of small-scale
research and tourism structure.

THE THING

Shabnam Hosseini + Hamish Rhodes

Essay by Adrian Blackwell

The Thing is a network: Its nodes connect physical and virtual space. Where these realms intersect is known as 'The Assembly'. Member can log-in, at any time and place, and observe or contribute to the operations of the Assembly. Floating within this space is 'The Map', an uneven patchwork of geospatial data which indexes all knowledge produced by *The Thing*.

What is *The Thing*?

The Thing is a proposal for a research station for the investigation of climate change in the arctic, a science fiction set in the near future. It is a capsule that can be dropped into impassable frozen landscapes by helicopter. Once situated, the container is forced open through the inflation of a pneumatic structure that triples its interior area, and acts as formwork for a self-structured, insulating ice dome. The resulting space provides accommodation and workspace for an interdisciplinary team of scientists, artists and activists, whose role is to measure and understand the reality of climate change. This small group is multiplied by its connections within a digital forum, through which thousands of people, from across the globe, are able to discuss this matter of concern.

Like the jug that Heidegger describes in his essay "The Thing," this thing is a vessel, whose emptiness acts as a gathering space. And similar to Heidegger's description of a thing, it is designed to create "nearness" or intimacy in a modern world damaged by "distancelessness." Heidegger points out that in Old German the word thing (*ding*), meant a place of assembly. Where Heidegger's jug gathers what he calls "the fourfold: earth and sky, gods and mortals," *The Thing* gathers together geologic, climactic, cultural and other matters of consequence. So *The Thing* is more closely tied to Bruno Latour's revival of the concept. Latour's thing is an assembly as well, but one that puts people, objects and concepts on the same plane, as potentially equal players in the constitution of things as matters of consequence to us. "Thingpolitiks" is his proposal for a political practice that could address the mysterious and irrational hybrids of nature and society, the monsters that were constructed throughout modernity. Perhaps the most urgent of these, and the one that opens his book *We Have Never Been*

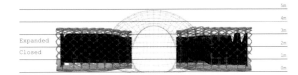

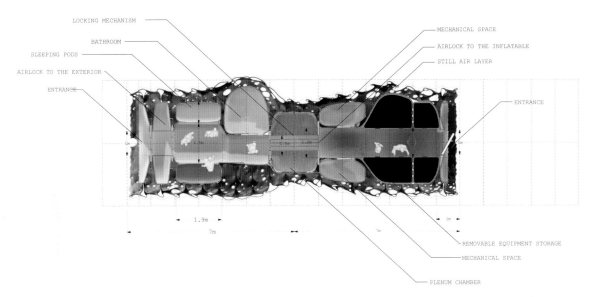

LOCKING MECHANISM

BATHROOM

SLEEPING PODS

AIRLOCK TO THE EXTERIOR

ENTRANCE

MECHANICAL SPACE

AIRLOCK TO THE INFLATABLE

STILL AIR LAYER

ENTRANCE

REMOVABLE EQUIPMENT STORAGE

MECHANICAL SPACE

PLENUM CHAMBER

Closed plan: Prior to inflation *The Thing* is compact and tight for the 6 crew members. A central corridor arranges the programmatic configuration.

Modern, is Climate Change. In this sense Hosseini and Rhodes's *The Thing* is at once a place of assembly and the monstrous issue around which people are gathering in their (dis)agreement.

That *The Thing* is a strange hybrid is clearly called out in its alien form. Materially it is a complex assemblage, a layered structure, like a Russian doll, with a set of skins separated by a spiraling truss-work whose spacing provide both insulation and structural integrity. The structure's muscular form—part plant, part animal—give it the character of the terrifying alien things that appear in science fictions. In this sense *The Thing*'s real architectural precedents are the alien invaders found in the Antarctic in John W. Campbell's novella *Who Goes There?* (and the sequence of movies called *The Thing* that have been based on it). In these stories "The Thing" appropriates the bodies of Antarctic (or sometimes Arctic) explorers. While certainly *The Thing* plays on these references, with its internal capsules that act as sentient skins for intrepid bodies, or with the capsule's giant inflated and frozen electronic brain that fuses the minds of both capsule dwellers and remote participants, *The Thing* also operates in a deeper psychoanalytic register.

In his Seventh seminar, Jacques Lacan fuses Freud's and Heidegger's concepts of the thing, to designate a central void around which desire is structured. The thing is not comprehensible, it cannot be rationally discussed in language (symbolized), or integrated into everyday images (imagined), it is rather what Lacan calls the Real—the terrifying meaninglessness at the heart of our desire. In the narrative structure of *The Thing*, it is both the white emptiness of the arctic winter, and the hole in the ozone layer. While the arctic operates as a metaphoric thing, a void that cannot be occupied, Climate change is the Real thing that collectively we cannot believe or legislate. However Lacan's concept of the thing also operates in another register. At the level of architectural design itself, Hosseini and Rhodes' process involves an incessant and inspiring repetition, circling around an unknowable goal. Design operates as desire here, the desire to realize *The Thing*. And while it can never be finally realized, this circuit of seemingly unending iterations, that make use of multiple computer programs, and fabrication techniques, is simply that open and desiring experiment with forms that exemplifies the work of all inventive artists or architects.

Collaborators since 2009, **Shabnam Hosseini** and **Hamish Rhodes** form MACGUFFIN—an interdisciplinary design practice that probes the intersection of architecture and cinema. Influenced by science fiction and Modernism, MacGuffin is a meditation on iteration, fabrication and narrative.

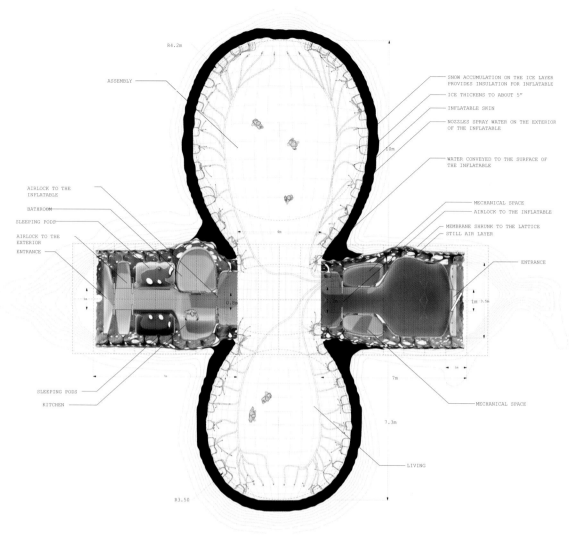

ASSEMBLY

SNOW ACCUMULATION ON THE ICE LAYER
PROVIDES INSULATION FOR INFLATABLE
ICE THICKENS TO ABOUT 5"
INFLATABLE SKIN
NOZZLES SPRAY WATER ON THE EXTERIOR
OF THE INFLATABLE

WATER CONVEYED TO THE SURFACE OF
THE INFLATABLE

AIRLOCK TO THE
INFLATABLE
BATHROOM
SLEEPING PODS
AIRLOCK TO THE
EXTERIOR
ENTRANCE

MECHANICAL SPACE
AIRLOCK TO THE INFLATABLE
MEMBRANE SHRUNK TO THE LATTICE
STILL AIR LAYER

ENTRANCE

SLEEPING PODS
KITCHEN

MECHANICAL SPACE

LIVING

Expanded plan: Additional space is gained through inflation. Network of pipes convey water to the surface of the inflatable to accelerate the generation of ice. The thin ice layer works as a structural shell. Snow accumulated on the ice layer creates sufficient thermal insulation for the crew.

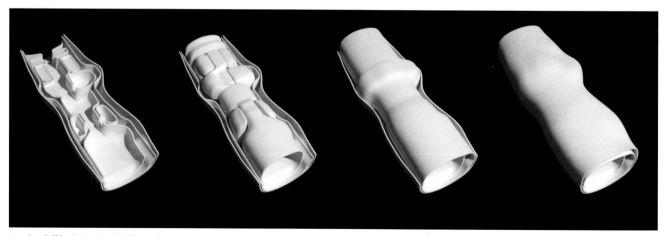

Russian doll logic: A series of offset surfaces constitute the insulation strategy of The Thing.

FRONTIERS AND BORDERS IN THE AMERICAN LANDSCAPE

Brian Davis

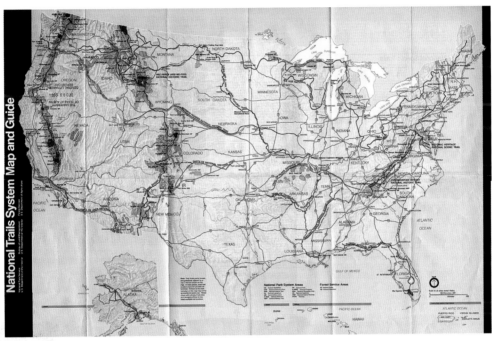

The US National Park system: These landscapes have most often been described in terms of romantic idealism or environmental conservation movements. However, seen as an adaptation to a frontier condition, these landscapes can be understood as a geopolitical instrument, allowing distant bureaucracies to bring administrative powers to bear on a contested territory with a sparse population.

The American frontier is sharply distinguished from the European frontier—a fortified boundary line running through dense populations. The most significant thing about the American frontier is that it lies at the hither edge of free land.
— Frederick Jackson Turner, 1893[1]

The European frontier has been synonymous with the idea of a borderland since its adoption from Old French into the English language in the 14th century. Throughout the Americas we find a more ambiguous definition, one coloured by, and affecting, the roiling landscapes of heterogeneous and contested colonial and post-colonial territories. The American frontier concept has changed through the centuries, coming

into, and falling out of, fashion. It has served as the object of study for generations of historians before being left aside, only to be revived as a metaphor for the space race and pop culture. What might be revealed by a more systematic, rigorous study of the difference between borders and frontiers in the American landscape? Is the American frontier a one-time historical anomaly, relevant only in the United States?[2] Or might we find it to be a Trans-American landscape condition, one that confronts us in contemporary cities throughout North and South America, the thawing polar regions, the American Cordillera and other places undergoing change at a massive scale, thereby compelling us to action?

Frederick Jackson Turner's original 'Frontier Thesis' stated

1. Turner, Frederick Jackson. "The Significance of the Frontier in American History," 1893 American Historical Society President's Address. *The Frontier in American History* (New York: Henry Holt and Company, 1920.), 3.

2. Webb, Walter Prescott. *The Great Frontier* (Boston: Houghton Mifflin, 1952.), 280.

that the American frontier, marked by continual westward expansion across the northern continent, was critical in shaping the people and institutions of the United States. He suggested that its disappearance in the late 19th century signaled a cultural crisis for the country. This thesis was especially noteworthy in recognizing, for the first time, that the rules of the European frontier did not apply in the Americas. Historian Walter Prescott Webb more clearly described this landscape, noting that in the Americas a frontier was "not a line to stop at, but an area inviting entrance. Instead of having one dimension, length, as in Europe, the American frontier has two dimensions, length and breadth." [3] His contribution allowed for the frontier to be understood as a multi-dimensional and dynamic geography. This concept of the American frontier is particularly interesting when one combines this representation with that of another prominent historian of the American frontier, Herbert Eugene Bolton.

In 1933, Bolton gave the President's Address to the American Historical Association, the very same occasion where Turner had first elucidated his Frontier Thesis forty years earlier. During his speech, Bolton argued that the American frontier could not be understood in terms of an inexorable, Anglo-centric march west. Rather, the American frontier must be understood as a hemispheric condition of contested terrains; while the Anglo-Americans marched west, the French moved south, the Spanish moved north, the Russians moved east, the British controlled Canada, and the Portuguese expanded over the entire Amazon basin.[4] Bolton's thesis was also decidedly Eurocentric, but by expanding the horizons of American history beyond the political borders of thirteen English colonies to a more geographical, hemispheric condition, it set a course that we might follow today to gain an insight into the settlement patterns and politics at play in contemporary urbanism throughout North and South America.

Redefining the Trans-American Frontier

A certain philosopher asserts that a space is something that has been made room for, something that is cleared and free, namely within a boundary. A boundary is not that at which

something stops, but that from which something begins its presencing. [paraphrased]
— William T. Vollman, *Imperial*[5]

Combining the work of these frontier historians with that of geographers, archeologists and landscape architects such as JB Jackson[6], Ruth Shady Solis, Alceu Ranzi[7], and Elizabeth Meyer[8], it is possible to understand the American frontier as a *landscape*: *a constructed place consisting of autonomous objects in dynamic relation to one another within a bounded terrain*. The characteristics that define this landscape--overlapping and contingent jurisdictions stretched over expansive territories, characterized by *bigness* and *collisions*—are endemic throughout the Americas. As Bolton showed, the American frontier must be understood as *non-directional*. It is not a line dividing civilization from wilderness, nor is it a thick band of open, receding land at the edge of society, but rather it is a heterogeneous and uneven agglomeration of difficult and contested territories where myriad indigenous and external interests are colliding with one another over and over. The frontier in the American landscape is not merely Turner's blank space or Webb's thick zone; it is marked by overlapping and ambiguous administrative jurisdictions. In the American frontier, control is ambiguous; there are real and perceived dangers,[9] and there is latent potential. This contingency and potential generates the frontier conditions that the Scottish recognized in the Darien Gap, the United States recognized in the Southwest, and the French saw in the Mississippi Valley.[10]

The American frontier is also marked by outsized investment and precarious control methods, administered by a massive, distant bureaucratic structure. A well-known example of this is the Spanish colony of Alta California, and its presidios and missions and sparsely populated territories established as a defense against the imperial aims of Tsarist Russia. This historical pattern was repeated throughout the colonization of the Americas: from the Treaty of Tordesillas and the disputed terrain of the Amazon basin[11], to the creation of the US National Parks[12], and in the ongoing fight over the Beagle Channel.[13] This pattern remains with us today in the geo-political ruderals[14] of Boliva Mar, Puerto Rico, and

3. ibid, 2.
4. Bolton, Herbert E. *Wider Horizons of American History* (University of Notre Dame Press, 1939), 11–17.
5. Vollman, William T. *Imperial* (New York: Penguin Group, 2009), 247. Vollman's lengthy anthology of Imperial County is a particularly interesting study in American frontiers and borders and the difference between them.
6. Jackson, John Brinkerhoff. *A Sense of Time, a Sense of Place* (New Haven and London: Yale University Press, 1994)
This collection of Jackson's essays examines the North American landscape and allows for insight into the ways that the historical condition of the American frontier in some ways both predates Columbus and persists to the present day, be it in his descriptions of the Anazi settlements at Pueblo Bonito, traditional Spanish-American settlements in the southwestern US, or the bizarre and convivial landscapes created by trucks.
7. In recent years advances in aerial photography and the development of methods of landscape archeology have lead to a wealth of new information attesting

to the contested and complex history of the cultures indigenous to the Americas. One of the most significant of these works is the discovery and documentation of the urban center Caral by the Peruvian archeologist Ruth Shady Solis. The article "1491" and subsequent book of the same name by Charles C. Mann offers an accessible compendium of all of this work, and begins to sketch some of the implications.
8. Meyer, Elizabeth K. "Uncertain Parks: Disturbed Sites, Citizens and Risk Society" in *Large Parks*, ed. by Julia Czerniak (New York: Princeton Architectural Press, 2007), 59–83.
9. Historically in the American frontier landscape there was a marked difference in reality and perception when it came to danger. This can be seen in everything from the mythical/historical accounts of European colonists at Jamestown or Jesuit priests in the southern cone of South America. See Muhn, Juan, *La Argentina Vista por Viajeros del SIglo XVIII. Buenos Aires: Editorial Huarpes S. A.*, 49.
10. Webb, Walter Prescott. *The Great Frontier* (Boston: Houghton Mifflin, 1952), 203–230.
11. The Treaty of Tordesillas was established in 1494 by

papal decree and divided the newly discovered non-European lands of the world between Spain and Portugal. The Line of Demarcation in the American Hemisphere passed through the Amazonian basin; encroachment beyond that line by European settlers of varying origin from either direction would become a point of contention for the next three centuries in South America.
12. The establishment of US National Parks entailed the eviction of residents from these lands, in particular indigenous inhabitants. In her book on the history of the first national park, Yellowstone, Aubrey Haines notes that "there appears to have been no concern for Indian rights in the area. Probably, they were unaware that a portion of the proposed park overlapped the Crow Indian Reservation established May 7, 1868- an oversight which was not rectified by the Congress until Apr. 11, 1882". http://www.cr.nps.gov/history/online_books/haines1/ieee.htm#354, accessed November 9, 2013.
13. Kelly, Phillip. *Checkerboards and Shatterbelts: The Geopolitics of South America* (Austin: University of Texas Press, 1997), 67.

Gas tank, Detroit City Gas Company, Detroit, USA, 1905: Often the continued presence of these structures or their residues creates a frontier landscape condition in cities.

the Triple Frontera of Brazil, Paraguay, and Argentina. As a landscape condition, the frontier is endemic to the Americas; marked by difficult terrain, massive capital investment, a tantalizing mix of potential commercial success and imminent disaster, and overlapping and ambiguous jurisdictions. And now the frontier is in our cities.

American Frontiers and Urban Landscapes

Today, the landscape condition of the American frontier is encountered at post-industrial sites, in city zones marred by interstate highways and '60s-era urban renewal, in the forgotten urban edges, near old industrial shipping canals, and now in the back lots of big box retail centers. As frontiers, these landscapes are not empty space, nor are they thick slices of real estate awaiting settlement and exploitation along the borderlands of the city. They are contested zones: they have a history, they are inhabited, they are dangerous, and they are marked by potential. The issue of jurisdiction is often murky in these zones: industry has largely fled and deliberations on

the site's future are endlessly being passed back and forth between municipal, state, and federal agencies. Further, there is always a perception of danger or undesirability, and often there are real issues of contamination or physical violence. Often times there are vast, obsolete structures from the past which must be dealt with: the factory that is too expensive to tear down, the massive landform created by waste landfilling or for defense, the old gantries and piers dangerously decaying, or a seductive tangle of linear transportation infrastructures. Lastly, the mobilization of a massive bureaucratic structure — be it the 17th century Scottish Darien Company or the US Environmental Protection Agency — lends the place a sense of inevitability, creating further conflict and possibility.

These places have other qualities: the vastness and openness, the ecological fecundity of a place left untouched, the embedded history, the perception of danger that creates an operating space for the weeds, hobos, kids, and birds typically excluded from the productive circuits of the modern city. Sola Morales identified the significance of

14. Literally meaning "from rubble", a ruderal is typically understood to be a weedy plant growing in a leftover or wasted patch of ground such as a roadside or cracked concrete pad. Here I use the term more broadly, referring to a territory that has sprung up from the rubble of a geopolitical conflict such as the Bolivia Mar on the coast of Peru, which resulted from the 1879 War of the Pacific.

these places in our cities and then posed the question, "*how can architecture act in the terrain vague without becoming an aggressive instrument of power and abstract reason?*"[15] In the context of the American landscape, the answer is two-fold: a landscape approach is essential, and that landscape must be understood as a *frontier condition*.

Defining a Landscape Approach

Traditionally, a landscape approach simply embraces the methods and techniques inherent to landscape practice. By landscape practice I do not mean solely landscape architecture or any discipline that is traditionally dominated by the art-historical approach, but a set of land-based cultural practices implicating aesthetics, territory, and productivity. This might include undertakings by everyone from army engineers to farmers as well as gardeners, architects, and landscape designers. The fact that the concept of landscape is so ill-defined, over-utilized, and vague suggests a need to further examine the concept and practice in an ontological sense.[16] Below I offer four concepts that might serve as a guide to a future definition of landscape.

Territorialization: The demarcation and control of a specific piece of the earth's surface. This can be seen in both the history of landscape practice and by examining the etymology of the word itself. The Peruvian landscape theorist Wiley Ludeña Urquizo shows that the term landscape (*paisaje* in Spanish) relates directly to the word for nation (*pais*). Drawing from Cesar Naselli, Urquizo shows that landscape signifies "the place of primordial experiences of a specific group of humans."[17] The etymological link between "nation" and "landscape" suggests that acts of surveying, map making, notational systems, or otherwise "taking stock", as well as bounding, fencing, patrolling, policing, or otherwise controlling the land — acts which are typically understood as part of creating a national territory — are fundamental to landscape-making.

Landscape is a Medium: Denis Cosgrove[18] argues persuasively that landscape is a cultural product. Expanding this notion, we can view landscape as a medium (which cultural product can be a subset of), a cultural product and cultural producer. Following Marshal McLuhan landscape-as-medium is both an object in its own right, and one that acts as an intermediary between other objects, transforming and transporting them.[19] It is the result of processes and intentions, yet once a landscape exists it possesses its own agency and affective potential.

Generative Capacity: A landscape's ability to create new objects and relations, to give rise to novelty, may be understood as its *generative capacity*. Generative capacity is the landscape between the arcadian and imperial nature, between source and resource.[20] While acts of territorialization are fundamental to human occupation of landscape, there is a simultaneous and opposite impulse at work. A gap between intent and reality is always present.[21] Consider the gully that opens up on a newly graded hillside of a highway project despite the presence of the geotextiles intended to counteract any erosion. Or, the invasion of a reforested planting bed by pine seedlings, or a newly created sandbar that materializes in a shipping channel after a flood event.

The use of contract specifications and the development of interchangeable parts in the last two hundred years was an effort to eliminate this gap between intent and reality — one that always fails, as any experienced designer can attest. Even now, the rise of computation and the great faith placed in systematic conceptions of landscape aspire to minimize it. But this gap — the difference between intent and reality, and the importance and persistence of novelty is fundamental to landscapes themselves.[22] This generative capacity of landscape serves to open up routes of deterritorialization, transgressing boundaries and creating new relations and objects.

Difference: Because of their capacity for novelty and surprise and their rootedness in a specific place, landscapes are defined in part by difference. This is difference in a positive sense, defined by what something is becoming, rather than by what it is not.[23] Therefore landscape practice valorizes the singular. While certain objects within the landscape — for instance a new retaining wall — might be created according to accepted models, the landscape itself cannot be. In this way landscape practice is first an experimental and educational project, not a formal or spatial pursuit.

Pulling from historical as well as speculative observation, we can reach some conclusions about ways in which a landscape practice might be developed for these frontier sites enabling a synthesis of new programs and forms. In the past, grappling with the Trans-American frontier gave rise to new landscape types such as the national park, new technologies such as barbed wire, and policy innovations such as the Laws of the Indies. Understanding post-industrial sites as new frontiers, rather than conceptualizing them according to the European concept of a shrinking city, may offer a way to create novel landscapes that are instrumental and appropriate to the Americas.

15. ibid, 123.
16. Timothy Morton's critique of landscape "Zero Landscapes in the Time of Hyperobjects", while a bit hyperbolic and unfair, is a good example of someone not taking the notion of landscape for granted and pointing out just how vague and problematic the term itself is.
17. Urquizo, Wiley Ludeña. "Paisaje y paisajimso peruano. Apuntes para una historia critica." *Textos-Arte*, No. 4.

Lima: Facultad de Arte Ponficia Universidad Catolica del Peru. 59–84.
18. Cosgrove, Denis. *Social Formation and Symbolic Landscape* (Madison, University of Wisconsin Press, 1984)
19. McLuhan, Marshal. *Understanding Media: The Extensions of Man* (London: Routledge, 2001), 7.
20. Worster, Donald. *Nature's Ecolonomy: A History of Ecological Ideas* (New York: Cambridge University

Press, 1998), 3–55.
21. Davis, Brian. "Landscapes and Instruments", *Landscape Journal*, 32-2. 161–176.
22. Galí-Izard, Teresa. *Los Mismos Paisajes: Ideas y Interpretaciones* (Barcelona: Editorial Gustavo Gigli S.A. 2004), 18-21.
23. Deleuze, Gilles. *Difference and Repetition* (New York: Continuum Press, 2004), 359.

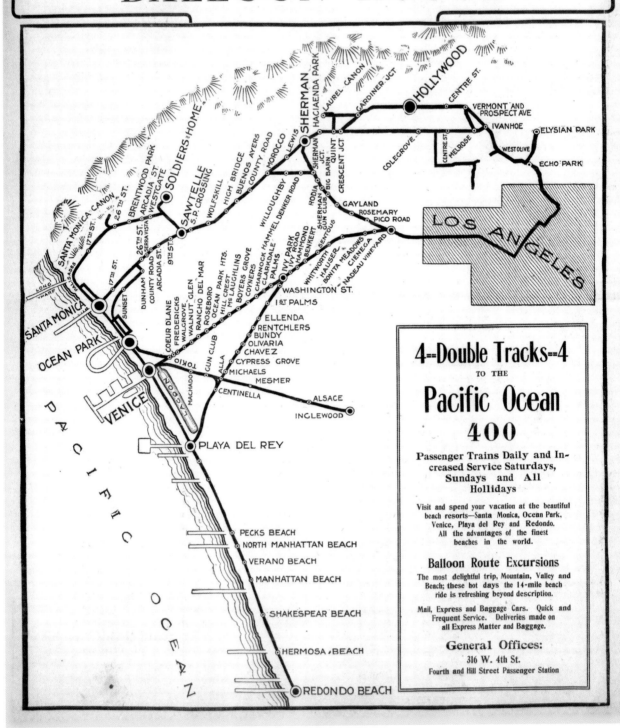

Los Angeles-Pacific Company
ELECTRIC LINES
"BALLOON ROUTE"

4=Double Tracks=4
TO THE
Pacific Ocean
400

Passenger Trains Daily and In-
creased Service Saturdays,
Sundays and All
Hollidays

Visit and spend your vacation at the beautiful
beach resorts—Santa Monica, Ocean Park,
Venice, Playa del Rey and Redondo.
All the advantages of the finest
beaches in the world.

Balloon Route Excursions

The most delightful trip, Mountain, Valley and
Beach; these hot days the 14-mile beach
ride is refreshing beyond description.

Mail, Express and Baggage Cars. Quick and
Frequent Service.   Deliveries made on
all Express Matter and Baggage.

General Offices:
316 W. 4th St.
Fourth and Hill Street Passenger Station

1906 Electric trolley lines between Los Angeles and the Pacific: This map of the electric trolley lines shows Los Angeles located well inland and connected to the coast by a network of transit lines; the location of downtown Los Angeles is a result of the historical institution known as the Spanish Law of the Indies, which dictated that cities in the New World be located twenty miles inland for protection from pirates.

California-mammoth trees: 1870, near Fresno; lumberjacks cutting up a tree with a seventy-eight foot circumference; The size of trees and extensiveness of forests in the Americas were such that new techniques for making axes were created, new methods for using longer crosscut saws were developed; The development of new technologies goes so far as to include ways to live on trees while they were being worked.

Technologies: A frontier landscape demands the development of new technologies and the deployment of existing ones in novel ways. The development of barbed wire, the Colt .45 [24], and new methods of surveying using the old Gunters Chain are testaments to this fact. While current landscape practice emphasizes the redevelopment of post-industrial sites through the real estate market and the regulatory instruments of bureaucracies such as the Environmental Protection Agency, a focus on the creation of novel technologies, and the application of existing ones in new ways, promises to open up new lines of action within post-industrial landscapes. These innovations will likely range from the newest technocratic gizmos with high barriers to entry, to lo-fi inventions deployed at massive scales.[25] Monitors that create spectacle and provide an alarm system for elevated levels of benzene might be installed at the site of an old gas works, semi-portable hydroponic digesters might be designed to allow vacant lots to act as temporary soil factories, while 5-gallon bags are affixed to old bulkheads creating new fish habitat and coir logs are inoculated with mycorrhizal spores and deployed like booms across a canal prior to sewer overflow events.

Social Institutions: The frontier landscape not only demands new technologies but also new social institutions. An institution can be understood as "a complex of positions, roles, norms and values lodged in particular types of social structures and organising relatively stable patterns of human activity with respect to fundamental problems in producing life-sustaining resources, in reproducing individuals, and in sustaining viable societal structures within a given environment." [26] That is, they are a reciprocal structure of persons in specific roles and the associated practices they employ toward specific outcomes. In the history of the Trans-American frontier the creation of the Texas Ranger and the Argentine gaucho, and the adoption of cultural practices such as primogeniture and homesteading are historical examples.

In each instance these institutions offer a way to pair local knowledge with new technologies and the power of a distant, centralized bureaucracy towards some problem encountered in the frontier landscape. The creation of the Texas Ranger bundled the local knowledge of farmers and ranchers with the technological advance of a handheld gun that could discharge rapidly and the financial might of a distant federal bureaucracy in Washington, D.C. in an effort to control a vast terrain contested between Mexico, the United States, and indigenous Comanches. In today's American cities there are some green shoots that suggest this is already happening, albeit at a different scale.

A recent example is the Aguas y Trabajo (AyT) project in Buenos Aires. Under the direction of river basin authority ACUMAR, the Argentine Water and Sewer Authority is paired with local colectivas — local labor organizations — to install

24. Webb, Walter Prescott. *The Great Frontier* (Boston: Houghton Mifflin, 1952), 239.

25. Davis, Brian. "Mycorrhizal Extrastructures", *Kerb* 19, 2011.

26. Turner, Jonathan. *The Institutional Order* (New York: Longman, 1997), 6.

27. ACUMAR, which stands for the Matanza-Riachuelo River Basin Authority, is a new agency that spans traditional municipal and federal jurisdictions and has capital funds. This makes it a unique organization—typically water basin authorities do not span jurisdictional boundaries, or more commonly do not have capital funds and are limited to an advisory role. The capital funds administered by ACUMAR come from a 2009 World Bank loan to the nation of Argentina, with much of the funding going to infrastructure in conjunction with the Argentine Water and Sewer Authority (AySA).

new water and sanitation infrastructure.[27] The AyT institution pairs the capital funds and technical expertise of the federal bureaucracy with the specific embodied knowledge of local workers who are daily affected by the results of the projects. Similar situations can be seen in New York City where surprising new partnerships are springing up in relation to the harbour and the intention to restore oysters to the estuary, or the efforts to reconstruct the recreational space and habitat zones in Jamaica Bay.[28] If post-industrial urban sites are understood as the contemporary frontier, then leveraging this tendency toward the development and adaptation of institutions becomes a critical component of the design project.

Frontier Landscapes as Borderlands of Intentionality

Today's urban landscapes — the plaza, the town square, and the street, as well as the port, the office park, the industrial shipping canal, and the parking lot — are the result of historical processes.[29] And some of these were the result of an American frontier condition. National parks, presidios and missions, and town plans based on aliquot parts (the system of land subdivision used in the Public Land Survey System) are all striking examples of this fact. Chimera-like landscapes arose from networks of bureaucratic inertia, the everyday minutiae of inhabitants' lives, the deployment of strange new technologies, and bacteria and mega-fauna in the throes of ecological release, all colliding. The result was the creation new territories at the extremes of accepted knowledge.

In the post-industrial sites strewn throughout the Americas, we are faced with a new frontier full of instability[30]; fraught and exciting places where it is unclear what should be done or who is in charge.[31] Yet precisely because of these facts, these sites offer "the expectations of mobility, vagrant roving, free time, and liberty"[32]. The recovery of a landscape approach alongside the construction of a nuanced and authentic understanding of the Trans-American frontier offers a precarious and exciting way forward for would-be settlers, rangers, outlaws, and natives but also the jaguar, mycorrhizae, and the Andean condor.

History suggests the results will almost certainly be uneven and at times violent, but we might learn some lessons from the past and embrace the historical condition of the frontier as a way to subvert the dominant modes of operating. Conceptualizing these landscapes as American frontier foregrounds new possibilities for technological innovation, both hi-tech and low-brow. As Frederick Jackson Turner recognized, new institutions, more adapted and appropriate to the contingencies of a shifting landscape, might spring to

life. Turner's work, which he himself admitted was not only Eurocentric but Anglo-Eurocentric, had important shortcomings. In particular, Turner's understanding that societies progressed from 'primitive' to sophisticated is a concept that has been shown wanting, analogous to the ecological theory of succession. Yet for all of its shortcomings the work of Turner points a way forward:

> For a moment, at the frontier, the bonds of custom are broken and unrestraint is triumphant. There is not tabula rasa. The stubborn American environment is there with its imperious summons to accept its conditions; the inherited ways of doing things are also there; and yet, in spite of environment, and in spite of custom, each frontier did indeed furnish a new field of opportunity, a gate of escape from the bondage of the past; and freshness, and confidence, and scorn of older society, impatience of its restraints and its ideas, and indifference to its lessons, have accompanied the frontier.[33]

A study of the American frontier as a landscape condition allows for a novel historical reading of our own geopolitical situation. Taking on frontier studies with a reconstructed landscape approach offers the chance to examine the effects of intention and agency, and the gap that is created between the two. The objective is nothing less than the development of new instruments and new modalities of landscape practice, and ultimately the creation of a more lateral spatial politics.[34]

Brian Davis is an assistant professor in landscape architecture at Cornell University, where he teaches runs the Borderlands Research Group which examines issues and potentials related to public landscapes and infrastructural projects in Latin America and New York State.

28. For a comprehensive write up of many of the various actors, capital and research partners, and overlapping jurisdictions acting on this situation see the "Oyster Reclamation Research Project" on the Urban Omnibus, http://urbanomnibus.net/2011/07/the-oyster-restoration-research-project/, accessed February 8, 2012. See also Brash, Alexander, et al. Gateway: *Visions for an Urban National Park* (New York: Princeton Architectural Press, 2011)

29. Jackson, John Brinkerhoff. *A Sense of Time, a Sense of Place.* (New Haven and London: Yale University Press, 1994), 173- 174.

30. Belanger, Pierre. "Landscape as Infrastructure," *Landscape Journal,* 2009 28:79-95.

31. Alan Berger's *Drosscape* publication does an excellent job of making the case for the prevalence of these places. He also brings up some of the issues – toxicity, economics, and politics— associated with them, and points an optimistic eye toward how we might act.

32. Solá-Morales Rubio, Ignasi de. "Terrain Vague" in *Anyplace* (Cambridge: MIT Press, 1995), 38.

33. Turner, Frederick Jackson. "The Significance of the Frontier in American History," 1893 American Historical Society President's Address. *The Frontier in American*

History (New York: Henry Holt and Company, 1920), 37–38.

34. Latour, Bruno. "Spheres and Networks." *Harvard Design Magazine 31: Sustainability and Pleasure, Volume II, Landscapes, Urbanism, and Products* (Fall/Winter 2009/2010) 141.

FULLY SERVICED

Martin Hogue

Bruce Davidson, Campground No. 4, Yosemite National Park (1966). Copyright Bruce Davidson/Magnum Photos.

[T]he romantic sportsman and traveler brought with him mementos of the civilized world he pretended to leave behind. These were important to keep him both physically comfortable and to prevent him from feeling that his connections to home life had been severed. He carried with him artifacts like neckties and champagne to keep up appearances and to avoid the sense of living in an uncouth or barbarous way he applied a civilized vocabulary to his wilderness campsite and activities to make them seem less hostile.[1]
— Philip G. Terrie, *Forever Wild: Environmental Aesthetics and the Adirondack Preserve*

Want more? You've got it. Level sites for your R.V. Grassy tent sites. Convenience store. Laundry facilities. Utility hookups. Swimming pool. Game rooms and playgrounds. Dump stations and advance reservations.
KOA—More of what you go camping for, '70s era advertisement

Modern campsites embody a peculiar contradiction: they are marketed to perpetuate the cherished American ideal of the backwoods camp yet serviced by an increasingly sophisticated range of utilities and conveniences. This phenomenon is not recent: the first tourists to the Adirondacks were privileged 19th century merchants and aristocrats from New York, Hartford, and Boston who, steeped in sophisticated garments and surrounded by experienced guides looking after their every need, spoke of the rejuvenating qualities of a few weeks spent "roughing it" in the backwoods. Fifty years later, electrical lighting in public campgrounds allowed campers to remain on the road longer, artificially lengthening the day so they would not be caught pitching their tent in complete darkness. Nowadays, the emergence of technological comforts like cable television and wi-fi begs the question: just how foreign, seductive, and mysterious is the realm of the campsite from the private domicile left behind?

    Bruce Davidson's wonderfully ironic 1966 photograph of Yosemite National Park draws critical attention to this continuing debate: the camp, which in earlier times had been a site of intense

---

1. Philip G. Terrie, *Forever Wild: Environmental Aesthetics and the Adirondack Preserve* (Philadelphia: Temple University Press, 1985), 50.

2. As Terrie suggests, this production was mostly accomplished by experienced guides, not the camper/tourist.

"My! how we slept last night. We'll stay here until to-morrow morning and hit the road again."

Early 20th century camping advertisement: The automobile still constitutes perhaps the most significant technological intrusion in the camping landscape, a source of continuing innovation and hybridization that yielded the tent trailer and the RV.

production[2], has been merely reduced to a glorified pantry—a place where goods are imported and consumed. Spread amidst the visual field of debris that is the campsite, a box of Ritz crackers near the geometrical center of the picture is identified as the true narrative focus of the scene: even the food is common-place, prefabricated.

Intended as a brief historical primer, this assembled collection of images explores the notion that the "cutting edge" of utilitarian excess is a paradoxical and continually evolving part of the camping experience. The goal of this exploration is to bring unvarnished attention to the programmatic diversity in camping culture. Like Davidson's work, these images pose an interesting challenge to the conventional rhetoric of camping and its emphasis on poetic optimism, independence, and personal empowerment. Of particular interest are alternate forms of representation such as maps, directories, matrixes, gear catalogs, advertisements, and the like.

While hardcore enthusiasts might scoff at the range of services offered on campsites, these multiple amenities celebrate the ingenuity with which intersecting narratives and desires surrounding the camping experience in America (wilderness, individuality, access, speed, comfort, nostalgia, profit) have been strangely and powerfully hybridized.

The automobile still constitutes perhaps the most significant technological intrusion in the camping landscape, a source of continuing innovation and hybridization that yielded the tent trailer and the RV.

The *Campmor 2011* collage examines the recent proliferation of gear in popular culture. The scene features four occupants sampled from Arthur Fitzwilliam Tait's celebrated 1878 Currier and Ives illustration of early campers in the Adirondacks, outfitted with gear selections from the spring 2011 edition of the Campmor catalog, one of the foremost retailers of camping gear in the United States. The retailer's distinctive graphic style constitutes a self-conscious throwback, with black and white, folksy hand-drawn depictions of its products. Each of the 32 individual items lifted from the catalog becomes part of a greater, scenic whole that recalls Davidson's congested campsite. Camping instrumentation is no longer simply limited to old, discarded items from the kitchen back home. Instead they are brand new, shiny pieces of gear custom-made for the rigors of the campsite. Indeed who could refuse a waterproof salt and pepper shaker (sold as a pair for only $3.95)? Campmor and other retailers like REI and EMS are banking on the fact that modern camper can be seduced by technological wizardry—not simply by the campsite's pastoral setting. Record sales reported by these sporting utility stores owe largely to successful efforts to associate their equipment with the out-of-doors and the prospect of healthy living. High-performance gear like hiking boots and mountaineering vests have become staples not just of camping outings but of everyday casual chic.

While the range of equipment brought by campers to campsites continues to impress, the programmatic specialization of fixed infrastructure surrounding campgrounds is equally remarkable in its own right. As a representation strategy, the origins of this type of services-matrix are grounded in efforts as early as the '20s to publicize newly emerging utilitarian features at municipal facilities across the country. Chapter XIII of *Motor Camping* by J.C. and J.D. Long stands out as perhaps the first true

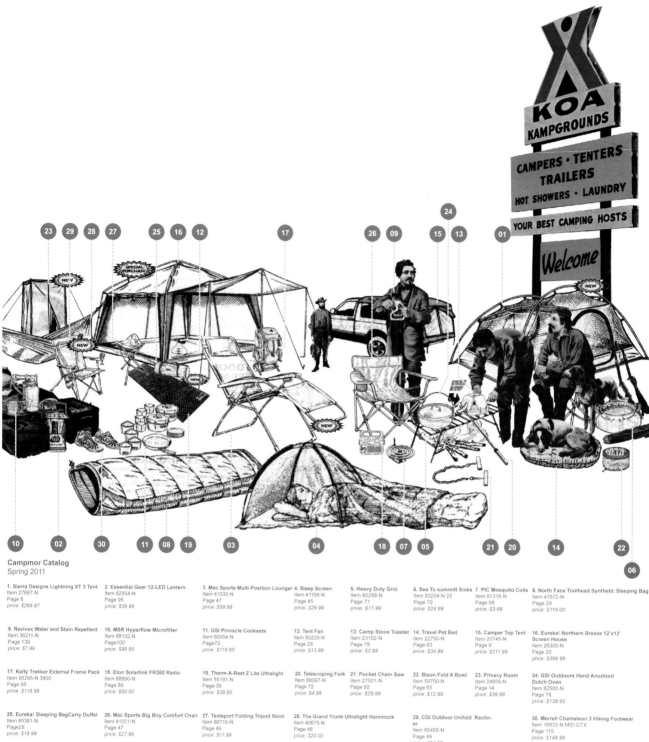

Campmor Catalog
Spring 2011

1. Sierra Designs Lightning XT 3 Tent Item 27667-N Page 8 *price: $269.97*	**2.** Essential Gear 12-LED Lantern Item 82954-N Page 95 *price: $39.99*

1. Sierra Designs Lightning XT 3 Tent · Item 27667-N · Page 8 · *price: $269.97*
2. Essential Gear 12-LED Lantern · Item 82954-N · Page 95 · *price: $39.99*
3. Mac Sports Multi-Position Lounger · Item 41030-N · Page 47 · *price: $59.98*
4. Sleep Screen · Item 41166-N · Page 45 · *price: $29.99*
5. Heavy Duty Grid · Item 80288-N · Page 71 · *price: $17.99*
6. Sea To summitt Sinks · Item 83204-N 20 · Page 79 · *price: $24.99*
7. PIC Mosquito Coils · Item 81316-N · Page 99 · *price: $3.99*
8. North Face Trailhead Synthetic Sleeping Bag · Item 47672-N · Page 29 · *price: $119.00*

9. Revivex Water and Stain Repellent · Item 36211-N · Page 139 · *price: $7.99*
10. MSR Hyperflow Microfilter · Item 88102-N · Page100 · *price: $99.95*
11. GSI Pinnacle Cooksets · Item 60054-N · Page73 · *price: $119.95*
12. Tent Fan · Item 85229-N · Page 25 · *price: $13.99*
13. Camp Stove Toaster · Item 23102-N · Page 78 · *price: $3.99*
14. Travel Pet Bed · Item 22750-N · Page 63 · *price: $34.99*
15. Camper Top Tent · Item 20745-N · Page 9 · *price: $211.99*
16. Eureka! Northern Breeze 12'x12' Screen House · Item 26300-N · Page 20 · *price: $399.99*

17. Kelty Trekker External Frame Pack · Item 90295-N 3900 · Page 56 · *price: $119.99*
18. Eton Solarlink FR360 Radio · Item 88890-N · Page 89 · *price: $50.00*
19. Therm-A-Rest Z Lite Ultralight · Item 55191-N · Page 72 · *price: $39.95*
20. Telescoping Fork · Item 88097-N · Page 72 · *price: $4.99*
21. Pocket Chain Saw · Item 27001-N · Page 92 · *price: $29.99*
22. Bison Fold A Bowl · Item 59700-N · Page 63 · *price: $12.99*
23. Privacy Room · Item 24659-N · Page 14 · *price: $39.99*
24. GSI Outdoors Hand Anodized Dutch Oven · Item 82500-N · Page 78 · *price: $139.95*

25. Eureka! Sleeping BagCarry Duffel · Item 45381-N · Page28 · *price: $19.99*
26. Mac Sports Big Boy Comfort Chair · Item 41021-N · Page 47 · *price: $27.99*
27. Textsport Folding Tripod Stool · Item 86716-N · Page 49 · *price: $11.99*
28. The Grand Trunk Ultralight Hammock · Item 40675-N · Page 46 · *price: $20.00*
29. CGI Outdoor Unifold Recliner · Item 65458-N · Page 49 · *price: $54.99*
30. Merrell Chameleon 3 Hiking Footwear · Item 16833-N MID GTX · Page 115 · *price: $149.99*

Campmor collage: Collage by the author. 2011. One of the foremost retailers of camping gear in the United States, Campmor's distinctive catalog style constitutes a bit of a self-conscious throwback, with back and white, folksy hand-drawn depictions of its products. As the collage demonstrates, both the diversity and degree of specialization found throughout Campmor's 64 densely printed pages is at times stunning.

MOTOR CAMPING

BY

J. C. LONG

AND

JOHN D. LONG

WITH ILLUSTRATIONS
AND DIAGRAMS

NEW YORK
DODD, MEAD AND COMPANY
1923

---

216   MOTOR CAMPING

by automobile and were prepared to camp." This number was exceeded in the season of 1922.

Much of the National Forest area is accessible to automobiles and more roads are being constructed all the time by State or National agencies. Owing to the activities of the Forest Service and the automobile clubs, California can now claim to have the best signed mountain roads in America.

The Forest Service has arranged a great number of camping places for motor tourists.

COLORADO

Municipal Camp Sites

Town or City	Charge or Free	Toilet	Drinking Water	Fireplace or Stove	Lights	Bath or Shower
Alamosa	F	Y	Y	Y	Y	
Arriba						
Ault	F	Y	Y	Y	Y	
Berthoud	F	Y	Y	Y	Y	
Boulder	F	Y	Y	Y	Y	Y
Brush	F	Y	Y	Y	Y	
Buena Vista	F	Y	Y	Y		
Burlington						
Canon City	F	Y	Y	Y	Y	Y
Castle Rock	F	Y	Y	Y		
Cheyenne Wells	F	Y	Y	Y		
Colorado Springs	25c.-50c. a day	Y	Fuel	Y		
Creede (2 parks)	F	Y	Y	Y	Y	
Cripple Creek	F	Y	Y	Y		
Denver	F	Y	Y	Y	Y	Y
Eagle						
Flagler						

LIST OF CAMPING SITES   217

COLORADO—Continued

Town or City	Charge or Free	Toilet	Drinking Water	Fireplace or Stove	Lights	Bath or Shower
Florence	F	Y	Y	Y	Y	
Fort Collins	F	Y	Y	Y	Y	Y
Fort Morgan	F	Y	Y	Y	Y	
Fowler	F	Y	Y	Y	Y	
Fruita						
Glenwood Spr'gs	F	Y	Y	Y	Y	
Grand Junction	F	Y	Y	Y	Y	Y
Greeley	F	Y	Y	Y	Y	Y
Green Mountain Falls						
Holyoke	F	Y	Y	Y	Y	
Hotchkiss	F	Y	Y	Y	Y	
Idaho Springs	F	Y	Y	Y	Y	
La Veta	F	Y	Y	Y	Y	Y
Leadville						
Limon						
Littleton						
Loveland	F	Y	Y	Y	Y	Y
Manitou						
Matheson						
Meeker	F	Y	Y	Y	Y	Y
Monte Vista	F	Y	Y	Y	Y	
New Castle						
Ordway	F	Y	Y	Y	Y	
Ouray	F	Y	Y	Y	Y	
Pagosa Springs	F	Y	Y	Y	Y	
Palisades						
Peyton						
Pueblo	F	Y	Y	Y	Y	
Ramah						
Red Cliff						
Rocky Ford						

Long directory: Sample directory pages from John Cuthbert and John Dietrichjoint Long, *Motor Camping* (1923. Reprint, Charleston, SC: Bibliolife, 2009)

---

example of a matrix on a large scale. The authors assembled from a number of disparate sources information on over 2,000 municipal, state, and federal facilities across the country. Arranged by state in a standard six column format pertaining to individual utilities (*cost; presence or absence of toilets; drinking water; fireplace or stove; lights; bath or shower*), the matrix allowed campers to debate *in advance of arrival* the relative merits of several potential campgrounds under consideration for the night.

This comparative mode of description has historically proved not only seductive but generative as well, acting both as an inventory *and* an agent of change and innovation. There exists within the logic of the Long matrix a tendency to work towards a certain level of density: a campground interested in competing with others should offer all services listed. Moreover, it could also expand its services beyond the original list.

Featured preeminently by the Longs in their book, Denver's municipal campground in Overland Park (1917–30) is among the first to try and aggressively broaden its approach with regards to its peers. Billed as "the Manhattan of auto camps"[3], Overland Park spread 160 acres along the Platte river, building its national reputation on offering a wide range of attractions that became the envy of municipal autocamps around the country. Further, its brutal size — 800 lots, each 25 x 30 feet — was designed to accommodate as many as 6,000 autocampers on any given night. At its height of operation in the mid-1920's, the campground, which was situated at the perimeter of the local automobile racetrack, offered a 400 seat movie theater, tourist information services, evening lectures, a restaurant, a barber shop, a gas station, an automotive repair garage, a grocery store, and laundry accommodations. As is customary in camping rhetoric, advertisements of the day strove to reconcile the prospects of being big and the camper's desire for pastoral settings. Overland Park anticipated Kampgrounds of America's (KOA's) revolution in camping utilities by more than 40 years, and in its urbanity rivals any campground built since.

KOA's own growth as a new, nationally branded system of franchises was remarkable: from a single campground in 1962, it had grown to 829 facilities nationwide by 1979.[4] By the late '60s it had surpassed the National Park Service in the number of individual campsites.[5] A crucial component

---

3. Warren James Belasco, *Americans on the Road: From Autocamp to Motel, 1910-1945* (Baltimore: The Johns Hopkins University Press, 1997), 72.

4. KOA has several franchises in Canada and Mexico, too. It also briefly and unsuccessfully developed campgrounds in Japan.

5. Susan Sessions Rugh, *Are We There Yet? The Golden Age of American Family Vacations* (Lawrence: University of Kansas Press, 2008), 131.

The club house at Overland Park, built when horse racing was in its palmy days, now the nerve center of the Denver automobile camp for tourists. The remodeled club house contains twenty-four rooms, hot and cold showers, laundry room, restaurant, refreshment stand, grocery store, steam table, lunch counter, dance floor and numerous ac-

commodations for the tourist. In preparing the camping grounds for the tourist the park authorities were confronted by fields of dandelions and daisies. A flock of sheep was turned into the park to reduce this crop. The camping area includes 800 lots, but may be increased to hold 6,000 or 8,000 people if necessary

Overland Park, Motor Camp De Luxe

Tourist Campers Now Have Freedom of Denver's Quarter Million Dollar Automobile Park, with Free Sites, Water, Electric Light, Shower Baths, Comfort Stations and Laundry---Twenty-four Room Club House, with Grocery Store, Steam Table, Lunch Room, Soda Fountain, Filling Station and Garage, Provided in Motor City

Overland publicity image: "Overland Park, Motor Camp De Luxe." Denver Municipal Facts 6-7 (1920), 3-5. As is customary in camping rhetoric, advertisements of the day strove to reconcile the prospects of being big and the camper's desire for pastoral settings.

of KOA's information strategy was its exclusive, annual directory. Complete with location maps and service matrixes for each state, KOA directories in effect instituted and perpetuated the image of its campgrounds as a self-sufficient system of facilities. To the camper, the directory, like the matrix, promised that the quality of the camping experience would be reassuring familiar: "Travel free from worry about where you will stay each night."[6] With this information at their disposal, campers could now plan their next stop and even call in a reservation to ensure availability.

Central to founder Dave Drum's approach were strategies of systematization and diversification both internal (services) and external (location) to the campground itself. Drum believed in offering the camper literally everything he wanted, often to the point of shameless excess. The brief summary highlights some of the utilities introduced in the fields of advance reservations, communications, lodging diversity, entertainment and ease of access: building on a consultation of directories published by KOA, a national location map including every franchise developed in its 50-year history indeed confirms the crucial emphasis placed by KOA on this last criteria, with most facilities often minutes away from major thruways. No longer a destination activity, camping takes its rightful place at highway exits everywhere with the likes of McDonald's, Holiday Inn, and the Home Depot.

It is reasonable to ask, in an era where campers have routine access to wi-fi and access to powerful databases that list information on individual campgrounds and campsites nationally, where this proliferation of comforts is likely to end. Bruce Davidson's alarming 1966 photograph marking the

6. Kampgrounds of America, *Kampground Directory: 1970 Winter Edition* (Billings, MO: 1970), 8.

Kampgrounds of America (KOA) utilities fact sheet*
(1962-2009)

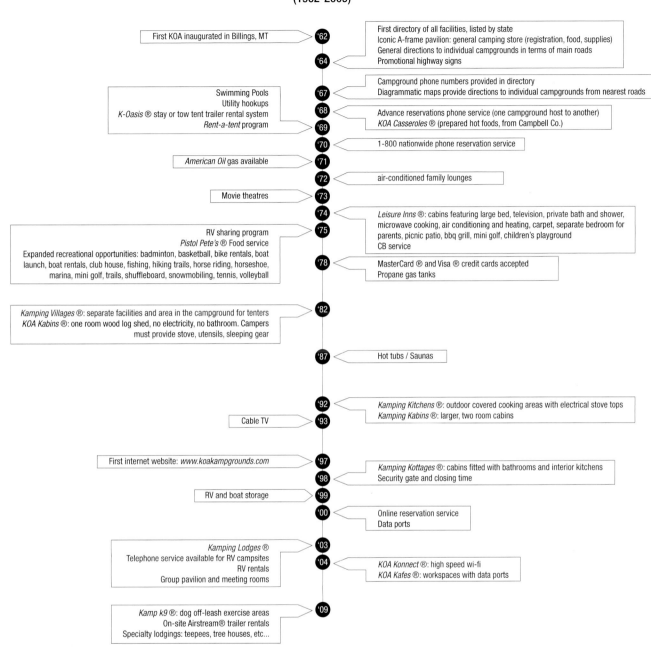

First KOA inaugurated in Billings, MT — '62

'62 — First directory of all facilities, listed by state
Iconic A-frame pavilion: general camping store (registration, food, supplies)
General directions to individual campgrounds in terms of main roads
'64 — Promotional highway signs

'67 — Campground phone numbers provided in directory
Diagrammatic maps provide directions to individual campgrounds from nearest roads

Swimming Pools
Utility hookups
K-Oasis ® stay or tow tent trailer rental system
Rent-a-tent program

'68 — Advance reservations phone service (one campground host to another)
KOA Casseroles ® (prepared hot foods, from Campbell Co.)

'70 — 1-800 nationwide phone reservation service

American Oil gas available — '71

'72 — air-conditioned family lounges

Movie theatres — '73

'74 — *Leisure Inns* ®: cabins featuring large bed, television, private bath and shower,
microwave cooking, air conditioning and heating, carpet, separate bedroom for
parents, picnic patio, bbq grill, mini golf, children's playground
'75 — CB service

RV sharing program
Pistol Pete's ® Food service
Expanded recreational opportunities: badminton, basketball, bike rentals, boat
launch, boat rentals, club house, fishing, hiking trails, horse riding, horseshoe,
marina, mini golf, trails, shuffleboard, snowmobiling, tennis, volleyball

'78 — MasterCard ® and Visa ® credit cards accepted
Propane gas tanks

Kamping Villages ®: separate facilities and area in the campground for tenters
KOA Kabins ®: one room wood log shed, no electricity, no bathroom. Campers
must provide stove, utensils, sleeping gear — '82

'87 — Hot tubs / Saunas

'92 — *Kamping Kitchens* ®: outdoor covered cooking areas with electrical stove tops
Kamping Kabins ®: larger, two room cabins
Cable TV — '93

First internet website: *www.koakampgrounds.com* — '97

'98 — *Kamping Kottages* ®: cabins fitted with bathrooms and interior kitchens
Security gate and closing time

RV and boat storage — '99

'00 — Online reservation service
Data ports

Kamping Lodges ® — '03
Telephone service available for RV campsites
RV rentals
Group pavilion and meeting rooms

'04 — *KOA Konnect* ®: high speed wi-fi
KOA Kafes ®: workspaces with data ports

Kamp k9 ®: dog off-leash exercise areas
On-site Airstream® trailer rentals
Specialty lodgings: teepees, tree houses, etc... — '09

*availability subject to location

KOA utilities history fact sheet [1962-2012]: Data
compiled by the author from a comprehensive analysis of
all campground directories published by KOA since 1964.

Wal-Mart campsite: Posted on Flickr.com.

centennial anniversary of the opening of Yosemite National Park seems almost quaint by comparison now. KOA's decline from nearly 900 facilities nationally in the late '70s to a mere 440 in 2012 seems to suggests a spike in the camping craze, with a return perhaps to more traditional values driven by a new ecological awareness.

On the other hand, retailer Wal-Mart's decision 10 years ago to open its parking lots nationally to overnighting RVers free of charge indicates a further and potentially radical devaluation of the campsite. With its only goal being to attract new customers, Wal-Mart's decision created (literally overnight) a new campground system with thousands of facilities that could rival camping giants like KOA. With no services whatsoever except the lure of low prices, Wal-Mart campers must be completely sustainable from the standpoint of electricity and water consumption, waste accumulation and disposal, security, etc… Indeed, who needs anything more than a parking space when you're at the wheel of a fully autonomous, $300,000 RV with three televisions and room for five?[7] Who even needs outdoor space? Saddled with an 8.5 mpg average fuel consumption, these proud owners might be tempted to settle more permanently in one of these parking lots than they would to take the wide open road.

Martin Hogue is the W. M. Kennedy Jr. Fellow at the State University of New York's Department of Landscape Architecture. Trained as an architect and landscape architect and working primarily with analytical drawings as a mode of inquiry, his research explores the notion of "site" as a cultural construction.

---

7. The 2013 Fleetwood Providence retails for $328,000. These seem modestly priced in comparison to the $2.5 million Vantre Platinum Plus, which includes indoor parking space for an automobile below the living quarters.

ENVIRONMENT—WEBS

Lola Sheppard

Architecture has recently renewed its fascination with the notion of environment, as a dynamic and an atmospherically tangible space of design. This has been driven by a number of trajectories and positions within the discipline. On the one hand, the ever-expanding discourse on sustainability has brought debates of technology-driven versus passive means of control to the fore. On the other hand, architecture has embraced responsive design anew, testing the possibility of environments that contain instruments for sensing and responding to atmospheric conditions and human occupants. Simultaneously, responsive design has sought out biological and ecological models, embracing the notion of architecture an as organism able to physically react to changing interior and exterior environmental conditions.

Reacting to the strictures of modernism in the 1960s, interest in ideas of environment served as a provocation to conventional models of architecture, and was part of a design counter-culture. Architects Buckminster Fuller and Francois Dallegret, and theorist Reyner Banham, as well as several Viennese and British architects[1], were advocating for architecture to reduce—if not shed entirely—its envelope, in favor of more technological means of producing controlled environments. In parallel, architects were speculating on the possibility of environments driven by informational feedback mechanisms rather than atmospherics. Recent renewed interest in the writings and work of this constellation of thinkers has influenced an evolving set of discussions and design provocations, centered around the consideration of environment and its external linkages.

Environment of Control

In many of the visions produced in the 1960s, including Fuller and Sadao's *Dome over Manhattan* (1960), Banham and Dallegret's *Environment-Bubble* (1965), or David Greene's *Living Pod* (1966), among others, architecture is reduced to 'bubble', located in the thin membrane that establishes this threshold. Banham and Dallegret's paradigmatic *Environment-Bubble* suggested that habitation was no longer a question of shelter, but rather, of conditioning, embracing the dematerialization of envelope and the augmentation of technology. Describing the "Standard-of-Living Package" which would anticipate a full eradication of the architectural envelope, Banham advocates that "to the man who has everything else, a standard-of-living package such as this could offer the ultimate goody—the power to impose his will on any environment to which the package could be delivered; to enjoy the spatial freedom of the nomadic campfire without the smell, smoke, ashes and mess..."[2]

The image of Banham and Dallegret in the bubble, suggests an environment in service of comfort, with the eradication of all bodily encumbrances, including furniture and indeed clothes. Environment here is technologically controlled and is neutralized to remove, as Banham proposes, the messy realities required to maintain a conditioned environment. In a certain irony, the climatic and environmental differences between interior and exterior demarcated by the bubble remain abstract, as does the material reality of envelope, yet the architects knew exactly where the hi-fi stereo, television and speakers would go. In her essay "Ecology without the Oikos," theorist Amy Kulper examines the relationship between morphology and ecology in Banham and Dallegret's work, in contra-point to contemporary architectural practice. She argues that Banham brought an interest in thinking the ecological, evidenced in books such as *Los Angeles: The Architecture of Four Ecologies* (1971), where ecology is understood not as a science, but as "lived environment."[3] Describing the *Environment Bubble*, Kulper writes the project "shifts architectural priorities from enclosure to building systems, from the monumental to the temporary...the Environment-Bubble embodies a diagram of architecture's capitulation to technological imperatives, its envelope or skin reduced to a token gesture of enclosure, nearing invisibility, and quite literally stretched to both its material and disciplinary limit."[4]

Operating at a much larger scale of environmental envelope, Fuller, in his unrealized *Dome over Manhattan* project, offered an articulate scenario for how the urban metabolism, the envelope's structure, and the environmental systems of this visionary urban bubble might work. He describes methods for water management, indicates the need to heat the skin in order to shed snow and ice in the winter, and to manage solar gain in the summer, among many other issues.[5] Here, the ecological complexity and mechanics necessary for maintaining

1. Projects such as Hans Hollein's *Mobile Office* (1969); Coop Himmelb(l)au's *Restless Sphere* (1971); Haus-Rucker-Co's *Oase No. 7* (1972), and in the UK, works such as Archigram's *Suitaloon* were later projects that continued, in part, the legacy of Banham and Dallegret's *Environment Bubble*.

2. Reyner Banham, "A Home Is Not A House," *Art in America* Number Two (April, 1965): 75.

3. Amy Kulper, "Ecology without the Oikos: Banham, Dallegret and the Morphological Context of Environmental Architecture," *Field Journal*, vol.4 (1) (January 2011): 72.

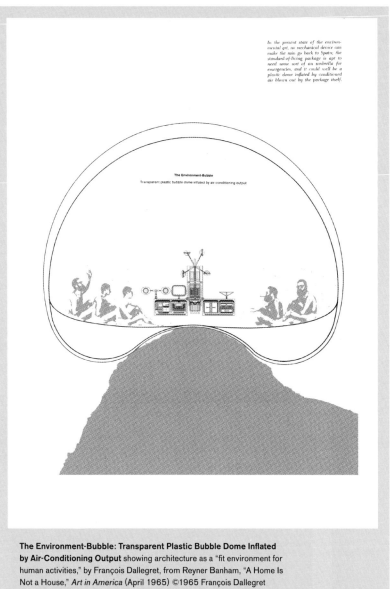

In the present state of the environmental art, no mechanical device can make the rain go back to Spain; the standard-of-living package is apt to need some sort of an umbrella for emergencies, and it could well be a plastic dome inflated by conditioned air blown out by the package itself.

The Environment-Bubble: Transparent Plastic Bubble Dome Inflated by Air-Conditioning Output showing architecture as a "fit environment for human activities," by François Dallegret, from Reyner Banham, "A Home Is Not a House," *Art in America* (April 1965) ©1965 François Dallegret

an isolated environment begin to be acknowledged. The ambition of mechanically producing and sustaining artificial environments reached its apogee in the 1991's *Biosphere II* experiment in Oracle, Arizona, which sought to reproduce—in a hermetically sealed spaceframe envelope—the web of interactions within life systems, including the provision of various ecological biomes, an agricultural zone and human living space. No exchange of air, moisture, or gas between the interior and exterior environments was permitted for the purposes of this grand experiment. However, ultimately, the complexities of humans, species, and ecologies cohabiting in a synthetic environment proved incompatible. In an ironic turn of events, the ambitious enterprise failed

because ants chewed through the building caulking, causing multiple leaks in the structure, thus rendering the experiment void. "The unanticipated behaviors of the biotic life within the system threatened this clean separation of an independent container and the self-organized ecosystem it contained."[6] What becomes evident across the range of bubbled environments is the struggle with, and in many cases disregard for, how to integrate biological matter; the unpredictability of plant and animal species was irreconcilable with the need to control environment. Even humans, in this context, are understood as technologically-dependent rather than biological beings.

4. Ibid., 84.
5. Buckminster Fuller. See *St. Louis Dispatch*, Sept 26, 1965 and *Scientific American*, Jan/Feb. 1970.

6. Meredith Miller, "Spheres, Domes, Limits and Interfaces: The Transgressive Architecture of Biosphere 2," *ACSA Annual Conference Proceedings* (2011), 102-110.

Biosphere 2: a 1.3 hectare structure built to be an artificial, materially closed ecological system. Envisioned as a self-sustaining organization, it explored the web of interactions within living systems. Image courtesy of the University of Arizona.

Many of these architecture bubble projects were being developed within the context of the 1960s and 1970s environmental movement and the Cold War. Tacit in a number of the proposals was a defensive strategy against an exterior environment deemed to be potentially threatening or toxic, or at the very least, uncontrolled. This trait was evident in the later work of the California-based architecture and media collective known as Ant Farm. Ant Farm played off a "survivalist rhetoric and military tropes"[7] and their provocative installations were largely a response to the growing national nuclear weapons research program and an increasing awareness of environmental concerns. However, as theorist Felicity Scott argues, with its almost invisible skin, the bubble is evoked not for the promises of survival, but rather, to participate in a battle over the future of the environment. "Far from refusing technologies of control, or defending the discipline against their vicissitudes, Ant Farm situated their architecture within this very technological milieu."[8] Peter Sloterdijk, in *Terror from the Air*, underscores the fundamental transformation that occurred in the twentieth century, when "the discovery of the 'environment' took place in the trenches of World War 1."[9] Sloterdijk suggests that with the release of poison clouds upon enemy lines, Europeans created an ecologized war. In this new era of "atmoterrorism," no protective envelope is possible; we are indissociably one with environment, and this very medium can be turned against us.[10] This

awareness, alongside an ever-growing consciousness of climate change, renders our dependence and complicity with environment acute. Environment in the twenty-first century has becomes more extreme in its material, social, and political identity, raising the question of how architecture's envelopes might respond, and what new roles might they take on.

Given the range of interpretations of the term environment, it is telling to review its multiple meanings. The term is understood as "the action or state of circum-navigating, encompassing, or surrounding something;" or "the physical surroundings or external conditions in general affecting the life, existence, or properties of a person, an organism or object." Other meanings of the term embrace environment as "the social, political, or cultural circumstances in which a person lives, in particular as it affects behaviour, attitudes, etc." or the overall physical, systematic, or logical structure (including operating system, software tools, interfaces) within which a computer or program can operate.[11] Also implied in the term is the notion of environment as a material entity; the air, moisture, and gases that sustain life. Embedded in each of these definitions is an idea of environment as a territory under the influence of a given force – be it political, technological, or ecological. Most architectural discussions on environment imply architecture at the scale of the bubble or singular spatial unit; architecture as envelope, intended to separate interior conditions from exterior surroundings. Yet the

7. Felicity D. Scott, *Architecture or Techno-utopia: Politics after Modernism* (Cambridge: 2007), 215.
8. Ibid., 213.

9. Peter Sloterdijk, *Terror from the Air* (Lost Angeles: Semiotext: 2009), 18.
10. Ibid., 20.

11. "Oxford Dictionary," http://www.oxforddictionaries.com/definition/english/environment. Last accessed August 15, 2014.

 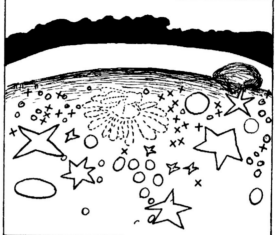

Umgebung and *Umwelt* of the honey bee. *Umgebung* or surroundings comprise all the elements present in the territory of a species; *Unwelt* or environment consists only of those elements that are instrumental. Image source: Jacob von Uexküll (1934), reprinted in *A Foray into the Worlds of Animals and Humans*, University of Minnesota Press, 2011.

multiplicity of meanings outlined above suggest a more ambiguous and productive understanding of environment's edges.

The Instrumentality of Environment

In the 1930s, German biologist and philosopher Jakob von Uexküll outlined the relationship between individual species and their physical surrounding in his treatise *A Foray into the Worlds of Animals and Humans*. Uexküll observed how living beings perceive their environments and articulated the difference between *umgebung* (surrounding) and *umwelt* (environment). *Umgebung*, he argues, consists of everything that is physically present in the territory of a species, while *umwelt* consists only of what is useful or instrumental to that species, or what Uexküll describes as a species' "perceptual-life world."[12] He argues that "an animal is not immersed in a given milieu but at best engages with certain features that are of significance to it, that counterpoint in some sense, with its own organs."[13] The environment of the organism is precisely as complex as the organs of that organism. Uexküll suggests that each species has an environment bubble, albeit one bounded not by a physical limit, but rather an operational one, defined by the constituent elements required for survival. These elements serve as perceptual stimuli or cues to help define a species' specific world within the surrounding. The *umwelt* of different organisms may overlap with one another; the relations between

things expanding and meshing with one another in the intricate web of life. Embracing a comprehensive understanding of environments, Uexküll writes: "Nature conforms to a 'super-mechanical principal' that has no formative plan but that extends across all things, both organic and inorganic."[14]

Extending from Uexküll's suggestion of environments as webs of overlapping rather than isolated bubbles, the role of architecture in the production of environment—and the scale at which it might contribute—is challenged. In this scenario, architecture becomes but one milieu within a series of intersecting environments of people, species, plants, and machines. Architecture must work as a platform—an infrastructure or armature—that should be conceptually, if not literally, porous; able to allow movement of air, moisture, gases, materials, and species.

Only in the past few decades, has it been universally recognized that natural ecologies are deeply intertwined with human forces. Simultaneously, evolving metaphors embraced by the discipline of ecology have been shifting from a boundary and organism-based model to a systems-based one in which organisms and species are understood through energy flow or exchange maps.[15] Landscape architect Kristina Hill describes evolving paradigms of ecology, shifting towards a non-linear/equilibrium system, in which nature is driven by multi-directional change.[16]

12. Jakob von Uexküll, *A Foray into the Worlds of Animals and Humans with A Theory of Meaning*, trans. Joseph D. O'Neil (Minneapolis: Minnesota University Press, 2010)

13. Ibid., 214.
14. Ibid., 258.
15. Ibid., 135.

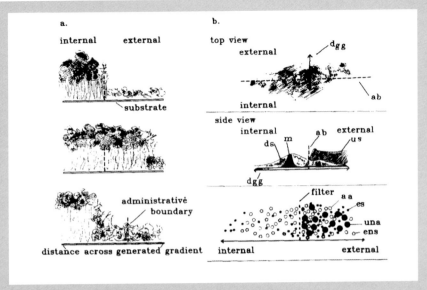

Boundary Conditions: Diagram of three hypothetical generated edges relative to administrative boundaries (ab) Filter properties of administrative boundaries (ab) Image source: C. Schonewald-Cox and J. Bayless, 'The Boundary Model: A Geographical Analysis of Design and Conservation of Nature Reserves'.

Boundaries of Exchange

There is increasing acknowledgement of the role of temporal transformations within ecological systems, suggesting it is an unstable and changing set of dynamics. In order to understand ecological systems, flows, and exchanges, the boundaries of exchange must also be studied and conceptualized. Ecologists classify boundaries as having exogenous or endogenous origins, resulting, respectively, from processes outside or inside the system of boundaries or territories being studied.[17] The species and ecologies within the territory or zone might transform the boundary, as might exterior conditions such as wind, water currents, and species migration. These forces can maintain, augment, or weaken boundaries over time.

In the mid-1980s, Christine Schonewald-Cox and Jonathan Bayless analyzed ecological performance boundaries in relation to administrative demarcations, using National Parks as test cases. They proposed that the boundary of a reserve be viewed conceptually as a filter, that it is tied to biological forces as well as human culture, economics, and physical geography. They produced a series of planimetric and sectional studies documenting reserve boundary conditions, which can vary in nature and porosity along their edge. These boundaries are often defined by a "generated gradient or edge;"[18] a zone, with thickness that changes in abundance of species, resources and human activities, and that can move under the influence external pressures acting on the reserve. Schonewald-Cox and Bayless' diagrammatic analyses demonstrate ecological boundaries as temporal, multiple, thickened, differentiated along their length, and mediating political, cultural, and ecological forces. Transferring such ecological models back to architectures and mediated environments raises questions of how envelopes and boundaries might operate under both interior and exterior forces—including flows of air, vehicles, human bodies, animal species, or plants.

Many landscape architects, most notably Gilles Clement, have argued for the consideration of landscapes "in evolution" that are based on how species take hold, migrate, thrive, and fail within the immediate landscape and the extended ecological network.[19] To a large extent, this is in contrast with landscape architecture's historically static aesthetic tendencies, in which a design, once implemented, is imagined to remain unchanged over time. In Clement's model, design accommodates temporal change rather than enforcing

16. Kristina Hill, "Shifting Sites," in *Site Matters: Design Concepts, Histories, and Strategies*, edited by Andrea Kahn and Carol J. Burns (New York: Routledge, 2005), 143.

17. Ibid., 131.

18. Schonewald-Cox and Bayless define the generated or gradient edge as follows: "The generated edge is distinct in that its location and characteristics develop in response to the condition and effectiveness of the first filter. This edge, generated by protection, also affects protection. It includes ecologic, geologic, climatic, economic, and demographic gradients, such as varying land-use practices."

Christine M. Schonewald-Cox, "The Boundary Model: A geographical Analysis of Desing and Conservation of Nature Reserves," *BioScience*, Vol. 38, No. 7, Oxford University Press on behalf of the American Institute of Biological Sciences (July/August 1988) Stable

URL: http://www.jstor.org/stable/131095. Accessed: 08/10/2014 14:47

19. See Gilles Clement's essay within *Meaning in Landscape Architecture and Gardens*, ed. Marc Trieb (Routledge: London, 2011)

predetermined end results, thus relinquishing control over outcomes.[20]

This design model is somewhat easier to envision within the medium of landscape architecture, which inherently works with dynamic processes of succession and evolution. Even so, Clement's propositions were considered provocative when introduced in mid 1980s. Within any design field, relinquishing control is often at odds with aesthetic intent. However, similar discussions are now beginning to pervade architects' design approaches, which respond to varying programmatic, economic or ecological demands. To embrace dynamic conceptions of environment, at the scale of buildings and urbanism, might suggest architectures able to evolve, transform, and weather; envelopes as surfaces of exchange, seeding or even cross-contaminating interior and exterior environments.

Most research into building envelopes has concentrated on furthering the comfort of its human inhabitants, or at best, to reduce energy loads. Other research has examined the transformation of buildings' envelopes over time, albeit with a focus on aesthetic and performance questions.[21] While these ambitions are laudable, they maintain an anthropocentric bias and leave unchallenged the paradigm of architecture resisting environment rather than contributing to it. What if the boundaries and territories of buildings were able to sustain multiple species simultan-eously—human, plant, and animal? If the envelope is understood as both *acted upon* but also *acting on* the exterior environment—impacting it and benefitting from it—architecture would need a far more reciprocal relationship with an extended environment.

Materializing Environment

Over the past decade or more, the question of environment has been rekindled, in part due to the recovery of interest in Reyner Banham's works and writings in contemporary architectural discourse, in particular his *Architecture of the Well-Tempered Environment* (1969). Banham's metaphor of the campfire,[22] and subsequent projects such as his and Dallegret's "Power-Membrane House" (1965) which removed the house enclosure entirely, opened up the potential for environment to be envisioned as zones—attractors of comfort or repellants of discomfort—in which boundariless

micro-environments overlap. This position has been extended by practices such as Philippe Rahm, DeCostered Architectures, and Weathers, among others, continuing to reshape the discussion of environmental systems from the technical and performative to the spatial, programmatic, and experiential. Philippe Rahm argues for a "meteorological architecture" in which environment is understood as dynamic, defined by thermal strata and flows of air, governed by human behavior and needs, and demarcating zones of activity based on interior climates.[23] The work of such practices opens up new possibilities for architecture's environment, rethinking the idea of spatially segregated and fully controlled environments defined by bubbles or envelopes. They also challenge the notion of undifferentiated comfort as a desired end goal, proposing instead a material understanding of environment that is tactile and tangible. While most of the work to date tends to focus on an immersive experiential sublime, there is the potential to consider such environments in relation to overlapping ecological, energetic, and atmospheric networks. Embracing the notion of micro-climates, at any scale, could enable new choreographies of people, plants, and animal species in a kind of soft geo-engineering of environments.

There is a growing body of work and architects looking at the under-belly of environments; what theorist David Gissen has provocatively termed "subnatures" or environments historically deemed undesirable by architecture, because they contravene our collective cultural notions of comfort, cleanliness, or control. These are environments constituted by insects, mold, dust, smoke, humidity, or toxicity, among others. Simultaneously, there is a growing interest to understand architecture's environments as substrates for both human and animal species.[24] In these scenarios, architecture's environments become the bio-physical substrate for plant and animal species, an armature both for natural processes and for human inhabitation. How human and animal species cohabit, the degree of spatial intertwinement, and the mutualistic benefits of such cohabitation and spatial co-speciation offers new design challenges. Architecture could become the armature or prosthetic for symbiotic environments that embrace the natural and the technologically enhanced, the stable and the dynamic. The true potential of architecture

20. See Gilles Clément, Philippe Rahm and Giovanna Borasi, *Environ(ne)ment, Manières d'agir pour demain / Approaches for Tomorrow* (CCA, Skira Édition : 2007).
21. See Mohsen Mostafavi and David Leatherbarrow, *On Weathering: The Life of Buildings in Time* (Cambridge: MIT Press, 1993)
22. See Reyner Banham's comparison of different ways of demarcating comfort and environment: the construction of an envelope and the building of a campfire;

the former requiring more effort and resources; the latter risking the draining of resources. The campfire, Banham argues creates concentric zones of heat (and comfort) defining different zones of activities, but which risk being disturbed by external forces such as wind, smoke, and so forth. Banham, *Architecture of the Well-Tempered Environment*, 20.
23. See Philippe Rahm's discussion of architecture's shifts from a focus on form to performance and interior

environment. Philippe Rahm,"Form and Function Follow Climate," Department of Architecture ETH Zurich. *Bauten / Bauen — Architekturlabor schweiz*: Interview 3: 89. https://admin.arch.ethz.ch/vortragsreihe/pdf_archithese/Rahm_AR_2-10_s088-093.pdf
24. See the work of contemporary practices such as Cero9 Amid, Weathers, Ants in the Prairie, Francois Roche, the Living, and the writings of theorist David Gissen.

Domestic Astronomy. Functions and furnishings rise off the floor and
stabilize at certain temperatures determined by the body, clothing and activity.
Philippe Rahm architectes, Domestic astronomy, Louisiana Museum, Denmark,
2009. Photo: Brøndum & Co

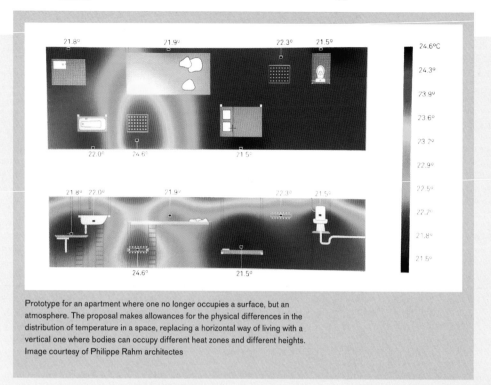

Prototype for an apartment where one no longer occupies a surface, but an atmosphere. The proposal makes allowances for the physical differences in the distribution of temperature in a space, replacing a horizontal way of living with a vertical one where bodies can occupy different heat zones and different heights. Image courtesy of Philippe Rahm architectes

participating in the production of environment-webs will in fact materialize when architects shift the discussion from environments to ecologies, and embrace conditions of instability and variability.

Understanding architecture not only in the service of humans, but also species, is part of a larger discourse on post-humanism permeating the humanities and increasingly, architecture. In *What is Posthumanism*, theorist Cary Wolfe suggests that post-humanism questions the role and hierarchy of the human in relation to ecological, evolutionary, or technological paradigms, problematizing the relationship between anthropocentrism and speciesism, and arguing that "the environment is thus different, indeed sometimes radically different, for different life-forms."

From Environment to Ecologies

Fifty years ago Reyner Banham advocated for architecture to be pure environment, embracing an erasure of the envelope in favor of technology as producer of environment. Describing the *Power-Membrane House*— a project that was an extension of the *Environment-Bubble*— Banham wrote that "the basic proposition is simply that the power-membrane should blow down a curtain of warmed/cooled/conditioned air around the perimeter of the windward side of the unhouse, and leave the surrounding weather to waft it through the living space."[25] Such a proposition, if seriously embraced, would compel designers to consider the full complexity of such an interaction—the nature of the boundaries,

and the potential of such interaction within a much broader understandings of environment.

Such an approach advocates for a shift away from technologically deterministic conceptions of architecture's envelopes, privileging instead a more radical and extreme notion of enclosure and boundary; as interface of exchange between a vast number of forces. It might even be conceived of as an environment in its own right—a thickened, ecologically active surface, capable of producing gradient conditions which could overlap with those of other species—whether plant or animal—for mutualistic purposes.

Such models of envelope and boundary, if embraced, would force inhabitants of architecture to consider interaction with the full physical materiality of an environment. It does not represent a call for bio-memetic models of architecture, in which structures emulate traits of species, but rather that buildings and urbanism embrace their role as habitat and producer of *umwelts* within competing webs of species and ecologies. Architecture and urbanism might at certain times be producers and at other times be consumers of environments and the resources within it. Architecture and envelope would necessarily be dynamic—required to transform, evolve, or decay over time—acknowledging its inherent environment-webs.

25. Banham, "A Home Is Not A House," 76.

tapping resources

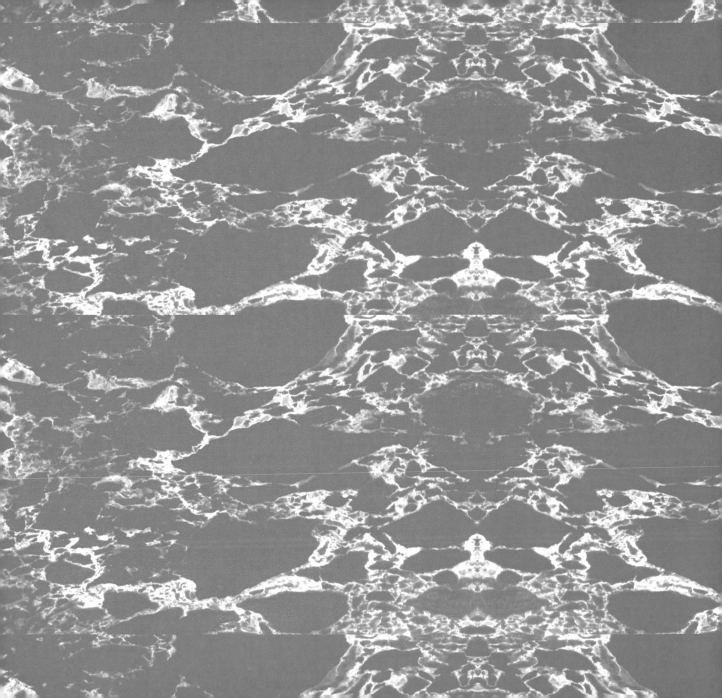

HARBOURWORKS TERRITORIES

Johnathan Puff

Before the last Ice Age: Georges Bank had been exposed as dry land, separating the Gulf of Maine from the Atlantic Ocean. Today, the Gulf is oceanographically distinct from the Atlantic, which accounts for its richness as both a fishery and a source of petroleum. Geology naturalized the Harbourworks site selection process.

Sometimes architecture is far more effective as a fiction. Between 1958, when it was first recognized by the Department of Defense, and 1982 when it was roundly rejected by international convention, an ambiguity existed in the United Nations Conventions on the Law of the Sea: a country could build its own maritime borders. By promoting an imaginary form of urbanism known as Harbourworks Territories the United States would buffer its coastline with massive bulwarks of unregulated offshore industrialization, all for the purpose of claiming sovereignty over massive tracts of marine resources.

The Cold War produced sublimated modes of aggression that relied on a nation's capabilities for controlling and exploiting nature. New fishing technologies and the development of factory vessels for processing fish at sea made it profitable for distant water fleets to permanently occupy offshore areas just beyond the conventional three-mile boundary of international waters. Clearly visible from land, these economic armadas were described by one coast guard observer as "floating cities." While the 1958 United Nations Convention on the Law of the Sea (UNCLOS) did little to actually guarantee maritime sovereignty, an ambiguity existed in Article 8 of this convention: "For the purpose of delimiting the territorial sea, the outermost permanent harbour works which form an integral part of the harbour system shall be regarded as forming part of the coast." Thus a nation willing to dedicate the resources could literally build additional Harbourworks Territories.

This opportunity to expand the sovereignty of the United States was not lost on a newly formed branch of the Defense Department, the Advanced Research Projects Agency (ARPA). While their work was generally more focused on developing weapons and communications systems, the potential to implement a technological solution to sovereignty issues proved irresistible. Research focused on Georges Banks, a shoal off the coast of New England, which was identified primarily

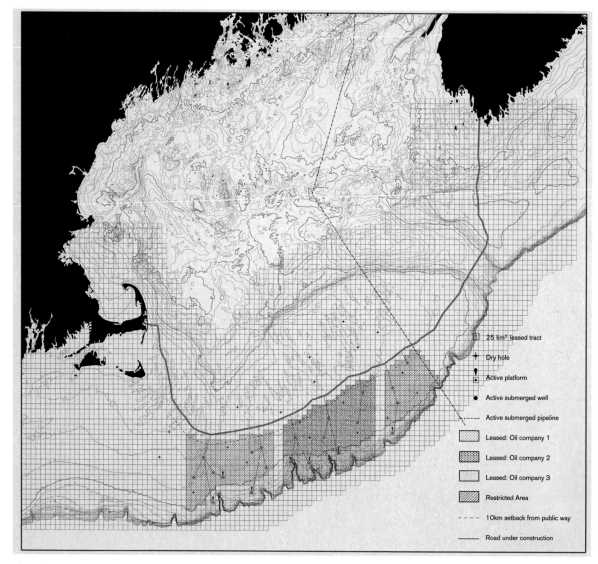

Legend:
- 25 km² leased tract
- Dry hole
- Active platform
- Active submerged well
- Active submerged pipeline
- Leased: Oil company 1
- Leased: Oil company 2
- Leased: Oil company 3
- Restricted Area
- 10km setback from public way
- Road under construction

The Defense Department determined the path of the Harbourworks. It used a grid of 25-squre kilometre plots to divide up the continental shelf into leasable oil development sites. An approximate path was charted by balancing political, structural and economic concerns, which was then refined by incorporating data taken from a series of test wells. Subsequently, the Harbourworks developed as a game-scenario.

for its significant oil development potential and depth:area enclosure ratio. A 500-mile highway bridge linking Cape Cod, Massachusetts to Shelburne, Nova Scotia would provide the backbone for the project, creating a federally sponsored tax haven for fishing, container shipping and oil exploitation. By incorporating Canada in its scheme, the United States immediately established an international coalition and further empowered the project on the world stage. Based on projections that maximized ease of constructability and proximity to likely oil reserves, it was estimated that the *Harbourworks* would provide approximately 112,000 km² of additional territory for Canada and the United States. Massive offshore colonies would be built along the bridge to support the commerce created by this scheme. As a new form of urbanism, the *Harbourworks* represented a democratization of the waterfront, opening up hundreds of miles of "coastal" properties for a booming middle class.

By 1973, mediated propaganda bled into the built world—itself another form of media. An initial construction was completed at the offshore terminus of the Canada-US border, known as the *Harbourworks* Installation. Choosing this site served a secondary purpose of resolving a longstanding dispute over fishing rights between the two countries. Yet the physicality of the installation made it susceptible to counter-narratives. Cape Cod Representative Gerry Studds quickly recognized that this project was a hoax for the purpose of legitimizing oil exploration on Georges Banks. Tireless campaigning by Studds led to a Congressional probe, and by 1977, all work on the Installation was halted, pending hearings. At the same time, a long overdue overhaul to the UNCLOS was convened in New York in 1973. Over the course of several years, the convention moved toward establishing

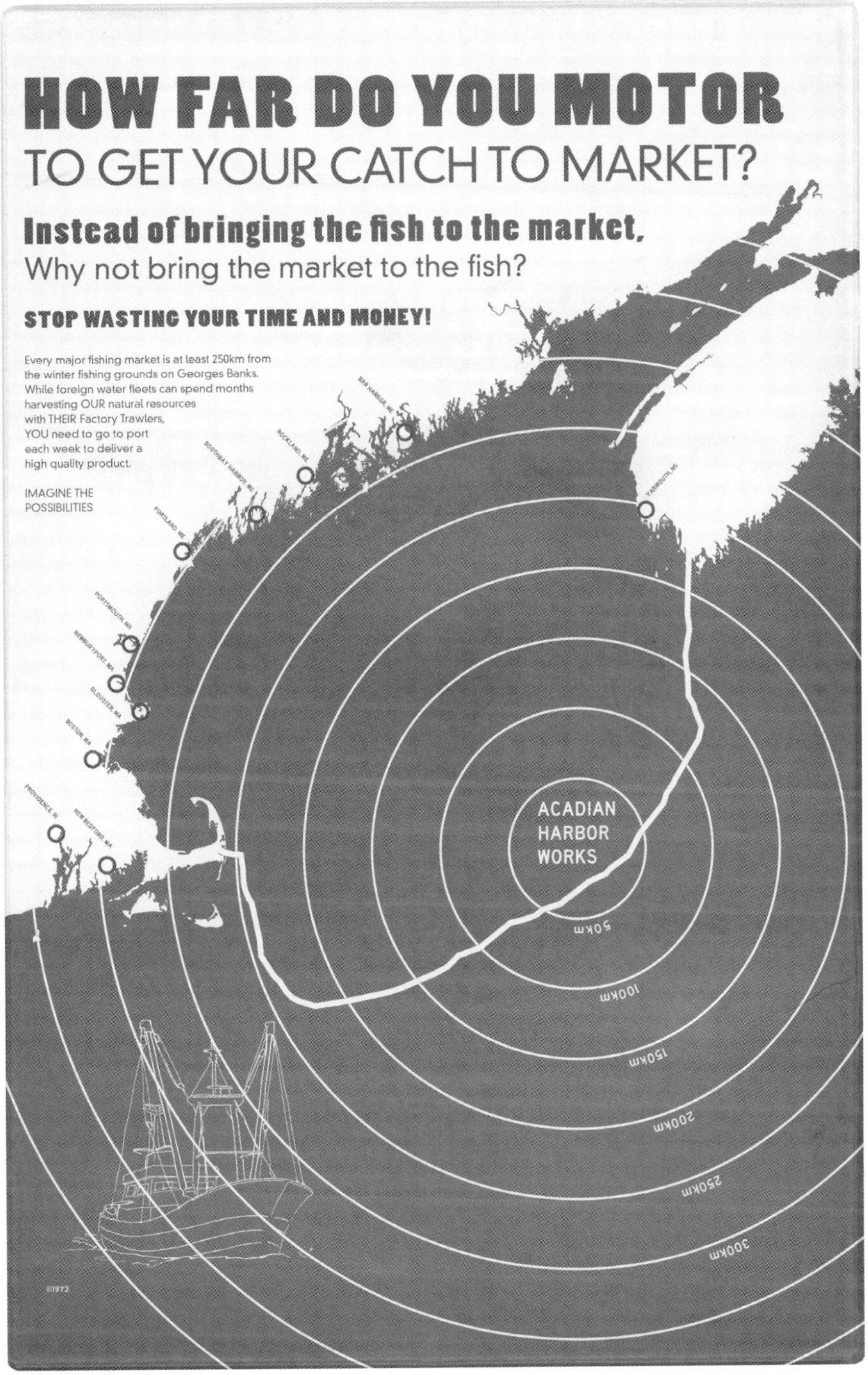
HOW FAR DO YOU MOTOR
TO GET YOUR CATCH TO MARKET?
Instead of bringing the fish to the market,
Why not bring the market to the fish?
STOP WASTING YOUR TIME AND MONEY!
Every major fishing market is at least 250km from the winter fishing grounds on Georges Banks. While foreign water fleets can spend months harvesting OUR natural resources with THEIR Factory Trawlers, YOU need to go to port each week to deliver a high quality product.
IMAGINE THE POSSIBILITIES
BAR HARBOR, ME
ROCKLAND, ME
BOOTHBAY HARBOR, ME
PORTLAND, ME
PORTSMOUTH, NH
NEWBURYPORT, MA
GLOUCESTER, MA
BOSTON, MA
PROVIDENCE, RI
NEW BEDFORD, MA
YARMOUTH, NS
ACADIAN HARBOR WORKS
50km
100km
150km
200km
250km
300km
©1973

Propaganda: An arm of ARPA targeted port towns and industry periodicals to enlist the important constituency of fishermen: who were likely to resist construction on Georges Banks. Posters could be seen at wharfs and co-ops from Long Island to Halifax promoting the advantages of the Harbourworks, specifically, the benefits of relocating ports and fish markets to the actual fishing grounds.

a 200 nautical mile Exclusive Economic Zone, which would secure access to the offshore resources adjacent to each nation. Such an outcome completely undermined the basis for the *Harbourworks*. Ironically, it was the surreal absurdity of bridging the ocean that demonstrated to the delegates the frightening consequences of offshore urbanization. Based on this premise, the wealthiest nations would eventually claim the regions of ocean richest in resource by incrementally deploying a sprawling matrix of *Harbourworks*. Thus the installation became a straw man, creating a sense of urgency whenever negotiations stalled.

A congressional censure in 1979 marked the end of the Harbourworks Territories as an active Federal project, stranding the installation hundreds of miles from shore in the Atlantic Ocean. It was dismantled in the early 1980's, cited as both a navigational hazard and international embarrassment.

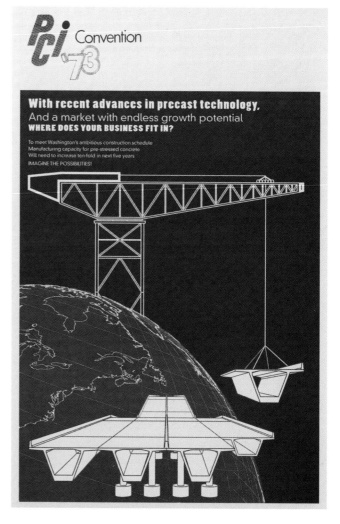

Full-page advertisements represented the Harbour-works as a realizable urbanism. Pre-fabricated living units would nest into the protective framework of the bridge and be served by a "frontage road." The visual presentation of the advertisements imitated familiar, real estate literature, depicting simple floor plans that were capable of being configured in multiple arrangements of two-, three- or four-unit homes. The system was recognizable, affordable and endlessly expandable, with a logic tied snugly to the linear expanse of the highway bridge.

Construction: In the fall of 1973, the Prestressed Concrete Institute held its 19th Annual Convention at The Palmer House in Chicago, Illinois. The program prominently featured the Defense Department's unveiling of the Harbourworks scheme, and the announcement of a series of competitive contracts for the immediate construction of the initial Harbourworks installation. Indeed, the presentation elaborated on the pressing need to expand industrial capacity to accommodate an anticipated growth in demand.

September 30, 1976   Cape Cod Chronicle   Page 7

The Harbourworks installation: became a site for negotiation between different actors. A 1976 newspaper article describes a study on the impact of the installation on local fisheries by researchers from the Woods Hole Oceanographic Institute. The photograph, however, also captures a CTL container ship, traveling from Halifax, NS to New York Harbour. This congested pilotage became an important indicator of the outer limits of the territorial waters shared by Canada and the United States.

Johnathan Puff is a doctoral candidate at the University of Michigan in Architecture History and Theory, and a student in the Graduate Program in Science, Technology, and Society. His research examines the intersection of design and infrastructure in 19th and 20th century America.

TAR CREEK SUPERGRID

Clint Langevin + Amy Norris

Aerial photo of Picher, Oklahoma: Town at the center of the Tar Creek Superfund site, one of three Superfund sites in the 1,188 square mile Tri-State mining district that straddles North-eastern Oklahoma, southwestern Missouri, and South-eastern Kansas. The photo was taken by local blimp photographers, one of the recreational uses of the piles by local residents.
Photograph by J.S. Alber

The history of Picher, Oklahoma begins and ends with the Tar Creek lead and zinc mines. Operational for just under 80 years, the area's mines provided over 45 percent of the lead and 50 percent of the zinc consumed by the U.S. during the Great War.[1] The by-products of this intense operation transformed the local prairie geography, creating dozens of waste rock piles — known as chat — some over 30 metres in height. Discontinuation, in the '70s, of the pumps required to clear water from the underground shafts, led to a gradual accumulation and eventual overflow of water to the surface,

carrying with it lead, zinc, cadmium, and arsenic.[2]

The mines that created Picher ultimately lead to its downfall. Although billions of dollars worth of ore was extracted from the Tar Creek area, the money available to clean up the environmental fallout from mining activities — in the form of the Comprehensive Environmental Response, Compensation, and Liability Act of 1980 (commonly known as the Superfund) — is extremely limited compared to the scale of the mine's impact. Lacking the funds to substantially remediate the site, the majority of available Superfund

1. Oklahoma Historical Society. http://digital.library. okstate.edu/encyclopedia/entries/T/TR014.html

2. U.S. EPA Superfund. http://www.epa.gov/region6/6sf/ oklahoma/tar_creek/index.htm#infob

The grid breaks to allow full sunlight to reach the chat piles in order to aid plant growth and to emphasize the defining quality of these features for the site. Though massive in its potential overall scale, the structure strives towards a maximum span in order to tread lightly on the damaged landscape.

money has thus been spent on moving the remaining inhabitants of Picher.[3]

The *Tar Creek Supergrid*[4] emerges from a proposition that landscapes disturbed by human industry, such as abandoned mines, could become frontiers for human settlement and innovation. Solar energy generation, as part of a proposed national grid of clean energy research and development hubs, is introduced as a financial catalyst for the site, but with a twist: a structure that raises the solar energy infrastructure off the ground, creates the opportunity to host other activities on the site, while treading lightly on a landscape in repair. In addition to providing the armature for energy generation, the concrete structure, pre-fabricated using waste rock material from the site, also acts as a conduit to carry water, energy, waste—all the infrastructure for human habitation—to inhabited areas of the site.

The result is a three-tiered plan. The topmost level is devoted to solar energy development and production, testing the latest technology and producing a surplus of energy for the site and its surroundings. This layer is also the starting point for water management on the site; rainwater is collected and flows to one of several treatment plants around the radial grid. The middle level is the place of dwelling and circulation. As the need for space grows, beams are added to create this inhabited layer: the beams act as a pedestrian and cycling circulation system, but also the infrastructure for dwelling and automated transit. Finally, the ground level becomes a laboratory for bioremediation of the soil and water systems. A combination of active and passive treatment systems for waste water and the acid mine drainage are coupled with a connected system of boardwalks to allow inhabitants and visitors to experience both the industrial inheritance of the site and the renewed hope for its future.

Based in Toronto, **Clint Langevin** and **Amy Norris** co-founded the research and design studio, Captains of Industry, to investigate the problems and potentials of our industrial heritage. Recent work explores the relationship between human activity and natural ecosystems and human complicity in the occurrence of natural disasters.

3. Ibid.
4. The title of this project *Tar Creek Supergrid*, comes from a post on BLDG Blog (http://bldgblog.blogspot.com/2011/09/tar-creek-supergrid.html)

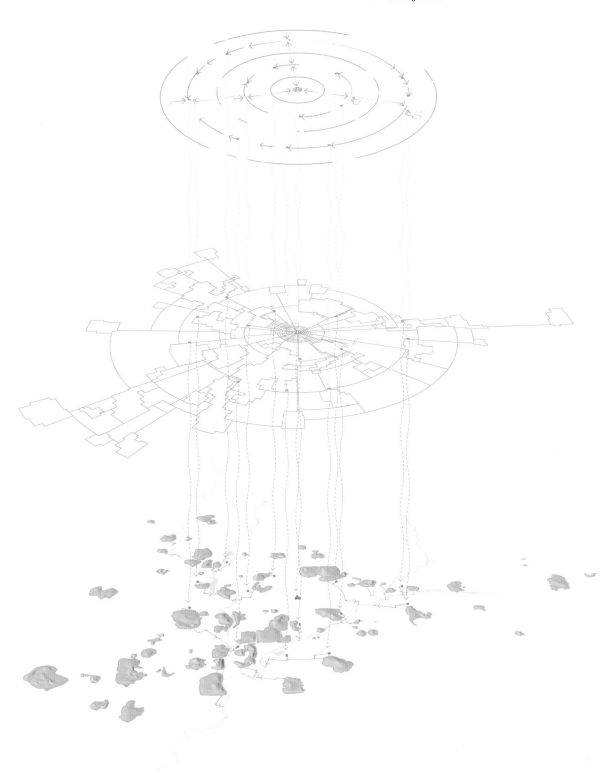

Water Collection

Water Flow

Water Treatment/Tourist Centre + Vertical Circulation

Passive Water Treatment

Existing Stream

Water management as key formal driver. Water is collected and transported by the structure to pre- and post-use treatment facilities before entering the passive treatment system at grade.

The extent of the Supergrid at an advanced stage of expansion. The Personal Rapid Transit (PRT) and self-propelled circulation systems extend to all the chat piles, creating opportunities for settlement and exploration of the site.

Solar level: The immensity of the endeavour is apparent
from the top of one of the site's defining waste piles,
optimistically depicted in a state of remediation amidst
a reclaimed infrastructural landscape.

Tar Creek chat pile: Dozens of waste rock piles, some up to thirteen-storeys high, and weighing several million tons are the visible legacy of mining operations in the area. Photograph by Jacky Brinkman.

Ground-level boardwalks: running alongside
the passive water treatment system, these walkways
reveal the tension between this new landscape and the
underlying damage from past mining activities.

Tar Creek Supergrid   **Langevin + Norris**

WITH/WITHOUT WATER

Christina Milos

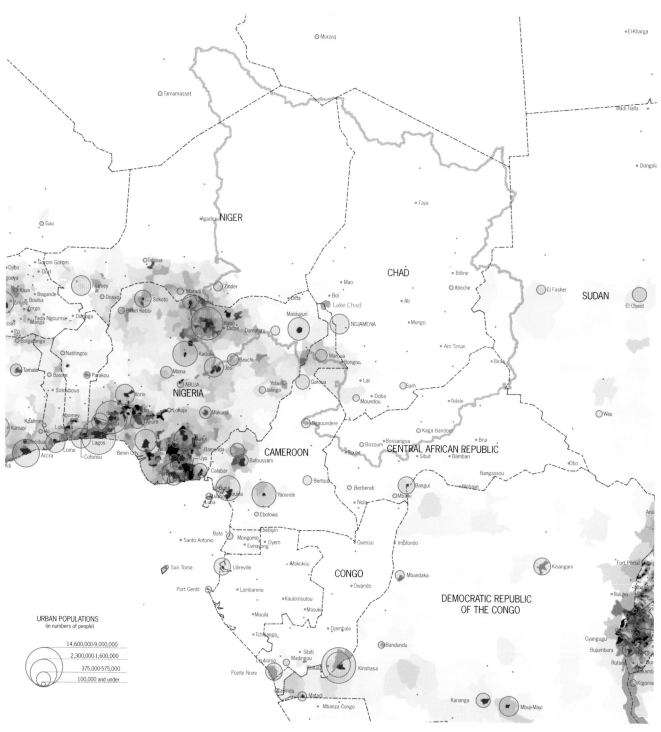

URBAN POPULATIONS
(in numbers of people)

14,600,000-9,000,000

2,300,000-1,600,000

375,000-575,000

100,000 and under

Home to 22 million people: the Lake Chad Basin
population is expected to rise dramatically this century,
increasing demand for water and arable land.

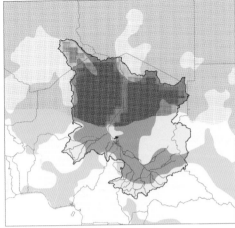

MAJOR SUBBASINS WITHIN THE LAKE CHAD BASIN

PRIMARY AQUIFERS

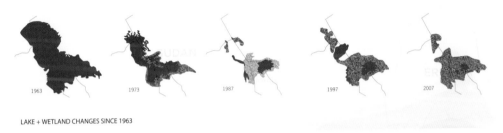

1963   1973   1987   1997   2007

LAKE + WETLAND CHANGES SINCE 1963

Water flows: Historical water trends in the Lake Chad Basin are highly variable but show a significant decline in the past 40 years. Though recently levels have started to rebound, future predictions indicate Lake Chad may disappear entirely within as little as 15 years.

The Lake Chad Basin is a region at a tipping point, with Lake Chad having shrunk from 25,000 square kilometres in 1962 to about 2000 square kilometres today—a decline of over ninety percent. A changing climate and anthropogenic pressure from dams, irrigation infrastructure, and poor water management are believed to be equally responsible for its demise.[1] The Food and Agriculture Organization calls the shrinking of Lake Chad an "ecological catastrophe" and warns of an impending humanitarian disaster without a radical change in water management practices.[2]

With/Without Water does not try to 'save' Lake Chad, but instead proposes an adaptive infrastructural scaffold to augment the resilience of ecosystems and populations to increasing water scarcity and desertification. While this work does not ignore strategies to rehabilitate the lake, it acknowledges the reality that the current water management practices may lead to the lake's complete disappearance within fifteen years or less. This would potentially create a region rife with famine and conflict over precious land and water resources. The work speculates as to how development projects can move beyond single-solution engineering and instead accept, enhance and complement changing ecological and social flows to support multiple viable outcomes.

A Region in Flux

Lake Chad is a large, shallow freshwater lake located at the southern edge of the Sahara desert in the Sahel region. The Sahel is situated between the arid Sahara to the north, and the sub-humid savanna to the south. Four countries—Nigeria, Niger, Cameroon, and Chad—share the riparian shores of the lake, and an additional three—Algeria, the Sudan, and the Central African Republic (CAR)—share the larger hydrographic basin. Currently home to twenty-two million people, the Lake Chad Basin population is expected to rise dramatically to thirty-five million people by 2020, sharply increasing the demand for water and arable land.[3] In addition to the difficulties arising from resource shortages, all countries in the basin are identified as having 'low human development' according to the 2013 United Nations Human Development Index, which limits their capacity to adjust to climate change and resource scarcity.[4]

During the past twenty-five years, rainfall has decreased by up to thirty percent across the Sahel—the most substantial and sustained regional rainfall decrease in recorded climate history.[5] This trend may persist, with the potential to exacerbate desertification and its attendant consequences—declining agricultural yields, higher livestock mortality, and decreasing vegetative cover. While some climate experts believe the trend

1. Pearce, Fred. *When the Rivers Run Dry: Water–The Defining Crisis of the Twenty-first Century.* 1st ed. (Beacon Press, 2007)

2. Food and Agriculture Organization of the United Nations. "Lake Chad Facing Humanitarian Disaster", October 15, 2009. http://www.fao.org/news/story/en/

item/36126/icode/.

3. Pearce 2007.

4. United Nations Development Programme. Human Development Report 2013. United Nations Development Programme, 2013.

5. McCarthy, James, Osvaldo Canziani, Neil Leary,

David Dokken, and Kasey White. "10.2.6.3 Climatic Factors in Desertification." In *Working Group II: Impacts, Adaptation and Vulnerability* (Cambridge University Press, 2001) http://www.ipcc.ch/ipccreports/tar/wg2/index.php?idp=403.

Nigeria–Chad border: Boats carry petrol, goods, and smoked fish to the Nigeria–Chad border. Four countries share borders in the middle of Lake Chad's labyrinthine network of wetlands and small channels, making the borders notoriously porous and difficult to police.

Sand dune stabilization pilot project: A Toshua village elder walks across a field of sand dunes migrating across formerly agricultural land. A pilot project with the University of Maiduguri Department of Forestry and Wildlife has planted Balanites aegyptiaca in an attempt to stabilize the dune field and prevent further intrusion on productive land.

Sand dune field: Goats are herded across a shifting field of sand dunes near Toshua, a village on the border of Niger and Nigeria, in search of vegetation to graze.

will continue, others believe climate change may actually trigger a reversal of this trend.[6]

The flow of water — seasonally, yearly, and over decades — drives the social and ecological systems of the basin.[7] Livelihoods in the basin are highly adapted to shifting water and vegetation flows. Pastoralists practice transhumance, or seasonal migration from dry northern areas to wet southern areas in search of greener grazing lands during the dry season. Farmers practice rotational and recessional agriculture — adapting their crop locations and cycles to water and nutrient availability.[8] The ability of basin farmers and pastoralists to sustain themselves under spatially and temporally unpredictable rainfall conditions testifies to the resilience of their techniques. Though these traditional land-based livelihoods are capable of adapting to a certain degree of disturbance or shock, their continued success depends on the health of the ecological networks in which they are rooted. Increasing population density coupled with increasing desertification has put pressure on limited land and water resources. Small-scale adaptation, while clearly necessary, may not go far or fast enough to resolve regional management issues such as food insecurity — which relies on coordinated

management of regional water sources as well as sustainable local management practices.

A Legacy of Failed Infrastructure

The Sahel has a legacy of poorly designed regional infrastructure built in response to the drought and subsequent famine in 1969–1974. During this time, Western media headlines proclaimed traditional productive systems had "collapsed" in a "major environmental emergency" that left six million people at risk of starvation. Scientists asserted the entire Sahelian ecozone had reached "carrying capacity" years before, and was incapable of supporting its current population with traditional methods.[9] As a result, radical large scale proposals such as irrigation infrastructure accompanied by enforced resettlement, extensive shelterbelts, and top-down land use zoning— all of which would have drastic impacts on the flexible vernacular land use strategies of rural Sahelians—were considered.[10]

Government infrastructure and aid projects have thus far proved incapable of designing large-scale interventions in the Lake Chad Basin with lasting success.[11] Unlike micro-scale traditional land management practices, proposed

6. Held, I. M., T. L. Delworth, J. Lu, K. L. Findell, and T. R. Knutson. "Simulation of Sahel Drought in the 20th and 21st Centuries." *Proceedings of the National Academy of Sciences of the United States of Amer* 102, no. 50 (December 13, 2005): 17891–17896.

7. Batello, Caterina. *Future Is An Ancient Lake. Traditional Knowledge, Biodiversity And Genetic Resources For Food And Agriculture In Lake Chad Basin Ecosystems.* Food & Agriculture Org, 2004.

8. Sarch, Marie-Therese. "Fishing and Farming in

Lake Chad: Implications for Fisheries Development." *Development Policy Review* 15, no. 2 (1997).

9. Adams, W. M., and M. J. Mortimore. *Working the Sahel.* Routledge, 1999.

| BEFORE 1969 | | 1969-PRESENT | | TRANSHUMANCE VOLUMES |
| Wet Season | Dry Season | Wet Season | Dry Season | |

Peuls

Toubous

Arabs

Kouris &
Budumas

● starting point
○ waypoint
━━━ greater than 15,000 people
─── 5000-15,000 people
‐‐‐ 500-5000 people

Niger

Chad

Nigeria

Cameroon

Central African Republic

**Transhumance is pastoralist movements from north
to south with following seasonal rainfall.** Pastoralists
and farmers have successfully shared lands for centuries
with a minimum of conflict. However, as populations
increase and resource scarcity rises, these movement
patterns are shifting, leaving farmers and pastoralists
fighting over limited arable land.

macro-scale interventions like the Baga Polder Project and the South Chad Irrigation Project were conceived entirely outside of cyclical environmental systems. These large-scale projects were engineered to operate successfully only under one set of conditions—when water levels of the lake were at a specific level. When conditions changed and water levels fell both irrigation projects were rendered inoperable. Instead of alleviating the effects of the drought, the conversion of land from small-scale traditional agriculture to unproductive large-scale industrial agriculture merely exacerbated the difficult circumstances Sahelian populations already faced as a result of the drought. While these projects offer substantial opportunity for critique, the intent of the development projects based on this model was laudable—the infrastructure projects sought to respond to the scale of an immense problem at an immense scale.

The Lake Chad Basin Commission (LCBC), originally formed in 1964 to address trans-boundary water and environmental management issues, today appears on track to repeat many of the same mistakes of earlier infrastructure projects. The Oubangui Inter-Basin Water Transfer project proposes a 150–170 km transfer of water from the Oubangui River of the Congo River Basin to the Chari River, which empties into the Lake Chad Basin. Although LCBC officials claim the new project takes environmental and social considerations into account, a review of the Original Procurement Notice for the project indicates the LCBC still seeks a permanent infrastructural solution to an unpredictable, shifting problem.[12] It is not clear how the Oubangui project would be any more successful than the many skeletons of other failed infrastructure projects that litter the Sahel.

Large-scale projects that follow an engineering resilience model are emblematic of what we could call landscape 'shock therapy'. The organizations and governments that propose and implement development projects in resource scarce areas frequently enlist a 'narrative of crisis' as defined by Milligan and Binns, as a justification for large-scale interventions during environmental crises. Instead of relying on local residents for information and insight, the crisis narrative permits the local actor to be ignored in favor of a frequently ill-conceived collective good. This often leads to a dismissal of traditional water and land management practices as broken, and thus in need of landscape 'shock therapy' to jumpstart productivity.

With the assumption that traditional methods failed because they were unable to optimize resource use, any intervention that maximizes use of precious resources is seen as an improvement. The very cause of the problem in the first place—an environmental shock—is thus addressed with yet another environmental shock, this time entirely anthropogenic in origin. As ecosystems rarely respond predictably to a massive input, the ill-effects of this secondary shock frequently rival the effects of the first—throwing off the ability of the ecosystem and its populations to bounce back.

Designing for Resilience

With/Without Water considers how technologies used to prevent desertification and sustain livelihoods can be designed to succeed where they have failed in the past. In contrast to the typical model of rigid, large-scale development interventions, this work proposes a flexible regional development backbone that supports nodes of appropriate, contextually-responsive activity. The goal is to use infrastructure development to build the adaptive capacity of smaller, local populations so that the total effect is multiplied exponentially across the larger region.

The uncertainty regarding future water flows, coupled with the difficulty of predicting future regional water management practices, is the reason why *With/Without Water* is designed to respond to three hypothetical future scenarios: (1) with water (2) status quo and (3) without water. Regardless of which future scenario comes to fruition, the basin is expected to experience increasing desertification, which in turn is likely to result in increasing food insecurity.

The primary method currently employed to prevent desertification across the Sahel region of Africa is the shelterbelt: a strategic plantation of trees and shrubs that creates a windbreak—thereby decreasing evapotranspiration and wind erosion to improve crop yields by up to 140 percent.[13] By combining shelterbelts with road development, this project responds to two needs of the lake and its larger basin—the need for better transportation infrastructure and increased crop production.

A series of other infrastructure typologies respond to the range of conditions encountered throughout the lake area. When combined, these typologies act as a long linear system, with the transportation network as the backbone. In plan, the shelterbelts expand and contract along the road, based on village location and size. In section, the shelterbelts concentrate and disperse based on the condition in which they are located—rural farmland, small village, or town.

The infrastructural system is deployed on the shifting edge of the lake and moves with changing climatic conditions. Currently, this edge consists of a gradient of moisture regimes supporting different livelihoods ranging from farming to fishing. Baga, a town of 15,000 people in northern Nigeria on the lake's edge, served as a case study for the deployment of the shelterbelt system. The town has moved several times in the past to follow the lake's changing shoreline. Shelterbelts are concentrated in two areas: (1) along linear road systems extending from the lake's edge and (2) around existing villages with arable land. Even if the community no longer has access to water based resources in the without water scenario, preventing future desertification before it can begin will build the resilience of local populations to the unpredictable climate of Lake Chad. In all scenarios, the resulting network of shelterbelt-road

10. Ibid.

11. Pearce 2007

12. "Feasibility Study of the Water Transfer Project in Africa". Lake Chad Basin Commission, April 21 2008. http://www.devex.com/en/projects/feasibility-study-of-the-water-transfer-project-in-africa

13. Gritzner, Jeffrey A. *The West African Sahel: Human Agency and Environmental Change.* (Chicago: Univ of Chicago, 1989).

Low-lying area at the edge of Lake Chad with shelterbelts.

systems across the basin will provide a solid backbone for development, providing 250,000+ hectares of arable land and access to local and regional markets, healthcare, and education.

In addition to functioning in a range of climatic scenarios, the project is also intended to respond to a range of funding and implementation possibilities. For example, while the best possible outcome would be an interconnected regional network of roads and shelter belts with a cascade of spill-over benefits, the project could still be successful even if only a handful of farmers improve their crop yield by implementing the shelterbelt planting strategy. For the project to reach its full potential at the regional scale, a number of management and implementation challenges would need to be overcome as the project develops. As the series of failed shelterbelt projects across the Sahel attest, changing land use practices is a difficult task. Each step would require substantial community buy-in and support that could only come through intensive participation and capacity building throughout the process. The project's success hinges on the ability to convince farmers that planting trees on their property will increase crop yields even though the total area of arable land would be reduced.

From a governance perspective, the proposed transportation infrastructure in particular requires coordination of local, regional, national, and international governing bodies. Regional conflict, including a recent surge in violence in Northern Nigeria, could either prove a stumbling block towards implementation or convince regional leaders of the importance of building sustainable livelihoods for young men who may otherwise take up arms. Ideally, a successfully managed project would convince each small-scale farmer that improved land management practices are a worthwhile investment, and persuade each governing body of the importance of linking productive agricultural lands with transportation infrastructure. Though the regional project hopes for large-scale implementation to provide maximum benefit, the effectiveness of the small-scale planting interventions does not rely on it.

With/Without Water argues that to design for resilience is to design for a changing landscape. Instead of attempting to 'save the lake' with another rigid infrastructure project doomed for failure, this work seizes the opportunity to build an infrastructural model of resilience designed to accommodate any number of potential unknown futures—With/Without Water.

With/Without Water is a masters thesis completed under Christian Werthmann while pursuing a Master in Landscape Architecture at the Harvard University Graduate School of Design. Christian Werthmann provided invaluable advice and support for this thesis. The University of Maiduguri Department of Forestry and Wildlife, in particular department head Dr. Adeogun and GIS specialist Garba Sambo, also contributed to the development of the project with their data, helpful insights and generous hospitality during field research in Nigeria.

Christina Milos is a Research Associate and Ph.D Candidate at the Institute for Landscape Architecture of Leibniz University Hannover, Germany. Her current research explores mapping and planning methods to anticipate urbanization associated with resource extraction in least developed contexts.

P.L.A.T.F.O.R.M.

Brian Lee

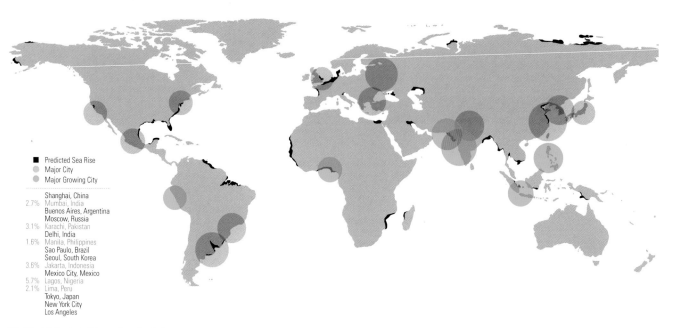

Predicted Sea Rise
Major City
Major Growing City

Shanghai, China
2.7% Mumbai, India
Buenos Aires, Argentina
Moscow, Russia
3.1% Karachi, Pakistan
Delhi, India
1.6% Manila, Philippines
Sao Paulo, Brazil
Seoul, South Korea
3.6% Jakarta, Indonesia
Mexico City, Mexico
5.7% Lagos, Nigeria
2.1% Lima, Peru
Tokyo, Japan
New York City
Los Angeles

The World's largest cities and sea level rise.

Lagos, Nigeria is a city of rapidly shifting conditions and perpetual crisis. The city faces issues of over population, pollution, circulation, waste management, sanitation, density, poverty, and social disparity.

Many of these difficulties result from the city's extreme growth, which happens in its slum territories. As poor regions continue to grow, weak existing infrastructures fail to manage demands. Garbage collection efforts are insufficient and predicted sea rise puts much of the coastal areas under water. Despite dramatic social and economic obstacles, Lagos seems to face these challenges with adaptability, positivity, and a will to survive. *P.L.A.T.F.O.R.M.*, The Public of Lagos Agency of Trash Formation, Organization, Remediation, and Management, seeks to utilize the local qualities of resourcefulness and adaptability in mitigating the challenges faced by the city. An organizing of the garbage-collection infrastructure minimizes contamination, accommodates for growing slum settlements, and provides a barrier against sea rise.

Growth and the Slums

For Lagos, an estimated population growth of nearly six percent equates to about a half a million new residents per year.[1] The largest and fastest growing city in Sub-Saharan Africa, Lagos barely manages to support the influx of migrants and rural transplants seeking work in the region's financial and commercial center. This migration growth is compounded by the stunning internal birth rate of its own people. The average woman in Lagos will have four children in her lifetime.[2]

The growth of Lagos has led to a conflict between two types of development: formal and informal. As the formal, publicly-planned urbanization strategies have failed to keep pace with current growth rates, new inhabitants advance the expansion of informal slum settlements. These rising informal developments have introduced new independent economies that confront and elude existing systems. A large part of the slums rely on access to water for transport, commerce, and vitality. Large, dense communities have arisen along coastal regions, some settlements actually built on the water. The slums act as infill to the cities' already minimal vacant space and ignore the geographic boundaries of the city by expanding into the coastal waters of Lagos Lagoon. The disconnect from public utilities such as running water, sewer, and electricity, causes the slum areas to suffer poor sanitation.

Sea Rise

The coastal growth and density of Lagos places the residents of the slums at extreme risk of displacement from predicted levels of sea rise. A rise of only 20 cm would displace 740,000 of the people in Nigeria, while a rise 1m, would make 3.7 million homeless people in the country. The predicted increases in sea-level rise over the next one hundred years indicate that the majority of the coastal slums will be

1. City Mayors: Statistics, accessed 4-14-2012, http://www.citymayors.com/sections/rankings_content.html.
2. All Africa Daily Independent(Lagos): Nigeria Citizens Groan Under High Cost of Hospital Delivery, accessed 4-14-2012 http://allafrica.com/stories/201105190546.html.

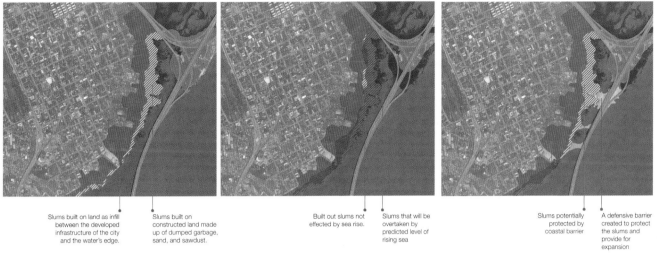

Slums built on land as infill between the developed infrastructure of the city and the water's edge.

Slums built on constructed land made up of dumped garbage, sand, and sawdust.

Built out slums not effected by sea rise.

Slums that will be overtaken by predicted level of rising sea

Slums potentially protected by coastal barrier

A defensive barrier created to protect the slums and provide for expansion

Rising sea's threats.

over taken by water.[3] Though the proximity to water facilitates the informal systems of transport and commerce within the slums, it also presents a major danger to the expanding zones. No formal plan to resist rising water currently exists in Lagos.

Waste

The intense growth of the city and the slums has also lead to a burgeoning waste management problem. Large dumpsites have developed in the central and northern regions of the city to deal with increasing amounts of trash. It is estimated that around 9,000 tons of garbage is delivered to the Lagos dumpsites each day.[4] The crisis of waste management is an opportunity for many and has given rise to innovation within Lagos. Entire communities have sprung up around the disposal and organization of trash. Bands of sorters wait alongside dump trucks searching for valuable materials that can be sold and reused. Along the coastal edges, garbage is used as fill; the trash is dumped into the water, then covered in sawdust and sand. Slum settlements are then built on top of the newly acquired land. An industry of informal sand and sawdust harvesting has resulted from the continual growth and expansion.The unregulated dumping of garbage has contaminated much of the water surrounding the slums.

Adaptability

Somehow, the social and ecological extremes of the West-African center have not thrown the city into an imbalance or disorder, as traditional models of urban planning would predict. Collective efforts of an entrepreneurial citizenry have largely managed these problems, seemingly unaware. Seen as opportunities, the processes of the city are its means of survival. Of Lagos, Koolhaas said, "[the] shortcomings have generated ingenious, critical alternative systems, which demand a redefinition of ideas such as carrying capacity, stability, and even order."[5] Each extreme in Lagos generates

industries and activities that seem to unintentionally manage possibly harmful outcomes.

P.L.A.T.F.O.R.M.

The Badia slum is the opportune site to investigate the potentials of the slums and attempt to balance issues of sea rise, population density, and waste management. The site is along a major garbage route. The water is shallow, and the barrier can be supported by the existing infrastructure of the highway bridge. A formalized trash dumping facility along Third Mainland Bridge, a major piece of transportation infrastructure, acts as a cut-off between the dense urban Lagos Island and the official dumpsites in the north. The facility connects the existing trash routes and the residents of the coastal slums. A hybrid defense system made of trash-filled gabions would allow for the disposal of garbage, containment of toxins, and establishment of a barrier to protect the coastal slums from sea rise. The triangular geometry of the gabion provides structure to the module and facilitates two processes.

Ramps bring garbage trucks down to the platform upon which dumping and sorting take place. Slum dwellers have access to the waste resources passing along the roadway bridge. On the platform surface, trash is sorted and separated into three types: re-sellable material, solid non-toxic waste, and contaminated waste. These resources allow for new commercial endeavours along the platform and in the coastal slums. Re-sellable material is kept on the platform and sold as salvage to slum dwellers and market customers. Non-toxic waste is used as the initial mass of coastal expansion and provides for a coastal defense system.

P.L.A.T.F.O.R.M. maximizes efficiency and minimizes contamination. The project makes use of Lagos' waste management system to facilitate slum expansion, forming a defensive barrier against rising water while mitigating the harmful effects of contamination. Contaminated waste is contained within a closed geometric unit remediated by planting and

3. Klaus Paehler. "*Nigeria in the Dilemma of Climate Change,*" Konrad-Adenauer-Siftung. July 19, 2007, retrieved August 8, 2013.

4. Bloomberg Businessweek. "Biggest Garbage Dumps;" August 5, 2009, retrieved August 20, 2013

5. Rem Koolhaas *Mutations, Project On The City: Lagos*

(Barcelona: Actar, 2001), 652.

Dumping of contaminated waste within the contained gabion.

Sediment accretion and sand dumping for planting of remediating vegetation. **Remediating plants** remove toxins from dumped garbage. Sediment accretion and sand are used for planting and barriers.

Burning of toxic plant life after remediation and clearing of land for slum habitation.

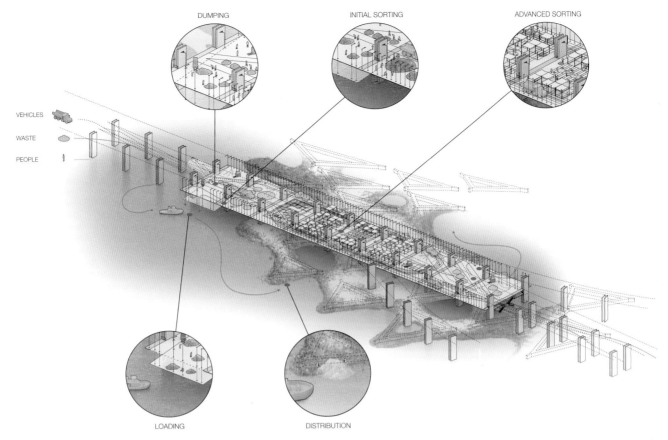

DUMPING   INITIAL SORTING   ADVANCED SORTING

VEHICLES

WASTE

PEOPLE

LOADING   DISTRIBUTION

Platform process.

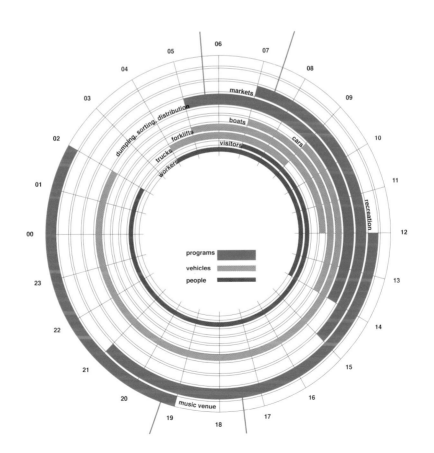

markets

dumping, sorting, distribution

boats

forklifts

cars

trucks

visitors

workers

recreation

programs
vehicles
people

music venue

Daily platform schedule.

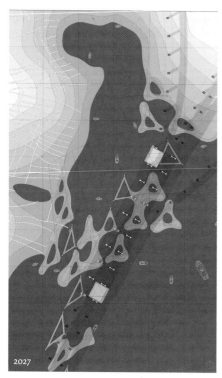 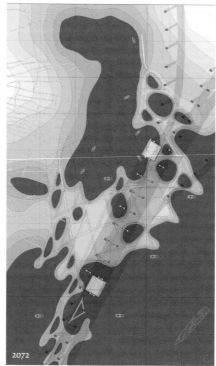 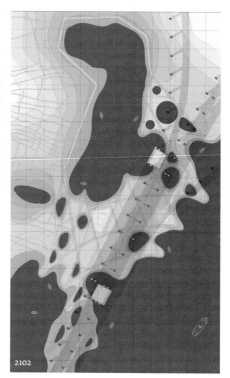

2027   2072   2102

Growth cells and land over time.

proper disposal. First, a closed unit allows for the containment of toxins and contaminated waste, which are dumped
within the center. Second, the module can collect and retain
passing sediment, dumped garbage and sand. As sediment
accumulates vegetation will grow and remediate contami-
nants, cleansing the water within the interior pools. As waste
is sorted and collected, gabions of compacted trash would be
organized in a pattern cohesive with coastal protection techniques in order to maximize energy absorption and sediment
accretion. Solid, non-toxic waste would make up the mass of
the gabion, establishing a framework for future dumping.

As the network gained strength and stability, passing sediments would accrete along the modules' edges, becoming a
framework for a defense against rising coastal waters. The
modules would begin to join and allow space for plant growth.
The vegetation on the modules adds support to sediment and
would begin to remediate the water in the central pools that
would be contaminated by dumping. The smaller pools within
the triangles would begin to fill in with garbage and sand and
the role of filtration would shift to larger pools formed at the
intersections of modules. As the water in the interior pools
becomes remediated, the toxic vegetation would be burned.
The module surface now becomes a programmable space
allowing for the expansion of the slum settlements in addition
to providing the necessary mass and strength for protection
against rising water.

These conditions of adaptability and resourcefulness present an opportunity to better exploit the particular economies
of Lagos. Within each of these so-called problems reside
inherent processes and qualities that can be reframed for
interdependence and mutual benefit. This project seeks to
rationalize the inconsistencies of the two modes of development, acting as a top-down urban-scaled plan-of-action while

embracing the bottom-up informalities of slum settlement
formation and the systems of commerce and productivity that
accompany their chaotic and organic growth.

Brian Lee earned an M. Arch degree from Rice University in
Houston, TX, where he received the Darden Award for Outstanding
Thesis. He currently works as a designer in New York City.

The platform: allowing for alternative programs
and appropriations.

Dumping and distribution: waste moving from the
platform to the gabion trashscape.

AIRNODES

Brandon Hall + Brian Vargo

Loading: Traffic momentarily stopped for loading of passengers.

Air travel has evolved into the most complex infrastructure in modern culture. The industry supports approximately 800 million passengers annually within the United States alone; all the while negotiating changes in regulations and technology with unprecedented precision.[1] Air travel's extremity lies in both the magnitude of its mobility and the complexity of its infrastructure.

Yet despite the massive scale and importance of this infrastructure, the airline industry has posted a $63 billion deficit within the past ten years. The increasing inefficiency of an aging system has driven operating costs up 162 percent since 2000.[2] Despite a persistently growing demand for air travel, airlines sell only 82 percent of their available seats because large scale airports are often no longer strategically located or, are situated remote from areas experiencing high population growth. The infrastructure has become increasingly congested, expensive, and inefficient.

Perhaps the cost of maintaining the current system actually limits its potential to grow. We propose a renewed airport typology to supplement these issues by addressing a systemic flaw. Why do airports limit the indefinite medium of aviation to only finite points? What if air travel can further propagate its mobility by finding a more adaptive system to truly become the most flexible of infrastructures?

Simultaneously accepting the consequence left by urban sprawl while providing a more adaptive system for the future affords new possibilities. Why not repurpose the 4 million miles of existing highway in the US to create temporary runways? By rescaling the 'airport' into a mobile *Airnode*, a new infrastructural typology can provide unprecedented opportunity.

The highway system provides a malleable substrate — already wide enough in most locations and well within structural limits to land commercial jets — it can easily facilitate the basic requirements of an average commercial runway. Airnodes divide the same functional, security, and mechanical requirements of a conventional airport into individual mobile gates that supplement the highway network. These gates are designed to the dimensions of a flat bed truck, and are thus easily moved to where

---

1. Smallen, Dave. "Summary 2008 Traffic Data for U.S and Foreign Airlines," U.S. Department of Transportation, Bureau of Transportation Statistics. (April 23, 2009.): Accessed February 9, 2012. http://www.rita.dot.gov/bts/ sites/default/files/rita_archives/bts_press_releases/2009/ btso19_09/pdf/btso19_09.pdf
2. "Toward Global Competitiveness, Economic Empowerment and Sustained Profitability," Airlines for America, Feburary 19th, 2012, Accessed Feburary 19, 2012. http://www.airlines.org/Documents/ A4AIndustryReview.pdf

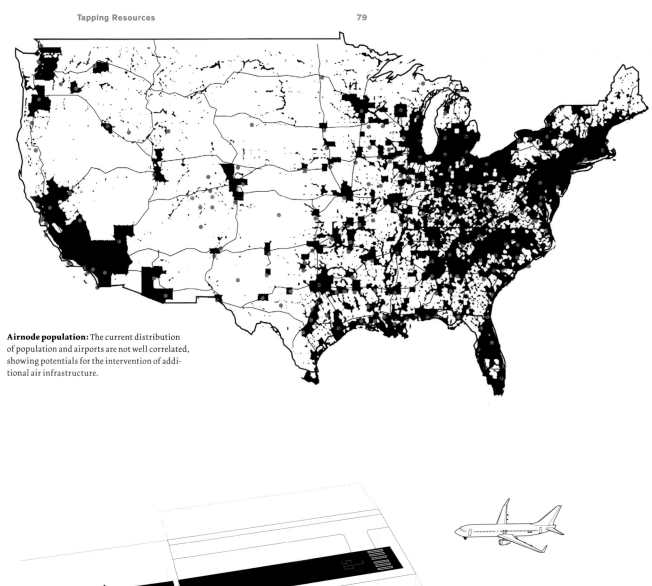

Airnode population: The current distribution of population and airports are not well correlated, showing potentials for the intervention of additional air infrastructure.

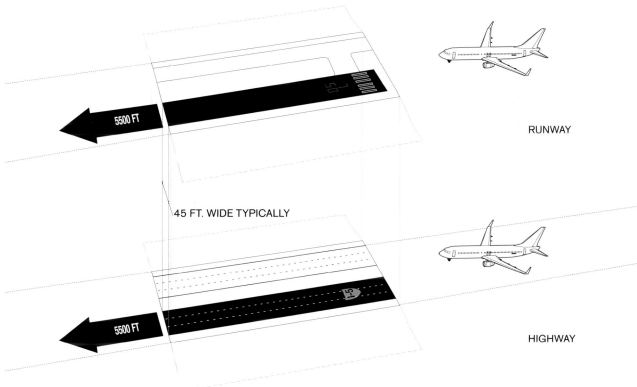

Requirements: Highway requirements provide a malleable substrate for the utilization as runways.

AIRPORT SEQUENCE

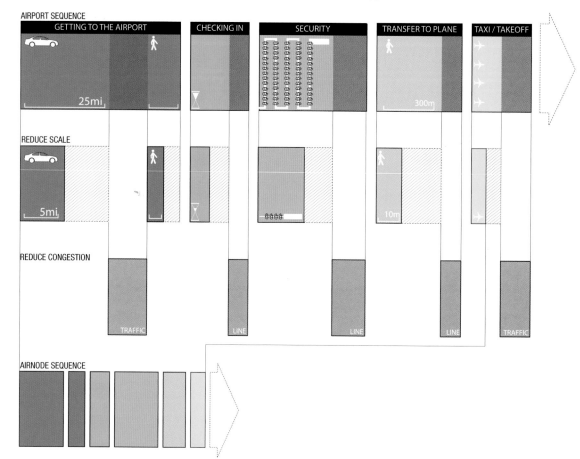

Sequence: A study of the current airport sequence demonstrates inefficiencies which provides the basis on which Airnodes can redefine this paradigm in the creation of a more efficient system.

they are most needed. 'Hotspots' will emerge and disappear over time, and routes can dynamically adjust to customer demand, models of efficiency, and the flows of existing ground traffic.

The potential of this typology is far reaching. In Los Angeles, for example, 12,000,000 residents spread over 5,000 square miles, but share only three major airports.[3] Airnodes can take advantage of the expansive highway system to create temporary runways during periods of low traffic, facilitating a hyper-efficient transportation network for one of the world's most congested cities. Airnodes can also be easily gathered into areas of very high demand, such as massive sporting or entertainment events, adjacent to existing large-scale parking lots. The flexibility of an adaptive system provides a synergy of transportation for all scales, more users, and in a wide range of contexts.

Airnodes is the logical response to the extreme inflexibility of a conventional airport. Can the global mobility afforded by air transit coalesce with the regional network provided by the highway system? This typology could push the boundaries of mobility by connecting the potential of two infrastructures into an infinitely more adaptive system.

Brandon Hall is a graduate of Yale School of Architecture, where he was a recipient of the James Gamble Rodgers Memorial Fellowship. He has practiced in Europe and Asia, most recently with OMA in Hong Kong. His work has been widely published and exhibited.

Brian Vargo has a background in architecture and urban design, and currently studies real estate and development at Harvard University. His Highlink proposal for Interstate 280 has been widely published.

Hall and Vargo pursue research together through *thisispre*.

3. "Los Angeles," Last Modified Feburary 20, 2012.
http://en.wikipedia.org/wiki/Los_Angeles

Stadium: Airnode at the Superbowl.

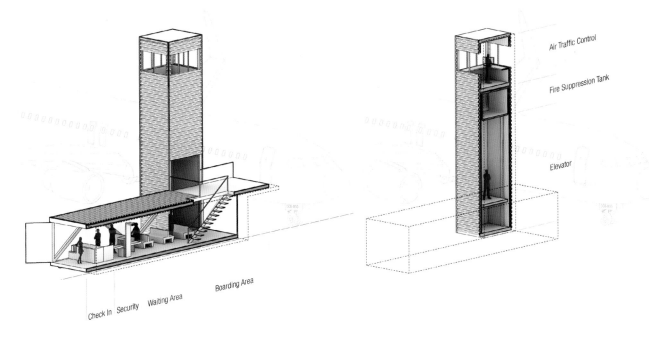

Air Traffic Control

Fire Suppression Tank

Elevator

Check In   Security   Waiting Area

Boarding Area

Airnode: Sectional axonometrics showing the public
and service areas of Airnode.

Highway: Interstate cleared for takeoff.

LE PARI(S) DE BKK

François Roche

English interpreter Camille Lacadee

(... betting on BKK/)

Charles de Gaulle Airport (CDG) is a transactional transitory zone, a transdoor[1] opening to a parallel, simultaneous, negotiable universe... The escape it offers may be narrow, it's wonderful anyway... just right for a native emigrant. Every other week, at a minimum, over the last ten years, to extricate myself from the museum city, frozen, transfixed in its conservatism and pedantic degradation... CDG Airport Terminal 1... "Beam me up, Scotty."

Complaint/

Paris, Charles de Gaulle Airport, Terminal 1, vanishing point... Escape the bourgeois city, capital of voluntary hostages huddling themselves up in sleepy ideals, where alienation is considered as good as a union contract. Flee this accretion of corrupt sycophantic institutions whose state clerks are amassing in Colbert's shadows, with their moral stench, vomiting their universalism to mask their pettiness.

Bataille's Paris was a wager, a city where you came willingly to get robbed, where people traveling across town knew they risked falling into a trap.[2] The danger of that Paris was intrinsic to its nature. There was no line between its heterotopia and its display case.

Haussmann was the first to perceive the danger of that tangled city planning. And in 1871, traveling down the avenues he cut through the city to allow for parades and military repression, the Versailles troops drowned the Paris Commune in blood. The mechanisms of circus and enslavement of today's "urban displays,"[3] to revisit Étienne de La Boétie,[4] have put an end once and for all to the popular and transgressive nature of the city. The alienation they produce among its inhabitants are far longer lasting than the substances of the previous kind.

They lull people to sleep while giving them the illusion of existence.

What was once a paranoid urban area has been replaced by a hygienic, moral, passive city life punctuated by ecstatic celebrations (such as La Fête à Neu-Neu),[5] each one spreading contamination further into the suburbs like Sarkozy's Le Grand Paris[6], disguising the coming servitude as territorial equality.

Line of escape/

BKK seems to last longer this time... It can neither be simply a rejection, a repulsion turned pathological, nor a stop-over, quarantine, transience... Nor a sort of "Interzone," the improbable grounds of which, made of experimentation and subversion, have already been tread by Burroughs[7]... Even less excused by the immersion in a humid and sweaty biotope, here in the heart of this entirely made up colonialist polyethnic neologism "Indochina"... with the affective, sexual, and economic transactional corollary of the aging man performing a platform of exchanges, to borrow from Michel Houellebecq.[8]

Le pari(s) de BKK is precisely here, ... a time machine for the price of a one-way ticket to rejoin in this Pari(s)... the one of Bataille... dirty, smelly, a swarm of men, women, rats, and cockroaches, of interloped mores, the Pari(s) of society-men and "Il est cinq heures"[9]... Whenever it rains, Alphaville's[10] macadam is covered with gray seeping soot, in daytime rasping the lungs, blackening the slightest apparition... at night coating the stooped grounds.

Le pari(s) de BKK would mean to embrace the street theater, human and machinist, erotic and tragic; the self-contradictory, never-ending messy interlacement; the polyphony of beings and encounters protected and/

1. In Dan Simmons' novel *Hyperion*, the transdoor is a vector of physical translation.
2. The Bataille' Paris is a kind of "portmanteau-word", the Battle of Paris (*Bataille* is French for battle) or the bet of Bataille (*pari* means bet), including unlimited disorder as a precondition of the order of the discourse, coming from the notion of Heterology developed by Georges Bataille (Documents #2, 1929); a text battling monumental and totemic architectural production as the expression of an urban-human domination. See Denis Hollier, *Against Architecture: The Writings of Georges Bataille*, trans. Betsy Wing (Cambridge: MIT Press, 1989).
Georges Bataille is a protean French philosopher and writer, involved in many domains—economy, anthropology, history of art and erotism. Disqualified by André Breton and J.P. Sartre in 1943, he was rehabilitated by Michel Foucault's preface in 1970 to the publication of his complete works. See Georges Bataille, *Œuvres complètes*, (Paris: Gallimard).
3. Public festivals such as Paris Plage, Paris Nuit Blanche, Paris Marché des Fiertés, Paris Fêtes des Tuileries, Paris Carnaval Tropical, Paris Famillathion, Paris Quartier d'été, Paris Techno Parade, Paris Fête de la musique, Paris Future en Seine, Paris..., a Paris of boredom and tourists suggest the city as a display.
4. See Etienne de la Boétie, *The Politics of Obedience: The Discourse of Voluntary Servitude*, trans. Harry Kurz (New York: Black Rose, 1975).
5. La Fête à Neu-Neu is an annual celebration in the Bois de Boulogne established by Napoléon I in 1815—the first drug-display for "Valium-ing" citizens.
6. Le Grand Paris (Greater Paris project) is an initiative launched by former French President Nicolas Sarkozy for "a new global plan for the Paris metropolitan region."
7. See William S. Burroughs, *Interzone* (New York: Viking Penguin, 1989).
8. *Plateforme* is a novel by Michel Houellebecq, published in 2001 by Flammarion, the theme of which is Thailand's prostitution, its affective and economic transactions.
9. "Il est cinq heures, Paris s'eveille," a song by Jacques Dutronc and Jacques Lanzmann.
10. *Alphaville*, a 1965 science fiction film by Jean-Luc Godard shot in the natural setting of Paris.

or exhibited in filth and noise, and yet freed from time and space. "Unplugged," in a mute, blind, and deaf zone [11]... creating simultaneously and in parallel the conditions for a city open to the world, to its species... disrupting and challenging its transactional modes day after day.

BKK/

The dust enshrouds the city and its biotope, modifies its climate. Within this fog of specks and particles [12] Bangkok turns into a melting pot of hypertrophic human activity, of convulsive exchanges of energy. At the antipode of the canons of modern urbanism and its panoply of instruments of prediction, planning, and determinism, the city of Bangkok [13] is conceived in between aleatory rhizomes where the arborescent growth is at the same time a factor of its transformation and its operational mode. It is an urban environment made of protuberances and emergences, where capitalist merchandise flows through a profusion of gigantic, aseptic, cold, and deterritorialized malls, immersed in an intoxicating urban chaos.

Le pari(s) de BKK is a mixture of dirtiness and beauty, of metabolism and verticality, of traffic jams and flat-smashed motorcycles swiftly finding their way through. It is the fly-over concrete-bridge-networks snaking their trajectories through a stochastic urbanism, with a permanent confusion, indistinction, and de-identification between publicness and privacy, exhibitionism and intimacy, repulsion and magnetism... It's an apparatus whose emergences do not pretend to be long-lasting or eternal.... Surviving, dying, resurrecting, dying again in a logic of contingency and vitalism, the logic of a palpitating organism stuttering between life-and-death drives, Eros and Thanatos are a second nature where the urban tissue is alive, and where the city is not limited and framed by its "representation," not frozen in a normative and panoptical system of survey and representation...

Le pari(s) de BKK is an inter-zone where the possible is uncertain and the impossible plausible... an ad hoc principle of urban (un)planning.

Stuttering/

In the hotchpotch entanglement of flux, friction, trifle, and cum, a few spots sparkle, ingrain, identify as the temples of normalized shopping mall exchanges. These 19th-century temples of commerce work under ritualized transactional modes, as the first penitentiary worlds of exchange, socialized and hierarchical biospheres, from the cashier to the department head, where the customer, machine subject and object of desire, is able to exercise the fiction of his/her power, of his/her supposed *jouissance*. The climate as well as the ambulatory and relational social modes are codified, formatted, artificialized, as the counterpoint to the swarming and untameable city blighting its accesses... But in Paris these capitalized zones have malevolently reversed inside out, and the city itself is now confused with their merchandized display, originally limited, contained and recognizable within geographic (id)entities.

Paris and BKK, two points on the planet, two asymmetrical evolutions, as if following two divergent, contingent space-time cynosures... one confusing the client with the citizen, the other still relying on the original contradiction between the object and the "subject" of capitalism. [14]

This is not so much an opposition between two cities as it is an opposition between several temporalities: Le pari(s) de BKK is the Paris of a future anterior eviscerated of all nostalgia, projecting a time when the city was not (yet) conditioned by the subordination of the bourgeois Ecolo plugged into his/her iPod mini, on a Velib ride, whatever his/her origins, education, salary and gender, to a standardization of appearances, willingly becoming the symptom of a global intellectual fraud.

Psycho transfer and Digression /

This apparently ideal "Parisian way of life" increases the schizoid negotiation of double belonging and double membership, framed by local reactionary injunctions on "living together" and, simultaneously, by the need to escape, to go anywhere. On one side, the local forces of permanence and immobility seeking to conserve a supposed "authenticity" regulated by rules and policies... a

---

11. The three wise monkeys are a pictorial maxim well-known throughout Asia. Each monkey is depicted as covering its ears, eyes, or mouth with its hands to embody the proverbial saying, "Hear no evil, see no evil, speak no evil."

12. The city is covered by $CO+CO_2$ particles that filter the light through spectral frequencies of grey, creating a glossy, luminous, hazy, suffocating, grey atmosphere that both reveals the degree of pollution and wraps the city in a sophisticated coat.

13. On the one hand, the bottom-up, under the freeway, is a self-organized, "messy," excessively rustling human zone, where frictions and encounters are intrinsically embedded. They embody a potential of adaptability,

tolerance, and indeterminism, from the shapelessness of the city to human pathologies and improvisations, where everything is dedicated to the logic and illogic of the swarm. It is in the exchanges' dynamism, in the smelled, digested, shitted substances, in the confusion between the taste of stir-fried food, the flagrance of rain on asphalt... the dirtiness and the beauty in the hell of human energies. On the other hand, the top-down, the freeway is a disseminated downtown dedicated to its own representation, self-satisfaction which embodies the running of the financial ideology through multiple condominiums of personal social "successes," stacked and disconnected from each other... both *alive and dead*: alive through the upward high-rising of the city, symbolizing the activity,

working potential, and efficiency of the economic model; and simultaneously dead for the same reasons, especially when the condos are completed... when working as financial products more than as actual living places.
The freeways, organized as a gigantic network floating in the urban tissue, are the "horizontal" line separating and distinguishing these two types of human habitudes of self-representation or social strata... enabling a myriad of connections, flirts, touches, caresses, and collision points between the two.

14. "Subject" here refers to a subordinate, as in a King's subject.

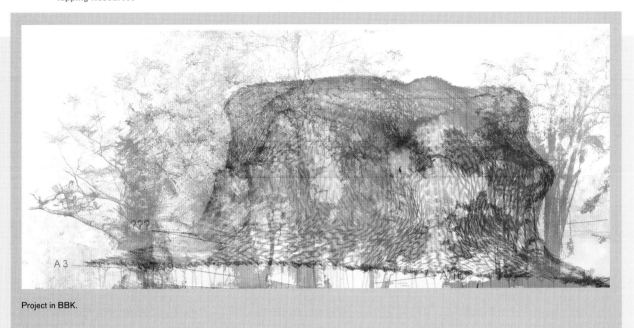

Project in BBK.

Project in BBK.

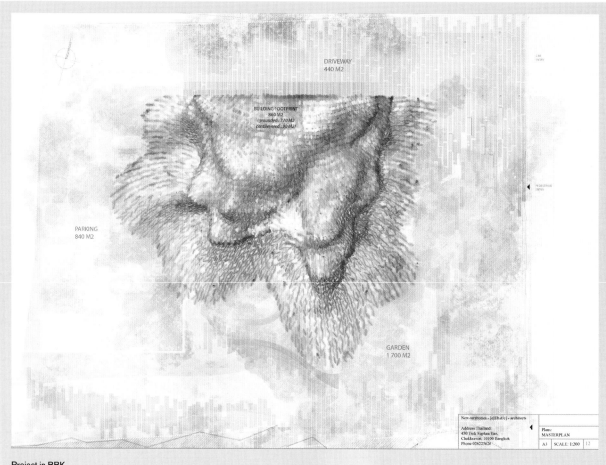

DRIVEWAY
440 M2

BUILDING FOOTPRINT
860 M2
(grounded: 770 M2)
(cantilevered: 90 M2)

PARKING
840 M2

GARDEN
1 700 M2

New-territories - [c]f/b/t/c] - architects

Address Thailand:
450 Trok Saphan Yao,
Chakkrawat, 10100 Bangkok
Phone 026225626

Plans:
MASTERPLAN

A3 | SCALE: 1:200 | 12

Project in BBK.

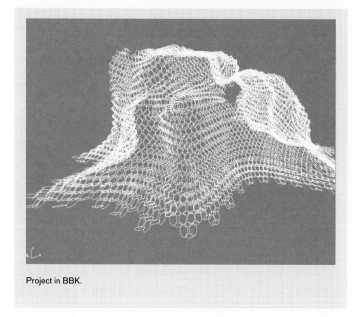

Project in BBK.

revived Puritanism driven by society-friendly standards for "good behavior", moralistic totalizing scrutiny, recipes for organic health food and hyper-moisturizing soap for a perfect body in the idealized Truman Show village.

In escaping all this, fulfilling irreducible needs such as reaching, touching the forbidden, jumping through the only window, authorizing objectionable behavior in the multiple infra-zones of electronic machinery doors (socializing, virtualizing, fictionalizing, pornoizing, criminalizing, and playing the game), the recognition of a contradictory, Siamese dualism... A symmetrical antagonism between the physical hoax of sedentary statements and the illusion of dematerialized nomadism... A permanent schizoid contingency, naturally intertwined.

It seems that our times have invited two demons to the same cozy dinner party, thus provoking a permanent schizophrenia. This basic and symptomatic opposition imposes itself like a cliché; a two-way caricature showing both the petrification of the local and the artificialized eroticism of the illusory-but-necessary objective of freedom, as a natural compensation for the stone-aged statement of the former.

Paris is becoming, with sublime effort and talent, the "sinthome"[15] of this capital(ist) city evolution... Urbanism as a regressive knot, a format of constraints, rules, policies... Smart speeches, small talks, flirts, merchandises, and all the "online" inhibited pathologies, on psychoactive antidepressants, on compulsive gambling officially organized by the French national lottery, La Française des Jeux. In opposition, Le pari(s) de BKK could run as an experiment in which the "village" is a matrix across multiple doors, articulating the immanent conflict of living together without denying the unpredictable nature of this very conflict, directly revealing the sophistication or the lack of social contract, of neighbourhood protocols, adjusted in real time, articulating phantasms and realities, obstacles and possibilities, garbage and fresh blooms, threats and various forms of protection, technical prowess and forces of

nature... interlocked... in keeping with the vitality of the species inhabiting them.

The "restoration" of the notion of democracy has to extend its potential of refabrication to the tooling and procedures that structurally produce city planning. Western democracy developed such a high level of control through the legitimate delegation of power as described and analyzed by Michel Foucault, that the energies of the multitude are framed, ghettoized in a predictable determinist master-planning agenda opposite of the notion of a heterotopic agenda, preliminary stones of urban contract emerging from the Multitudes.

In this sense, BKK, simultaneously "tragic" and "expectable," can be seen as the pursuit of Rimbaud's poetry,[16] including its (un)predictable fragility and failure.[17] Not in terms of the political structure of the system, but in the logic of (un)planning, through flux and reflux between "top-down" and "bottom-up", the loophole between the looseness of an administration and the individual dynamic innovation able to infiltrate this tolerance, is reconditioned. In a succession of extension, entropy, graft, a permanent mutation of the "tissue" is created, neither constrained by the ideology of tabula rasa, nor by archaeological preservation.

Schizoid apparatuses /

What perhaps is most relevant in Le pari(s) de BKK is the potential confrontation between the antagonistic forces of two urban models, a permanent union and divorce of the "Commune and the Capital," intrinsically intertwining to generate a systemic live output. The first model is made of the sound of the human swarm, musical and terrestrial, on the city's ground, and includes permissiveness of transformation, adaptation, graft, and necrosis, on its first four-five floors from the ground... where one can erect, destroy, alter, gangrene, and nest one's familial, commercial, or amicable system without having to report to public authority, as if in the midst of a judicial vacuum. The other is looking down on the first, appearing as a skyline, a vertical succession of malls, condos, and hybrids[18] emerging without creating

---

15. The *sinthome* (an archaic French spelling of the word symptom) is a concept introduced by Jacques Lacan to redefine the psychoanalytic symptom in terms of his topology of the subject. Moustapha Safouan, *Lacaniana: les séminaires de Jacques Lacan* (Paris: Fayard, 2001). In this sense we could consider that Paris represents the *sinthome* of its citizens.

16. "The Communards defending their revolutionary Paris against the government forces attacking from Versailles roam about the city like ants (*fourmiller*) in Rimbaud's poetry and their barricades bustle with activity like anthills (*fourmilières*). All of Rimbaud's poetry is full of insects, particularly their sounds: buzzing, swarming, teeming (*bourdonner*, *groullier*). 'Insect-verse' is how one reader describes Rimbaud's poetry, 'music of the

swarm.' The reawakening and reinvention of the senses in the youthful body—the centerpiece of Rimbaud's poetic world—takes place in the buzzing and swarming of the flesh. This is a new kind of intelligence, a collective intelligence, a swarm intelligence, that Rimbaud and the Communards anticipated." Michael Hardt and Antonio Negri, *Multitude* (New York: Penguin, 2004) 92–93.

17. The riots in BKK between the "Red Shirts" (People's Power Party) and "Yellow Shirts" (People's Alliance for Democracy) during the Thai political crisis from 2008 to 2010 were reminiscent of the Paris Commune in 1871 and the revolts of 1830 and 1848, where the city was not only zones of consummation, works, play, and sleeping but the territory of tension, where public space as the theater of the antagonisms

stretching and pulling human society.

18. One hundred high-rise buildings are currently planned and/or under construction in Bangkok.

any centralized downtown, subject to opportunities, speculations and resistances, themselves subject to strict rules of materiality, normality, and global representational aesthetics.

Le pari(s) de BKK is this friction territory… It makes possible the encounter between the one who only exercises his/her power through the compulsive merchandise of turnkey life models, and the one who, in contrast, is in synchronicity with the animal pleasure of things and beings, smells and sounds, illusions and ripe fruits. One makes a skyline, the other humming asphalt. One is capitalizing his/her economy by freezing it in the standardization of an imaginary vertical home (a condo 70 percent unoccupied, like so many financial products where habitability is a fiction), a producer but not consumer of a horizontal urban line, a financial transfer zone. The homogenization of desires and satisfaction allows for the flow of merchandise and the circulation of the money-narrative [19] (the city has turned into a transactional economic vector), which disincarnates in the construction of pseudo-luxurious, pseudo-comfortable, pseudo-designed, pseudo-inhabited, speculated, and volatile products in a skylinization process… before the financial bubble bursts into a myriad of collateral effects, junk bonds, and fatal contingencies -— the predictable de-organization of profits. The other has nothing to capitalize except its daily ritornello of "difference and repetition" in an erotic pornographic rustle conditioning.

Le pari(s) de BKK stutters on two models of *jouissance*, between the city-as-product-of-the-capital and the city-that-doesn't-give-a-shit, busy getting pleasure from it, in the superimposition of two strata, two morphologies, two mechanics of nonlinear exchanges… But Paris only has one model left: the human bourgeois, or bourgeois-becoming,[20] insulated in his/her sound-proofed home, listening for the least untimely noise that might get through the partition-walls to immediately denounce it, confusing life with its representation… with its corollary of sadness, and its dependency on the display organized by the central system of power

delegation, the political, social, monarchical operator: la Mairie de Paris.

On the other side, BKK, where two stories of time are still plausible… Like an urbanism simultaneously dead and alive, a contingency, a place of parallel stories… exuding the possibility to navigate in their frictions without subscribing to the one or the other as the unique mode of existence.

 The jump has been made, one year ago… Le pari(s) de BKK… Could it only be a 14-hour flight, a glass of whisky, three meals, two movies, some writing, half a drawing…? A normalized distance, linear, almost disappointing, inasmuch as one carries one's psyche in one's baggage… and the distance travelled will not metabolize its dependencies….

---

19. "Capitalism is nearly indifferent to the contents of the stories of which it enables the circulation. The money-narrative is its canonical story because it brings together its two properties: it tells us that we can tell any stories we like, but that the stories' profits must return to their author, or at least to those who convey their narratives (green washing, social washing, security washing). Jean-François Lyotard, Instructions Païennes (Paris: Éditions Galilée, 1977).
20. Paris is used like a beta development zone for the luxury industry. International magazines often depict Paris as a place where people on the street look like fashion models, provoking the Paris Syndrome: a transient psychological disorder encountered by tourists visiting Paris, and Japanese visitors in particular. It is characterized by a number of psychiatric symptoms such as acute delusional states, hallucinations, feelings of persecution (perceptions of being a victim of prejudice, aggression, or hostility from others), anxiety, and also psychosomatic manifestations such as dizziness, tachycardia, sweating, and others. See "Paris Syndrome," *Wikipedia*, http://en.wikipedia.org/wiki/Paris_syndrome.

advancing tools
and materials

WHOLE ARCTIC CATALOG

Pamela Ritchot

In the 1960's, as the post-war world developed in an age of technological innovation and social liberty, an American counterculture movement was brewing. An unyielding group of cross-disciplinary stakeholders sought immediate resolution in global ecological stability. Boasting ideas previously heard under the umbrella of Environmentalism, this radical offshoot foretold the future of a rapidly changing globe at the hands of industrialization, oil domination, and militarization. The '70s oil embargo that wreaked havoc in the US exemplified their concern that a crises elsewhere across the globe could spark local problems. The popular environmentalist slogan "We only have one Earth" was a quiet scream in the face of global ecological destruction.

In 1966, Stewart Brand emerged as a leading activist in this American counterculture. He lobbied for NASA's public release of the Earth's image from space in part to heighten awareness of its fragility and in part to arm the masses with visual propaganda. An author as well, Brand strategically responded to NASA's released images by publishing the *Whole Earth Catalog* in 1968, which offered a toolkit for ecological action. Brand hoped the catalog would help reconcile the technological prowess of global-industrial society with the very real ecological crises of the day. A graphic and encyclopedic-like anthology, its pages depicted the tools available to a militarized, industrial society, which he believed could be paradoxically leveraged to mobilize a grand-scale ecological revolution. Indeed, by its cover's subtitle, "access to tools," the catalog positioned itself as a survival guide for the flailing environmental and human condition, using the very tools and technologies—both physical technologies, as well as strategic, eco-centric thinking—that brought it to the brink.

The comprehensiveness of Brand's counter-philosophy is evident by the catalog's vast artillery. It combined species information; mathematical facts, such as the solutions to geometric puzzles; technological how-to's, such as how to transform a sheet into a geodesic dome structure similar to those found in the counterculture community of Drop City; and pertinent advertisements, such as excerpts from Stromberg's *Falconry Bulletin*. At a time when society was seemingly operating through a lens of black and white, the pages of the *Whole Earth Catalog* gave space to unexpected and often paradoxical pairings. It was a venue where nature met machine and where ecology met technology—and, importantly, where these pairings were rendered palatable. It provided its readers access to new ideas that might remedy the day's ecological destruction. The mandate of the *Whole Earth Catalog* was to scour the problem for a solution, to turn the tools on themselves.

As those touting Brand's earth conscience have today found common ground, the *Whole Arctic Catalog* posits that the current concern should be focused on our northern territory. This time, the catalog for the 21st century turns the view of the earth on its poles, allowing the viewer to see the less-seen: a contemporary Arctic in crisis. At the hands of our modern, industrialized society that Brand so passionately foresaw, the Arctic faces some of the most drastic impacts of climate change. The region struggles with ecological imbalance and a disappearing landscape, its melting icecaps leading to drastically rising sea levels that redraw its landmass with each passing season. The destruction of the Arctic threatens not only its land, people and species, but also the whole earth's ecological stability.

The *Whole Arctic Catalog* builds off of the prior belief that the designer—the architect—is driving the direction of this ecological mandate. This catalog posits that the history of innovation specific to the Arctic started, in fact, with the discussions of Brand and his contemporaries, as they activated a riotous era that empowered designers to boldly step outside of their conventional roles and uphold their place in the construction, and reconstruction, of new and sensitive environments. Their design and innovation has had a marked impact—both directly and theoretically—on Arctic development.

As their professional role has expanded over time, designers have positioned themselves alongside Brand's ecological agenda. Commanders of the built world, they capitalized on their power to alter and adapt human living conditions—constructing the built world as the 'machines' for living in harmony with the earth. These machines became quickly likened to the alternative environments of space travel, and this profession—equipped with spatial and systemic thinking—became obsessed with the challenges and obscurities of constructing new realities in far-off galaxies. Some of the first schemes for Arctic new towns offered structures that gave life to this space-age obsession, feeding into their fantastical visions of what it might be like to inhabit the far-off territory.

In tune with space travel, the work of Buckminster Fuller greatly advanced this ecologically minded agenda. Peder Anker noted that Fuller's obsession with finding earth-conscious solutions to sensitive and often remote regions, providing us with the proof that "Fuller's technological designs for a better environment did capture the counter-culture of the '70s."[1] As a multi-lingual designer, Fuller combined an interest in the rigor and efficiencies of militarized devices and operations with his interest in science, ecology, and engineering. His solution for the geodesic radomes for the DEW Line Radar stations demonstrate his ability to find smart, impactful solutions that have a maximum impact in a remote place with limited resources. The more the world seemed imperiled and its future unclear, the more the architects obsessed over the construction and habitation challenges that unfriendly environments presented.

Just as Brand had predicted of industrialized society, today's Arctic has seen several waves of development, interest and innovation that are akin to the historic environmental "space captains." Obsessing over the conquest of inhospitable lands has, throughout history, promised an array of rich rewards at the end of dubious struggles. Seeking to find innovation in the unknowns of its vast lands, the earliest Arctic explorers initiated the territory to the ongoing struggle for its geopolitical control and sovereignty. Martin Frobisher's 1577 expedition captures the mindset of understanding this "meta incognita" as the ultimate test and the ultimate reward in tackling what Queen Elizabeth deemed a land "beyond the unknown things."[2]

This mindset persisted into the mid-20th century, as its attractive possibilities reinvigorated an interest in defending, populating and exploiting Canada's so-called last frontier. During the onset of the Cold War, a growing concern for the permeable boundaries separating North America from its Soviet enemy drove an era of territorial expansion in the name of US and Canadian defense. Canada's Diefenbaker administration, for example, coordinated the construction of the Distant Early Warning (DEW) Line across its 69th parallel. Fuller's DEW line stations have become significant markers of Arctic innovation, but they also demonstrate the impact of Canada's sovereignty agenda and the militarized innovations that come with it—the very tools that have become fundamental to the Catalog itself. Matthew Farish describes this time in Arctic development as "a dual geopolitical and scientific frontier...

when fear of a Soviet assault led to an alternate invasion of Arctic landscapes by research teams, administrators and troops; all pushing northwards to occupy and materialize the region."[3]

Further to this, Diefenbaker's "Northern vision" helped accelerate the emergence of tools for Arctic development, catalyzing a push toward declaring the untold riches of the North as Canada's own. His "Road to Resources" program in 1957 sparked national support for rapid northern infrastructural development so as to explore and exploit the resources of this "new world to conquer".[4]

This attitude has carried through to the present day as oil companies such as BP and Shell position themselves for exploration in the contested subterranean territories of the Arctic waters. Their presence acknowledges that the pursuit of energy has become a very real spatial project, both challenging and advancing the construction of the Arctic landscape. "Spatial" in the sense that these resources begin to influence both our territorial understanding of the Arctic—the lens through which we map and analyze the geography—and our capacity to advance the infrastructural constructions of physical space in this lucrative region. The race for oil in ice, therefore, becomes a geopolitical fight to stake claim over the melting mass and what lies beneath. As well, this political and economic will provides the impetus to innovate Arctic construction both on- and off-shore, reconstructing the landscape at a scale and pace that this region could not spark or manage on its own.

Today, designers confront the challenges of construction and development in the fierce, unwelcoming Arctic, but they do so with the very real potential to deploy the technological know-how illustrated in the *Whole Arctic Catalog* and to author new ideas for the next generation. As we utilize our tools for construction, destruction, habitation, expansion and exploitation, we once again turn them upon themselves to steer the Arctic into a sustainable and optimistic future. As commanders of the built environment, we have found inspiration in hostility. We have invented construction tools and strategies purely borne from the utilitarian response to the North's volatile climate and ground condition. The challenges of an ever-changing landscape that oscillates between viscous and solid characteristics are only compounded by the logistical challenges of material transport, prefabrication, smart foundations and advanced thermal barriers for the harsh climate—reminiscent of the inventions of Buckminster Fuller. And as much as the "captain of Spaceship Earth" once argued that a multilingual toolkit could save the world from ecological disaster, so too can our Arctic mandate echo Fuller's agenda.

The Arctic needs our know-how, right now. The territory is already facing climate change and geopolitical contention. This *Whole Arctic Catalog* repositions Brand's model to now posit that while we only have one Arctic, we already have the tools and technologies that can secure its future. The *Whole Arctic Catalog*, with its collection of techniques, knowledge and announcements, speaks to its predecessor in philosophy, but it speaks beyond it—it speaks to our contemporary predicament, confronting the very real need to reverse global environmental problems—a terrifying, but exciting, prospect indeed.

Pamela Ritchot's design research is focused on the development potential and challenges of remote regions like the Arctic. Particularly, where issues of resource extraction, sovereignty and traditional settlements incite the need for innovative and impactful development. She is currently working as an Intern Architect and Urban Designer in Baltimore, Maryland.

1. Peder Anker. "Buckminster Fuller as Captain of Spaceship Earth." *Minerva* Vol.45. 2007: 417-434.
2. Andrew Waldron. Frobisher Bay Future: Megastructure in a Meta-Land. Architecture and Ideas. Retrieved from http://architectureandideas.com/issues_PDF/ Ai_issue08/Ai_v8_Waldron.pdf: 21.
3. Matthew Farish. "Frontier Engineering: from the Globe to the Body in the Cold War Arctic." *The Canadian Geographer*. Vol 50, No 2. (2006): 179 .
4. Coates, Kenneth. Canada's Colonies: *A History of the Yukon and the Northwest Territories* (Toronto: James Lorimer and Company, 1992), 1999.

WHOLE ARCTIC CATALOG

access to tools
for survival at the edge of the Earth

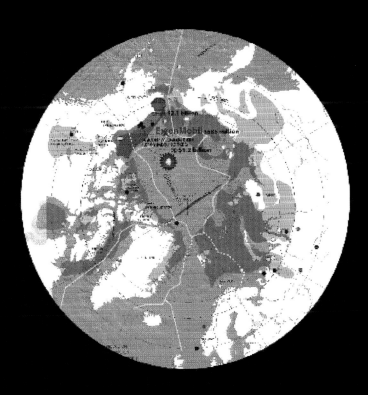

WINTER 2014

$32

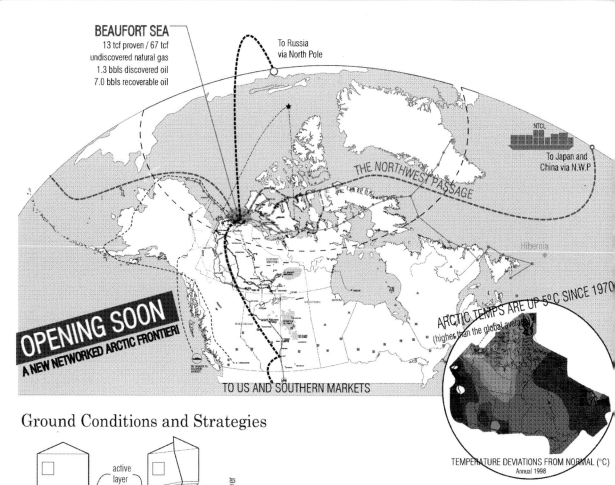

BEAUFORT SEA
13 tcf proven / 67 tcf
undiscovered natural gas
1.3 bbls discovered oil
7.0 bbls recoverable oil

To Russia
via North Pole

THE NORTHWEST PASSAGE

To Japan and
China via N.W.P

Hibernia

OPENING SOON
A NEW NETWORKED ARCTIC FRONTIER!

ARCTIC TEMPS ARE UP 5°C SINCE 1970
(higher than the global average)

TO US AND SOUTHERN MARKETS

TEMPERATURE DEVIATIONS FROM NORMAL (°C)
Annual 1998

Ground Conditions and Strategies

active layer

active layer

thaw bulb

permafrost

permafrost (over time)

Adfreeze Piling

residual heave

active layer

permafrost

early fall | early winter | late winter | late summer

Premise

Adfreeze foundation piles often experince frost heaving that can cause differential uplift and structural failure. As the Active Layer experiences phases of freeze and thaw, it exerts varying periods of frictional stability on a pile. As this layers freezes, the ground exerts frictional force on the pile that drives it up, slightly heaving that point of the foundation. As it thaws, this frictional force is lost and the foundation is allowed to settle at its new height.

Winter Movements

DRIFT !

SNOW DRIFTS AND SITE DISTURBANCES OCCUR

SLUMP !

THERMAL BRIDGING   THAW BULB

PERMAFROST MELT CAUSES STRUCTURAL FAILURE THROUGH GROUND SLUMP

LIFT !

BRRR !

TOTAL PHYSICAL SEPARATION OF PERMAFROST AND HEAT SOURCE. PILES CREATE AN EXPOSED UNDERBELLEY - A TRADEOFF, COOLING CONDITION.

Permafrost Subsidence

3 mm / year

CAUSES:
Subsidence: thawed permafrost
Climate Change: melting Ice Caps

INUNDATION !

CAUSES:
Increased storm surge
Warming ocean currents
undercut the permafrost base of
landmass

2 m / year

EROSION !

The Triodetic Space Frame!

high single point capacity !

torsional stiffness

30,000 lbs

top chord

diagonal

10" max. adjustment

Adjustable Bearing Plate

base plate on permafrost

triodetic connector

bottom chord

Allows for even settlement upon ground shifting

ARCTIC RETROFITS

uniform settlement

Typical Differential Ground Settlement

Arrives by BARGE!

tubular packable components

Order Today!

Transportable Space Frame systems offer an ease of transportation and on-site fabrication by local, unskilled labour. Its standardized assembly ensures quality construction in even the harshest climates!

no skilled labour required !

The Utilidor

Insulated corridor for liquid resource transportation in permafrost zones.

INSULATED PIPING:
Reduces heat transfer that causes permafrost thaw

INSULATED FOOTING:
Prevents thermal bridging

LIFT !

Creating uninterrupted mobility across terrains that bisect fragile ecologies

1.5 m

LIFT !

Ability to find stability on an uneven, shifting groundplane

Screw-Jack adjusts for differential settlement maintaining a mat condition.

Screw-Jacks are adjusted by local residents to account for heave in the winter and drop in the summer

The Screw-Jack Foundation!

Equal Distribution Loading

adjustable footing creates mat condition

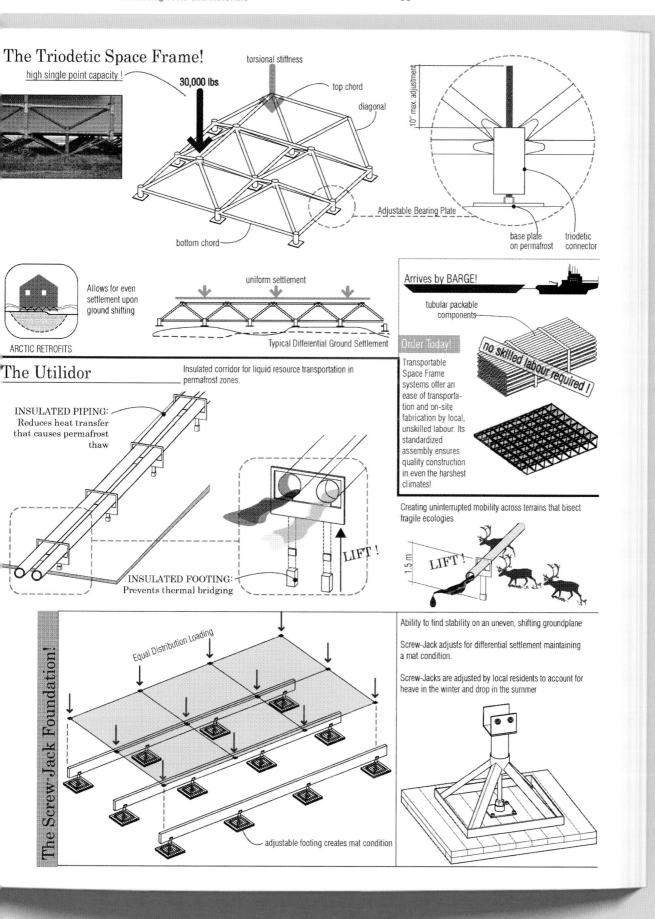

Geodesic Radomes

30 Rhombic Faces

RHOMBIC
TRIACONTAHEDRON

Buckminster Fuller developed the Geodesic Radome for a string of Distant Early Warning Line (DEW Line) Radar Stations along the 69th parallel of the North American Arctic. His concern for the global ecological crisis led him to find design strategies for sensitive territories that had light earthly impacts through geometric intelligence and attention to energy consumption. These smart skins survived with little and infrequent maintenance.

Combining the sphere with the tetrahedron, minimal materials are stretched over a maximum area to achieve maximum structural strength without the need for internal supports. The rapid deployment of 361 lightweight, self-bracing polyhedrons could withstand winds of up to 210 mph - an Arctic conquest! Further still, the mass production and flatpack shipments of their fibreglass and plastic components could be rapidly assembled with only the use of 1 plane, 1 engineer, and a small force of skilled labourers. The structural resilience of these smart skins allowed Fuller's Geodesic Domes to respond to the complexities of their remote Arctic conditions.

wind direction

drift patterns

wind direction

Spherical shell

Open Crawl Space

The Quonset Hut

flat pack transportation !

STRUCTURAL SPANNING SKINS

Rapidly deployable structures provide easy assembly in remote terrains. The Quonset Hut provided a clear span, prefabricated, lightweight shelter for military use throughout areas of the Arctic and throughout regions of military deployment.
These iterative huts have been arranged in various configurations to create a range of community spaces.
Their innovation has resulted in numerous patents for folded skin structures.

ETFE SKINS

Material rolled into bolts and placed in cannisters that are bundled and labeled per section to be assembled on site

Ease from transportation to assembly

Arrives by BARGE!

Fibreglass-Reinforced Panels

1973 IGLOOLIK RESEARCH LABORATORY, IGLOOLIK, NV

What FRP can do for buildings.

INTRODUCTION

Arctic innovations?

FRP cladding

steel structure

service core

prefabricated concrete substructure

drift pattern

Caisson-Retained Island (CRI)

PACK OFFSHORE LAND TODAY!

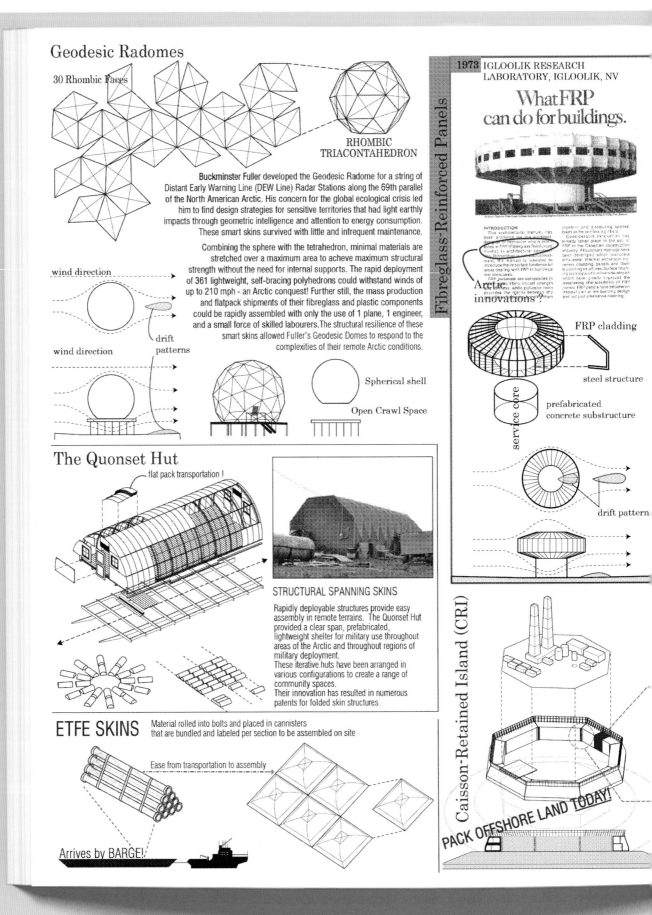

2007 HALLEY VI RESEARCH BASE, ANTARCTIC

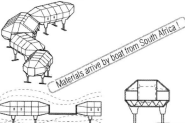

Materials arrive by boat from South Africa !

Raised off of the ground and containing the open space between two pods, reduces snow buildup from perpendicular winds.

Jack-up legs are recalibrated each season as ice conditions change. Ski footings provide mobility in snow.

The repetition of a single unit for six structures and only one varying unit as the social space allows for repetitive construction methods.

Adjustable jack-up legs allow the pods to rest lightly on the ground

A regularized structural steel space frame allows for a lightweight, easily deployable structure that properly counters the weight capacities of sea ice.

A linear deployment traps air between the pods as well as the ability to thermally seal one unit off from the rest in case of emergency.

2011 SPANISH ANTARCTIC BASE, LIVINGSTONE ISLAND, ANTARCTIC

MODULAR FRP MONOCOQUE RINGS !
Taking the structural Fibreglass Reinforced Panels to an ever-advanced staged, this tubular geometry resists past needs for additional steel structure supporting the panels. Instead, the rigidity of the monocoque extruded fibreglass rings maintain clear span and structural rigidity when fully assembled. This reduces the quantity of materials transported to this extreme remote location.

MODULAR CONSTRUCTION
Rapid construction for worker housing

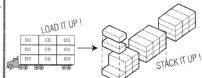
LOAD IT UP !
STACK IT UP !

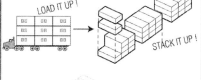
SPREAD IT OUT !

IT'S THE MANCAMP MODEL !

SINGLE UNIT - REPEATED

STACK IT UP !

OWNER: OIL INDUSTRY
OCCUPANTS: FOREIGN WORKERS

The Stressed CRI utilizes 8 caisson units held in an octagonal ring configuration by two pre-stressed bands of steel cables.
This offshore caisson structure reduces the amount of land needed to construct a drilling island, and its structural SKIN protects the drilling surface from wave action and erosion

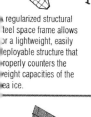

At the mitred ends of each caisson unit, vertical and horizontal shear keys prevent rotation
380 mm diameter pins are strung through mating coupling heads of each caisson.

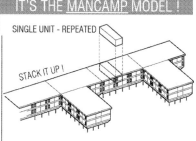

CAUTION !

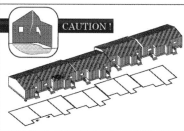

Structurally Insulated Panels SIPS!

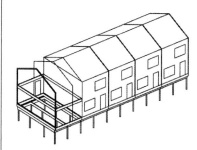

Arctic Construction Concepts

REPETITVE MODULES
Prefabricated SIP panels arrive by barge in repetitive modules that allow for rapid construction efficiency.

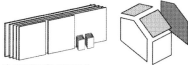

FLAT-PACK COMPONENTS
This material innovation allows for ease of transportation to on-site fabrication by unskilled, local labourers.

SNOW STRATEGY: LIFT UP!
Lifting the structure off of the ground allows for snow to pass under the building and reduces the occurance of snow drifting.

THERMAL STRATEGY:
Building units are constructed linearly, to reduce exposure of the envelope to extremes on the exterior.

Don't repeat the monotony and failed housing strategies of Arctic past!

GOVERNMENT ROW HOUSING TYPOLOGY

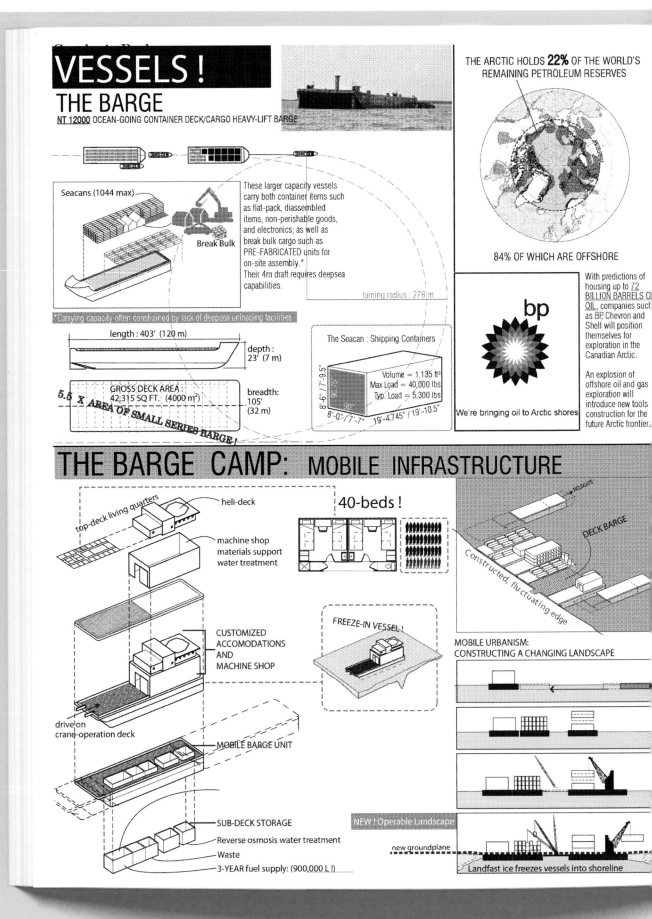

VESSELS!
THE BARGE
NT 12000 OCEAN-GOING CONTAINER DECK/CARGO HEAVY-LIFT BARGE

Seacans (1044 max)

Break Bulk

These larger capacity vessels carry both container items such as flat-pack, diassembled items, non-perishable goods, and electronics; as well as break bulk cargo such as PRE-FABRICATED units for on-site assembly.*
Their 4m draft requires deepsea capabilities.

turning radius : 278 m

*Carrying capacity often constrained by lack of deepsea unloading facilities

length : 403' (120 m)

depth : 23' (7 m)

GROSS DECK AREA : 42,315 SQ FT. (4000 m²)

breadth: 105' (32 m)

5.5 X AREA OF SMALL SERIES BARGE !

The Seacan : Shipping Containers

8'-6" / 7'-9.5"

90.75°

Volume = 1,135 ft³
Max Load = 40,000 lbs
Typ. Load = 5,300 lbs

90°

8'-0" / 7'-7"   19'-4.745" / 19'-10.5"

THE ARCTIC HOLDS **22%** OF THE WORLD'S REMAINING PETROLEUM RESERVES

84% OF WHICH ARE OFFSHORE

bp

With predictions of housing up to 72 BILLION BARRELS OF OIL, companies such as BP, Chevron and Shell will position themselves for exploration in the Canadian Arctic.

An explosion of offshore oil and gas exploration will introduce new tools construction for the future Arctic frontier.

We're bringing oil to Arctic shores

THE BARGE CAMP: MOBILE INFRASTRUCTURE

top-deck living quarters

heli-deck

machine shop
materials support
water treatment

CUSTOMIZED ACCOMODATIONS AND MACHINE SHOP

40-beds !

FREEZE-IN VESSEL !

RELOCATE

DECK BARGE

Constructed, fluctuating edge

MOBILE URBANISM:
CONSTRUCTING A CHANGING LANDSCAPE

drive on crane-operation deck

MOBILE BARGE UNIT

SUB-DECK STORAGE
Reverse osmosis water treatment
Waste
3-YEAR fuel supply: (900,000 L !)

NEW ! Operable Landscape

new groundplane

Landfast ice freezes vessels into shoreline

ce Islands!

An expanded interest in Arctic oil and gas has advanced the knowledge of offshore drilling in harsh conditions. The construction of **ice islands** in shallow water provide a seasonally-manufactured surface for peak winter drilling.

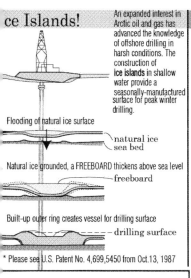

Flooding of natural ice surface

— natural ice
— sea bed

Natural ice grounded, a FREEBOARD thickens above sea level
— freeboard

Built-up outer ring creates vessel for drilling surface
— drilling surface

* Please see U.S. Patent No. 4,699,5450 from Oct.13, 1987

Artificial Islands!

The inconsistent Arctic sea ice demands new strategies for the CONSTRUCTION OF NEW GROUND PLANES. Artificial islands -- of both ice and earth -- recreate an industrial landscape that oscillates with the changing seasons.
In the SUMMER, these structures require defence against erosive wave actions and over-topping storm tides.
In the WINTER, their foundations must withstand significant lateral loads exerted by the movement of landfast ice sheets.

cable
netting
over
chain
link
fencing

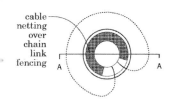

A ——— A

Mobile Assets! Vessel Relocation & Retrofit

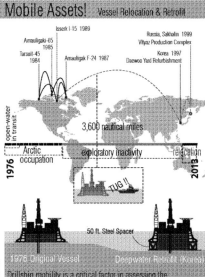

Isserk I-15 1989
Amauligaki-65 1985
Tarsuit-45 1984
Amauligak F-24 1987
Russia, Sakhalin 1999
Vityaz Production Complex
Korea 1997
Daewoo Yard Refurbishment

open-water in transit
3,600 nautical miles
1976
Arctic occupation
exploratory inactivity
relocation
2013

TUG !!

50 ft. Steel Spacer

1976 Original Vessel   Deepwater Retrofit (Korea)

Drillship mobility is a critical factor in assessing the infrastructure's lifespan. In volatile Arctic conditions, moving ships between drill sites with fluctuations in open water season ensures the most lucrative asset. From these economic and climatic conditions, a mobile, adaptable infrastructure was born.

Cost of RIG RELOCATION
• 60 tonnes fuel/day X 3,600 nm X 30 days
• $8,000,000 for fuel / trip
+ escort vessels = $18,000,000 fuel cost

Cost of DECOMMISSIONING :
• Scrap Metal Sales: Typically 12,000 tonnes
• World steel price: (approx.) $200 / tonne
+ $240,000 scrap value GAINED
• Energy Use: $500,000,000 disassembly, cleanup, disposal, transport, etc.

SELLING TO A RIG BREAKER =   (est.) $500,000

ADVANCED VESSEL FLEETS:
LEARNING FROM ARCTIC OPERATIONS IN THE 1970s & 80s :

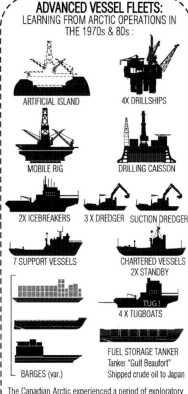

ARTIFICIAL ISLAND   4X DRILLSHIPS

MOBILE RIG   DRILLING CAISSON

2X ICEBREAKERS   3 X DREDGER   SUCTION DREDGER

7 SUPPORT VESSELS   CHARTERED VESSELS
                         2X STANDBY

                         TUG !
                         4 X TUGBOATS

BARGES (var.)   FUEL STORAGE TANKER
                        Tanker "Gulf Beaufort"
                        Shipped crude oil to Japan

The Canadian Arctic experienced a period of exploratory drilling following the global oil crisis of 1973. Thus, an advanced offshore vessel fleet developed. Technological advancements allowed access to increasingly deep reserves, and found integral solutions to Arctic drilling.

VS. **39** MARINE UNITS FOR DRILLING IN BEAUFORT SEA *
    27 MARINE UNITS IN ALL CANADIAN ARMED FORCES

* in the 1970s

1. Sea bottom dredging builds initial base

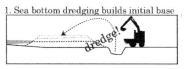

dredge!

2. Off-site gravel trucked on ice roads to infill

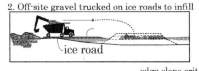

ice road

3. Final drilling surface is attained

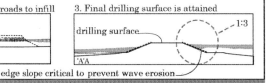

drilling surface   1:3

'A'A
edge slope critical to prevent wave erosion

Vessel Evolution
Progression from seasonal artificial islands and drillships to robust caisson structures

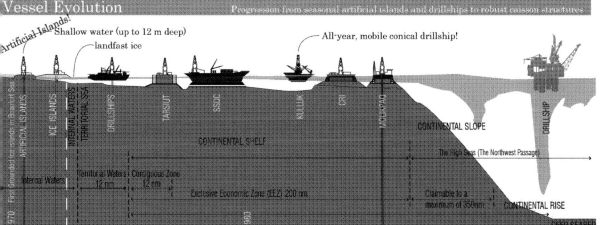

Artificial Islands!
Shallow water (up to 12 m deep)
landfast ice
All-year, mobile conical drillship!

ARTIFICIAL ISLANDS | ICE ISLANDS | INTERNAL WATERS | TERRITORIAL SEA | DRILLSHIPS | TARSIUT | SSDC | KULLUK | CRI | MOLIKPAQ | CONTINENTAL SLOPE | DRILLSHIP

1970 First Grounded ice islands in Beaufort Sea

CONTINENTAL SHELF
The High Seas (The Northwest Passage)

Internal Waters | Territorial Waters 12 nm | Contiguous Zone 12 nm
Exclusive Economic Zone (EEZ) 200 nm
Claimable to a maximum of 350nm

1980

CONTINENTAL RISE
DEEP SEABED

OPERATION EARLY BREAKFAST

Fionn Byrne

Seed rain: over the Yukon, near Dempster Highway.

Evolvability

Darwin's theory of evolution, driven natural selection and survival of the fittest, recognized that a species best able to reproduce its genetic material in a given environment would flourish. Without exception, all life today is the genetic descendant of previously living organisms who were able to survive until able to successfully reproduce.[1] Regardless of the variable time scale between the beginning of an organism's life and the moment of reproduction; all organisms must negotiate the demands of their survival in an environment subject to change.

Environmental change then is a driving force of evolution: individuals who are not able to adapt to dynamic external conditions fail to reproduce and those who survive do so by migrating to more favourable conditions, or by adapting in place to the changing environment.[2] The latter, *in situ* adaptation, is accomplished either by an organism resisting change, on account of its *robustness*, or accommodating change, on account of its *evolvability*.[3] A growing body of experimental data is beginning to suggest that the traits of robustness and evolvability may also be the subject of selection.[4] In other words, research suggests that Darwinian evolution may not only select the individual best evolved, but also the one best able to evolve.[5] This potential is particularly interesting when we consider the velocity of environmental change.

While environmental change is a constant, its velocity is not. Today we find ourselves in a situation where the pace of environmental change has accelerated beyond evolutionary historical rates, due to human modification and consumption of resources. Thus, we must accept that the unprecedented rate of environmental change corresponds to a shift in the selection process of Darwinian evolution from the natural to the anthropocentric. Relating this idea back to the notion of *evolvability*, defined as "the capacity to generate heritable, selectable phenotypic variation," it can be inferred that the outcome of evolution by anthropocentric selection may favour species with a high level of phenotypic plasticity.[6] In short, humans are forcing rapid change in environmental conditions where the fittest organisms are those best able to adapt to change.[7]

1. Richard E. Lenski et al., "Balancing Robustness and Evolvability," *PLoS Biology* 4,12:e428 (2006): 2190.
2. Gabriel G. Perron et al., "The rate of environmental change drives adaptation to an antibiotic sink," *Journal of Evolutionary Biology* 21, 6 (2008): 1724.
3. Andreas Wagner, *Robustness and evolvability in living systems* (Princeton: Princeton University Press, 2005), 367.
4. Gunter P. Wagner and Lee Altenberg, "Complex adaptations and the evolution of evolvability," *Evolution* 50, no.3 (1996): 967–976.
5. David J. Earl and Michael W. Deem, "Evolvability is a selectable trait," *Proceedings of the National Academy of Sciences* 101, no.32 (2004): 11536.
6. Marc Kirschner and John Gerhart, "Evolvability," *Proceedings of the National Academy of Sciences* 95 (1998): 8420.
7. David J. Earl and Michael W. Deem, "Evolvability is a selectable trait," *Proceedings of the National Academy of Sciences* 101, no.32 (2004): 11536.

Unnatural Selection

It is interesting to consider that organisms which are favored to survive and flourish in a fast-changing environment are often also introduced, invasive or alien species.[8] Again, evolvability and phenotypic plasticity are critical to the discussion. Professor Steven Chown, the Head of School of Biological Sciences at Monash University had affirmed: *"The extent of phenotypic plasticity has also long been considered a major difference between introduced and indigenous plant species"* and these differences "are likely to be particularly important in mediating responses to climate change".[9] The reason this is a critical issue is because invasive species have a severely negative impact on indigenous biodiversity, ecosystem services, and human health and economy.[10] Indeed so much so that biological invasion has been identified as a major threat to global biodiversity and human welfare.[11] While this remains a global phenomenon, one terrestrial zone expected to face

significant challenges is the forest-tundra ecotone, more commonly referred to as the arctic treeline.

Treeline

The arctic treeline is the most northerly extent of tree growth. It is defined by the zone where trees are replaced by non-trees along an environmental gradient.[12] At extreme environments such as this, even small shifts in environmental conditions can mean the difference between the survival of a species or its failure. As global temperatures rise, trees expand into territory that was previously inhospitable.[13] The implications of migrating into a previously un-colonized area extend beyond the lack of competition, predation, or herbivory; at a newly expanded treeline, the colonizers make up the entirety of the woody plant material, an extreme monoculture lacking the critical biodiversity for a functioning food web.[14]

The combination of a species with a high degree of evolvability, namely the colonizing non-native tree, and the

8. For an compelling discussion on invasive species, migration and climate change see Jason Groves, "Nonspecies Invasion," in *Telemorphosis: Theory in the Era of Climate Change Volume 1*, ed. Tom Cohen (Michigan: Open Humanities Press, 2012), 183-202.
9. Steven L. Chown et al., "Phenotypic plasticity mediates climate change responses among invasive and indigenous arthropods," *Proceedings of the Royal Society B: Biological Sciences* 274 (2007): 2531.

10. Invasive Species Specialist Group (ISSG), "The Invasive Species Problem," www.issg.org/about_is.htm.
11. Millennium Ecosystem Assessment, "Ecosystems and human well-being: biodiversity synthesis," (Wahsington, DC: World Resources Institute, 2005).
12. George C. Stevens and John F. Fox, "The Causes of Treeline," *Annual Review of Ecology and Systematics* 22 (1991): 177.
13. Camille Parmesan, "Ecological and Evolutionary

Responses to Recent Climate Change," *Annual Review of Ecology, Evolution, and Systematics* 37 (2006): 637-669.
14. Perhaps even more drastic, ecologically speaking, is Marilyn Jordan's (a Senior Conservation Scientist with The Nature Conservancy) assertion that "in ecosystems where 90 percent is non-native, there is no functioning food web left." The Dirt, "The Rise of Novel Ecosystems," http://dirt.asla.org/2011/04/06/the-rise-of-novel-ecosystems.

SEED RAIN : natrual means of seed dispursal

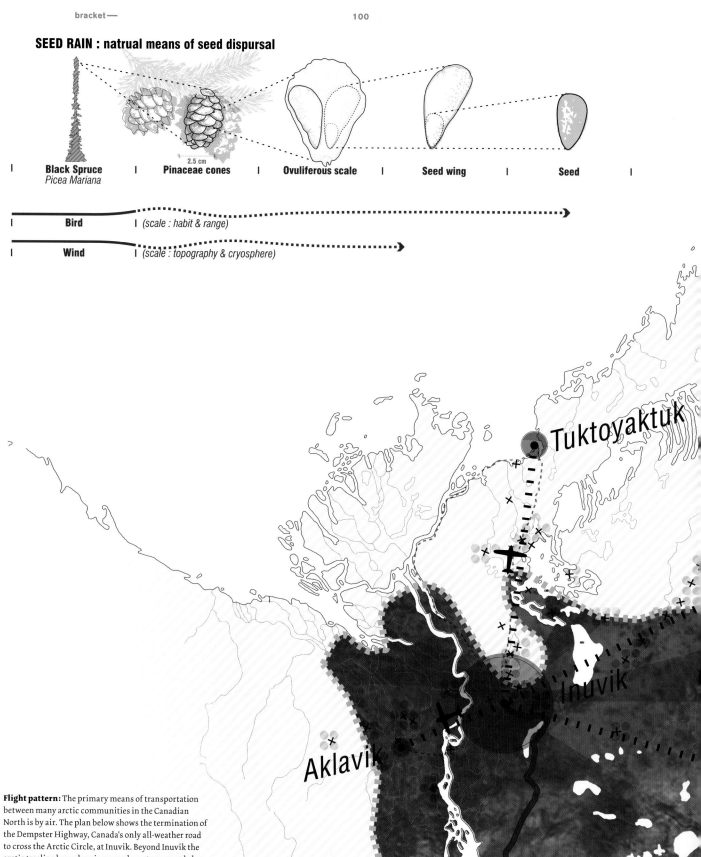

Black Spruce *Picea Mariana*	**Pinaceae cones** 2.5 cm	**Ovuliferous scale**	**Seed wing**	**Seed**

Bird — (scale : habit & range)

Wind — (scale : topography & cryosphere)

Tuktoyaktuk

Inuvik

Aklavik

Tsiigehtchic

Flight pattern: The primary means of transportation between many arctic communities in the Canadian North is by air. The plan below shows the termination of the Dempster Highway, Canada's only all-weather road to cross the Arctic Circle, at Inuvik. Beyond Inuvik the arctic treeline boundary is crossed most commonly by airplane. Carrying repurposed cluster munitions with modified anti-personnel fragmentation mines, vast quantities of seeds sourced from native species can be delivered to territory previously inhospitable to tree growth. The evolutionary means of seed dispursal is augmented to match the accelerated pace of environmental change.

AT EXTREMES

AUGMENTATION : antropogenic means of seed dispursal

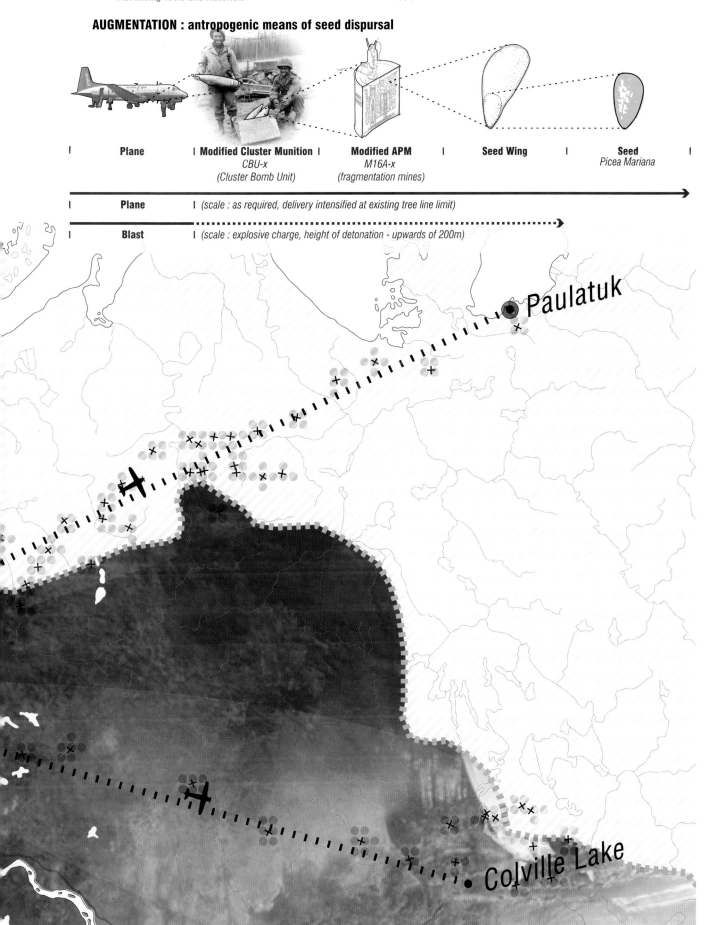

| Plane | | Modified Cluster Munition |
CBU-x
(Cluster Bomb Unit) | Modified APM
M16A-x
(fragmentation mines) | | Seed Wing | | Seed
Picea Mariana | |

	Plane		(scale : as required, delivery intensified at existing tree line limit)
	Blast		(scale : explosive charge, height of detonation - upwards of 200m)

Paulatuk

Colville Lake

Action at a distance: a previously deployed modified fragmentation mine detonates and disperses seeds over a maximum range when the temperature sensitive trigger detects the warming of local conditions to those suitable for tree growth.

expanding treeline is especially worrisome. If climate change and the amount of human activity in the arctic continue to increase, then large areas of the tundra may be colonized by invasive plant species, negatively impacting local wildlife.[15] The vast circumpolar area which will increasingly support the growth of trees, is projected to reach far north into the high arctic.[16] Should such a vast territory be left to transition un-monitored and un-aided, enormous tracks of land will be colonized by non-native introduced species leaving a severely reduced functional capacity in terms of biodiversity and ecosystem services.

Assisted Migration

While non-native species may have an advantage over native species in colonizing new territory, a rate-limiting obstacle for both species type is their method of seed dispersal.[17] This is especially true at range margins; the edges of a species' territory usually signified by a change in environmental conditions. Along this territorial perimeter survival pressures are most extreme, and in the case of the forest-tundra boundary, lack of viable seed is a critical factor in limiting plant establishment.[18]

This is important because any improvement in seed dispersal will directly improve a plant's ability to colonize new territory.

Plant species have evolved physiological and morphological characteristics to improve their ability to more quickly migrate over longer distances, but every advantage was selected by Darwinian evolution in environments undergoing significantly slower rates of climactic change. For example, the seeds of the black spruce (*Picea mariana*) have a non-reproductive projection: a wing, which allows the seed to be carried by the wind. Other trees of the same family have larger seeds with smaller wings. The larger seeds are heavier and cannot be carried as far by the wind, but they store greater resources, increasing the chance of seedling survival. The same morphological adaptation (the wing) in two different environments produces unique strategies for species propagation. Both of these species find themselves today in a new environment, the faster changing and warmer global anthropogenic environment that is making new territory habitable at a historically and evolutionary unprecedented rate. We could project that a third dispersal strategy: a very small seed with a very large wing, would enable a species to out-travel the competition and colonize the expanded habitable

15. Milissa Elliott et al., "Non-indigenous plant species along roadsides and other transportation routes in the Mackenzie Valley," (Toronto: York University, 2010), http://pi.library.yorku.ca/dspace/bitstream/handle/10315/6345/Invasive_species_Danny_ENR.jpg?sequence=1.

16. NunatsiuqOnline, "Warming Arctic climate may mean trees for Nunavut in 100 years," www.nunatsiaqonline.ca/stories/article/65674warming_arctic_climate_may_mean_trees_for_nunavut_in_100_years.

17. Robert D. Holt, "On the evolutionary ecology of

species' ranges," *Evolutionary Ecology Research* 5 (2003): 159-178.

18. Åsa Lindgren et al., "The Impact of Disturbance and Seed Availability on Germination of Alpine Vegetation in the Scandinavian Mountains," *Arctic, Antarctic, and Alpine Research* 39, no.3 (2007): 449-454.

territory, but the speed of evolution by natural selection is not as fast as the human capacity to modify the environment. In an unnatural environment, natural selection isn't effective. There is no greater evidence of this than the fact that the current rate of biological extinction is estimated to be upwards of ten thousand times higher than expected background (natural) rates.[19]

Assisted migration has emerged as a strategy for bypassing such limits. In order to accelerate the migration of species, humans are intervening by selectively moving species or planting seeds in desired locations. In effect, with this strategy, methods for biological systems to respond to environmental change are anthropogenically augmented to match our acceleration of environmental change, with the ultimate goal of maintaining biodiversity and important ecosystem functions (such as carbon sequestration). A call to arms for assisted migration has been delivered by Biologist Jason McLachlan et al.:

> Regardless of forthcoming scientific progress, the magnitude of impending climate-driven extinctions requires immediate action. Delays in policy formulation and implementation will make the situation even more urgent. We advocate developing management strategies with the flexibility to respond to emerging insights from basic and applied research, but we cannot wait for better data. To an uncomfortable extent this war will have to be fought with "the army we have, not the army we want."[20]

In this call to arms, *Operation Early Breakfast* imagines a human intervention into the evolutionary means of biological reproduction and vegetal migration of native species. This project begins to question and explore methods for increasing the distribution of native seed at the treeline boundary, reducing the advantage of non-native vegetation and accelerating the growth of biologically diverse habitats.

Area of Effect

No human endeavour has been more explicit in its destruction of the environment than war. As Peter Sloterdijk argues "the 20th century will be remembered as the age whose essential

thought consisted in targeting no longer the body, but the enemy's environment."[21] Beginning with chemical warfare during World War I, where the opponents' air and atmosphere was the target, modification of the enemies' environment reached a climax during the Vietnam War.[22] The extent of these activities and their far-reaching implications resulted in a globally accepted need to ban the hostile use of environmental modification post 1978.[23]

Today, the military continues to provide ample precedents and many innovative technologies to rapidly, efficiently, and effectively modify environments.[24] The majority of these weapons operate at smaller scales, but are resolute in their targeting of the environment. Consider the host of titles such as area denial weapon, land mine, anti-personnel mine, fragmentation mine, or improvised explosive device (IED). It is worth pointing out, because it is often taken for granted, that these weapons are the invention of human ingenuity, research and design. In terms of affected area, the cluster munition (CBU or cluster bomb unit) is particularly well designed. This insidious device, when dropped from the air releases many smaller submunitions. Indeed, the design of these devices was to make the largest area possible momentarily damaging to humans. *Operation Early Breakfast* redeploys the intelligence and technology of the military to carry out tasks of environmental modification, with the goal not of destruction, but greater biological productivity and success.

Operation Early Breakfast

In the Canadian Arctic, mobility is reliant on air travel as environmental factors make the construction of roads an onerous task. Indeed, it is by air that the arctic treeline is most commonly crossed. *Operation Early Breakfast* proposes the dropping of modified cluster munitions (CBU-x) from aircraft once they reach proximity to the treeline. Upon release, these munitions will distribute multiple fragmentation mines (M16A-x), which upon detonation release a dense cloud of native seeds. The trigger mechanism is imagined to be two fold. The first is temperature sensitive. With this strategy, seed fragmentation mines can be dropped in locations beyond the current habitable range of the desired

19. International Union for Conservation of Nature (IUCN) Red List, "Species Extinction – The Facts," http://cmsdata.iucn.org/downloads/species_extinction_05_2007.pdf.

20. Jason S. McLachlan et al., "A Framework for Debate of Assisted Migration in an Era of Climate Change," *Conservation Biology* 21, no2 (2007): 301.

21. Peter Sloterdijk, "Terror from the Air," (Los Angeles: Semiotext(e), 2009): 14.

22. Some examples of ENMOD programs include Operations Trail Dust and Ranch Hand which involved the large scale aerial dispersal of herbicides. Operation Popeye and Projects Cirrus and Stormfurry disrupted weather patterns by either increasing or decreasing cloud cover though the dispersal of dry ice and later silver iodide. The Commando Vault Program saw the above ground detonation of 15,000 pound bombs in order to clear any organic matter in a 300 metre radius without creating a blast crater, to be later used as helicopter landing zones. Operation Fishbowl was a series of near-space high altitude nuclear detonations carried out to test the

capability of such explosions to manipulate atmospheric conditions with the desired outcome of disrupting communication systems. These are only a few examples of environmental modifications for military purposes of which there are many more. For more on environmental modification and the military see Mike Hill, "Ecologies of War," in *Telemorphosis: Theory in the Era of Climate Change: Volume 1*, ed. Tom Cohen (Michigan: Open Humanities Press, 2012), 239-269.

23. In 1978 the Convention on the Prohibition of Military or Any Other Hostile Use of Environmental Modification Techniques (ENMOD) was entered into force and prohibits the hostile use of environmental modification techniques. The particular of this convention are available online: UN Documents: Gathering a Body of Global Agreements, "Convention on the Prohibition of Military or Any Oth er Hostile Use of Environmental Modification Techniques," http://www.un-documents.net/enmod.htm.

24. DARPA continues to pioneer much of this research. DARPA's Blue Angel Program has been established to

accelerate the manufacture of pharmaceuticals by using plant-made proteins and to accomplish this is exploring means of rapidly growing enough tobacco plants to realize their goal of greater than 10 million doses in one month. The program is described further online: DARPA, "DARPA Makes 10 Million Strides in the Race to Contain a Hypothetical Pandemic," www.darpa.mil/NewsEvents/Releases/2012/07/25.aspx. Or consider the EATR Program. The Energetically Autonomous Tactical Robot is designed to forage for plant biomass which is then converted to fuel, allowing the robot to theoretically autonomously operate indefinitely, described online: John Byrne, "Military Death Cyborg Synergy Come True," Rawstory (2009) http://rawstory.com/blog/2009/07/new-military-robots-could-feed-oncorpses.

species. When temperatures reach a predetermined level where the plant is known to survive, the trigger detonates the mine, dispersing seeds in the appropriate microclimate. A second trigger relies on keystone species. For example the woodland caribou (*Rangifer tarandus caribou*) whose habitat encompasses the arctic treeline, is expected to migrate north with increasing global temperatures. In this case, bounding fragmentation mines which deploy tripwires are modified such that when tripped they are launched not to waist height for detonation but higher, clear of the species below. In both cases, the naturally evolved means of species propagation of arctic vegetation (seed wings) is augmented in order to accelerate their colonization of territory made newly habitable by anthropogenic global climate warming. Evolution by unnatural augmentation is the end game of assisted migration. Human culture selects which species to support and their survivability is maximized by way of existing technology and logistics, our weapons in the war on the environment.

While the technology for *Operation Early Breakfast* is military, the work of deploying the seed mines is completed by the public or private corporations. Any flight passing in proximity to the treeline would be enlisted More flights into remote environments beyond the treeline will correspond with the deployment of more cluster seed munitions and will result in the production of more bio-diverse habitats.

Beyond Shallott

Operation Early Breakfast is a design of assisted migration writ large. The *Operation* parallels the developments in reforestation, primarily the work of Mark Hodges who is actively testing aerial planting techniques to *"assist or accelerate nature."*[25] The military would be the technological apparatus that enables the survival of the non-human. The process will be designed into the very system that is today primarily responsible for creating the ecological crisis. This will have an initial economic cost but the dystopian scheme is designed with the same impulse for efficiency that drives weapons research: maximizing effect, minimizing cost. While James Lovelock's Gaia hypothesis defined the entire planet as a 'living' system because of its ability to self-regulate and defy entropy, so to shall the same definition apply to capitalism.[26] We must heed this *"call to service"* in the war on the environment.[27] Should we hesitate we may be forced to consider the outcome of the following question: When human survival, predicated upon access to some minimal limit of natural resources is at odds with an economic system that is predicated upon consuming those resources, who will the state protect?

The ecological example of Hurricane Katrina in New Orleans saw the localized exclusion of ethics and politics as the state put the protection of property (capital) before life and intervened with military power to assert population control.[28] With a 'looming ecological crisis' that is argued to be global and totalizing, *Operation Early Breakfast,* if it operates correctly, is designed as a mirror against which alternative scenarios can be tested. It is not design as a conclusion, nor as a solution. Instead, it offers questions and strives to be a starting point, a turning point.

Fionn Byrne welcomes discussion, praise or criticism. Send digital communications to him via mr.fionn.byrne@gmail.com.

25. Hodges, Mark, "Use of Military Aviation Assets for Restoration of Grasslands and Forests. 2009" (presented at annual Environment, Energy Security & Sustainability (E2S2) Symposium & Exhibition, 2009) http://e2s2.ndia.org/pastmeetings/2009/tracks/Documents/8190.pdf
Last accessed August 12, 2014.
26. Mick Smith, "Against ecological sovereignty: Agamben, politics and globalization," *Environmental*

Politics 18:1 (2009): 101.
27. Call to service is the military language that James Lovelock employs in his recent novel. James Lovelock, "The revenge of Gaia," (London: Allen Lane, 2006): 153.
28. Mick Smith, "Against ecological sovereignty: Agamben, politics and globalization," *Environmental Politics* 18:1 (2009): 111.

LAND MANAGEMENT TRIBES

Matthew Spremulli + Fei-Ling Tseng

1.

2.

3.

4.

Currently the region of the Great Plains is fraught with social, capital, and ecological issues.
1. Eco-strain shows degrees of human influence on the land.
2. Agri-exodus shows counties experiencing negative population growth alongside urban agglomerations that have recently expanded in territory.

3. Agri-speculation Three indicators to measure the likelihood of current and projected agri-innovation: speculative bio product investment, state-supported bio industry and industrial farming by type.
4. Overlap Finding the place of most overlap between the three maps, an ephemeral and ever-changing territory emerges, shown as the darkest area in 4. This area of

extremes is the habitat of the Land Management Tribe, where they exist mediating between these challenges.

Agriculturally converted grasslands represent a major source of food, fuel, and fiber for all of humanity. However, both the host ecologies and the techniques to farm these regions are approaching critical limits due to stresses incurred by increased productivity demands and ecosystem failures. Globally, temperate grasslands represent the most 'at risk' terrestrial eco-region having been affected by the most amount of landscape conversion and receiving the least amount of protected/conserved land (Hoekstra's Conservation Risk Index 2006). Rethinking how grasslands are farmed is unavoidable if we are to continue relying on these regions for agriculture.

Grasslands have historically supported the world's largest mammals, often found herding, grazing, and migrating with the growing seasons. In turn the migration and grazing created a co-evolutionary relationship where grasses began growing deeper roots and were able to resist more damage. The result of this paring created the world's most productive "earth-making" landscape, capable of yielding both rich soils and grains. Once their consumable and storable products were discovered, the grasses were converted to intensive croplands by farmers. Farmers replaced perennial polycultures with annual monocultures in order to maximize yields. Instead of symbiotically developing rich soil over multiple years and benefiting from mixed roots and nutrients, the annual monocultures absorbed nutrients for their one-year cycles and did not create beneficial soil relationships with their neighbouring plants since they were all the same. Further, in order to farm these grasslands, farmers needed to evacuate the animals who would otherwise be consuming their crops or disrupting their lives on the farm; the grazing migrators. These farming preferences have significantly slowed the cyclical ecosystem services that were offered by the perennial polycultures and the symbiotic relationships with the migrating grassland animals. Carbon sinking, soil building (both nutrient creation and anti-desertification), and species diversification are but a few of the ecosystem services that temperate grasslands used to offer before being agriculturally converted. Nowhere is this conversion most extreme than in the North American grasslands, which is more commonly referred to by its agricultural uses as "the corn belt", "the grain belt", or "the bread basket".

America's Great Plains is an interesting region in which to explore alternative grasslands farming techniques, not only because of its current extreme conditions, but because continuing advances in automated farming and a shrinking population have created a condition of fewer people managing more land. Long hailed as the 'mecca' of the farming world, the advances in automation made across the prairies have liberated farmers from the land, but also left a large vacancy. The recent depopulation has hit such severe lows that many counties are returning back to their "frontier" designation (less than six people per square mile). Machine technologies that now work in place of absent land managers have created a land use of paradoxical character; that of a "productive frontier".

Land Management Tribes envisions a landscape future for the Great Plains that finds new design opportunity for intelligent automation in the farming of the ecologically-challenged grasslands. The project intervenes on the very technology that began the landscape conversion processes and are already being developed in the region: the robotic farming systems. But rather than looking only at production efficiency, the proposals consider the spatial, symbiotic, and experiential potentials such technology might offer in this context. As a result, these alternative land-management machines are less engineering-like and more species-like as they mediate between ecosystem rehabilitation, productive farming, and new human experiences. The design considers human vacancy to be a design opportunity, and pushes this current trend to an extreme where humans assume new modes of grassland occupation such as safari adventurists, soft herd-management veterinarians, or migrating mechanics.

The "hoofed wheel", an autonomous, hyper-sensory, mono-wheel is the base component of a modular equipment library, which effectively becomes the new tractor for the grasslands. The porous wheel design is inspired by the soil stimulating impact of ungulate hooves, which in combination with lighter, continuously operating, intelligent, and more numerous machines, mimics herds of animals. The "hoofed wheel" can combines with both implement and stationary equipment from the library making the resulting machines capable of scaling between tasks and conditions.

One example of a combination the "hoofed wheel" can make with implements is the "bison herder." As a team, a series of "bison herders" crowd source several herds, distributing their ecological services (soil aeration and fertilization) with their management services (grass mowing) over an area. While providing benefits to farms these machines also protect bison by guiding them between conservation areas, feeding grounds, and wintering havens.

Together the machines build symbiotic relationships with the larger grasslands ecology, on the basis of machine-to-machine shared data across the region. As a result of working with their surroundings, the distribution between the machine activities become blurred; farming, wildlife conservation, or soil remediation all become one as they roam the grasses. Humans are purposefully decentred in the Land Management Tribe future, but provide a new opportunity to engage with the prairies that has never been provided in the past, as a process-aware observer and participant. The machine tribes become a new interface to hear, feel, and see the complexity of the grasslands that have been so easily overlooked, and they call into question the very practices of agriculture that our civilization has taken for granted.

Matthew Spremulli is a designer and educator interested in architecture as an interactive interface with our environments. His work explores the topics of resource flows and co-speciation through crossover between ecology and technologies.

Fei-Ling Tseng is a planner interested in how we use cities as an interface for resource and knowledge flow, transformation and consumption.

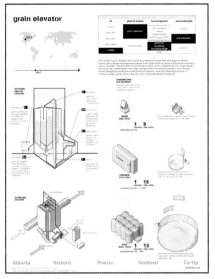

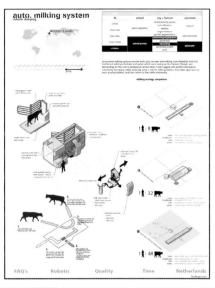

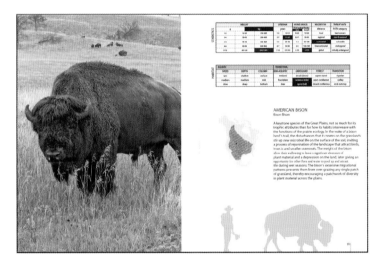

The Agri-Tech Catalog explored various techniques and technologies employed by farmers on the Great Plains to create and distribute agricultural products from the landscape.

The Animal Index explored numerous Great Plains species, tracking their adaptive traits in response to specific micro-climates, their ecosystem services, and their current status in the grassland.

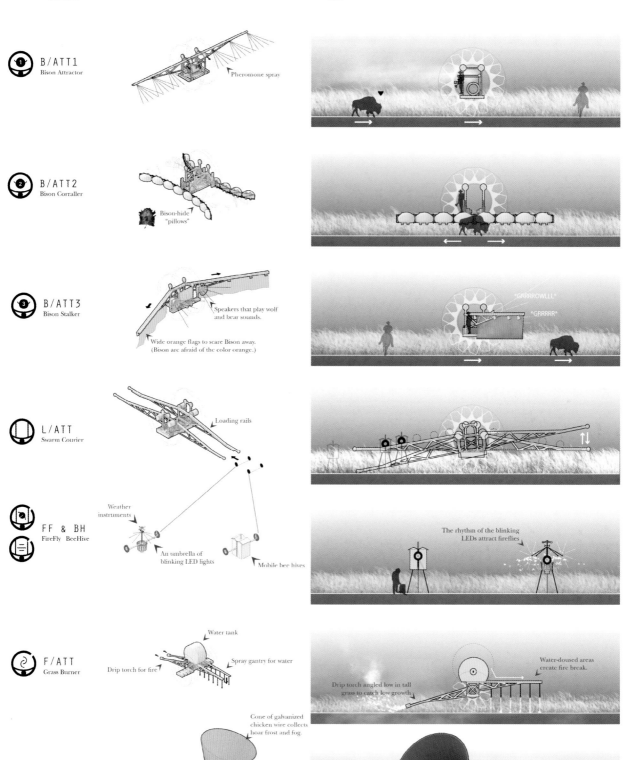

Each horizontal band of the Adaptive Tallgrass Transporter (ATT) sub-species chart describes both the anatomy of the implement kit (left) and their predominant behaviour (right).

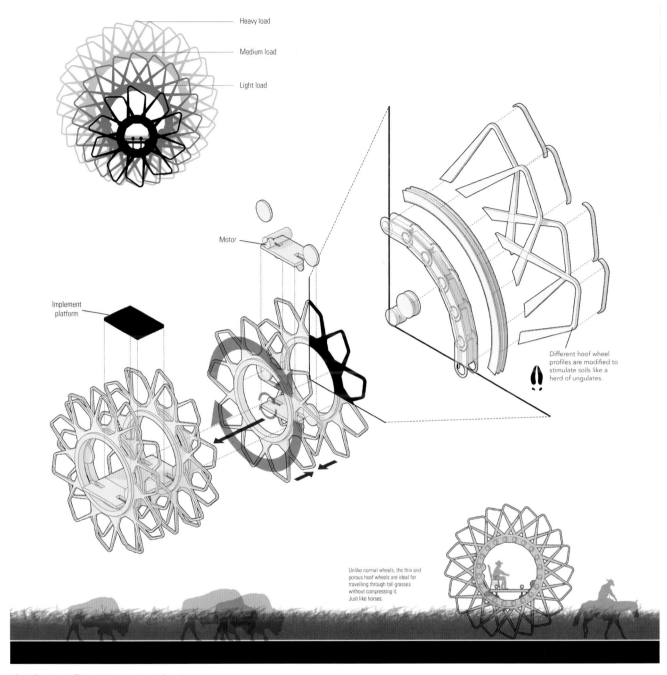

Heavy load

Medium load

Light load

Motor

Implement
platform

Different hoof wheel
profiles are modified to
stimulate soils like a
herd of ungulates.

Unlike normal wheels, the thin and
porous hoof wheels are ideal for
travelling through tall grasses
without compressing it.
Just like horses.

The Adaptive Tallgrass Transporter is the primary
means of mobilizing a family of robotic fieldwork
implements.

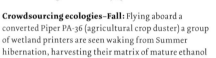

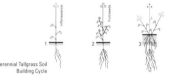

Perennial Tallgrass Soil
Building Cycle

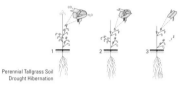

Perennial Tallgrass Soil
Drought Hibernation

Crowdsourcing ecologies–Fall: Flying aboard a converted Piper PA-36 (agricultural crop duster) a group of wetland printers are seen waking from Summer hibernation, harvesting their matrix of mature ethanol rich crop. Bison are herded between a network of these rehabilitated prairie potholes on their reverse migration route.

Domesticated Cattle "Lounging" Behaviour

Bison Grazing Behaviour

Crowdsourcing ecologies–Spring. From on board a B/ATT, a herd of bison are seen resting by a "printed" wetland, letting calves drink as they migrate from their winter fields to more nutrient-dense spring grass.

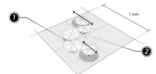

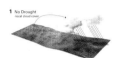

Moisture-to-Grass Relationship

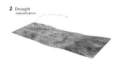

Migrating microclimates: A cluster of buoyant rotor-kites have been deployed with a network of solar collecting canvas to shield the drought-stricken grassland below. F/ATT's scurry through the grasses replenishing water to the dry ground while locals from a nearby town take advantage of the shade.

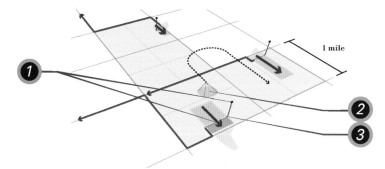

1 mile

DRY

Pothole/Playa Ephemeral Ecologie

The majority of prairie potholes and playas (an extensive system of small wetlands across the Great Plains) have been converted to flat crop-land since the 1920's. Their disappearance has also disabled their ecosystem services of ground water recharge and migratory bird stop-overs. The wetland printers reclaim these dormant wetlands but augment their productivity with tactical seed printing.

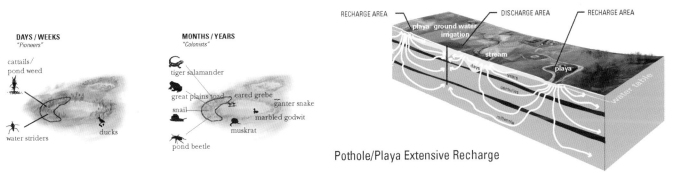

DAYS / WEEKS
"Pioneers"

cattails/
pond weed

water striders

ducks

MONTHS / YEARS
"Colonists"

tiger salamander

great plains toad   eared grebe

snail   ganter snake

marbled godwit

muskrat

pond beetle

RECHARGE AREA   DISCHARGE AREA   RECHARGE AREA

playa ground water
       irrigation

stream

days

years   playa

centuries

millennia   water table

Pothole/Playa Extensive Recharge

SINGING LANDSCAPES

Mazin Orfali

Archive of the Air: Users tuning in on the 25th
October 2015 17:01. A defined invisible architecture
of a single moment.

Flawed Aboriginal archiving system: detaching the user from the context of site.

*"To wound the earth," he answered earnestly, "is to wound your-
self, and if others wound the earth, they are wounding you. The
land should be left untouched: as it was in the Dreamtime when
the Ancestors sang the world into existence."* [1]

In 48,000 BC[2], the first groups of Aborigines landed in
Bandaiyan[3], having migrated from the African continent after
approximately 20,000 years of habitation en route. In 1788
AD, the first fleet of ships landed in Botany Bay, Australia.
This was to be the initial colonisation of Great Britain, relocating convicts to establish the new settlement before the French
or Spanish had a chance. The land however, had already
been established as the spiritual landscape of the Australian
Aboriginal, the custodians of the oldest living culture on earth.

However the Aboriginal emergence within the Australian
landscape led to their severe maltreatment by the colonists.
Aboriginals were used as guides, locating water holes in the
outback, and were displaced from their lands to be relocated
to alien landscapes. The most fundamental issue that still
underlies the Aboriginal community today is the displacement
of tribes from their defined territories, resulting in the near
extinction of their culture and history. The main culprits were
the Woomera test launches and drought.

In 1946, British colonists had set up their missile base
in Woomera; an area the Australian Government claimed
was a testing corridor, considered large enough for tests, yet
containing minimal population. The test spaces also included
a satellite range towards eighty miles of beach in Western
Australia. This Australian-Anglo project would test missiles in

an area which covered approximately 270,000 square kilometres at its peak.[4] However, this region was the home of the
entire indigenous population. The bombardment on the landscape was permanently destroying segments of their home
with no remorse. Whilst it would be easy to point the finger
directly at the military, J. B. Jackson, in "The Landscape as
Seen by the Military" describes how the military understand
landscape:

We did not speculate about the environment and its psychological impact nor about the relationship between the environment
and man…. We came to think of the environment as a kind of
setting or empty stage upon which certain alarming and unpredictable decisions and actions took place… the stage continues
to be vacant and uninteresting except when some military action
was taking place.[5]

Little did the military know, a vast piece of landscape
in the satellite region was home to the Martu Aborigines
whose history dated back over 20,000 years. Because the
Aboriginal culture is defined by its oral traditions, the knowledge that had been built up over the thousands of years in
this landscape, was and still is on the verge of extinction; as
they had been displaced from their homeland into neighbouring cattle ranches and mission settlements located in
other tribal lands.

The Aboriginal people of Australia believe in the Dreamtime, 'a metaphysical now, a mystical time outside of time,
a spiritual yet nonetheless real dimension of time and space

1. Chatwin, Bruce, *The Songlines* (London: Picador,
1988), 11.
2. This is an approximation. Some experts even predict
the year to go back as far as 125,000 BC.
3. The Australian Aboriginal word for 'Australia'.
4. http://www.defence.gov.au/news/raafnews/
editions/4702/features/feature02.htm
5. Jackson, John Brinckerhoff, *Discovering the Vernacular
Landscape* (New Haven: Yale University Press, 1986), 133.

The recording process is done digitally as its the most safe and secure method for archiving the oral information. The Archive of the Air is emitted in the shortwave radio frequency which has the capacity to travel 1000km during the day and further at night as the ionosphere cools and increases in height from the earths crust. The Archive of the Earth is emitted using Infraplants embedded in the landscape.

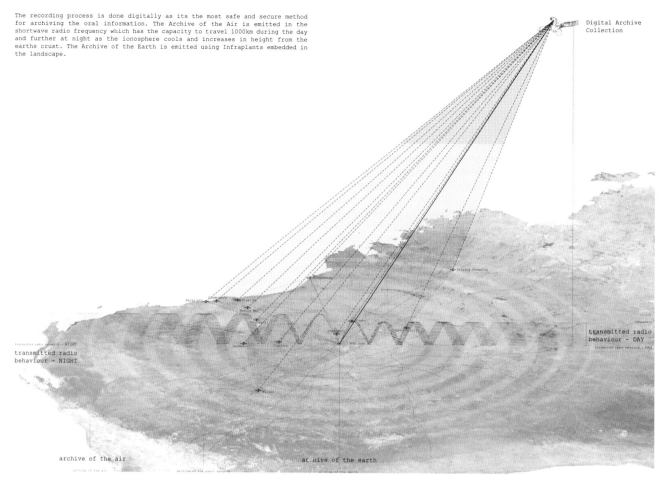

Digital Archive Collection

transmitted radio behaviour – DAY

transmitted radio behaviour – NIGHT

archive of the air   archive of the earth

Archive of the Air (AOA) & Archive of the Earth (AOE):
invisible architecture inhabiting the Australian outback.

somehow interpenetrating and concurrent with our own.'[6] The Dreaming was not formed recently, but as far back as the time when the Aborigine migrated from the African continent tens or even hundreds of thousands of years ago. The *Dreamtime* defines the sacred era where their ancestral Totemic Spirit Creatures formed their Creation of Australia. Depending on their territory within the landscape, an Aborigine could say he is a Kangaroo Dreaming, Honey Ant Dreaming, etc…, and could combine the Dreaming's together. The Dreaming establishes their rules of behaviours, the manner in which ceremonies are performed to ensure the livelihood of life and land, the overall structures of society and the intricate knowledge of the earth they resided on.

Singing Landscapes

Set within the dry and almost uninhabited territory of the Australian outback is an invisible landscape embedded with the *Songlines* and the *Dreaming* of the Aborigines. For many years, the Aboriginal people of Australia have been detached from their traditional homelands, running the risk that their 50,000 year-old oral culture would be diluted and essentially lost forever. Existing archival systems put in place to record and illustrate this oral culture are inefficient, as the information

is detached from the context of the landscape, which is so central to aboriginal knowledge.

Singing Landscapes analyzes radio and acoustic spectrums as possible sites of architectural intervention, in order to understand how these can redefine the way one can experience space. The Australian outback offers an ideal site to test and implement these two devices, in order to reveal the unique invisible landscapes of Aboriginal culture. Rather than being detached from its home turf, the instruments allow individuals to access their history, as well as crucial knowledge.

Singing Landscapes is comprised of instruments and buildings for recording and storing knowledge embedded in the air and in the earth. The *Archive of the Air* is transmitted through the obsolete shortwave radio spectrum, and the *Archive of the Earth* is embedded within the ground through the use of infrasound from the acoustic spectrum. The architecture serves to reveal these two invisible landscapes where one can experience space and knowledge simultaneously. The role of the physical instruments is to emit and tune into the information, allowing the user to experience this vast body of collective knowledge within the landscape rather than through the medium of a computer screen connected to the internet.

6. Harvey Arden, *Dreamkeepers – A Spirit-Journey into Aboriginal Australia* (New York: HarperCollins, 1994), 5.

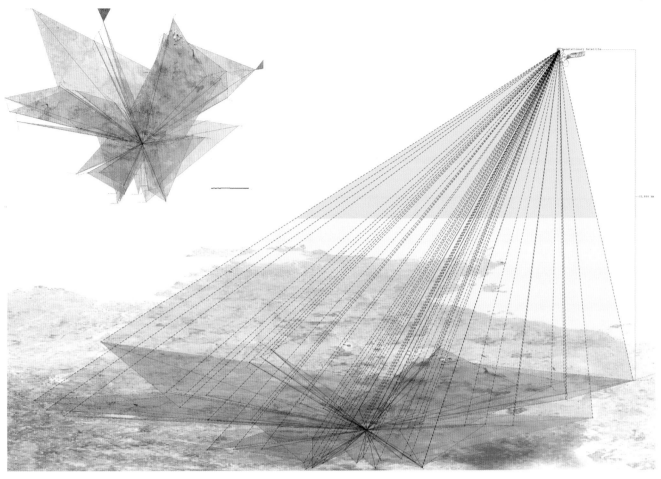

Invisible architecture: School of the Air,
Australian outback.

The *Archive of the Earth* is meant to be evolving, dynamic, and embedded within the landscape. It has the possibility of becoming a feedback loop; writing and rewriting valuable knowledge of place, and tunable using two scales. The *Infrasonic Aide* device is used for the personal experience of walking through the landscape and the *Acoustic Pavilions* offer a place where several members can listen collectively.

Archive of the Air provides a tuneable archive accessible to all, regardless of location. Stories can be listened to, food and medicines are uncovered with the information on aboriginal bush craft and traditional storytelling; some of the essential ingredients for surviving one of the world's most unforgiving landscapes.

The Archive is no longer a room with virtual information fed to the listener through the computer screen, instead, it is returned to the site from which it was dreamt.

> White man, when he came in here, he didn't understand about those lines. He didn't see the pattern they made. He trampled right over'm. He still doesn't understand. He bulldozes the land for his mines and cuts through it to build his roads. That digs all that pattern out. Destroys it. You can't recognise it anymore.

> That land only exists now in our stories and in our songs and in our ceremonies. When the land dies, we die.[7]
> —An Aborigine explaining the situation to Harvey Arden

Born in London and a product of the urban social conditions which the city had to offer, **Mazin Orfali** began his architectural adventure at the University of Brighton before migrating to the AA School of Architecture where he had a personal interest in extreme regional and intangible architectures. He has worked for UN Studio in Amsterdam, Benoy in London and cunently resides at Michaelis Boyd Associates.

7. Harvey Arden, *Dreamkeepers – A Spirit-Journey into Aboriginal Australia* (New York: HarperCollins, 1994) 201.

Archive of the Earth: Directional listening pavilion.

Archive of the Earth: Omnidirectional listening pavilion.

Infrasonic Aide artefact: A single user tuning into the Archive of the Earth and listening through bone conduction.

AVANT-GARDE REAL ESTATE:ARTIFICIAL LAND IN JAPAN, 1954–2000

Casey Mack

Fort-l'Empereur, Algiers. Le Corbusier, 1932:
Artificial land's debut as infrastructural platforms on
which "every architect will build his villa as he likes."

> *...unhappily as in a thousand student projects (from the time of Le Corbusier's Algiers project onwards),*
> *the romance of the idea of 'each man building his own house' on man-made platforms stands unsupported*
> *by a demonstration of how it is to be done.*
> *— Peter Smithson, "Reflections on Kenzo Tange's Tokyo Bay Plan," 1964[1]*

Perhaps the most famous concept the fewest have ever heard of, Le Corbusier's "artificial land" uniquely combines simplicity of idea with complexity of realization. This essay investigates how four Japanese projects translate this fantasy housing typology into actual housing. While each project engages the same basic concept, its interpretations within extremely different economic situations are highly diverse, indicative of the idea's fundamental flexibility. And though the typology fascinated Japan's Metabolist architects in the sixties, fulfilling their desire to bring "a time factor into city planning," it has actually had a much longer hold on the country's architectural imagination.[2] The prototypes presented here show that through the poverty of the fifties, the "income-doubling" period of

---

1. Peter Smithson, "Reflections on Kenzo Tange's Tokyo Bay Plan," *Architectural Design* 34 (1964): 480.

2. Noboru Kawazoe, "The City of the Future," *Zodiac* 9 (1961): 100.

the metabolic sixties, the global oil crisis of the early seventies, and the "Lost Decade" of the nineties, artificial land has repeatedly promised economic and environmental resilience in Japan. By illuminating an imported concept's translation through construction, the projects offer for export their own ideas on infrastructure, adaptability, and ownership. As Peter Smithson suggests, the typology is an ongoing romance with an allure far beyond Japan's border.

This is Not a Megastructure

Artificial land can be defined as a theoretically permanent platform or framework supporting an indeterminate infill of housing—a description essentially identical to the definition of the later term *megastructure*. First introduced in 1964 by the Metabolists Fumihiko Maki and Masato Otaka in their essay "Collective Form—Three Paradigms," this term went on to inspire Reyner Banham's book *Megastructure: Urban Futures of the Recent Past*, from 1976. Through these two influential texts, the term artificial land was effectively buried.

Maki and Otaka's term seems like a strategic re-branding. Signaling an anxiety over Le Corbusier's coining, megastructure definitely sounds better, like exciting science fiction. In comparison, artificial land sounds as bland as "processed cheese." Paradoxically, Banham's book calls Le Corbusier's 1932 Fort-l'Empereur project in Algiers the "most general ancestor" of the "megastructure international," although this is exactly the project where *terrain artificial* first appears in name.[3]

But a fundamental difference between the terms needs to be recovered: the French *terrain* and the English "land" both thematize a context of property transaction and a construction site. Later, the translation of *terrain artificiel* retains these associations in Japanese as *jinko tochi*—literally "manmade land."[4] Megastructure, however, has no such specificity. Artificial land is avant-garde real estate.

Stimulus Package

Unlike the starchitect condos that might be considered avant-garde real estate today, the typology is conceptualized more as a process than a form. Its invention may have been provoked by the extensive alterations residents made to Le Corbusier's 1926 housing at Pessac, which lead him to remark "it is always life that is right and the architect who is wrong."[5] Artificial land suggests a solution to this conundrum. Describing the Fort-l'Empereur proposal, the centerpiece of his Algerian planning, Le Corbusier writes:

> Here are 'artificial sites,' vertical garden cities. Everything has been gathered here: space, sun, view; means of immediate communication, both vertical and horizontal; water, gas, etc. thriftily supplied; ideally simple sanitation—sewers, garbage pails, etc. The architectural aspect is stunning! The most absolute diversity, within unity. Every architect will build his villa as he likes; what does it matter to the whole if a Moorish-style villa flanks another in Louis XVIth or in Italian Renaissance?[6]

Extreme serviceability led to ideal plots with "no faulty section," vitally important for a scheme imagined as a massive economic stimulus for the city. Modernization of municipal transportation, through construction of a new highway running in part through Fort-l'Empereur's middle, would be financed by the sale of these plots constructed by the French colonial government. Buyable in any size and able to accommodate a two-story home, the plots would be built out by their new owners. In an incredible hybrid of top-down and bottom-up planning, the scheme would put "billions" of francs into the city's coffers through a minimal initial investment. Expanding the diagram of the Domino House, the design transforms the free plan's separation of components enabling a compositional freedom in space to also provide a financial opportunity in time.

In two diagrams, Le Corbusier juxtaposes his proposal with what he considers the undesirable aspect of a garden city, where free-standing homes require horizontally dispersed infrastructure that he argues lead to increased municipal costs. This argument makes Fort-l'Empereur legible as a daring compensation for the garden city's attraction, now converted into a wish image reconciling the individual home's identity with the efficiencies of vertical density. As Mary McLeod has pointed out,

3. Reyner Banham, *Megastructure: Urban Futures of the Recent Past* (New York: Harper and Row, 1976), 7.
4. *La Ville Radieuse* (1933), where *terrain artificial* seems to first appear in print, was first translated into Japanese in 1956 by Junzo Sakakura, who worked with Le Corbusier from 1930 until 1937.

5. Quoted in Philippe Boudon, *Lived-in Architecture: Le Corbusier's Pessac Revisited*, 1969. (Cambridge: The MIT Press, 1979), 1.
6. Le Corbusier, *The Radiant City*, 1933. (New York: The Orion Press, 1967), 247. While the English translation of the book uses "sites" instead of "land," the phrase

"artificial land" is the term most frequently used in English-language Japanese publications such as *Japan Architect*.

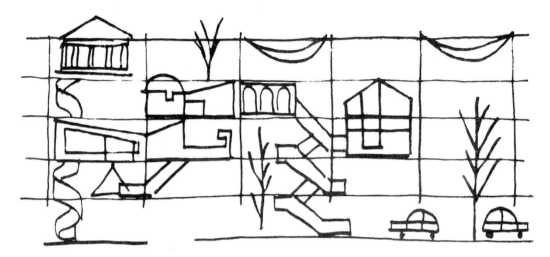

Ville Spatiale: Yona Friedman, c. 1957

Untitled #6: Filip Dujardin, 2010. Ongoing Romance Exhibit B

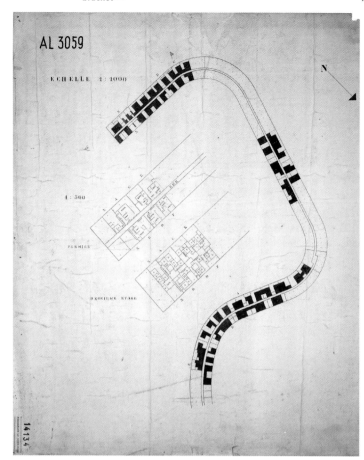

Fort l'Empereur: Plan of plots with "no faulty section"

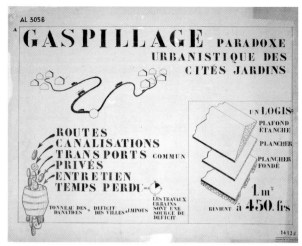

Problem: The inefficiencies created by the horizontality of fashionable garden city planning

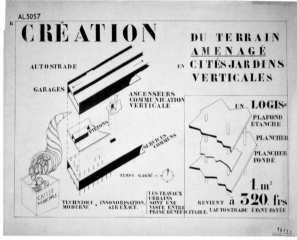

Solution: Fort l'Empereur as a "vertical garden city" reconciling identity with density

the urban plan of which Fort-l'Empereur is a part took the controversial position of combining Muslim and French areas of the city in ways that undermined the clarity of the colonial government's quarters.[7] Far from a postmodern joke, Fort-l'Empereur's similar strategy of combining identities—of vernacular and colonial styles of houses—works on the level of architecture. Had the plan been built, the city's growth into a culturally integrated and economically progressive future would be supported by this residential infrastructure.[8]

Tokyo Embryo

After two years in Le Corbusier's studio, Takamasa Yoshizaka returned to Japan in 1952 with the desire to make artificial land the answer to the country's housing crisis. In 1950, the housing shortage caused by the war was 3.4 million units.[9] The country was largely bankrupt, scarce land was made even scarcer by new property laws of the Allied Occupation, and of course the nation still faced its immortal threat of earthquakes. Japan's *real* land was in dire need of an *improved* land.

In 1954, Yoshizaka wrote "Artificial Public Land as a Solution to the Housing Shortage." Appearing in the influential journal *Kokusai Kenchiku*, the article reprised the description of Fort-l'Empereur, proposing that:

7. Mary McLeod, "Le Corbusier and Algiers," *Oppositions Reader: Selected Readings from a Journal for Ideas and Criticism in Architecture, 1973-1984* (New York: Princeton Architectural Press, 1998), 499.

8. While artificial land may be most associated with Fort-l'Empereur, it is clear from *The Radiant City* that the viaduct part of the 1932 master plan was artificial land as well. Another massive ribbon, Le Corbusier mentions

that the viaduct's provision of housing can happen "little by little" within its existing structure. See page 246.

9. The Building Center of Japan. *A Quick Look at Housing in Japan*. Tokyo: May 2014. PDF e-book. 26.

for public parking and shopping by lifting the fractured city from the ground onto a platform above, slipping the new below the old.

The platform is actually a group of platforms, assembled in four phases between 1966 and 1985. This extended phasing was a direct result of the Sakaide Housing Corporation's difficulty in buying lots from the existing property owners. Indeed, the project is not a transfer of ownership from ground to platform as originally envisioned, as all of the old housing replaced on top of Otaka's infrastructure is owned and operated by the city. The housing is also of course hardly the fulfillment of people building "their own homes as they want." However, what the platform does test is the engineering of this potential, one among various scenarios pushing the capacity of the free plan.

In the words of project engineer Yasuke Hachinohe, the design's hope was to "meet the various changes inherent in a dynamically growing city."[16] A 1968 memo by Hachinohe can be read as a manifesto for this structural future-proofing:

1. Maximum freedom in placement [of housing on the platform] to create variety and richness in apartment exterior spaces
2. Allowances must be made for the possibility of adding four-story apartment buildings in areas left vacant in the present plan
3. Provide for the possibility of dismantling the present buildings (if the foundation beams of the buildings on the platform and platform's own beams are one, dismantling becomes impossible)
4. Provide for the possibility of future extensions raising the heights of all the apartment buildings to four stories
5. To increase the freedom of use on the ground level by reducing the number of columns to a minimum[17]

Sakaide's moveable components are no longer merely walls as in typical free plan modernism, but in an extreme change of scale, entire four-story buildings. A grid of holes passing through the concrete beams on the underside of the platform furthers this flexibility by accommodating re-routing of pipes and wires. Unlike today's parametric obsession with shaving off any excess material to optimize between known conditions, the platform's major structural redundancies anticipate events that only *might* happen, investing in indeterminacy as civic durability.

Mega-appropriation

Artificial land was a major meme in Japan through the sixties into the seventies. As with many popular ideas, its meaning was often misinterpreted or willfully co-opted. The Metabolist Kisho Kurokawa, for example, would call the cores of his 1972 Nakagin Capsule Tower an "artificial-land base," using the now forgotten buzzword for a project whose standardization is far away from a bottom-up building site.[18] On a much vaster scale, *jinko tochi* is also the official description for Ashiyahama Seaside Town, completed in Osaka in 1979.[19]

Sponsored in part by the national Ministry of Construction, the 1973 competition for the project just preceded OPEC's embargo later that year, with the recession that followed often seen as Metabolism's death knell.[20] Won by the giant design-build company Takenaka Komuten, its proposal may have survived due to its artificial land approach of strictly separating infrastructure and infill. Takenaka pushed the concept to the extreme as a time- and cost-efficient strategy addressing the competition brief's request for detailed estimates.

Dramatically inflating the double-height bays of Fort-l'Empereur, each bay of Ashiyahama's steel frame holds four stories of concrete apartments, the system used for most of the development's 3,400 units. For Takenaka, the frame's attraction was speed rather than choice. The system allowed a fast-track process where the independence of frame from units meant both could be constructed simultaneously, with the units prefabricated in an on-site factory. The open truss work of beams and columns contains all of the project's circulation, and this ant farm crossed with an urban street grid is in fact what the designer's call "artificial land." Now synonymous with megastructure, artificial land is recast as sky gardens linking the rigidly defined apartments and forming perhaps the most ambitious skip-floor access ever built, with elevators stopping only every fifth level. The same year as Ashiyahama's competition, Yoshizaka added a library and an attic to his tiny incremental experiment.

16. Yasuke Hachinohe, "Memo on the Structure of the Artificial Land Project," *Japan Architect* (August 1968): 31.
17. *Japan Architect*: 31.
18. Kisho Kurakawa, "Challenge to the Capsule," *Japan Architect* (October 1972): 25.
19. See Michael Franklin Ross, *Beyond Metabolism: The New Japanese Architecture* (New York: McGraw-Hill Book Company, 1978), 41.
20. Regarding the oil crisis and its repercussions, see Zhongjie Lin, *Kenzo Tange and the Metabolist Movement: Urban Utopias of Modern Japan* (New York: Routledge, 2010), 227-228.

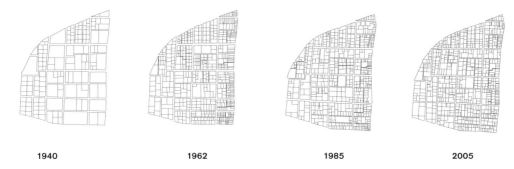

1940   1962   1985   2005

Plot sizes in Setagaya, Tokyo: Increasing subdivision of land constricting urban renewal (based on Zenrin Housing Map)

Ashiyahama Seaside Town: Takenaka Komuten, 1979. Photo in 2010

Ashiyahama Seaside Town: Takenaka Komuten, 1979. Photo in 2010

While Ashiyahama brought quantity, it lost artificial land's original bottom up possibilities. Slack had left the system.

Collective Concrete

Banham writes that by the end of the sixties, the concept of megastructure was "deserted by the avant-garde" and "left to the despised Establishment as a conventional method for maximizing the returns from urban development."[21] Ashiyahama is a prime example of this. All that was morally permissible for Banham's activist architect instead was the "spontaneous housing" built by the people, self-ejected from the state infrastructure previously seen to support it. But other possibilities exist: at the Tsunane co-op housing in Nara, residents *own* the infrastructure.

Unlike megastructure, artificial land has no necessary connection to being big, just as megastructure has no necessary connection to a negotiation and expression of property. Composed of two rectangular bars ranging from one to three stories high around a central yard, and housing twenty-three families, Tsunane is quite small. Completed in 2000, the project was initiated in 1995—the middle of the "Lost Decade" following the bursting of Japan's eighties bubble. A completely intentional community, it slowly formed from an original core of three families dissatisfied with Nara's public housing. Calculating that twenty-three families would be necessary to make the scheme financially viable, this initial group hired VANS Architects in 1996 as the main designer and referee both between and on behalf of the future residents.

With a rationale the polar opposite of Ashiyahama's, Tsunane uses an artificial land strategy to fully engage the residents' participation. Effectively one project divided into over twenty-three distinct parts, the façade-less free plan let the architect adjust to each family's budget and desires. This is helped by a migration from typical office design: Tsunane's slabs have a raised floor system for piping, allowing bathrooms and kitchens to be located at will, breaking the plans loose from the stacking of wet

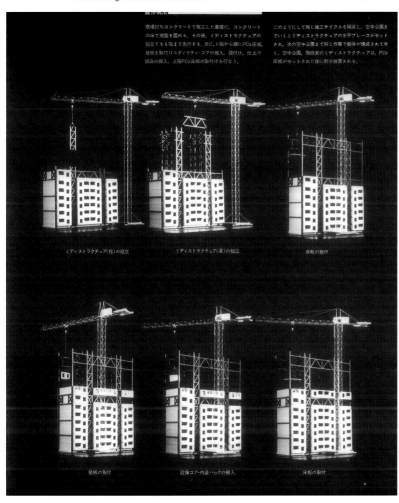

現場打ちコンクリートで施工した基礎に、コンクリート
の床で地盤を固める。その後、ミディストラクチュアの
組立てを6階まで先行する。次に、1階から順にPCa床板、
壁板も取付けユティリティ・コアの搬入、据付け、仕上げ
部品の搬入、上階PCa床板の取付けを行なう。

このようにして同じ施工サイクルを繰返し、空中公園ま
でいくとミディストラクチュアの水平ブレースがセット
され、次の空中公園まで同じ作業で躯体が構成されてゆ
く。空中公園、階段室のミディストラクチュアは、PCa
床板がセットされた後に耐火被覆される。

ミディストラクチュア(柱)の組立　　　ミディストラクチュア(梁)の組立　　　床板の取付

壁板の取付　　　設備コア・内装パックの搬入　　　床板の取付

Ashiyahama Seaside Town: construction diagram, c. 1973

services common to most of the world's apartment buildings. In a further loosening, the boundary of each unit's non-structural envelope is variable as well, with residents able to select external materials from a palette of sixteen options chosen by the architect. After a floor plan workshop in 1998, residents produced homemade models of their units that became the basis for the final designs.

As a co-op, the residents of Tsunane jointly own green space, parking, a multi-purpose room, energy systems, and the slabs of plots. Individual ownership includes both the interior and the envelope of each unit, allowing them to completely transform independently. That is, so long as residents follow the rules. VANS' principal, Tosiaki Ban, notes that "rules and guidelines that surpass those of the government or society is [sic] a definite requirement of Co-op Housing, which is a small commune, or a direct, democratically run project without any hierarchy."[22] This investment in process and determination of controls was significant—in time, money, and patience. But according to the residents, it was well worth it.[23]

Tsunane is both a fulfillment and a reversal of Le Corbusier's huge state-sponsored prototype. If Tsunane is seen as a replicable model, it suggests that large-scale social infrastructure can be an incremental infrastructure, assembled from small initiatives. Yoshizaka's house may be closer to the mark than he thought. Perhaps the reduced scale of an intentional community is best suited to commit to the economics and ethics—and the romance—of artificial land's fullest expression.

Futurist Vernacular

In the early nineties, Rem Koolhaas remarked that in postmodern Japan "incredible buildings are built about nothing, without any program, without any social ambition."[24] With a twist, this interpretation

21. *Megastructure*, 10.
22. Ban, Tosiaki. E-mail to the author. 17 July 2011.
23. Based on the author's interview of Tsunane residents on September 19, 2011.
24. Quoted in Hajime Yatsuka, "The Rise and Fall of Architects' Ambitions in a Modernizing Society" (paper presented at the Kenzo Tange Workshop, Harvard Graduate School of Design, Cambridge, Massachusetts, October 17, 2010).

Tsunane co-op housing: VANS Architects, 2000. Photo in 2011

can be inverted: that for housing, the absence of any *fixed* program *equals* social ambition. Indeed, in a sublimation of the artificial land concept, in 2008 the Japanese Parliament passed a new housing law giving tax incentives for creating and living in housing designed to last for 200 years, a lifespan meant to conserve resources through flexible designs able to adapt to new lifestyles.[25] This ambition to respond to changing demographics and their housing needs connects directly to recent developments outside Japan, such as the Making Room and adAPT initiatives that question the current regulations for apartment types in New York City.[26] Despite artificial land's flexibility, its emphasis on the external expression of a household might be unreasonable, even undesirable, if applied to emerging initiatives. In 1954, Yoshizaka was soon criticized for proposing a city like the "door-less clothing chests in the dressing rooms of bathhouses."[27] In a way, artificial land may seem too familiar, as merely a ubiquitous skeleton frame. But for problems of housing that do not seem to go away, describing a skeleton frame with this awkward term has provoked a host of explorations. May it continue to do so.

The author would like to thank Hajime Yatsuka for his guidance through the Metabolist nexus, as well as Riyo Namigata and Shohei Kawanaka of RAJP for their essential translation and image research.

Casey Mack is an architect and the director of Popular Architecture, a research and design office based in Brooklyn. This essay's content is from his book *Digesting Metabolism: Artificial Land in Japan, 1954-2202*, forthcoming from Princeton Architectural Press in 2016 with the support of the Graham Foundation for Advanced Studies in the Fine Arts and the New York State Council on the Arts.

25. For background on the so-called "200 year housing law," see Kazunobu Minami, "The New Japanese Housing Law to Promote the Longer Life of Housing and Example of Changes in the Layout of Public Housing over 40 years in Japan" (paper presented at the Changing Roles conference, Noordwijk aan Zee, The Netherlands, October 5-9, 2009).

26. See http://makingroomnyc.com/ and http://www.nyc.gov/html/hpd/html/developers/HPD-adAPT-NYC-RFP.shtml

27. Akira Ushimi, "Criticizing the Artificial Ground Theory of Yoshizaka," *Kokusai Kenchiku* (April 1954): 8.

UNPACKING EXTREME PERFORMANCE PERSPECTIVES

An Interview with Michael Hensel

Michael Hensel is an architect, researcher, writer and educator. His research interests and efforts include formulating the theoretical and methodological framework for Performance-oriented Architecture and developing a biological paradigm for design and sustainability of the built environment. Hensel is a professor for architecture at the Oslo School of Architecture and Design where he directs the Research Center for Architecture and Tectonics.

Maya Przybylski In preparing for this interview and seeking out fresh responses to your work, we found ourselves continuously coming back to the various definitions of extreme; we came to realize that your body of work addresses notions of extreme on a variety of fronts and in a variety of ways.

Given that one of Bracket's subtexts is the unpacking and expansion of the term's relationship to architecture, environment, and digital culture, we thought it could be interesting to carry out this unpacking of the term in relation to your work—as an architect, researcher and educator.

Extreme as in Approaching Limit-States / Highest in Degree

MP One meaning of extreme implies a state of "excessive in degree". In this sense, it is interesting to consider your work as it relates to complexity. In your writing on sustainability for the built environment you call on the reader to view the problem space through the lens of Fritjof Capra's notion of 'deep ecology'. Specifically, in advocating for the removal of the separation between humans and the natural environment, you foreground a systemic viewpoint emphasizing the super extreme-complex weave of interconnections and interdependencies that comprises our built environment.

With such an ecological approach, it seems possible that once we open the door to embrace this inclusion and the resultant, increasingly complex models; it may be difficult to know when to stop. What criteria do you use in evaluating the suitability of a model? How do you know when it's inclusive enough? How do you decide what is and is not included?

Michael Hensel Any reply to these questions will inevitably be coloured by different considerations and inclinations. One type of response may focus predominately on a methodological level based on a more narrow understanding of what constitutes a 'model'. Currently this approach tends to invariably yield formulaic responses that prescribe design methods in accordance with preferred outcomes that underpin the position of the respective protagonist. This reflex may benefit the individual, yet, more often than not also considerably obstruct genuine discourse.

Another take then may focus on a detailed analysis of the design problem at hand while at the same time incorporating it into a wide spectrum of interrelated aspects and processes that impact on architectural design and the built environment. Here the term 'model' is understood in a wider and more inclusive sense.

As an example it is interesting to examine the notion of sustainability. Today it has become an omnipresent and often rather superficially used buzzword, a box to be ticked in order to have a reasonable chance to acquire work or recognition. This is not at all to say that the notion of sustainability is useless but, instead, the prevailing approaches which are lacking in inclusiveness and complexity. Typically this limits questions of sustainability to energy calculations and material characteristics and processes.

We may simply need to try and do better both in terms of concepts of sustainability and increase in complexity in a step-by-step manner and with an inquisitive, critical and projective mindset. First of all it is important to get to an understanding what reductive approaches tend to lack and how to go about widening considerations in a manner that makes it possible to reach. If building up alternative concepts and more complex approaches are pursued, architecture and architectural inquiry are set to gain significantly.

A widened scope of inquiry might lead to a set of more relevant and involved questions than the ones that are generally asked. That alone is worth the effort even if the scope is not necessarily markedly more inclusive. Prof. Dr. Birger Sevaldson, my colleague in the OCEAN Design Research Association, has developed

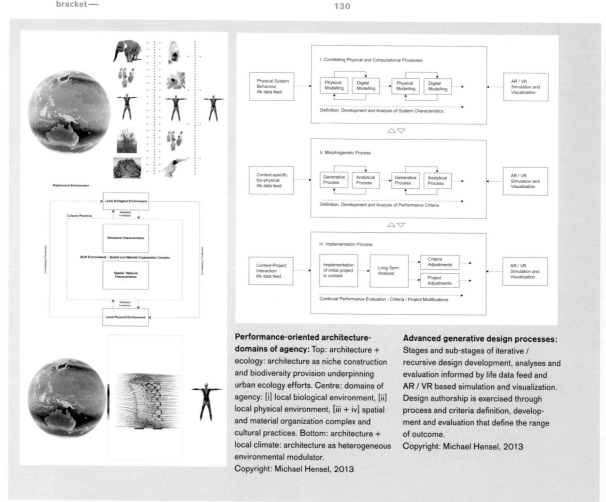

Performance-oriented architecture-domains of agency: Top: architecture + ecology: architecture as niche construction and biodiversity provision underpinning urban ecology efforts. Centre: domains of agency: [i] local biological environment, [ii] local physical environment, [iii + iv] spatial and material organization complex and cultural practices. Bottom: architecture + local climate: architecture as heterogeneous environmental modulator.
Copyright: Michael Hensel, 2013

Advanced generative design processes: Stages and sub-stages of iterative / recursive design development, analyses and evaluation informed by life data feed and AR / VR based simulation and visualization. Design authorship is exercised through process and criteria definition, development and evaluation that define the range of outcome.
Copyright: Michael Hensel, 2013

a technique for the purpose of an inclusive mapping of aspects and processes related to a given topic or design problem. This technique is called 'giga-mapping'. While it is an inclusive technique it also serves the purpose of reframing a design problem or inquiry in often quite unexpected ways. Criteria are thus established through a process rather than simply inherited from a given catalogue. We therefore do not simply use a fixed set of criteria. Instead we take the time to establish in a careful and extensive process and on a case-by-case basis what the relevant criteria might be.

The question of when a 'model', read 'approach', is inclusive enough cannot be answered in general terms. However, a model may be deemed sufficiently inclusive for a given period of time if it looks beyond established requirements and if at its base lays a critical approach and projective will. If and when this is the case, the question as to what is to be included or excluded will depend on the restated design aim and the capacity to process a more informed approach. This is not merely a question of data, but more so about vital traits, interrelations and interaction. We have termed this performance-oriented approach.

MP It is interesting to see your work as a continuum in which you seek to incrementally do better. This is a familiar approach shared and fostered within traditional research environments such as the sciences. It seems less commonplace, or at least harder to identify in research conducted within a design context. Can you share with us how you organize and strategize your own research activities so that they contribute towards incremental progress along a research trajectory?

MH Architects often view their discipline as straddling an uneasy position between the humanities and sciences. This entails a continuous struggle to define what architecture is about and what may constitute disciplinary specificity in architecture. While this struggle is unlikely to be solved any time soon it is nevertheless of useful to look across disciplinary boundaries in order to apprehend unexpected aspects that may be shared and that dissolve inherited preconceptions. The late Ernst Mayr, one of the foremost evolutionary biologists of the 20th century, pointed out the vital importance of concepts in the development of biology. This position, which also occurs in other sciences, may be unexpected to some. At any rate, in architecture too the importance of concepts cannot be overstated. Therefore quite some emphasis and effort needs to focus on the formulation and questioning of conceptual frameworks and approaches, whether past, prevailing or propositional.

Architecture and ecology: The Department of Architecture at Cornell University and the Research Centre for Architecture and Tectonics at the Oslo School of Architecture and Design collaborated on organizing two international symposia in 2012 and 2013 that focused on the relationship between architecture and ecology. The accelerating transformation of the natural environment by humans entails that the built environment is increasingly becoming the context for ecosystems. It is now no longer possible to consider the built environment as merely asserting negative impact on the natural environment; instead, built and natural environments need to be equally considered as habitats that are designed so as to provide for biodiversity. On an urban scale, such efforts have taken shape in the interdisciplinary field of urban ecology. Now architecture needs to respond to these efforts.

To my mind there is currently not enough effort invested into this, even though there are plenty of attempts to posit new paradigms in architecture. Yet, frequently these are barely masked and superficial attempts to justify claims for newness and thus legacy. A little more modesty and relevance on the side of these protagonists and a broader more serious effort would do our discipline well.

Regarding incremental development or improvement is a rather common trait across many human undertakings. What comes to mind, for instance, is the way in which things are 'advanced' in vernacular architecture. I have often wondered whether some of the iterative and recursive (computational) design processes that are pursued today can be understood in the way that they offer as it were a fast-forward simulation of the lengthy time based advances of the vernacular over many generations. Clearly a general statement would be too farfetched, but as a speculative thought it might be useful in suggesting trajectories of development for some of the approaches that operate on a defined search space within which design solutions are located that can be comparatively analysed.

In general what may be useful is a careful incremental probing of the output and consequences of alternative conceptual frameworks and approaches. Serious work of that kind will not be able to operate on the fashion clock, but instead require long term sustained efforts, similar to serious research efforts in other disciplines. An extensive analytical and reflective mindset is required for this.

MP Related to this approach is an awareness of change and dynamic factors present on a site of intervention. As part of OCEAN, specifically in the Synthetic Landscape project, you tackled the relationship between planned design interventions and contingencies that cannot be foreseen.

Can you elaborate on some of the strategies developed for confronting design problems as complex dynamic systems? How have these evolved since the Synthetic Landscape project from 2000? Does embracing this type of open-endedness contribute to our capacity to build sustainably? How so?

MH The big question is 'when is a project finished'? Some may say once construction is finished and the project is handed over to the client. Others may entertain different views. Complex projects such as airports or large hospital facilities require extensive project

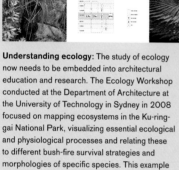

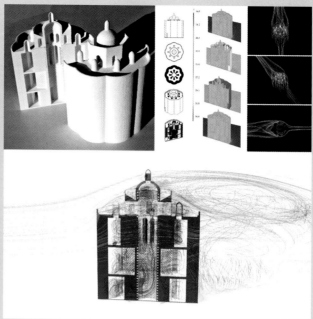

Understanding ecology: The study of ecology now needs to be embedded into architectural education and research. The Ecology Workshop conducted at the Department of Architecture at the University of Technology in Sydney in 2008 focused on mapping ecosystems in the Ku-ring-gai National Park, visualizing essential ecological and physiological processes and relating these to different bush-fire survival strategies and morphologies of specific species. This example focuses on an analysis of the habitat, physiology and morphology of the Australian grasstree [Xanthorrhoea].

Architectural history from a performance perspective: How does one design for other species? Detailed and linked Environmental Analyses of a Pigeon Tower from the Safavid period located in Isfahan, Iran. These buildings housed up to 10.000 pigeons and served the collection of the guano for the purpose of fertilizing fields. The knowledge that underlies the design of such architectures evolved in the vernacular tradition. With this the question arises how such results could be accomplished today and what this entails for the way knowledge is produced and design processes are configured. Copyright: Sustainable Environment Association, 2013

management. Vernacular environments may not find the question of completion relevant at all. In these contexts tectonics tend to underpin the possibility of change. In some contexts it is today a requirement to include material life-cycle considerations in the design. And for certain building types it is expected that some parts, such as the building envelope, will need to be changed at certain intervals during the lifespan of a building.

In general numerous aspects of context and circumstances of any given project change to some extent continually. The question is whether these changes are of relevance to a given project and in turn what kind of changes, if at all, these might necessitate in the design. This requires ongoing analyses and evaluation not only of the results, but also the criteria of analysis. Some aspects might be quantifiable and measurable, and others might not be so. Since the Synthetic Landscape project that focused on these questions we have worked mainly on developing theoretical and methodological frameworks for addressing these questions. These include the notion of 'performance-oriented architecture' and associated with this 'intensely local architecture', as well as 'systems-oriented design' with its associated methods and techniques such as

'giga-mapping', which often includes timelines and associated scenarios. This entire line of inquiry is one of the central problems of architecture, in particular in the context of the increasingly dense urban centers of today. New urban densifications models will require to quite some extend a time-based approach to be able to remain resilient. Clearly an intense amount of work will need to be invested in this field.

Extreme as in Border

MP Another meaning of extreme implies an approach toward a boundary or limit. In this sense, perhaps, we can think of your agenda as anti-extreme: Your work exploring the potentials of non-discrete architecture by way of expanded thresholds seems to ultimately strive for the elimination of borders between inside and outside in favour of a thickened, continuous zone of transition; the "elaboration of a new and deep middle-ground" versus the figure-ground.

Is this project ultimately advocating a seamless gradient, or is there something valuable or exciting to be preserved in creating and maintaining multiple boundaries that may interact or overlap but remain distinct?

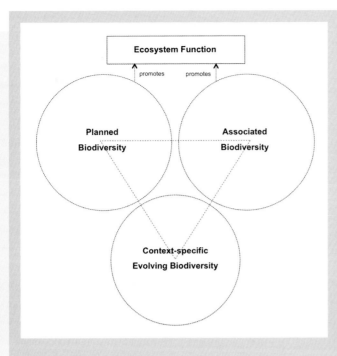

Learning from Agro-ecology: A key consideration of agro-ecology is the interrelation between designed, associated and freely evolving biodiversity. This entails what species farmers grow, which associated species emerge and how both fit into the context-specific biodiversity, thus maintaining ecosystem function. This field of study provides a promising inroad for defining the relation between architecture and ecology and a shift towards designing for biodiversity. Modified from Vandeermeer, J. and and Perfecto, I. (1995) 'Breakfast of biodiversity: the truth about rainforest destruction. Oakland: Food First Books. And: Altieri, M.A. (1994) 'Biodiversity and Pest Management'. In: Agroecosystems. New York: Haworth Press.

MH The central aim of non-discrete architecture is to offer an alternative to today's preoccupation with the (idiosyncratic) architectural object, which necessitates a sharp separation between a building and its surroundings. Discrete architecture, which places strong emphasis on the object, reinforces and is reinforced by entrenched dialectics that hardly ever get truly challenged, such as, for example, figure and ground, outside and inside, natural and man-made, etc. This leaves little room for a spatially enriched architecture that can provide for a much wider range of spatial, environmental and ecological aspects, as is usually the case.

However, non-discrete architecture is not based on a rejection of the material boundary and does not preclude enclosure and spatial partitioning. Instead it asks for a more versatile definition and use of boundaries. In some instances seamless spatial transitions may be of interest, but in the main multiple boundaries with different characteristics are very useful to articulate architectures that are more intensely embedded into their context. Multiple ground projects are not equivalent with and should not descend to become un-grounded 'Junkspace' of the sort that Rem Koolhaas criticised. There should remain a sense of groundedness, just as there always exist a sense of enclosedness in multiple envelope or boundary schemes. The boundaries that get challenged are the ones that underlie the aforementioned dialectics. These are notional boundaries that curtail the conception of different kinds of architectures that negotiate continuity with spatial heterogeneity. This indicates a quest for a more 'extreme' range of spatial organisations and transitions. In a forthcoming book entitled *Grounds and Envelopes — Reshaping*

Architecture and the Built Environment (Routledge, 2014) my colleague Jeffrey Turko and I pursue this argument at length and discuss various traits of non-discrete architectures that might help overcome todays spatially impoverished designs.

MP Some projects that you have cited as demonstrating eroded or permeable boundaries between interior and exterior are located in temperate climates. How does working in Norway, with its wide range of climate conditions, inform this ambition?

MH This question may be restated as follows: 'is the use of non-discrete architecture not limited to moderate climates'? Our argument is that distributed boundaries do not preclude effective climate envelopes, but instead add a greater variety of spaces with different exposure, whether climatic or in relation to public to private transitions. In Norway it is actually quite nice to sit outside during a sunny winter day for as long as one is not exposed to cold wind.

The question also touches on another interesting subject, which is that of local climate variation. Non-discrete architecture with its varied boundaries can deliver a real model for free running spaces as part of an overall architecture. Multiple boundaries with different characteristics can provide a variety of passively climatized spaces for different purposes while reducing the overall climate impact on the main climate envelope or the innermost spaces. The design approach can be adjusted to very specific local circumstances to not waste material and energy as a habit due to homogenous regulations for countries with greatly varying local climate conditions. Though, in order to do so we must relinquish the expectation that the entire available footprint (minus the thickness of the exterior wall) of a building should by fully climatized interior. For a good part of the year spaces with varying degrees of shelter are of tremendous use both in cold and hot climates.

MP It seems that one implication of a non-discrete architecture is the inclusion of things as part of architecture that architecture has traditionally tried to exclude. With such a reshaping of approaches, an expanded capacity of the design team is likely necessary. How can we build-in such capacity? How does the expertise of an architect get redefined, if at all, within such an interdisciplinary framework? As an educator, how do you support this redefinition?

MH Here again it is necessary to carefully avoid the reflex to deliver formulaic responses to such important questions. In particular since such questions may also reveal a certain unchecked bias. Can it be stated in the general that architecture has traditionally tried to exclude particular aspects? Or does this not apply to varied degrees to a much narrower section of often unreasonably dogmatic or self-absorbed idiosyncratic architecture?

Many of the great names associated with delivering illustrious descriptions of architecture over time have taken a relatively wide outlook and / or have frequently been polymaths.

From Vitruvius' (c. 80-70 BC–C. 15 BC) foundational *De Architectura* to the numerous undertakings of Nicolas-François Blondel (1618–1686) or Philippe de La Hire (1640–1718) architectural history before, during and after its formalization as a discipline is rich of such examples that seem often entirely contemporary in expertise range. Philippe de La Hire, for instance, wrote on structure, geometry, astronomy, hydrological systems, biology and mechanics (anticipating bio-inspired design).

In its formational period as a discipline architecture was in exchange with and informed by various other disciplines. Thus we may raise the question when have certain strands of architecture disconnected, why and to which consequences. At the same time we might lay open those strands of architecture that have not become detached, disinterested and solipsistic in inlook. Here we will find ample possibilities that can be taken forward and enriched.

The US-American architect, systems-thinker and writer Harold Nelson has pointed out a central capacity of architects that he termed 'adaptive expertise'. Foregrounding and nurturing this capacity is of vital importance for architects to play a key role in interdisciplinary undertakings. This requires first principle

knowledge in a variety of disciplines that are key to a given design problem. Needless to say, the aim is not to educate genius polymaths, yet, well and broadly educated architects that have the capacity to question, learn and reskill throughout their work life and in accordance with circumstance. To support this as an educator one needs to circumnavigate the negative consequences of education as a managed service industry on a day-to-day basis and interrelate education with research and interface it with practice. On a different level it is of increasingly critical importance to battle education as service industry, to resist the unquestioned processing of increasing numbers of students that will not find employment, lowering benchmarks to avoid liability issues, and to forcefully engage in formulating alternatives.

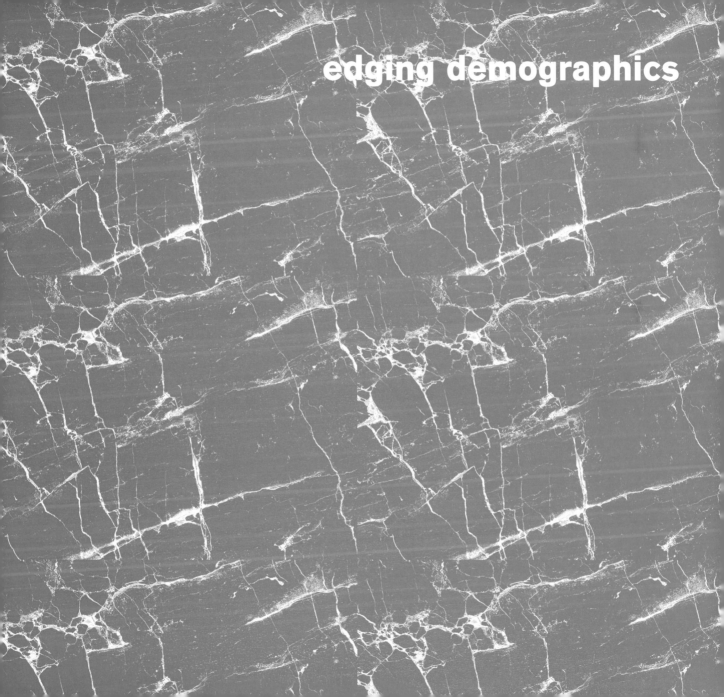

edging demographics

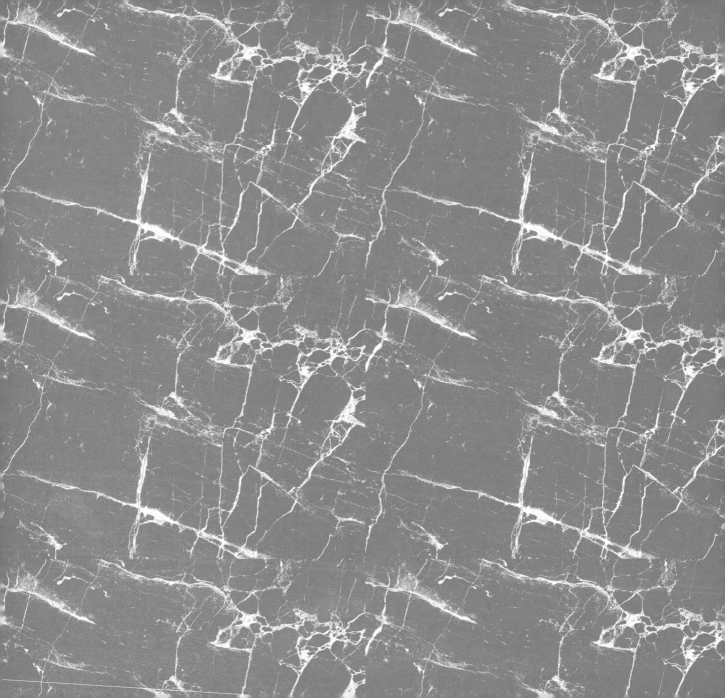

INFOSTRUCTURES

Ali Fard

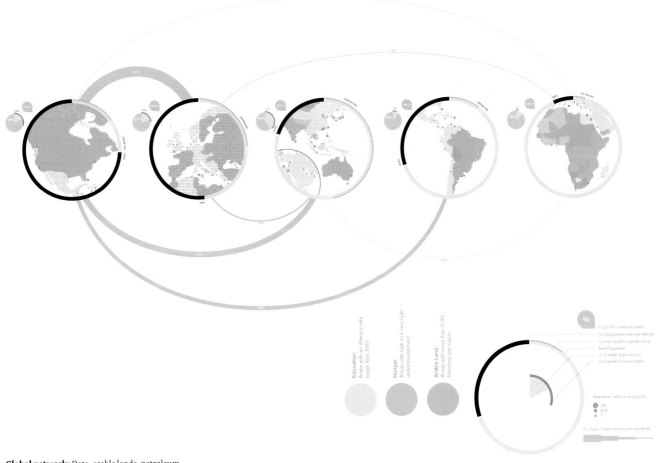

Global network: Data, arable lands, petroleum
production and consumption, hunger and education.

The rampant spread of Information and Communication Technologies (ICTs) has been a defining
factor of 20th and early 21st centuries. The Internet and its distribution network have become the
backbone for commerce, media, education, and research. The ubiquity of mobile devices, such as
mobile phones and laptops, has extended our connectivity to coffee shops, parks and other public
spaces. Yet, our fascination with the seemingly immaterial and virtual characteristics of information
technologies has prevented deeper research into the physical geography of information networks.
The prevalent reading of digital networks as the 'always-on, always-accessible network' tends to
ignore a set of power relations, which have resulted in a polarization of information distribution. The
submarine communication cables that connect continents to each other have largely followed the
telegraph lines of early 20th century, hence establishing poles of high and low information connectivity. These cables are the not-so-visible proof of our dependence on concentrated sources of information. These physical communication highways establish links between information super hubs, while
controlling the Internet's capacity to disseminate information.

As access to information becomes a common and increasingly necessary feature of cities
around the world, developing countries and emerging economies have begun to acknowledge ICTs
as important factors for development. This has given way to a rush towards securing 'info-resources'.
The recent landing of multiple submarine cables at Africa's coasts is testament to this push for connectivity. Africa's developing nations see ICTs as agents of growth. As far back as 1997, researchers
and analysts have maintained that African countries can leapfrog several stages in the use of ICTs by

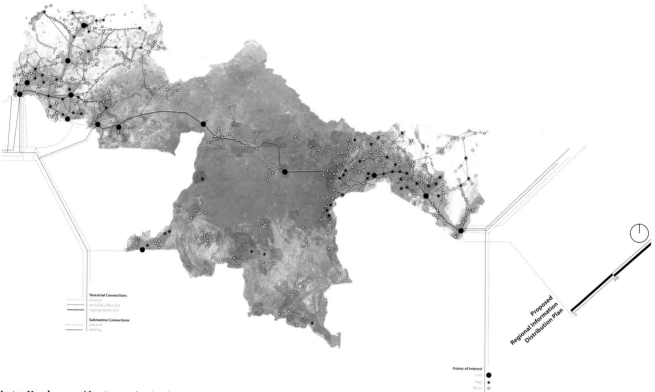

Lagos-Mombasa corridor: Proposed regional
information distribution network.

incorporating the latest technology available and learning from the experience of the more
advanced countries.[1]

The African Condition

There are two major trends in Africa's move towards ICTs: the proliferation of mobile use within
the continent by the general public and businesses alike, and the establishment of technology clusters
aimed at attracting the larger IT businesses. Although mobile communication and its proliferation
in Africa have been studied extensively, the influence of technology clusterization in African cities
remains relatively unexamined.

Technology Clusterization

As cities in the developing world vie for entry into the global information market, highly engineered
spaces of data efficiency are inserted into contexts which, until recently, were ignored, not only by
information networks but also other infrastructural developments. Due to the heavy dependence of
information technologies on more traditional infrastructures such as power, water and transportation,
the introduction of information infrastructure in developing countries is usually manifested through
establishment of IT parks. Clustering such uses into these parks, also known as Internet Villages
and Technology Campuses, enables the concentrated development of the necessary supporting
infrastructures.

  Typologically, the local effects of such parks are limited. Devised as hyper connected enclaves fitted
with walls, security fences, armed guards and defensive urban design, these 'info-bubbles' attempt to
bypass the barriers and constraints of local geography, by systematically ignoring the local condition,
while aligning themselves with global flows of information and economy. The current investments by
Kenya, Uganda, and Nigeria, among other African countries, towards developing IT clusters indicates
both the enormous potential for ICT growth in the region, as well as the lack of a future-oriented plan
for public engagement as part of a more widespread information economy. This clusterization will

1. Kwankam, Yunkap, and Ntomambang Ningo.
"Information Technology in Africa: A Proactive
Approach and the Prospects of Leapfrogging Decades in
the Development Process." *Internet Society (ISOC)* (1997).

Web. 17 Oct. 2011. <http://www.isoc.org/inet97/proceed-
ings/B7/B7_1.HTM>.

North America   **Africa**

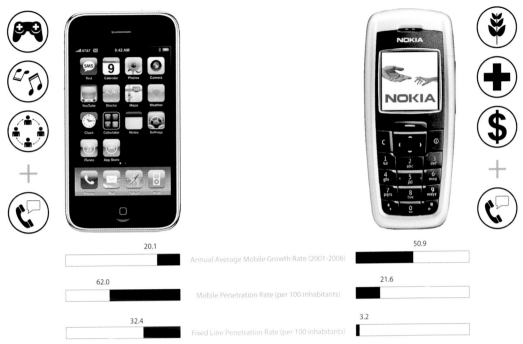

	20.1	Annual Average Mobile Growth Rate (2001-2006)	50.9	
	62.0	Mobile Penetration Rate (per 100 inhabitants)	21.6	
	32.4	Fixed Line Penetration Rate (per 100 inhabitants)	3.2	

Comparison: mobile telecommunication
culture in Africa and North America.

ultimately result in further polarization of access to information networks and will deepen the digital
divide already prevalent in most of these contexts.

Infostructures

Infostructures presents an alternative to the clustering of information technologies in IT parks by envi-
sioning a new breed of public spaces to address the formal and informal possibilities of the insertion of
high technology within the unique urban context of African cities. The stretch from Lagos, in Nigeria, to
Mombasa, in Kenya, is chosen for a regional investigation. This decision is based on three conditions:
first, the tremendous interest and investment of the region in entering the global information race;
second, the growing young English-speaking urban population; and third, the recent connections made
to the global information network by Nigeria and Kenya.

Inspired and influenced by existing digital network typologies that provide models for scalable network design, a regional distribution plan is established for the Lagos-Mombasa Corridor. Three major
types of information spaces (Cores, Hubs, and Nodes) are introduced, each dealing with a specific
type of activity, from data-heavy regional centers to rural access points. A matrix of building typologies
further breaks down the three major types into nine typologies (Cores: Market, Park, Arena; Hubs:
Digicenter, Digiport, Incubator; Nodes: Basic, Standard, Advanced). By incorporating specific sets
of inputs and outputs (digital consumption and production), each of these typologies-which range
in scale from wireless access poles in rural areas to large urban markets in city centers-use ICTs to
make digital information accessible to a wider segment of population. In addition to providing access
to information, these networked spatial constructs incorporate renewable energy production, environmental management systems (such as rain-water collection), educational digital workshops, and
workspaces for e-commerce. In turn, a new spatial economy emerges which is as much a product of
the local condition as it is the product of the technology.

Nairobi Digital Library (NDL)

Proposed within the larger *Infostructures* project, the Nairobi Digital Library (NDL) serves as a
case study to further investigate the application of these new types within a local context. Imagined
as the main branch of a regional digital library system, NDL's strategic location on the main fiber
line, and its proximity to the University of Nairobi, the National Theatre, the National Museum, and

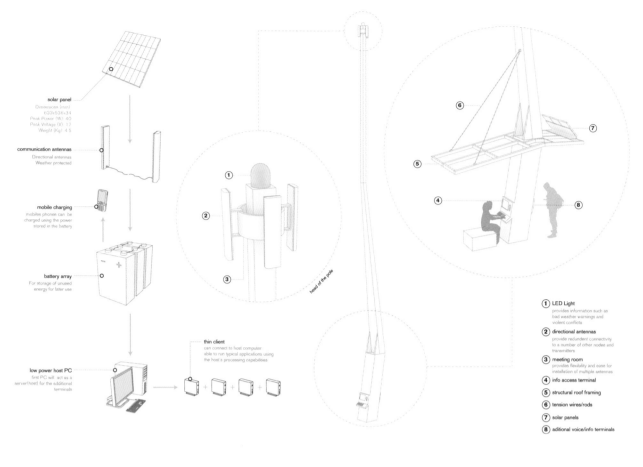

solar panel
Dimensions (mm)
633x536x34
Peak Power (W): 40
Peak Voltage (V): 17
Weight (Kg): 4.5

communication antennas
Directional antennas
Weather protected

mobile charging
mobiles phones can be
charged using the power
stored in the battery

battery array
For storage of unused
energy for later use

thin client
can connect to host computer
able to run typical applications using
the host's processing capabilities

low power host PC
first PC will act as a
server(host) for the additional
terminals

1. LED Light
provides information such as
bad weather warnings and
violent conflicts

2. directional antennas
provide redundant connectivity
to a number of other nodes and
transmitters

3. meeting room
provides flexibility and ease for
installation of multiple antennas

4. info access terminal

5. structural roof framing

6. tension wires/rods

7. solar panels

8. aditional voice/info terminals

head of the pole

Sector share for type

Programmatic breakdown

basic

Type: Node

Category: Basic

Services: Basic office services, Internet surfing, emailing, VOIP

Programmatic Breakdown:
This node type provides basic connectivity and information access for rural areas which are not on a power grid. Imagined as a self-powered node within the network, the basic type takes advantage of wireless mesh networking to create redundant connections to other nodes and hubs in the network. Solar panels generate enough electricity to power the communication equipment as well as a low-power PC which can be used to surf the Internet, run basic software and Voice Over IP (VOIP) service. Unused power will be stored in batteries for later use. Cellphones can also be charged at these stations. Remote IT service and maintenance is provided through connection to Hub typologies.

Node providing basic connectivity and information access for rural areas not on a power grid: As a self-powered node, this basic type takes advantage of wireless mesh networking to create redundant connections to other nodes. Solar panels generate enough electricity to power the communication equipment and a low-power PC to access the internet and run basic software, as well as charge cell phones. Unused power will be stored in batteries for later use.

a major broadcasting company, brings together a set of activities from research and education to entertainment and communication. The building's form responds to these activities with the extension of its programmed arms, to create passages towards a public park at the center, which acts as the roof for the reading environment below. The NDL houses a small data center, reading areas, private booths, and other forms of access to information, from local literature to global news and market information. Above, a digital park provides free public Wi-Fi and access to the digital library archives, as well as charging stations for mobile devices powered by a number of solar canopies. A data-free courtyard in the center of the building provides pause from the sometimes-overwhelming world of information flows.

Project Advisor: Mason White.

Ali Fard is a designer, researcher, and currently a doctoral candidate at Harvard University Graduate School of Design. He is the co-founder of Op.N, a design and research office based in Toronto and Cambridge, and an editor of the *New Geographies* journal.

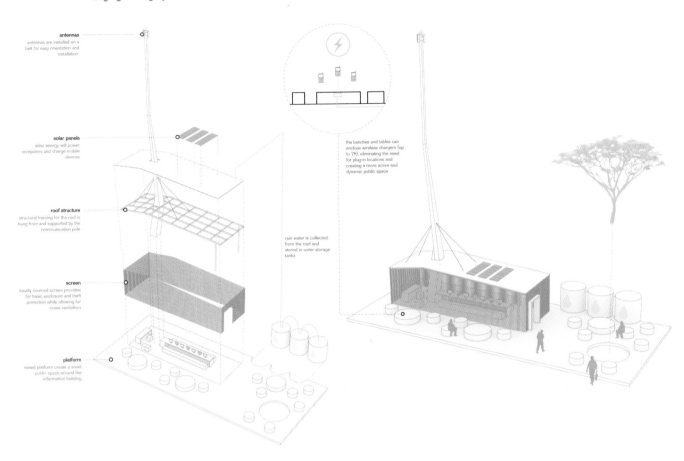

antennas
antennas are installed on a bolt for easy orientation and installation

solar panels
solar energy will power computers and charge mobile devices

roof structure
structural framing for the roof is hung from and supported by the communication pole

screen
locally sourced screen provides for basic enclosure and theft protection while allowing for cross ventilation

platform
raised platform create a small public space around the information building

the benches and tables can enclose wireless chargers (up to 7ft), eliminating the need for plug-in locations and creating a more active and dynamic public space

rain water is collected from the roof and stored in water storage tanks

Sector share for type

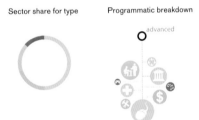

Programmatic breakdown

advanced

Type: Node

Category: Advanced

Services: All standard services + Wireless access to satellite places, education and vocational training, health advice.

Programmatic Breakdown:
Advanced type is seen a progressional growth of the standard type, but can be installed in unprecedented situations if a larger demand exists. In addition to general access terminals and government services, online and on-demand health advice is provided in a special room..

Evolution from the standard node type: It can be installed when a larger digital demand exists offering general access terminals and government services, online and on-demand health advice is offered. A public space is created around the building for informal gatherings and special events, as well as a place to charge phones and other mobile devices.

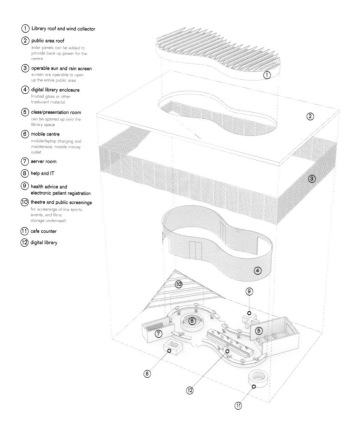

① Library roof and wind collector

② public area roof
solar panels can be added to
provide back up power for the
centre

③ operable sun and rain screen
screen are operable to open
up the entire public area

④ digital library enclosure
frosted glass or other
translucent material

⑤ class/presentation room
can be opened up onto the
library space

⑥ mobile centre
mobile/laptop charging and
maintenance, mobile money
outlet

⑦ server room

⑧ help and IT

⑨ health advice and
electronic patient registration

⑩ theatre and public screenings
for screenings of live sports,
events, and films
storage underneath

⑪ cafe counter

⑫ digital library

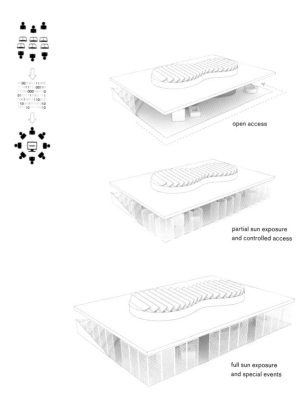

open access

partial sun exposure
and controlled access

full sun exposure
and special events

Sector share for type

Programmatic breakdown

✳ digi-center

Type: Hub

Category: Digi-centre

Services: all digiport services
and IT training classes,
in-house tech support, digital
library branch, mobile centre
charging and maintenance,
mobile money, health advice
room, free public Wi-Fi,
meeting spaces, access to
mentorship and classes,
community centre activities,
recreation.

Programmatic Breakdown:
Digi-centres are digitally oriented community centres. With a branch of the regional
digital library at its core, the centre will
provide the community with access to a
vast online library of local and international
literature, while promoting community
oriented activities. These activities are
encouraged through a collection of public
spaces arranged around the library.

This new public space is connected via
Wi-Fi and provides the local community
with screening areas (theatres streaming
entertainment, sports and special events),
a centre for mobile money and cell phone
maintenance, a health advise centre, and
a cafe.

**Digi-centres are digitally-oriented community
centres:** With a branch of the regional digital library at
its core, the centre provides the community access to an
online library, while promoting community-oriented
activities. This new public space is connected via wi-fi
and provides the local community with screening areas,
a centre for mobile money and cell phone maintenance,
a health advice centre which provides electronic patient
registry, and a cafe.

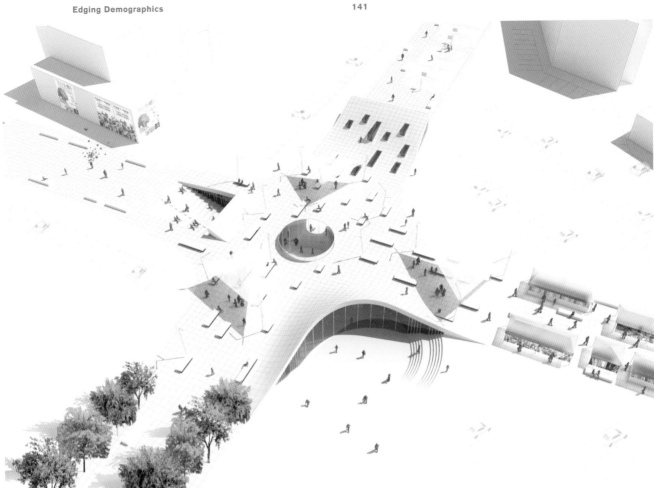

The Nairobi Digital Library: makes formal connections to the various cultural and educational programs nearby. Each extended arm is programmed with complementary activities that create direct links between the library and the neighbouring programs.

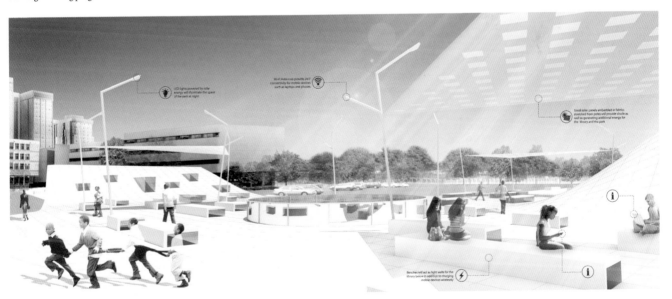

The top surface of Nairobi Digital Library: accommodates a diversity of programmatic opportunities that engage the public through environmentally flexible spatial elements. Solar canopies gather passive solar energy while providing shaded areas underneath for gatherings, leisure and educational activities.

THE OIL CHANGE

Eric Tan + Leon Lai

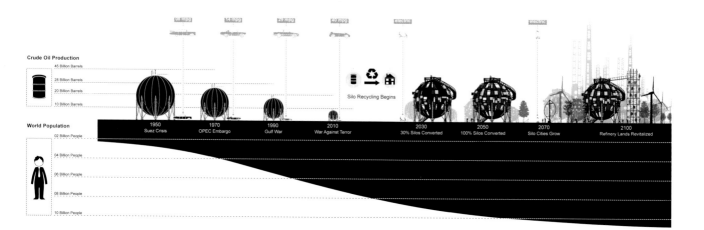

Flood/ Water Proof
An inherently Water-tight container firmly grounded by suspension structure

Hurricane/ Tornado Ready
Aerodynamic Shell + Reduction of uplift due to uniform pressures and airflow

Sand/ Blizzard Proof
Geometry prevents accumulation of sand and snow, reducing structural stresses

Earthquake Tolerance
Structural legs provide flexible suspension as well as rigidity to overall design

UFO Abduction Proof
Geometry makes alien abduction attempts extremely difficult

Oil timeline: As the human population increases at an exponential rate, oil discovery is decreasing at an exponential rate. Natural gas is becoming scarce and oil silos are now becoming abandoned as storage containers.

Global warming ready: Oil silos are inherently flood/ water proof, hurricane/ tornado resilient, and earthquake tolerant water-tight containers firmly grounded by a solid suspension structure.

Imagine the future world pushed to a new extreme—a world without petroleum, a world where the vast infrastructure of current petroleum storage and transportation will become obsolete and abandoned. These leftovers of industry could form the very foundation of a new breed of housing and community; *Silo Home* explores such a scenario.

Human population is increasing at an exponential rate, while the discovery of easily accessible oil is decreasing: domestic oil production in the US peaked in 1970 and global peak oil was reached circa 2005.[1] With the world's sources of easily accessible petroleum depleting, the remaining levels of petroleum found within the earth are becoming ever more difficult to extract, with unknown consequences on the environment and its inhabitants. The American Petroleum Institute estimates that the world's supply of "easy" oil will be depleted sometime between 2062 and 2094.[2] If this milestone is reached in a mere fifty years, a new paradigm will need to be established.

In the world of *Silo Home*, the foregone era of oil supports the transformation of desolate industrial land into unique urban realms. Such conversion is already evident in the post-industrial zones of many American urban centers, which are being transformed into desirable areas for the live/work/play model of 21st century modernity. The notion of architecture hijacking the holdovers of industry and converting them into a platform for environmental revitalization and community growth is one solution to the problems imposed by two centuries of environmental impacts and petroleum tensions in America.

Silo Home begins with the sustainable repurposing of silos into multi-family housing units. As an adaptive-reuse design, *Silo Home* builds upon Buckminster Fuller's Dymaxion approach of modular design and prefabricated components. The original silos along with the site are detoxified with in-situ oil bioremediation where soil microbes are dispatched to eat leftover pollutants. The silos are then

1. Matthew R. Simmons, "The Peak Oil Debate as the EIA Turns 30" (paper presented at the EIA 2008 Energy Conference, Washington, DC, April 7, 2008), http://www.eia.gov/conf_pdfs/Monday/Simmons.pdf.
2. Tim Appenzeller, "End of Cheap Oil," *National Geographic*, http://ngm.nationalgeographic.com/ ngm/0406/feature5/fulltext.html.

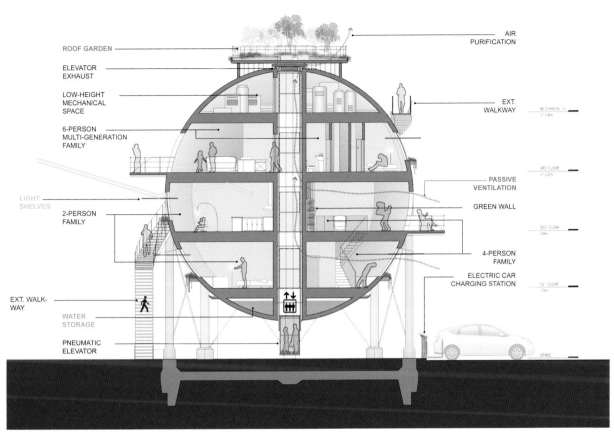

ROOF GARDEN

ELEVATOR
EXHAUST

LOW-HEIGHT
MECHANICAL
SPACE

6-PERSON
MULTI-GENERATION
FAMILY

LIGHT
SHELVES

2-PERSON
FAMILY

EXT. WALK-
WAY

WATER
STORAGE

PNEUMATIC
ELEVATOR

AIR
PURIFICATION

EXT.
WALKWAY

PASSIVE
VENTILATION

GREEN WALL

4-PERSON
FAMILY

ELECTRIC CAR
CHARGING STATION

Beyond carbon neutral: The Silo Home strives to
exceed a carbon-neutral classification and ultimately
achieving a carbon-positive rating.

disassembled and remodeled on site, including the insertion of new window openings, which then are
outfitted with new factory fabricated building elements and finishes. The shell of existing silos will be
combined with a modular kit of parts that are simple to manufacture, easy to install, and highly scalable. This reduces the cost of production and on site assembly is kept to a minimum.

An integrated set of passive sustainable installations, augmented by the silo's inherent spherical
shape, generate energy while reducing energy use and costs. Sunlight is harvested through surface
PV and solar thermal panels to provide electrical energy and hot water while rain is collected to
provide a free and clean water supply and conserve precious public water reserves. Surface plant-
ers assist in the bioremediation for recycling water. The silo's spherical shape aids heat distribution,
increasing comfort and cutting costs; passive ventilation is achieved by the dome through natural stack
effect through the central service core, sucking up hot air and allowing cool air to settle. The energy
generated by Silo Homes and their surroundings is shared within the community.

The traditional separation of industrial zones and cities will be erased as former blighted areas rein-
tegrate into their urban fabric. Contaminated lands of former oil refineries will go through an intense
detoxification process consisting of strategic landscaping and planting of greenery. These parks will
serve a dual purpose: naturally cleaning the soil as well as greening the site. Beyond sustainability, Silo
Home is designed to challenge and provoke existing notions of housing, industry, and recycling.

Project Team: Nico Schlapps (Berlin) and Sarah Roberts (Rotterdam).

Leon Lai is a graduate student at the University of Toronto fascinated by the changing global contingencies that
make our cities tick. **Eric Tan** is a GSAPP graduate, currently a New York based designer who recently exhibited his
work at the MoMA and was recognized as a Curbed Design and Real Estate "Young Guns". Both are founders of the
design collective PinkCloud.DK.

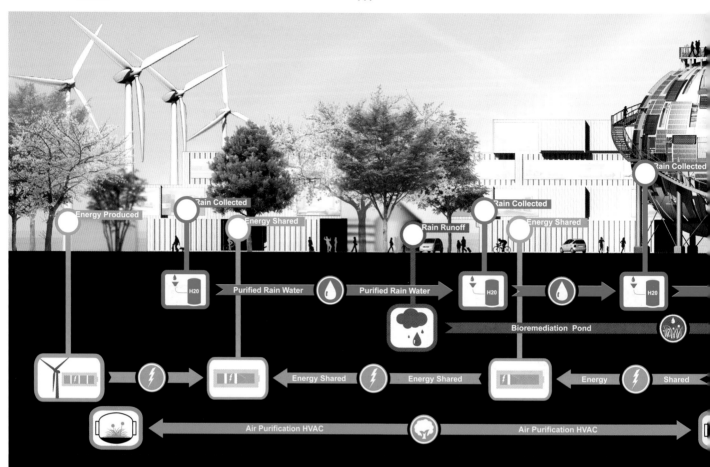

Energy Produced • Rain Collected • Energy Shared • Rain Runoff • Rain Collected • Energy Shared • Rain Collected

Purified Rain Water • Purified Rain Water

Bioremediation Pond

Energy Shared • Energy Shared • Energy • Shared

Air Purification HVAC • Air Purification HVAC

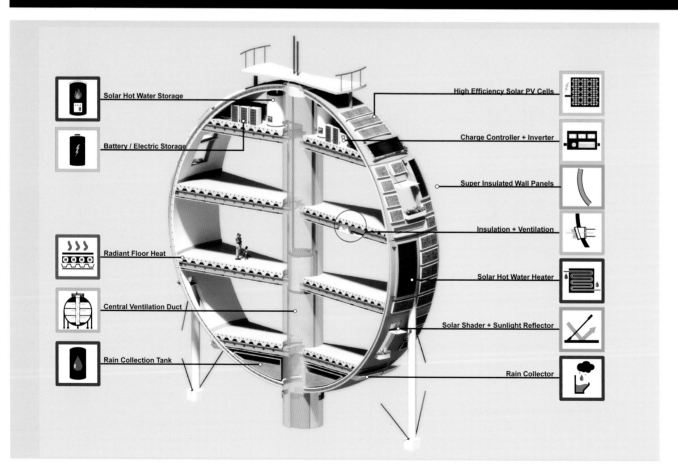

Solar Hot Water Storage • High Efficiency Solar PV Cells

Battery / Electric Storage • Charge Controller + Inverter

Super Insulated Wall Panels

Insulation + Ventilation

Radiant Floor Heat • Solar Hot Water Heater

Central Ventilation Duct • Solar Shader + Sunlight Reflector

Rain Collection Tank • Rain Collector

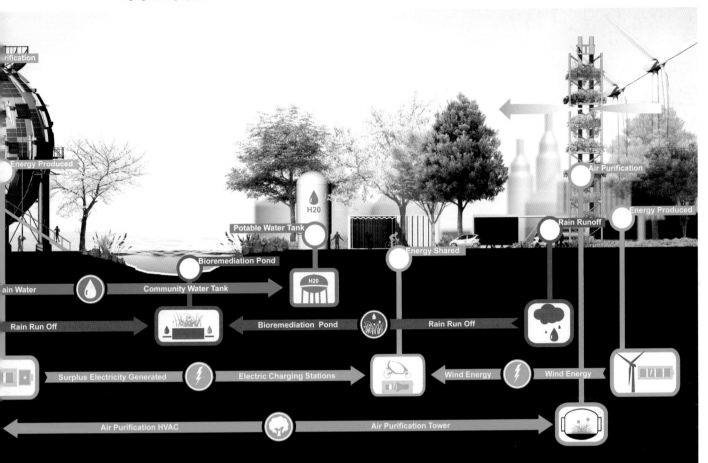

Shared resources: The Silo Home community is interconnected with a shared resource infrastructure. While resources are produced by individual mechanisms throughout the community, all resources are pooled and shared to maintain sufficient levels of energy, water, and clean air. This unified system of allocation meets the needs of all citizens of the community while conserving resources and minimizing waste.

ELDERQUARTERS

Beth Blostein + Bart Overly

An extreme demographic shift: Because of cultural advancement, the US population demographic is about to grow much older. The shift will, by 2050, dramatically skew the nation's Dependency Ratio, reducing the number of people in the workforce to "dependent" retired people.

Biological Aging: A Dependency Shift

A century of medical and scientific advancement allows us to live longer than ever before. Because of this extreme transformation, the US population demographic will shift; in less than forty years the number of people sixty-five and over will increase so that nearly one quarter of the population will be senior citizens. This shift will, by 2050, dramatically skew the nation's "Dependency Ratio", the age-related ratio between the segments of the population not in the work force (economically unproductive, dependent) relative to the segments who are. A full quarter of our population will be retired for a quarter of its increased lifespan.[1]

Despite advancements that curtail its effects, the process of aging is a biological inevitability and a crisis that invariably confronts each successive generation in every culture; it is seen as a progressive disease that must be combated. Take for example the legend of "setting adrift". Associated with Eskimo societies among others, the story tells of seemingly unproductive elderly villagers who, perceived as burdens for the resource-deprived community, were routinely set adrift upon ice floes to face a horrifying and solitary end.[2] Regardless of its authenticity, the mere existence of such a legend espousing a culturally sanctioned process of elder-corralling highlights the ubiquitous undercurrent of fear and uncertainty associated with aging. Each generation must define what it means to be "old" and answer the perplexing question of what to do with those who fit the definition. In the contemporary western world, the "old" often fall victim (literally or figuratively) to various kinds of institutionalization and societal expectations. This system has its own tempo and its own codes of conduct, often manifested through specialized facilities like retirement communities and nursing homes. While perhaps a more humane approach than being perched on the ice floe, the end result still becomes a forced placelessness and isolation from the continually evolving world. While each generation tries to improve upon the strategies of the last, the pending upheaval in the US demographic will mandate more than an incremental improvement or a dressing up of established institutional infrastructures; a radical reconsideration of its physicality will be necessary.

Architectural Aging: A Case for Reinvention

Culture's distaste for the "decrepit" extends to the environment we have constructed for ourselves. After all, architecture acts as an extension of our bodies. Looking only at commercial lease trends since 2008, at the start of the world-wide economic crisis, 133 million square feet of office space in the US, equal to sixty-three Empire State Buildings, has become vacant and unproductive.[3] While there are accepted assumptions that old-age justifies a reduced (or non-existent) set of productivity expectations for our parents and grandparents, the same does not hold true for buildings. The anecdote told by Robert Harbison in *The Built, the Unbuilt, and the Unbuildable* of the betrayal felt upon returning to his childhood summer camp only to find it in ruins, demonstrates our desire for architecture to withstand the tests of time.[4] The reality is that architecture rarely ages gracefully; it simply gets old and outmoded. These days architecture is deeply rooted in industrialized building systems and imposter materials. As a result, in the contemporary landscape of commercial buildings, structure gets hidden behind dropped ceilings and wrapped in materials that resist patina. When businesses fail or styles

1. "The Next Four Decades: The Older Population in the United States: 2010 to 2050," The United States Census Bureau, (May 2010) (based on data collected in the 2010 Census), 3-9.
2. "Eskimos: Old Age," http://www.theinitialjourney. com/features/eskimos_01.html, accessed on July 27, 2011.
3. Anton Troinovski, "Office Vacancy Rate Keeps Climbing," *The Wall Street Journal*, July 6, 2010. He compares the vacancy to the size of 2300 football fields, but we thought equating to The Empire State Building would be useful to this discussion.
4. Robert Harbison, *The Built, the Unbuilt, and the Unbuildable* (Cambridge, Mass.: MIT Press, 1991), 103.

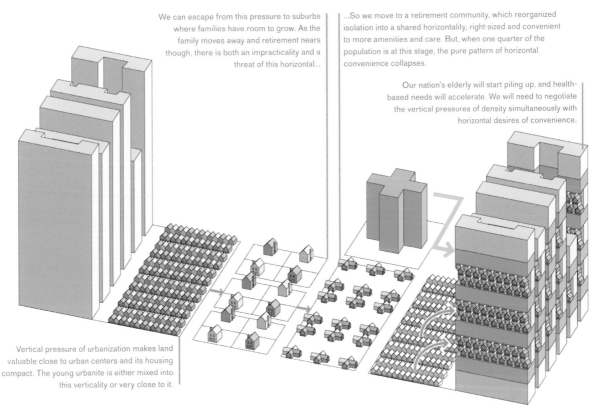

We can escape from this pressure to suburbs where families have room to grow. As the family moves away and retirement nears though, there is both an impracticality and a threat of this horizontal...

...So we move to a retirement community, which reorganized isolation into a shared horizontality, right-sized and convenient to more amenities and care. But, when one quarter of the population is at this stage, the pure pattern of horizontal convenience collapses.

Our nation's elderly will start piling up, and health-based needs will accelerate. We will need to negotiate the vertical pressures of density simultaneously with horizontal desires of convenience.

Vertical pressure of urbanization makes land valuable close to urban centers and its housing compact. The young urbanite is either mixed into this verticality or very close to it.

A shifting city: From vertical to horizontal and back again.

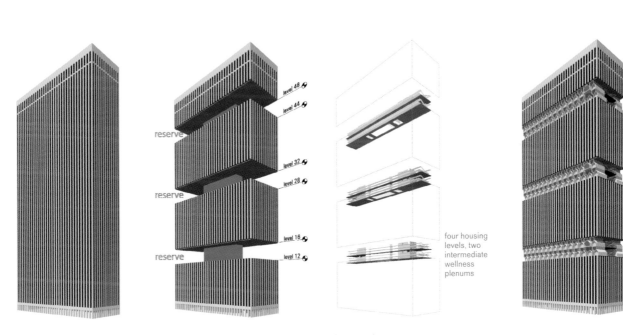

reserve

reserve

reserve

level 48
level 44
level 32
level 28
level 16
level 12

four housing levels, two intermediate wellness plenums

Shifting typology: Rezoning of permanently underutilized existing fabric would allow the city to infrastructurally accept this new and active elder housing typology. As a test case, we investigated a generic tall building: 1251 Avenue of the Americas, part of the nineteen building Rockefeller Center in Midtown Manhattan.

A Future City: elevated horizontal reserves reprogram the fabric of the city.

change, buildings almost overnight can be re-skinned and re-partitioned (within the limiting parameters of economics, building and zoning codes) to host the next commercial office venture. This saves the public from the unpleasant experience of watching swaths of their constructed world become irrelevant and compromised.

There are other examples where the image of the "aged" has been embraced, as something that holds a certain kind of potential, or power. One is the Victorian pleasure gardens and their orchestrated romantic, reconstructed ruins. Through the staging of events, old objects had the ability to spawn the latest in fashion and entertainment of the time. One might also look to James Wines and SITE's *Best Products* stores of the '70s–'80s. Intentionally fabricated in a state of suspended aging, there was a notion that visitors, reminded by the perceived decay of the architecture that the clock is ticking in in their own consumerist bodies and might be inspired to buy more.[5]

Despite these examples, the image of "aged" or "old" is fraught with difficulty, especially in a culture obsessed with youth and innovation. Moreover, unlike the picturesque qualities offered up by ruins in the Victorian garden, or SITE's ironic follies, abandoned glass and steel office buildings in American cities outwardly show minimal signs of age, and for the majority of people fail to evoke much in the way of good feelings. These nearly pristine ruins are the result of financial machinations that are not part of a distant history, but instead remain key features of virtually every evening news report. The continuing evacuation of commercial office space has been clean and swift. On one hand, the aforementioned pieces of urban fabric do not reflect utter architectural degradation, or a complete and total loss of capacity. On the other hand, given forecasts for the global economic future, one cannot help but consider the possibility that these spaces can never be recovered in the way intended and should just be set adrift.

5. Harbison, 108.

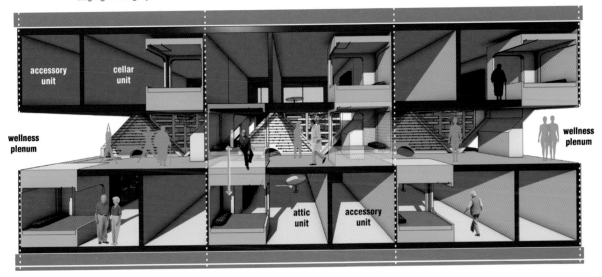

accessory unit

cellar unit

wellness plenum

wellness plenum

attic unit

accessory unit

The four level reserve: a layering of independent living with shared community.

Avoiding a repeat performance of '60s style urban renewal where the slate in many US cities was wiped clean for reinvention, another possibility for reuse exists. Fritz Lang's classic film, "Metropolis," superimposes two intertwined cities living at extremes: one for the elite, one for the oppressed masses that serve them. One is made of a supremely modern architecture: the other is more primal, existing in the interstitial spaces and margins. Independent of any critique of the exploitive social and political hierarchies presented in the film, there is an instrumental relationship between the two cities and their associated citizenry. Rather than scraping cities and starting over, the potential lies in these margins.

Vertical and Horizontal Dependencies

Ever since the first Otis passenger safety elevator was installed in New York in 1857, the organization of the city has been predominantly vertical. The dependency on this organization continues to grow as cities find themselves land-locked or bearing the weight of extreme real estate values. Over the last decade New York has piled an overall average of 35 feet of vertical space onto its skyline. Globally this upward trend is even more marked: Hong Kong, 241 feet; Shanghai, 263 feet; Dubai, 354 feet.[6]

Counter to this, as our demographic grows older, needs and desires for flatness and convenience drive the development of an alternate and separate horizontal universe. It strings together a trajectory of amenities and necessary resources: from the dwelling, to the attached garage, to the car, to the big-box grocery/pharmacy, to the health club/doctor. Whether "aging-in-place" or part of a retirement community or in an assisted-living facility, nearly three quarters of American senior citizens are in this alternate universe: sprawling suburban space where the horizontal conveniences

of living were made possible through the exploitation and development of cheap, flat farmland and the automobile.[7] Horizontal space invented typologies like "The Ranch," a popular Post-WWII housing option which accounted for ninety percent of American housing constructed in 1950.[8] Horizontal space acted to make dense vertical city dwelling less and less desirable, particularly to families and seniors. It represented a new kind of continuity that had limitations in the city: a horizontal, seemingly unending continuity of needs and desires.

There is an active battle between horizontality and verticality building. As the number of senior citizens in our nation piles up and health and wellness-based needs accumulate, our city-making patterns will have to renegotiate the pressures of vertical density with horizontal desire. The relationship between what are currently carefully zoned and separate lifestyles (the relaxed horizontal dispersal of the suburb/exurb and the active vertical aggregation of the city) will be radically reconsidered.

Re-Zoning the Horizontal: the Space for ELDERQUARTERS

Zoning has played a significant role in the way cities are imagined, built and used. Zoning negotiates access. In New York for instance, zoning was meant to mitigate the irreconcilability of the tower form and access to sunlight. The resultant buildings were a formal product of both its mandates and its loopholes. Rem Koolhaas saw a different kind of zoning potential in the city exemplified by the Manhattan's Downtown Athletic Club. He imagined an interior urbanity: a vertically-zoned pile of plots, independently programmed and choreographed by the opening and closing of elevator doors.[9]

6. "World's 25 Tallest Cities," http://www.ultrapolisproject.com. *The Ultrapolis Project* has formulaically tracked the average height of cities by averaging their tallest buildings in terms of inhabitable space.
7. United States Census Data, 2010.
8. Witold Rybcynski, *Last Harvest: How a Cornfield Became*

New Daleville (New York: Scribner, 2007).
9. Rem Koolhaas, *Delirious New York: A Retroactive Manifesto for Manhattan* (New York: The Monacelli Press, 1978), 152-159.
10. CoreNet Global Corporate Real Estate 2020 survey of 500 corporate real estate executives. The average square

footage for each American office worker has moved from 225 square feet in 2010 to 176 square feet in 2012. It is projected to reduce further to 151 square feet by 2017, and 40% of the respondents plan to be below 100 square feet by this time.

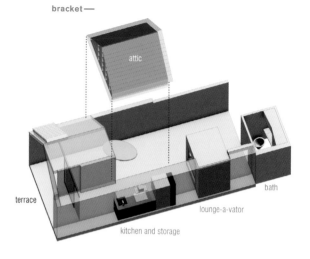

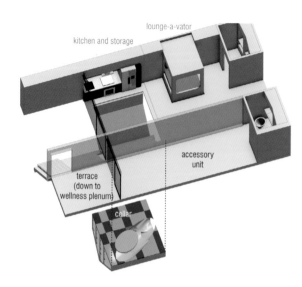

Attics and cellar units: used as personal storage and
support movement to the wellness plenum.

Since the economic events of 2008, it has become evident that our cities are piled with the wrong stuff, and the companies inhabiting it are finding ways to do more with much less of it. Private corner offices give way to flexible open officeing, shared support resources and office hoteling. Mobile connectivity makes all of this dedicated commercial "stuff" all the more questionable as Corporate America accepts more forms of remote work.[10] "Re-zoning" this permanently underutilized existing fabric would allow the city to absorb new typologies and new forms of living for the changing demographic.

ELDERQUARTERS imagines an urban scenario for a soon-to-be-exploding senior citizen population. As a prototypical infrastructural and architectural proposal to re-zone existing urban fabric, the project reformulates new relationships of lifestyle/wellness and comfort/desire. Deployed here as an experiment for Midtown Manhattan, a series of four floor "reserves" are reprogrammed every twelve levels (or a quarter of the overall tower) in the vertical space of the city. Over time, 25 percent of the nearly 600 million square feet of underutilized commercial office space would be re-appropriated as horizontal continuums throughout the city fabric. These reserves are to be reprogrammed with a world previously left in the isolated margins: two levels of independent living apartments layered with an expanse of shared community, longevity, wellness, and healthcare services on the other two.

Within the living unit the bed takes on an extended role, combining the rituals of domesticity with those of professional health care. In the modern hospital room, the bed is a device that monitors vitals, constantly modulates pressure on the body, and adjusts to allow for multiple programs of use: sleeping, reading, treating, lifting. In ELDERQUARTERS, the bed connects the residential private realm to a semi-public Wellness Plenum where full medical and wellness services are offered. From resting to transporting to treating, the bed morphs from an accessory of comfort and pleasure to a necessity of medical support. The literal maneuverability of

the bed through the section of ELDERQUARTERS allows each resident to seamlessly oscillate between health services and the comforts of home.

Acting as insertions into the expanse of the Wellness Plenum, individual storage is provided for each residential unit, its type determined by the movement of the bed: "attics" for movement up one level into the Plenum, "cellars" for movement down. This storage, absent or minimized in typical city living, allows residents to keep important mementos that have been accumulated over a lifetime but are often relinquished through the typical process of downsizing. As one moves from their residence to the Plenum, the mementos stored become accessible and visible, and in a sense personalize the space of the Plenum.

Much like our system of national park reserves throughout the country, as more generic commercial space empties and as entire buildings are re-zoned, a visually articulated system throughout the city will emerge. The elder-hipsters that inhabit this new system will vary wildly. Some might choose to start collaborative post-retirement careers with other like-minded people. Others may strategically relocate to reserves having consultancy opportunities in office space two floors up or two floors down. Still others might take in highly specialized wellness or medical offerings that materialize. In all cases, it's a connected infrastructure of lifestyle, wellness, and convenience. Each reserve becomes a unique floating neighbourhood to visit and touchdown with the city again, via socially programmed vertical public transportation (slow moving, floating coffee shops and speakeasies). In this sense these Ex-Expatriates find themselves out of the accelerating, fast paced world and in it at the same time.

Beth Blostein is an Associate Professor and **Bart Overly** is on the auxillary faculty at The Knowlton School of Architecture at The Ohio State University. **Blostein/Overly Architects** looks for idiosyncrasies in program, politics, site, and banal necessity that can be used to formulate unexpected narratives and new typologies for projects.

OPSPACE:OPEN SOURCE URBANISM

Mona El Khafif + Kory Bieg

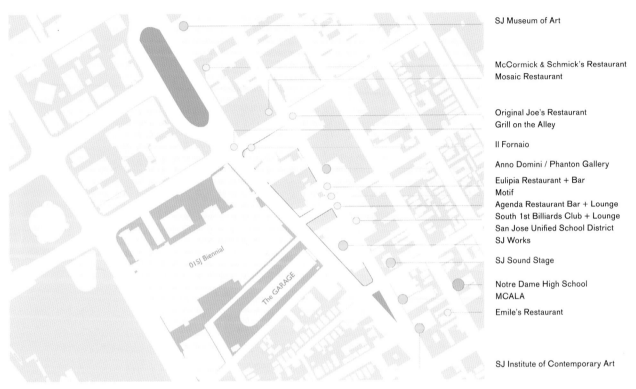

SJ Museum of Art

McCormick & Schmick's Restaurant
Mosaic Restaurant

Original Joe's Restaurant
Grill on the Alley

Il Fornaio

Anno Domini / Phanton Gallery

Eulipia Restaurant + Bar
Motif
Agenda Restaurant Bar + Lounge
South 1st Billiards Club + Lounge
San Jose Unified School District
SJ Works

SJ Sound Stage

Notre Dame High School
MCALA

Emile's Restaurant

SJ Institute of Contemporary Art

Absent everyday urbanism: An analysis of program and activity in SoFA.

OPspace transforms vacant inner city real estate spaces through a design framework that fosters and directs a range of flexible community-driven occupations. The project responds to unpredictable programmatic needs, unknown user groups and a diverse range of site conditions.

OPspace is a pilot project conducted by students and faculty at the CCA URBANlab, an advanced research and design lab in the Department of Architecture at California College of the Arts. During the 3rd ZERO1 Biennial, *OPspace* was installed inside the WORKS' storefront, where students tested the design through a series of programs created with the local community. The real-time testing of the prototype provided feedback on its potential to initiate a new form of open-source urbanism.

Urban Strategy: extremes of urban vacancies

Alan Berger's analysis in *Drosscapes* reveals that as cities rapidly expand at the edges, a vast landscape of vacant real estate is left at the urban center.[1] These territories, however, should not be understood as wastelands but as sites that demand new design strategies.

In 2010, the street-level storefronts in downtown San Jose's SoFA district, the selected testing ground for this project, suffered from a 40 percent vacancy rate, a situation also found in the Central Market neighbourhood of San Francisco and downtown Oakland.[2] Located in the center of NorCAL, one of eleven US mega-regions with a projected growth rate of 50.7 percent over the next 40 years, these communities are representative of broader national trends.[3]

A critical aspect of urban vacancy is a lack of social interaction among remaining communities, causing stigmatization. Lefebvre writes in *La Révolution Urbaine* that urbanity as a condition of social life and interaction evolves from both networks and boundaries. The friction between these differences can fertilize productive transformation.[4] The production of urbanity therefore, also exists in an immaterial world defined by human behavior, framed by organizational structures, and driven by perception. How can design initiate synthesis

1. Alan Berger, *Drosscape. Wasting Land in Urban America* (New York: Princeton Architectural Press, 2006), 18.
2. "CoStar Real Estate Database, 2012," *CoStar Group,* http://gateway.costar.com.
3. "Northern California," *America 2050,* http://www.america2050.org/northern_california.html.
4. Henri Lefebvre, *La Revolution Urbain* (Paris: Gallimard, 1970).

Unfolded modules: Each base shape unfolds at either side creating four total configurations. These sectional configurations are then aggregated in plan to create the varying OPspaces.

and support community life in an environment characterized by urban decline?

Based on theories of "Staged Urbanism,"[5] *OPspace* fills the void through the design framework and choreography of four spatial layers: architecture as hardware, programming as software, organizational frameworks as orgware, and finally communication strategies as brandware.

The project is defined by performance rather than architectural form. A "Zipcar" style short-term rental model accessible through an open-source Internet forum (orgware) defines a new economy and organization of the space. Formerly private space is democratized and transformed into a public domain with multiple users sharing rent and infrastructure. A flexible modular system (hardware) consisting of hexagons supports a variety of community-driven programs and unpredictable activities (software). Finally the implementation of social communication tools like Facebook and Twitter (brandware) help to build a community and make a place.

Working with the local community in SoFA, students researched demographics and proposed a program umbrella with five categories defined by different aggregations of the modular system: OPscene, OPstage, OPexhibit, OPtaste, and OPlab. These program umbrellas addressed the needs of the neighbourhood and created a range of possible activities. *OPspace*—which stands for opportunities, open, and operable—provides communities with the tools to fill the void

and to reactivate the cultural and economic development of their neighbourhoods.

Digital Fabrication: individualized solutions

The digital design and fabrication of *OPspace* is driven by the multi-layered conditions of spatial performance central to the project's socio-economic strategies for urban revitalization. The design accommodates individualized solutions within a framework that is both generic and specialized.

Though a continuous surface, differentiation of the interior is expressed through varied combinations of form, use and material. The exterior of *OPspace* is a billboard, identifying the brand and drawing to customers, but it is also a programmatic surface allowing additional uses such as the display of merchandise, storage, and the attachment of uniquely designed accessories. In the open position, the interior and exterior surfaces are conflated, mixing program and material into a multi-layered and multi-functioning space.

The project's core becomes a domain of integrated simultaneous operations.[6] *OPspace* is more than the shape of its profile. Voids are carved out to reduce weight and store seats. Fastening devices, lighting and other systems are integrated with structure, which is also shaped and perforated to ease the moving and reconfiguration of each module. The inclusion of the project's technical requirements, constrained by the formal variation of each module and its use, necessitated the development of a (co)operative and integrated detailing

5. Mona El Khafif, *Staged Urbanism*. Urban Space for Art, Culture and Consumption in the Age of the Leisure Society (Stuttgart: VDM, 2006).
6. The integration of multiple systems should not be confused with the simple organization of parts. The hybrid shapes of OPspace embody many functions

simultaneously. As Wiscombe points out, "curiously, the advent of building information modeling (BIM) in recent years, while spurious as a design tool, has increased awareness of coordinating building systems in a three-dimensional environment. Nevertheless, coordination is false integration." Wiscombe continues,

an "architecture of extreme integration, [is one] of nuanced transgressions, of dipping in and out of poché space and reconstituting them in a more complex way. Poché becomes vivid, active space." In Tom Wiscombe, "Extreme Integration," *Architectural Design* 80, no. 2: 82.
7. In an essay about the use of CNC for architectural

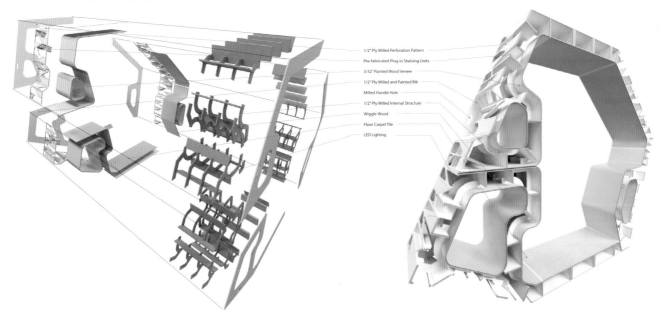

1/2" Ply Milled Perforation Pattern
Pre-fabricated Plug-in Shelving Units
3/32" Painted Wood Veneer
1/2" Ply Milled and Painted Rib
Milled Handle Hole
1/2" Ply Milled Internal Structure
Wiggle Wood
Floor Carpet Tile
LED Lighting

Module Fabrication: All pieces are attached together by wood glue, notching system, and nails. It takes on average 9 hours to put together the rib system for each section, prior to painting affixing wiggle wood, and finishing touches. The carpet is attached on top of the wiggle wood and it placed strategically to prevent slip hazards as well as adding an extra cushioned surface when acting as a seat.

OPspace during the Biennial: Presentation during Symposium Decoding Military Landscapes

On Site: OPspace occupies an exterior condition.

strategy with tolerances that could only be achieved by using digital fabrication technologies.

The flexible, user-directed design required details that were highly specific but also multi-functional. A slot for attaching two modules in one direction might be used for mounting audio-visual equipment or supporting merchandise. To achieve this level of structural and functional performance, hundreds of unique components were exported directly from the digital model to a CNC milling machine. The digital model was unfolded, labeled and milled, allowing for the quick and efficient assembly of what would have otherwise been a difficult and labor-intensive construction project.[7] Though a descendent of industrialized machines for mass-production, the use of current CNC technologies allowed for the immediate and extreme individualization of parts, supporting the overall design agenda of *OPspace*.

The Design of Multiplicity
As Stan Allen writes in *Landform Building*, "you need very specific design conditions in order to trigger the potential of [...] flexibility and the openness of the public domain."[8] In this respect *OPspace* creates a strategic fixity in order to support the unfolding of a bottom-up occupation.

OPspace is a mechanism for generating possibilities within an environment of indeterminacy. They are a response to a condition of programmatic and social unpredictability and reside in the multi-layered design of every form, detail, surface, and structural component. As much as the urban strategy operates like a framework for a diversity of urban programming and users fostering a form of open source urbanism, the modular system creates an alphabet of architectural elements and details, in which architectural form is

replaced with the concept of performance. Driven by the need for flexibility, the system offers multiplicity: of form, users, programming, and context.

Project lead Dr. Mona El Khafif; Adjunct Professor Kory Bieg; and the following students: Josh Campos, Alexa Getting, Brittany Glover, Richard Lyttle, Carlos Martinez, Jeronimo Roldan, Lauren Tichy, Fabiola Vargas, Mike Vargas, Rachael Yu, Carmen Smith, Pia-Jacqlin Malinis, Matt Adams, Hiram Boujaoude, Maryam Zahedi, and Justin Mason (TheOverLayGroup).

Collaborators: Andre Caradec of S/U/M Architects (Fabrication and Construction), David Maynard (Joint Detailing), Andrew Sparks and Ben Corotis (Construction), Cinthia Wen (Branding), Brandon Walker and the CCA fabrication team (CNC Milling), Karen Eichler (Very Public Art)

Mona El Khafif is an Associate Professor of Architecture at the University of Waterloo, and together with Ila Berman, Principal of SCALESHIFT located in Toronto. She received her professional degree from the RWTH in Aachen Germany and her doctoral degree from the TU in Vienna, where her research investigated interdisciplinary urban regeneration strategies and urban choreographies. Between 2008 and 2013 El Khafif lead the URBANlab at CCA in San Francisco.

Kory Bieg is an Assistant Professor of Architecture at the University of Texas at Austin and Principal of OTA+, an architecture, design and research office that specializes in the application of advanced digital technologies for the design and construction of projects of all types and scale. Bieg received his Master of Architecture from Columbia University in New York City and is a registered architect in the state of California, Colorado and Texas.

production, Bill Kreysler, an expert on composites and digital fabrication, acknowledges "digital tools and machines, invented to improve factory productivity, can be used to make custom components that outperform their mass-produced cousins." See Bill Kreysler, "Craft in Digital Design," *Composites, Surfaces, and Software: High Performance Architecture*, eds. Greg Lynn and Mark

Foster Gage (New Haven: Yale School of Architecture, 2010), 39.
8. Stan Allen and Marc McQuade, *Landform Building* (Princeton: Lars Müller Publishers), 257.

SALVAGED LANDSCAPE

Catie Newell

Arson House: A house in Detroit captured during an arson.

There is a short and fleeting moment when a house is burning that is perhaps the peak of its aesthetic beauty. A rolling and vibrant mix of oranges violently traces the familiar outline. Ghostly smoke fills the air, making visible the surrounding atmosphere and the burning property. The sounds give the construction a voice, and the urgency demands attention. It is impossible to turn away from such untouchable presence as the mind sustains conflicting emotions tied simultaneously to the beauty of the material performance and the pain of loss related to this familiar domestic setting. Irreversible and haunting, the act of arson gives the common material and volumes new attributes, and the story of the house a new weight.

In Detroit, arson and its results are not unfamiliar sights. Indeed, in its current state, the city is primed for this act. The abundance of abandoned homes, the diminished and strained civic infrastructure, and a history of mischievous fires combine to breed arson. It sparks from direct intent, boredom, insurance claims, and politics. The crime is usually not investigated and is often coupled with multiple conspiracy theories. Remnants of fires are rarely attended to, making the resulting charred wood an increasingly familiar material within the urban landscape. With each fire, a single house reveals another reality at play in Detroit, and collectively, arson becomes a visual cue to the complex circumstances currently defining the city.

As a city that is both an anomaly and the embodiment of ailing times, working creatively in Detroit necessitates on-the-ground maneuvering. It requires strategies that respond to derelict materials, questionable volumes, and the harsh realities of an anxious city. Creative methods driven by necessity can stage an approach to architecture that makes a state of extremity and imbalance productive.

The work on one particular house, 2230 14th Street, signaled an effort to strategically embrace existing circumstances, to see the conditions as a creative spark within the city. While the assembly of materials at 2230 14th Street ceased being a house as we know it, it never entirely stopped carrying

The cut ends: The wood as seen from the backyard.

the semantic weight of a domestic house. This relationship creates an opportunity to reflect on the cultural contingencies we currently live among, and the values that we ascribe to them.

Though empty of permanent occupants, the fallen house still maintains familiar volumes while carrying no meaning. Squatters used the spaces as needed, although they did not alleviate its ailing condition nor settle for very long. Irreversible, transformed, and impaired, the burning turned the wood a beautiful deep black, with an eerie reflective shine amongst a bulbous impure geometry, stricken with lightness and fragility. Severely damaged and unsafe, the space required demolition.

In response, by creating a purposeful teardown, *Salvaged Landscape* appropriates the charred wood from the arson to create new spatial configurations within the remaining structure. Using existing material from the house as the palette, and using the surviving stable walls as formwork, the salvaged charred wood is configured piece by piece into a new, denser volume that explores thickness, texture, occupation, and intentional darkness. The wood is sliced on one end to expose the raw conditions amongst the depth of the char. With the cut end strictly exposed to the exterior, the remaining extents of the wood suspends inward. As each piece punctured the space it did not bring light, but instead brought darkness. The interplay between the textural techniques provided occupants with a passageway through the material, an inhabitable texture. At its opening on Devil's Night, October 30th, a night notorious in Detroit for the extreme number of arsons, the new configuration of charred wood introduced new rooms to the house while simultaneously removing light.

Soon there after, with the required demolition of its formwork (the room and upper floor immediately surrounding the work) *Salvaged Landscape* was exposed as a dense stand-alone space solidifying a former interior. Leaving its lot in a heroic craned flight over the neighbouring house the material construction left its once familiar setting and entered the environment of an art gallery. Away from Detroit as the immediate context, both physically and legally, it could be seen as an object, freed again from being a house.

Only intended as a temporary disappearance from the circumstances of the city, *Salvaged Landscape* returned to Detroit. While in transit, it was unexpectedly denied a promised plot of land in

Haunting Addition: Half of the house as reconfigured back inside the other half of the house.

In flight: *Salvaged Landscape* being lifted out of the house by crane.

Released: *Salvaged Landscape* removed from its formwork.

Detroit as it was turned away for its 'controversial weight' as an arson home. Simultaneously, the city called for an emergency teardown of the house it originated from, citing the owners' slow progression in securing the land. Crated and sited on a driveway to nowhere, it resettled as an odd neighbour to its former residence. The original house—burned and set for demolition—was hit with arson yet again. For its part, *Salvaged Landscape* was spared from this most recent fire. Meanwhile, the other half of the house now appears as a fresh palette of charred wood and a crisis of safety and motivation.

It remains a delicate story: To burn it, though perhaps not unexpected, would be offensive, making a mockery of a painful urban situation. To place it in the landfill would be wasteful, mistaking these rarely harnessed material attributes of wood for trash. To remake it would dull its condition, as the presence of the remaining house would be missing. As a seemingly simple and ubiquitous set of materials, it is in essence unable to be concluded because it still remains a house. A house from Detroit.

Installation Team: Catie Newell, Chuck Newell, Joe Proper, Chip Newell, Lefty's Angels.

Catie Newell is the founding principal of *Alibi Studio, Detroit and Assistant Professor of Architecture at the University of Michigan. Newell's work and creative practice has been widely recognized for exploring design construction and materiality in relationship to location, geography, and cultural contingencies.

Devil's Night: Salvaged Landscape as it existed October 30, 2010.

A MAN, A TREE, AND AN AX

Keller Easterling

Contemporary mediagenic design is attracted to several default scripts.

One all too familiar script is that of the so-called "tech intellectual." TED, PopTech or any of its numerous clones have made the hipster standup conference into popular cultural entertainment and even big business. Cities, universities, arts organizations and others have joined the conference stagers as producers of the format, tuning up the academic conference to include music, demos, theatrical lighting, sound cues, podcast interviews on lounge furniture and other show biz production values. While innovations from many different disciplines are present, new technologies and cresting scientific developments are reliable crowd pleasers. New technology is a crucial component in this culture's regime of modernity, as is the upbeat, brisk, friendly ethos of openness and sharing. The startup-style demo calculates all the mechanisms for catapulting the previously obscure lecture into contact with a broad general audience and a celebrity-light status. A more entrepreneurial academic, previously lined with care and worry is in the glow a promotional tour, an individual as entertainment event, with and agent and polished sound bites and the equivalent of ratings on twitter and Facebook.

For architects just starting their career or poised to enter academia, this script appeals for obvious reasons. The choice is to work for geriatric pundits in low paying jobs or illegal internships or to transform into an artist/performer/hacker who works on projects reflecting the relevant innovations of the day. "Trained as an architect" becomes an added curiosity or credential to add to the promotion as one looks at biotech, high tech materials, software, digital sensing, nanotechnology, robotics, big data, etc. The sense is that architecture does not have anything that captures the cultural imagination—no demo, no drones not breathtaking (or in TED argot, jawdropping) dance of data. A career, when thus successfully transformed, suddenly gains a sense of relevance, funding from science or the art world, inclusion in lists of top young movers and photographs taken with crossed arms and a penetrating gaze. Conformity to every aspect of this role, down to its middle-aged swagger and jargon around all things "viral" may seem sad. Yet given what architecture offers as an alternative, it deserves to be left behind.

Also attractive to architects is the relatively recent script of design fiction. Including design at every scale from the microscopic to the urban to the planetary, design fiction arguably retains a focus on the technical object and as well as some of same fascinations with contemporary innovations. The scenarios are perhaps dramatized, maybe even over-dramatized, by a tradition of science fiction. The script also incorporates some of the selective revivals of cybernetic thinking that accompanied the late 20th century adoption of digital technologies. So occasionally the projects reflect a dystopic, techno-fantasy or steam punk patina or a MacGyver-style ingenuity. Design fiction often performs in some of the same standup festivals and so must be, as Bruce Sterling recently described it, "full of wow and amazingness."[1] Snidely avuncular, Sterling made those remarks in the process of cautioning design fiction about the start-up that is co-opted by the powers that be—echoes of the fun-loving Media Lab funded by the defense department or the technoart funded by Xerox Park. Often designed to be germs that influence or expose a larger organization, design fiction offers instead of comprehensive solutions, a swarm of independent anecdotal projects that vie for attention. At its best, design fiction travels to extremes to highlight something ubiquitous, building some bright, some solemn scenarios about "wicked problems" or about objects clasped in our hand, orbiting in the stratosphere or residing in the gut. This probing experimental work is also almost always informed by the deepest dives into the study of political consequence.

Another script attractive to architects—one that probably won't get any invitations from DEF CON—offers not the anecdotal but the comprehensive. With precedents in landscape urbanism and infrastructure design, these projects integrate a world of synergistic ecologies. Sober but cheerful aerials portray a bundle of political, environmental and logistical problem in which driverless vehicles stream over a smart highway lined on one side with energy producing and desalinating windmills that also just happen to be able to assist in the migrations of birds. The guano from the birds is recaptured to fuel the driverless vehicles and, avoiding any possible waste, is also used as fertilizer for the vertical farming and co-working centers that line the other side of the highway. These scripts often reside on the walls of design studios in the academy where they can remain pure and uncompromised. They might also be the winner honorable mention in architectural competitions—their authors convinced that the world was simply not ready for the innovations they propose. This script can reside quite easily as a parallel activity within a conventional practice.

Any of these scripts can be used to effect change and to press spatial studies onto a global stage. Any of them can also be used to stay safe. The new culture of intellectual entertainments can, ironically, make it can be quite practical to be rhetorical and quite risky to be practical.

It is reasonable to calculate that the space of urbanism can most readily capture the world's imagination only when it is a giant wiki, enhanced with digital devices—bristling with sensors as an internet of things, or inflected by a technological or biological gizmo.

Yet perhaps these nourishing and exciting projects also prematurely satisfy, or even foreclose on, an urge to explore a much more expansive territory. Even when resisting the vampiric modernist impulse to declare a new regime, these projects may be drawn into a cul-du-sac, and their production of artifacts risks being yet another anecdotal, even marginal, expression in a succession of ideas, when they have the potential to inspire much broader application.

A non-modern question—the artifacts of which have always been with us, the boundaries of which include but exceed all of the above experiments, and the answer to which we already know—is how space, without digital or media enhancement, is itself information.[2]

While accepting that a technology like mobile telephony has become the world's largest shared platform for information exchange, we are perhaps less accustomed to the idea of space as a technology or medium of information—undeclared information that is not parsed as text or code.

For some who foretold the digital revolution but who were not yet surrounded by all of its products, it was perhaps easier to understand that anything—dumb, inert, human, non-human, non-digital—could be a carrier of information. When the social scientist and cybernetician Gregory Bateson referred to a man a tree and an ax as an information system, he made self-evident the idea that not only the texts or telecommunications, but activities in space—space without sensors or drones—can be a medium of information. The information manifests, not in text or code, but in activity and relationship.

The softwares of our digital culture retroactively help to train this habit of mind in the sense that softwares are not content but content managers—not about things but about the way things are interacting. There are literal softwares for making buildings, digital platforms like Wikihouse for sharing and altering the building files and softwares like MIT's Urban Network Analysis.[3]

But a much broader project involves not a literal software but another approach to form making that is perhaps analogous to software. The world could use from architects and urbanists form in another gear or register. In addition to master plans, buildings or any of the usual object forms on offer, even in addition to the mediagenic offerings are forms, might there be active forms that simply specify the relationships between things over time? Active forms are expressions of interdependence between spatial variables—content managers in something like a spatial operating system.

Econometrics and informatics usually control the operating system. Remarkably, spatial variable variables rarely take the lead in development and governance. The most interesting thinkers in the social, political and economic sciences are looking for hidden relationships in more complex test beds like the almost infrastructural spatial products in which the world is swimming. Perhaps even more than architects and urbanists, they are well aware of underexposed underexploited opportunities at the dead center the most ubiquitous spaces.

Space, as central as air and water, needs no embedded technology to gain relevance. Most of the spaces in the world are extreme in their ordinariness—the malls, spatial products and free zones that create nothing less than a default medium of global polity. The world is filled with multipliers, switches, governors and countless other interdependencies. Like bits of code in the operating system, active forms that hack into these repeatable spatial products. There is no visionary utopia to portray because the field is not something that holds still long enough to be depicted, determined or prescribed in a constantly updating platform. Bypassing some of the default scripts or the ready political cautions of elders, these forms have undisclosed political powers and underexploited artistic pleasures—aesthetic regimes that are being enacted as well as depicted.

1. http://nextberlin.eu/2013/04/bruce-sterling-fantasy-prototypes-and-real-disruption/
2. Bruno Latour, *We Have Never Been Modern* (Cambridge: Harvard University Press,1993), 48.
3. http://cityform.mit.edu/projects/urban-network-analysis.html. This software arguably feeds data to an existing econometric marketing system that already informs the city.

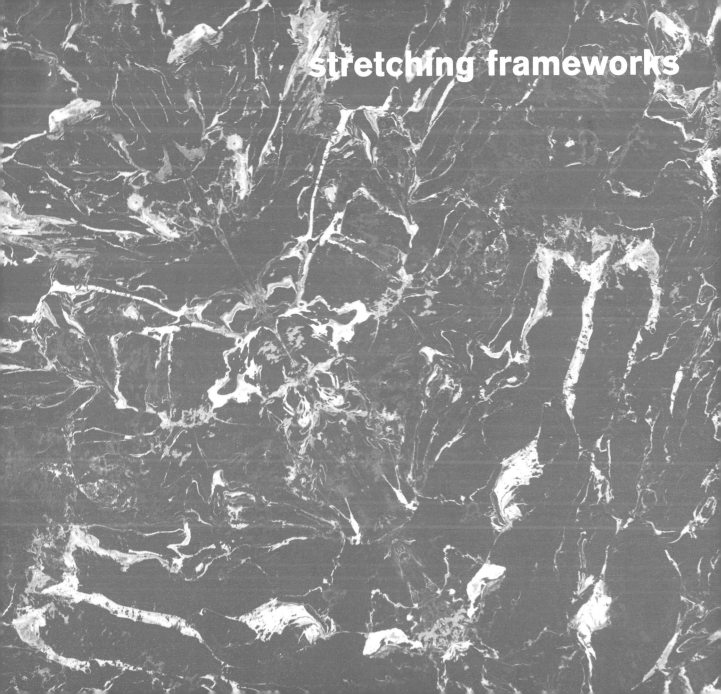

stretching frameworks

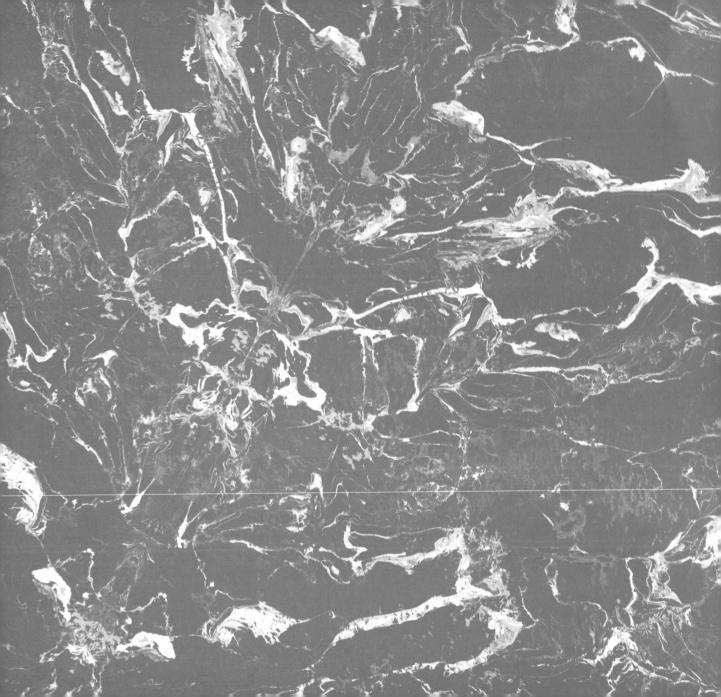

SUPERDIVISION DETROIT

David Freeland + Brennan Buck

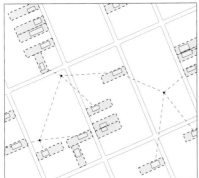
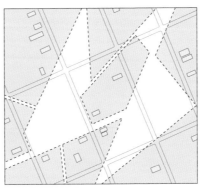
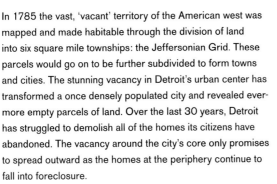

Superdivision algorithm: Currently, at left, occupied lots are isolated like islands in a sea of vacant territory. At center, hedgerows form new boundaries around larger plots shared by several houses. At right, they also connect a network of forest and farmland.

In 1785 the vast, 'vacant' territory of the American west was mapped and made habitable through the division of land into six square mile townships: the Jeffersonian Grid. These parcels would go on to be further subdivided to form towns and cities. The stunning vacancy in Detroit's urban center has transformed a once densely populated city and revealed ever-more empty parcels of land. Over the last 30 years, Detroit has struggled to demolish all of the homes its citizens have abandoned. The vacancy around the city's core only promises to spread outward as the homes at the periphery continue to fall into foreclosure.

The remaining small lots surrounded by empty territory call for an inverse strategy of *Superdivision*: one involving the scaling-up of property dimensions in occupied territories and the repurposing of unused infrastructure. Given a failed city structure, and the reality that an infrastructure built for over 1.5 million people will soon serve less than half that many, the project proposes a strategy of re-territorialization rather than construction.

The hedgerow, a technique of rural landscape division, may be able to stave off the city's urban decay by defining new, super-scaled, and occupied territories. We propose an algo-rithmic and interactive tree planting strategy in publicly-owned land parcels. This would form both a connective network of trails and a set of preliminary boundaries, scaling-up the existing pattern of property ownership to suit the collapsing population densities. Rather than resisting the city's inevitable depopulation over the next several decades, the superdivision channels and manages that depopulation, eventually stabilizing home ownership into archipelagos of dense neighbourhoods.

As an algorithm, the proposal is both geometric and social, involving homeowners, banks, local government and emerging rural populations, including farmers, fauna and wildlife. The city has been demolishing vacant houses for years, leaving the lots barren. The hedgerow planting would be run by the parks department, but configured annually by a computer pro-gram. Based on year-by-year patterns of building demolition and the surveyed interest in each neighbourhood, the algo-rithm pinpoints a set of hedgerows to be planted each spring. Geometrically, each hedgerow runs through the middle of a given vacant lot, splitting the territory exactly in half between the two closest occupied homes. From that midpoint, trees are planted in both directions until they terminate in an occupied lot. As new trees are planted in the following years, hedge-rows begin to intersect, defining enlarged territories for each occupied house and defining open parcels to be rededicated for community gardens, commercial agriculture or succes-sional forest. Initially a set of star-like ecological nodes, the hedgerows eventually grow into an interconnected network of forest and agricultural land, collecting the remaining houses into a set of distinct, vital neighbourhoods.

In collaboration with David Fletcher (FletcherStudio)

Brennan Buck is a critic at the Yale School of Architecture and principal at FreelandBuck in New York. His writing and editing focuses on architectural technologies and their associated aesthetic culture.

David Freeland is design faculty at the Southern California Institute of Architecture (SCI-Arc) and principal at the Los Angeles office of FreelandBuck. His research and writing focuses on the effects of technology on the discipline and conventions of architecture.

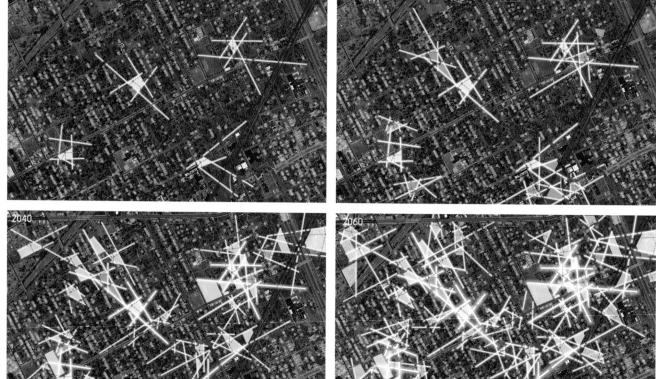

Growth: Beginning as a set of star-like ecological nodes, the hedgerows eventually grow into an interconnected network of forest and agricultural land.

Rural Land-use: Newly defined open parcels are rededicated for community gardens, commercial agriculture or successional forest.

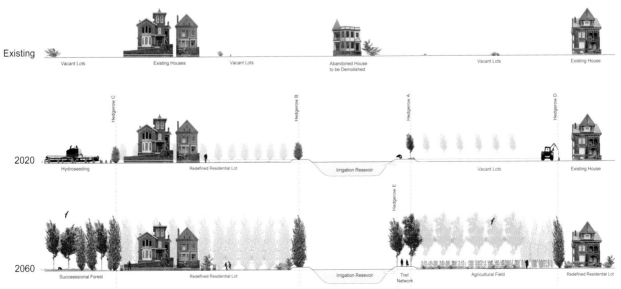

New boundaries: The hedgerows redefine the territory of the city, scaling up the existing pattern of property ownership to suit the collapsing population.

FREE ZONING

Georg Rafailidis + Stephanie Davidson

Central park plaza strip mall: view from front and side.

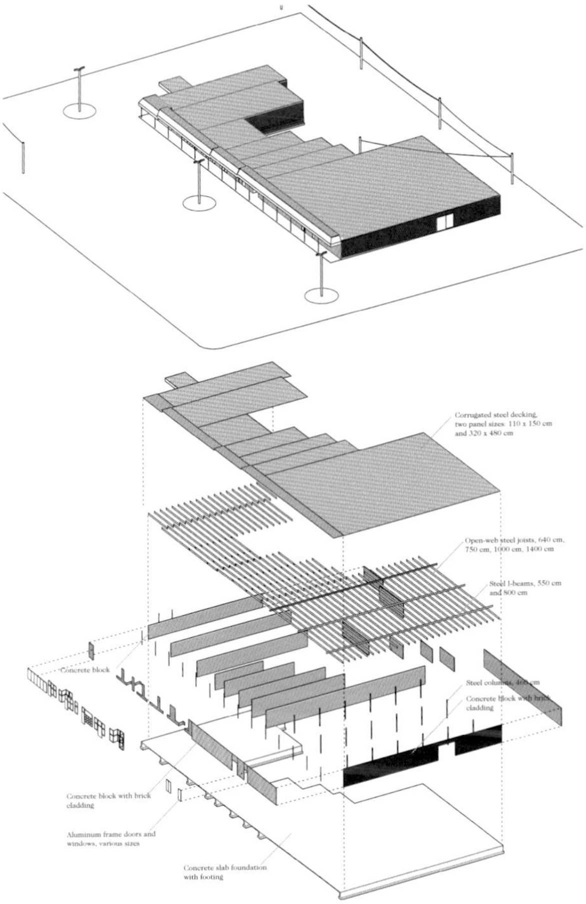
Corrugated steel decking, two panel sizes: 110 x 150 cm and 320 x 480 cm
Open-web steel joists, 640 cm, 750 cm, 1000 cm, 1400 cm
Steel I-beams, 550 cm and 800 cm
Concrete block
Steel columns, 400 cm
Concrete block with brick cladding
Concrete block with brick cladding
Aluminum frame doors and windows, various sizes
Concrete slab foundation with footing

Existing strip mall: disassembled into individual building components.

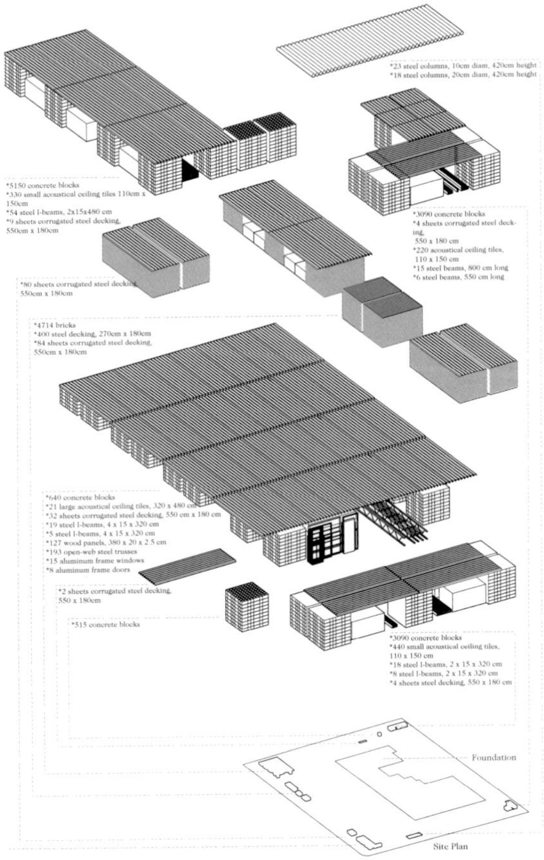
*23 steel columns, 10cm diam, 420cm height
*18 steel columns, 20cm diam, 420cm height
*5150 concrete blocks
*330 small acoustical ceiling tiles 110cm x 150cm
*54 steel I-beams, 2x15x480 cm
*9 sheets corrugated steel decking, 550cm x 180cm
*3090 concrete blocks
*4 sheets corrugated steel decking, 550 x 180 cm
*220 acoustical ceiling tiles, 110 x 150 cm
*15 steel beams, 800 cm long
*6 steel beams, 550 cm long
*80 sheets corrugated steel decking 550cm x 180cm
*4714 bricks
*400 steel decking, 270cm x 180cm
*84 sheets corrugated steel decking, 550cm x 180cm
*640 concrete blocks
*21 large acoustical ceiling tiles, 320 x 480 cm
*32 sheets corrugated steel decking, 550 cm x 180 cm
*19 steel I-beams, 4 x 15 x 320 cm
*5 steel I-beams, 4 x 15 x 320 cm
*127 wood panels, 380 x 20 x 2.5 cm
*193 open-web steel trusses
*15 aluminum frame windows
*8 aluminum frame doors
*2 sheets corrugated steel decking, 550 x 180cm
*515 concrete blocks
*3090 concrete blocks
*440 small acoustical ceiling tiles, 110 x 150 cm
*18 steel I-beams, 2 x 15 x 320 cm
*8 steel I-beams, 2 x 15 x 320 cm
*4 sheets steel decking, 550 x 180 cm
Foundation
Site Plan

Building component: inventory and storage.

Contemporary architecture projects are typically triggered by and tailored to specific uses, business plans, building codes and immediate economic interests. These project triggers are increasingly time-specific and dynamic, and often result in shortened lifespans for particular building uses. A quick succession of programs, changing building codes, updating mechanical services, economic shifts, land banking, are all forces that challenge buildings over time. Now more than ever, buildings are outliving their intended use.

On average, retail typologies change every ten to fifteen years. Architects, planners and administrators are struggling to acknowledge and reconcile the rift between the lifespan of buildings and their original use. When buildings no longer meet the spatial demands of their use, they are often abandoned, offered as leftovers for an "adaptive reuse" project, or simply demolished.

Central Park Plaza exemplifies this increasingly common rift between the lifespan of a building and its use. It is a derelict strip mall in Buffalo, New York which has been vacant for years, its vandalized shell is now an infamous site of crime and illicit activity. Built in 1957, partly on the site of a former rock quarry and partly on forested land, the strip mall thrived for the typical time span of fifteen years before it predictably lost its retail appeal. The City of Buffalo however, still treats its demise as an unfortunate, unforeseen event. The repeated searches for a commercial developer only underscore the inability to understand the changed economic, social and political context for typologies such as the strip mall, which are spatially inflexible and typologically outdated.

Central Park Plaza is typical of a new form of architecture that emerged in the second half of the 20th century. The plaza depends on mechanical services to produce vast and unusually deep spaces that don't rely on natural ventilation or lighting. The high running costs of mechanical ventilation, air conditioning and around-the-clock lighting were easily met by the large revenues these businesses initially produced. Ideally, after one or two decades, when the business model fulfilled its ambition and a new retail typology replaced the former one, this architecture would disappear. But of course the plaza did not disappear. It continues to exist with permanent construction materials: bricks, steel, wood, concrete, pipes etc. However, the mall cannot be used in its current form because it depends on high running costs of its mechanized space.

The question emerges: how can the intrinsic tension between the physical endurance of architecture and the fast-paced rhythm of business models be channeled into productive development? What is a viable way to re-use or re-interpret buildings such as strip malls?

In exploring these questions, two basic strategies were established. First, it is instrumental to define the whole site as a quarry of existing building materials. Central Park Plaza has no spatial value in its current form. Its value lies rather in its building components, its capable foundation and its infrastructural connections to city services (water, sewer, gas, telecommunications and electricity). The Central Park Plaza site could become a "zone of radical deregulation". Instead of limiting the site to one particular zoning constraint, deregulation would trigger a radical reconfiguration of the existing building components within the footprint of the existing foundation.

With these two guiding principles in place, *Free Zoning* proposes the following measures:

1. All building materials used in constructing the strip mall get dismantled and sorted. They can be used for free for any new building activity on site.
2. Given that the building foundations are the most expensive building element to build as well as to demolish, we propose to use the existing foundation as a seedbed for new construction.
3. All uses are allowed. No zoning variances are required.

Instead of relying on the tradition of a single profit-motivated financial investment, the proposal focuses on flexible ownership and *free zoning*. This model does not require any significant monetary investment. Instead of designing a new form for the strip mall, or proposing a new use, this proposal offers the legal and economic framework in which new form and use can emerge. It is an architectural solution to the lack of capital and other economic constraints plaguing many post-war retail malls. The City of Buffalo, by offering a space with no zoning restrictions or *free zoning*, would be inviting unpredictability, instability and risk. The result could be a new kind of economic and legal zone triggering open-ended typological evolution.

Numerous historic precedents show us how the strategy of imposing fewer formal and use restrictions on a site can spur new growth and complexity. The former state-run amphitheater in Lucca Italy, for instance, became an inhabited part of the city fabric by the interventions of countless independent private citizens who moved into the obsolete structure in the Middle Ages. It was common in Roman and Medieval times for buildings to be used as quarries for new buildings. Existing buildings were viewed afresh, through ambitious acts of re-interpretation.

Many building typologies, such as the strip mall, are becoming obsolete. These buildings are the result of a program-driven approach to architectural design, which tailors a building to a time-specific use. We are faced with a proliferation of obsolete, vacant buildings in our built environment. Simultaneously, we should question certain contemporary architectural design practices, which seem to avoid creating buildings that are physically able to house activities for many years, but are spatially unable to accommodate new activities. In addition to fulfilling a client's demand, designs should be evaluated as future ruins.

While architectural design shifts towards the design of spaces rather than the design for programs, a strategy like *Free Zoning* shows how the remaining lifespan of the materials in these obsolete buildings can be exploited if the economic and political framework for building activity is made less restrictive. *Free Zoning's* ambition is to transform the quasi-architecture of the strip mall into a dynamic and evolving process of construction and program, to create something radically new with what is already at hand.

Project Staff: Stephanie Davidson, Jia Ma.

Georg Rafailidis is a licensed architect in Germany and the EU and an Assistant Professor in architecture at the State University of New York at Buffalo.

Stephanie Davidson is trained in fine arts and architecture and is a Clinical Assistant Professor in architecture at the State University of New York at Buffalo.

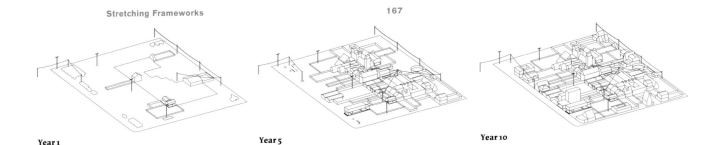

Year 1   **Year 5**   **Year 10**

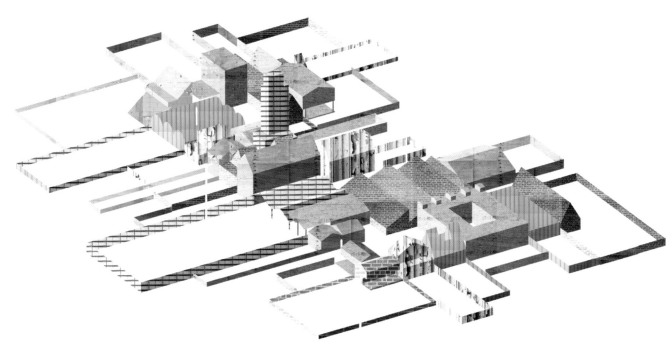

Year 25

Potential new urban build-up: Resurrecting the spirit of the late 1800's American Frontier, the *Free Zoning* plot offers an open invitation to potential inhabitants to build. This series of illustrations shows how the plot might develop over time, with a wide variety of functions and building typologies, all primarily constructed with the salvage material from the strip mall.

0-5 Years: a handful of small buildings are constructed around the perimeter of the foundation of the former strip mall using salvaged materials from the mall demolition. Building activity continues to be focused on the existing foundation edge, close to utility hook-ups and inhabitants demarcate private yards in the asphault parking lot.

After 1 year: a handful of small buildings are constructed around the perimeter of the foundation of the former strip mall using salvaged materials from the mall demolition. Building activity continues to be focused on the existing foundation edge, close to utility hook-ups and inhabitants demarcate private yards in the parking lot.

5-10 Years: The area of the former strip mall foundation has been saturated with a high density of new buildings. Alleyways, pedestrian paths and parking spaces are organized as each building is added to the cluster. The community takes on a village quality, because of its small scale, high density and wide range of programs.

After 25 years: the site of the former strip mall and parking lot is saturated by a wide range of building typologies and functions. It is a dense, lively, ad hoc urban fabric unlike anywhere else in the city.

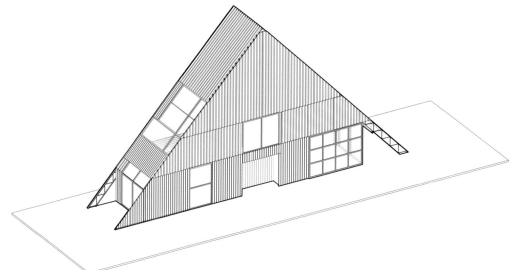

This small house is a little case study looking at what kind of dwelling could be constructed using a strict material palette of strip mall salvage.

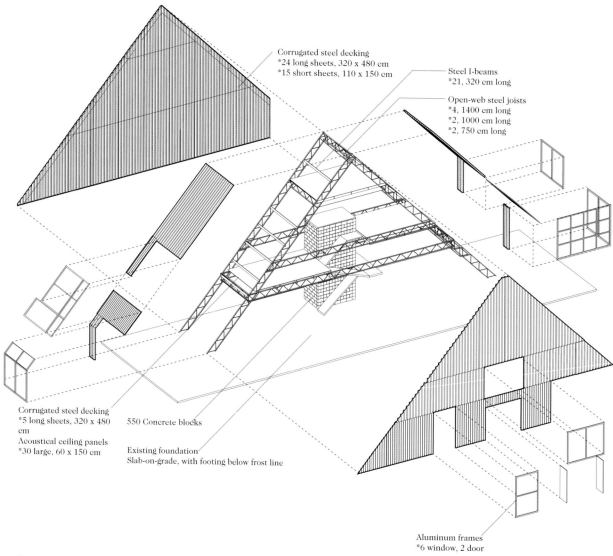

Corrugated steel decking
*24 long sheets, 320 x 480 cm
*15 short sheets, 110 x 150 cm

Steel I-beams
*21, 320 cm long

Open-web steel joists
*4, 1400 cm long
*2, 1000 cm long
*2, 750 cm long

Corrugated steel decking
*5 long sheets, 320 x 480 cm
Acoustical ceiling panels
*30 large, 60 x 150 cm

550 Concrete blocks

Existing foundation
Slab-on-grade, with footing below frost line

Aluminum frames
*6 window, 2 door

Sample transformation: Small House Built Using Strip Mall Building Components

MORPHING
MANHATTANISM

Jonathan A. Scelsa

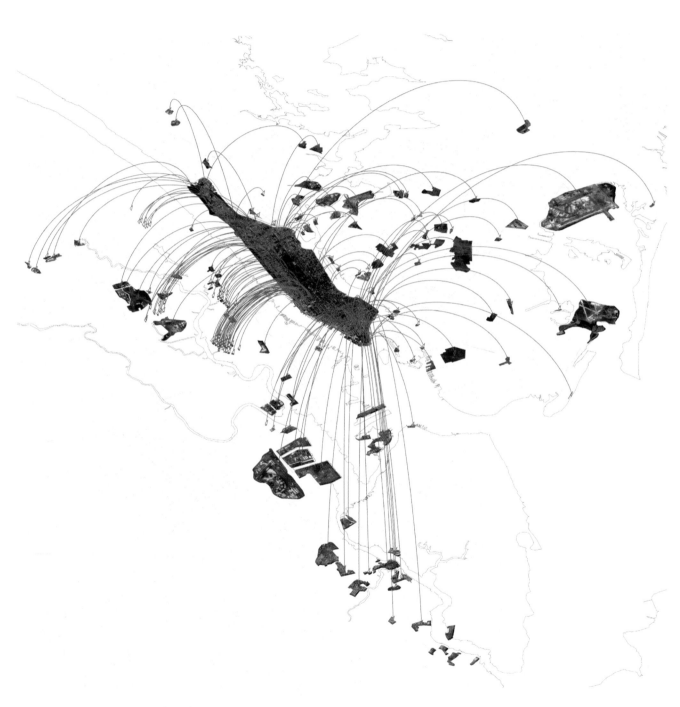

Hierarchical establishment: The paradigm of
Manhattanism oversaw the expulsion of many parts
of the urban equation from the center of the city,
establishing a hierarchical regional geography. The
project of the twenty-first century will be the dispersal
of these externalities via infrastructure, provoking a
more inter-regional continuum.

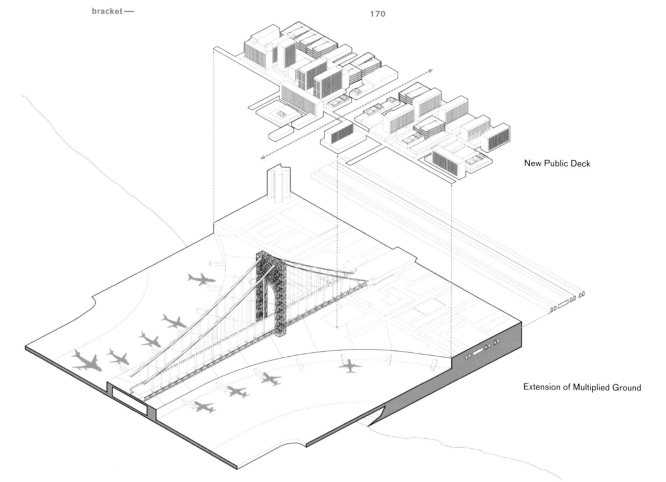

New Public Deck

Extension of Multiplied Ground

Laminated zoomscape: The bridge becomes the object via its verticality and is simultaneously the Megaform in its ability to inflect and catalyze the horizontal plane of the city.

Manhattanism is over. The paradigm that produced the skyscraper; the delirious grid of New York; the extremity of urban density; the congestion that in turn bred a heightened geographic exclusivity, is a dead paradigm.[1] The urbanization of places of finite geography, such as islands, deltas, and archipelagos has established certain social and political hierarchies endemic to a center-periphery relationship. It is this exclusivity of finite geography that pushes the detritus of urbanization out to the periphery, claiming the center for the promise of a few. Despite the rapid horizontal growth of cities in recent years, historic centers have clung to the center-periphery relationship embodied in Manhattanism and refuse to embrace the overwhelming inevitability of the Megalopolis or inter-regional city.[2] In the face of the inevitability of the continuous city, it is time to confront the exclusivity and social division that finite geography has wrought. We must empower a new urban player—not the verticality of Manhattanism but a horizontal mega-formal nature.[3]

The bridge is the vessel for this new paradigm. The bridge has the ability to undermine the discreteness of natural geography and impose an urban order at the inter-regional scale. The 19th century city was established around the commerce of the port of arrival and was therefore built at the confluence of waterways. Goods would meet piers and then be released into a land-based road network. This process sculpted the development and urban morphology of many American cities and is registered in the chaotic gridding of lower Manhattan as well as its gridiron north of Houston Street.[4] The densification of the finite geography at the center of the historic city led to the expulsion of larger land-uses and blue-collar industry to its periphery. In turn, bridges were manufactured to facilitate the overland importation of goods and services previously externalized to the hinterlands. With this center-periphery condition came class divisions and extreme social separation that are exemplified in contemporary Manhattan as well as many other North American cities. In order to subvert these divisions, we must envisage a new player capable of recapturing the pieces of urbanism that have been cast out of paradise.

1. Koolhaas, Rem. *Delirious New York: A Retroactive Manifesto for Manhattan.* (New York: Monacelli, 1994),Print.
2. Gottmann, Jean. *Megalopolis; the Urbanized Northeastern Seaboard of the United States.* (New York: Twentieth Century Fund, 1961), Print.
3. Frampton, Kenneth. *Megaform as Urban Landscape.* Ann Arbor, MI: University of Michigan, A. Alfred Taubman College of Architecture Urban Planning, 1999. Print.
4. Gandelsonas, Mario. *X-urbanism: Architecture and the American City.* (New York: Princeton Architectural, 1999), Print.

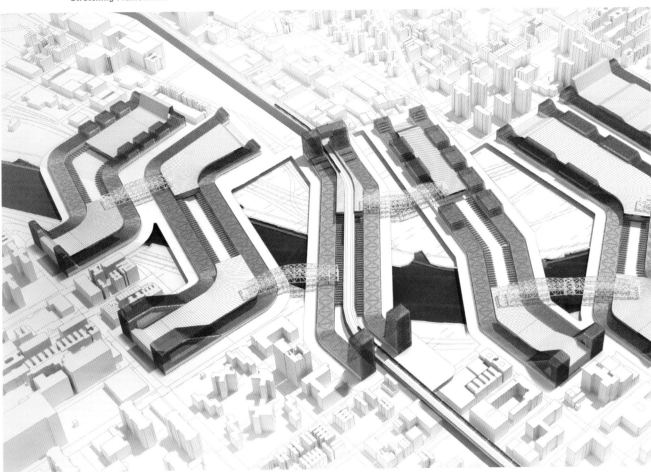

The bridge: as a device for urbanism allows a reposition-
ing of various infrastructural elements of the city—the
market, distribution housing—and questions the edge
of the city. Shown above the Harlem River in between
East Harlem of Manhattan and Mott Haven of the Bronx.

Morphing Manhattanism argues for the use of the bridge
as a device to promote inter-regionalism in lieu of the isolationism resultant from Manhattanism. Formally, the bridge has
always been an emblem or an icon of a regionalist project.
The sight of the bridge serves as a reminder that the city is
part of a larger interconnected web of urban life.

The bridge, as a piece of infrastructure, is a totality
composed of three discrete formal parts: the *emergence*, the
incline and the *object*. Each of these components perform
distinct roles in forming our perception of the city-region, and
together create a world that is both in and out of the city.

The *emergence* is the moment in the bridge when it is
neither a completely constructed geography nor a part of its
immediate ground surface context. At this moment, the bridge
is able to invigorate the area around it by catalyzing growth
and connections within the existing urban fabric.

The *incline* is the point of detachment from the city, when
the bridge is an oblique plane that carries users over the land-
divide. The incline marks the moment of the bridge's separation from land and introduces the threshold of another world.
Here, the occupant of the bridge is locked into a journey of
vehicular one-way traffic within the bridge's structural cage
and separated from the familiar buildings and geography.

The third component is the *object*, the center of the bridge-
world that is completely removed from land. Several bridges

have asserted objecthood through their vertical structural
piers built to suspend the vehicular deck with tension cables.
Historically these piers have been formed as monumental
arches signifying the threshold of departure from terra firma
to new land.

In this new urban paradigm, the *object* houses the cast-
away programs and land-uses of forgotten hinterland urbanism. The concourse of the object is the exposition of a new
type of urban geography, bringing thousands of users to the
nexus and hinge-point of inter-regionalism. This new space
for the public, neither in one land-mass or the other, creates a
viewing platform to visually compress the disjointed city into a
singular image of unified urban geography. These three parts
allow the deconstruction of natural geography both literally,
via its constructed linkage, and metaphorically through its
method of blurring together two distinct worlds within the
panorama of the city.

As Manhattanism ends, so too does the need for density
via verticality. New archetypes emerge for an inter-regional
order, linked by mobility corridors such as bridges and
highways. The airport, as a key economic generator is pulled
from the hinterlands and hung over the divided geography
of the Hudson River. The service industry, of food goods
and wholesale markets historically a part of the river-way
and later expelled into smaller ex-urban economies, is pulled

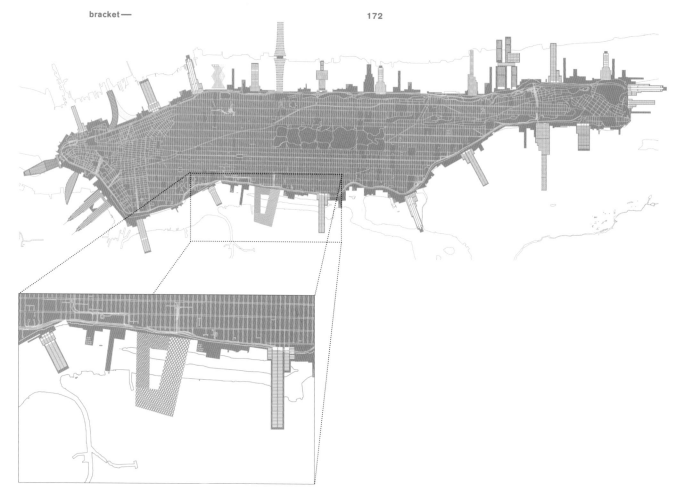

The island as a world into itself: is no longer a world;
it is enervated by the straps that bear it and diffuses the
energy into the cosmopolis beyond.

back and placed at the nexus of the flatland Harlem Riverbed as a Market Bridge. This commerce center enlivens the corridor in-between formerly separate municipalities, reusing the existing river-way rail transport. This logistic landscape includes programs and markets, creating new public space between formerly segregated urban boroughs.[5] The mega-mall, previously a gargantuan box in suburbia, now emerges from the commercial downtown and bridges the water into its surrounding boroughs. The Olympic parks and stadium spaces that had been pushed out of the city are now housed on the river, serving as event destinations to join neighbours. A new sense of urban geography is created, blurring the boundaries of the city by creating shared nexus points within a larger urban continuum.

The bridge is no longer a zoom-scape between two discrete places. It is now an urban event space; a place that reminds us of natural geography by lifting us to engage in the perception of the city as a whole, while simultaneously denying the shortcomings of ground condition in its ability to house larger programs and operate on the edges of the city.

The bridge now sits poised to be key player uniting the region, programmatically, physically and infrastructurally.[6] This new role for the bridge reduces Manhattan to a piece of a greater Megalopolis rejecting isolationism in favor of an interregional perspective, marking it as part of a dispersed world.

The island is broken; its shores have been breached.

The essay and images associated with Morphing Manhattanism *were created in the New Geographies Research Lab at Harvard University under the guidance of Professor Hashim Sarkis.*

Jonathan A. Scelsa's practice, OP/Arch-Land, focuses on the design of interventions in the public realm that are simultaneously autonomous and contextual, such as the bridge. Additionally, Jonathan is a Design Critic at RISD and an Adjunct Assistant Professor at the Spitzer School of Architecture, CUNY.

5. Waldheim, C., and A. Berger. "Logistics Landscape." *Landscape Journal* 27.2 (2008): 219-46. Print.
6. Sarkis, Hashim. "New Grographies: Notes on an Emerging Aesthetic." *New Geographies*. Ed. Neyran Turan. Cambridge, MA: Harvard University Graduate School of Design, 2008. N. pag. Print.

The bridge houses infrastructure: larger then that which fits within the confines of the gridded history city. It works a-hierarchically to serve both sides of the water and provides a social meeting ground amid a logistic landscape.

THE
SOPHISTICATED HUT

Jordan Carver + Andy Vann

A Not-So-Primitive Hut: Tax havenry as a spatial practice.

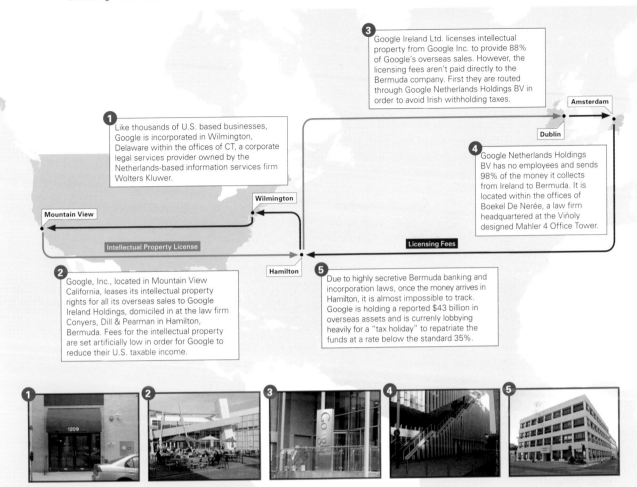

1 Like thousands of U.S. based businesses, Google is incorporated in Wilmington, Delaware within the offices of CT, a corporate legal services provider owned by the Netherlands-based information services firm Wolters Kluwer.

3 Google Ireland Ltd. licenses intellectual property from Google Inc. to provide 88% of Google's overseas sales. However, the licensing fees aren't paid directly to the Bermuda company. First they are routed through Google Netherlands Holdings BV in order to avoid Irish withholding taxes.

4 Google Netherlands Holdings BV has no employees and sends 98% of the money it collects from Ireland to Bermuda. It is located within the offices of Boekel De Nerée, a law firm headquartered at the Viñoly designed Mahler 4 Office Tower.

2 Google, Inc., located in Mountain View California, leases its intellectual property rights for all its overseas sales to Google Ireland Holdings, domiciled in at the law firm Conyers, Dill & Pearman in Hamilton, Bermuda. Fees for the intellectual property are set artificially low in order for Google to reduce their U.S. taxable income.

5 Due to highly secretive Bermuda banking and incorporation laws, once the money arrives in Hamilton, it is almost impossible to track. Google is holding a reported $43 billion in overseas assets and is currenly lobbying heavily for a "tax holiday" to repatriate the funds at a rate below the standard 35%.

Amsterdam
Dublin
Mountain View
Wilmington
Intellectual Property License
Licensing Fees
Hamilton

The Dutch Sandwich.

You've got a building in the Cayman Islands that supposedly houses 12,000 corporations. That's either the biggest building or the biggest tax scam on record.[1]
— Presidential candidate Barack Obama

It would not be a stretch to say that the history of civilization runs concurrent with the history of taxation. For as long as there have been forms of governance, there have been ways to levy taxes in support of them. No government works for free and every empire needs its roads. In the same breath, we can also say, that as long as there have been systems of taxation, there have been those trying to undermine it.

Today, the practice of tax havenry has become a distinctly spatial practice. Increasingly instantaneous technologies of communication, complex international juridical structures, inter-governmental competition, and the lack of a supranational sovereign power contributes to making the practice of tax havenry a commonplace occurrence in the global business world.[2] This practice is a derivative of the larger

spatial logic applied by contemporary multinationals, that of outsourcing. This approach organizes business as a set of activities to be partitioned, understood separately, and optimized to the fullest extent possible in radically different, customized spaces. This logic allows for businesses to be physically located wherever they want, moving their legal and financial incorporation to nations whose juridical structures have been specifically designed to incentivize such behavior.

The tax haven exists at the extreme edge of globalization and international monetary flows, displacing national systems of taxation and decentering standard business practices.[3] The tax haven can be thought of within similar systems of labor and capital displacement as the maquiladora, the special economic zone, and the territorial lease.[4] The tax haven is the *ur* system that allows all of these spatial and political anomalies to exist. It is the extraterritorial enclave reduced to an address and a series of filings within a sea of paperwork sitting in the basement of a non-descript offshore law firm. The address is of course crucial to the entire equation. The tax haven is

1. Comment made during a Presidential debate in Manchester, NH. January 5, 2008.
2. According to Dominique Strauss-Khan, former head of the International Monetary Fund, "More than half of world trade passes, at least on paper, through tax haven."

3. There is no one definition of a "tax haven" and in fact, the term can be problematic. But here we have used the term as defined by Nicholas Shaxson, from his book *Treasure Islands*, "A tax haven is: a state captured by financial interests from elsewhere."

4. Here systems of finance and banking are understood as a globalized site of production. (See Saskia Sassen's *The Global City: New York, London, Tokyo.*)

twinned with architecture and the two implicitly support each other. Capital needs an address to aim for, it needs a shelter. The territorial aspects and juridical inconsistencies are just as important as the filing cabinet and the mailing address.

Almost by definition the tax haven is a small territory, often either an island, or a nation that operates as an island. The Cayman Islands, Bermuda, Jersey, Luxembourg, and Singapore are all notorious tax shelters. But, in a sense, so is the island of Manhattan and the City of London, that strange city within a city entirely claimed by London's financial services industry. Each financial center is just one node within the global, decentralized network of finance, banking, production and the services that maintain them. The tax haven is a well-worn trope within the public imagination, often thought about within the context of drug money laundering, mob activity, weapons financing, terrorism, clandestine operations, and other nefarious activities. The less exciting truth is that tax havenry is simply an accounting method. It is standard business practice for most large, international corporations. Indeed, the practice of establishing an offshore tax structure *is* international business. They are one and the same. And perhaps most importantly, there is nothing illegal about it.

The revelation in 2011 that presidential candidate Mitt Romney was a habitual tax avoider and patron of tax havens was greeted by the news media with both condemnation and acclaim. He was both vilified for neglecting his social responsibilities, and celebrated as a shrewd businessman, the new ethical model for how a contemporary citizen should act. This recently enflamed debate, however, signals that taxation, as a central political question, mediating individual and collective interests, is again an existential question for our democratic society. As architects, this terrain appears beyond our commonly accepted field of expertise or area of concern. But by examining the tax haven as a spatial type that is intimately connected yet publicly distanced from the more visible corporate headquarters, we will show that architects are implicated in this debate by designing the spaces necessary for the functioning of tax havenry and by lending their symbolic capital to corporations who practice it.

The Dutch Sandwich
In a widely discussed *New York Times* article published in March of 2011, it was reported that General Electric, stalwart of the American image and economy, earned $14.2 billion in profits. Of that, $5.1 billion were reported from its domestic operations. And as April 15th approached, a day of fear and anxiety for many Americans, it appeared their total tax liability was not just zero, but G.E. had managed to claim a $3.2 billion tax benefit.[5] John Samuels, head of G.E.'s tax department and former treasury department official was able to effectively flip their tax liability by funneling their corporate profits

through a series of tax breaks and legal tax avoidance legislation towards offshore financial centers specifically established for companies and wealthy individuals to avoid taxation.

A few months earlier Jesse Drucker, a reporter from Bloomberg News who often writes of corporate tax evasion, broke a similar story concerning Google's tax avoidance techniques. Through a sophisticated tax maneuver colourfully known as the "Dutch sandwich" or "double Irish", Google, whose unofficial corporate slogan is "don't be evil",[6] has managed to reduce its tax liability by $3.1 billion over the last three years by reducing its overseas corporate tax rate to just 2.4 percent. By contrast the US corporate tax rate is 35 percent and in the United Kingdom, Google's second largest market by revenue, it is 28 percent.[7]

The process of setting up international subsidiaries and moving capital across several different sovereign jurisdictions is, by necessity, highly complex and confusing. Taxation, as it is currently structured in the United States, is predicated on a notoriously complicated tax code set up to create small widows where enormous amounts of money can easily flow. These small windows where laws misalign and tax codes become blurry, are where the tax policy of the United States seamlessly blends into a spatial network of offshore banking and finance.

Spatial Logics of the Googleplex
By now, it's almost common knowledge that Google is symbolically headquartered at the GooglePlex in Mountain View, California, in the middle of Silicon Valley. The core of the Googleplex is the former SGI Graphics campus, purchased by Google and retrofitted in 2003 by Clive Wilkinson Architects. The *Plex*, as it is known, is the most famous of tech campuses; it is an architectural manifestation of the Silicon Valley image and philosophy. Cafes occasionally interrupt open, vibrant workspaces where workers sit atop rubber exercise balls. Employees are encouraged to take advantage of the Plex's numerous gyms and workout facilities, as well as the free laundromat. Within GooglePlex, work is now overcoded with "experiences." The once holy separation of the work-life dichotomy, not to mention the eight-hour working day, is effectively shattered in this supposedly relaxed and creative environment.[8]

What matters at the GooglePlex is on the inside; its exterior is rather unremarkable. Its green spaces, eating areas and corporate sculptures are not out of place in the typical corporate campus. This absolute emphasis on the interior, with near total disregard for the exterior, marks a pinnacle in the development of corporate architecture since its shift away from designing for Fordist models of production. The heroic architect, as embodied in figures like Kahn, Mies van der Rohe, and Bunshaft is here replaced with the heroic interior

5. Kocieniewski, David. "G.E.'s Strategies Let it Avoid Taxes Altogether." *The New York Times.* 24 March 2011.

6. Google's unofficial "Don't Be Evil" motto was initially formulated as a cynical response to the perceived phoniness of corporate discussions on citizenship, values, and overall corporate responsibility at Google. For an in-depth telling of this allegory see Steven Levy's *In the Plex: How Google Thinks, Works, and Shapes Our Lives,* 2011

7. Drucker, Jesse. "Google 2.4% Rate Shows How $60 Billion Lost to Loopholes." Bloomberg. 21 Oct 2010. Web. <http://www.bloomberg.com/news/2010-10-21/google-2-4-rate-shows-how-60-billion-u-s-revenue-lost-to-tax-loopholes.html>

8. For an longer discussion on the corporate culture promoted by Google through the organizational logic of the GooglePlex see Steven Levy's *In the Plex: How Google Thinks, Works, and Shapes Our Lives,* (New York: Simon and Schuster, 2011)

architect, Clive Wilkinson. Consequently, the model of the corporate campus is accepted as is, and is simply retrofitted. Somewhat paradoxically, it's Google's concentration on the interior, its focus on human relations and the materialization of a post-Fordist model of production, which becomes its representation to the exterior.

The formal design of the GooglePlex produces symbolic capital for Google. Its place-making and architecture communicate its corporate philosophy of focused, yet emancipated creativity, its desire to foster a horizontal, less hierarchical workplace organization, and its quasi-spiritual "Don't Be Evil" ethic.[9] However, this contemporary model displaces and attempts to cover over some of the less-savory practices of business that must still go on in the pursuit of profit. While Google may be spiritually domiciled at the Googleplex, its true heart lies in a stodgy law firm taking up three floors of a converted parking garage in central Hamilton, Bermuda.

Paradis Fiscal

Bermuda markets itself in the traditional manner of an island paradise, and indeed sits counter to the image of a metropolis. Beautiful beaches line its shores, luxury yachts fill its harbours, and its picturesque Front Street is lined with palms and pastel-hued colonial style buildings. There is even a contented, easy-going character to the islands' business culture, known for their infamous Bermuda shorts. Outside the tourist set, Bermuda also markets itself as a paradise by way of the French term for tax haven, *paradis fiscal*. The island is a paradise for capital. Financial profits from around the world are legally funneled here in order to avoid the burden of taxation from "high-tax jurisdictions" located onshore. This paradisiacal relationship to international business centers makes the sleepy capital of Hamilton one of the most important financial outposts in the world.

Bermuda is technically an Overseas Territory of the United Kingdom located in the middle of the Atlantic Ocean over 1,000 km from the nearest land mass, yet it is easily reachable by plane from either New York or London. As an Overseas Territory, it is able to craft its own internal laws while benefitting from a close economic relationship and the protection of the UK. This island nation, with a population of 60,000 is home to nearly 20,000 corporations, the overwhelming majority of them foreign-owned. Business legislation in Bermuda has made this corporate friendly attitude into public policy with the creation of a special entity: the foreign-owned, Bermuda-domiciled corporation. Consequentially, the island nation is now home to a wealth of expertise with regards to the founding and operation of these special entities. As a result, three-quarters of the top 500 U.S. companies have captives and subsidiaries based in Bermuda. The benefit these companies receive includes no corporate

income tax and strong secrecy laws, allowing money to easily enter, and be hidden from outside oversight.

There are, however, minimum requirements that companies must fulfill, in order to be in accordance with Bermuda's incorporation laws. It is within these laws where the formal language of the tax shelter manifests itself in very subtle architectural details. Importantly each business is required to maintain a registered office. Yet this office is almost always that of an acting agent, designated by the subsidiary, usually a law firm. By law, the acting agent for one company can be the same for an unlimited number of other subsidiaries. Following this logic, a single office space can be the head office for thousands of Bermuda-domiciled subsidiaries of multinational corporations. And indeed, this is exactly what happens. This effectively reducies the technical office space to the width of a piece of paper, slipped into a filing cabinet and stored onsite.

The largest and most prominent of the Bermuda law firm-cum-subsidy magnet, and Google's firm of choice, is Conyers, Dill & Pearman (CDP). Their worldwide headquarters occupies all five floors of the Clarendon House, at the corner of Par-la-Ville Road and Church Street in central Hamilton (CDP's own subsidiaries also occupy the building). The Clarendon House is rather mundane, a 60,000 square foot concrete and steel building which previously held a warehouse, auto showroom, and parking garage. Purchased by CDP in 1980 it was renovated and redesigned by Fraser Butterworth, a British expat architect and, at the time, partner-in-charge of the local firm OBMI. Headquartered in this building is Google Ireland Holdings, the subsidiary that, in effect, is the end-of-the-line for Google's worldwide profits.

Aside from the stucco façade renovation, the main architectural feature of the Clarendon House is its outdoor atrium, connecting its southern face with the Bank of Bermuda (now HSBC) headquarters. The atrium, first of its kind on the island, symbolically and literally unites the financial and juridical forces into one shared corporate space. Shielding the shared atrium from the Bermudian climate, the techno-enclosure is covered in a rather inelegant space-frame structure, disguising its short span necessities with open-space structural solutions. Atop the frame are inset solar-tinted polycarbonate pyramid-shaped panels. Access to the space is controlled by a steel gate, closed outside of office hours, and topped with polycarbonate facades built to withstand hurricane-force gales. Inside the atrium, sculptures and plastic plants occupy the controlled environment, proposing a shared space with benches and seating, but in actuality providing little more than a back door to both buildings. As a designed space, the atrium defies the circulatory and logistic needs of the buildings, yet unites it with other such spaces that have become to symbolize a specific formation of global financial architecture.[10]

---

9. Google's unofficial "Don't Be Evil" motto was initially formulated as a cynical response to the perceived phoniness of corporate discussions on citizenship, values, and overall corporate responsibility at Google. For an in-depth telling of this allegory see Steven Levy's *In the Plex: How Google Thinks, Works, and Shapes Our Lives* (New York: Simon and Schuster, 2011).

10. For more on the atrium as a symbolic space of global capitalism see Fredric Jameson's book *Postmodernism, or, The Cultural Logic of Late Capitalism*. While the atrium space at the Clarendon House is not at all comparable in scale or luxury to that of Portman's Bonaventure Hotel, its seemingly obligatory, useless presence is still symbolically significant.

The building was redesigned— in recognition of CDP's expanding involvement in global corporations. The redesign took advantage of the structural steel skeleton of the existing building, necessary for the housing of large quantities of paperwork and filing cabinets. The major design moves included adding a fourth and fifth floor, in addition to the complete façade makeover. At the time of renovation, CDP had over fifty years of experience practicing tax law in Bermuda and were able to pair this experience with specific needs in running an international firm dedicated to foreign-domiciled companies.

If the interior design of the GooglePlex embodies the image of Silicone Valley and its entrepreneurial spirit, the Clarendon House is a physical manifestation of the spatial production of global finance. While the GooglePlex is organized according to a contemporary, post-Fordist model of production, the Clarendon House is organized specifically according to the local legal regulations and requirements that allow global finance to sidestep the inconvenience of taxation. The Clarendon House is an amalgam of the sparse efficiency of the parking garage, matched with the wood panels of the corporate boardroom, effectively becoming a parking garage for international business.[11]

The interior layout of the office follows the logic predetermined by Bermudian subsidiary law. Of the few restrictions, the most prominent is a requirement for each domiciled business to hold annual board meetings at their address of domicile. The core and shell building has been fit with numerous boardrooms allowing for many of the thousands of domiciled companies to fulfill their annual requirements at any one time. The boardroom thus becomes the major organizing principle of the Bermuda law firm. Quite often firms have entire floors given up to rows of boardrooms, each wrapped in sound insulating materials, and fitted with high-speed data connections to enable trans-global board meetings between local lawyers and representatives on site with CEOs in other global cities.[12,13] Occupying a central location both in its physical layout and its spiritual *raison d'etre*, it is possible to understand the remaining spaces of the firm in service to the boardroom. Along with the overwhelming presence of the boardroom, there are other companies that need a more permanent and private "headquarters." The result is little more than a small room outfitted with a computer and telephone, the sign on the door noting the particular firm who has it reserved for the time being.[14]

There is one last architectural trace of the existence of the giant multinational subsidiaries inhabiting these small offices: the vault. The Clarendon House, like other law practices in Bermuda, must keep a physical paper trail of its subsidiary documentation. Located deep beneath the Clarendon House is a room surrounded by one-metre thick concrete walls housing important papers, servers and back up data. The vault is, in essence, the end of the paper trail starting in Mountain View, and countless other offices worldwide. The logistics of the tax shelter is that of file management and proper data organization and it comes to rest in a subterranean vault impervious to natural disaster. The vault provides a secure storage facility but the fault lines of tax law are located within the documentation it contains. And it is these very fault lines that are exploited to the tune of billions of dollars in taxes deferred.

Globalized Spatial Practices

A spatial analysis of the contemporary multinational corporation produces a reading of the principal spatial logic through which it operates, that of outsourcing. The tax haven is a radical spatial product of this very same logic. The accounting and financialization of a multinational's books is effectively outsourced to other jurisdictions, like Bermuda, that optimize them for the sake of efficiency. From the perspective of capital, this outsourcing efficiently minimizes the "friction" created by taxation, and allows capital to finance business operations without the "burden" of regulations. In order to outsource these ephemeral monetary flows, however, physical traces must exist, and in the case of Google, the Clarendon House stands as that trace. In this banal office building on an island outpost in the Mid-Atlantic, Google effectively dodges U.S. taxation, making it a highly significant node in Google's global network of production.

At the same time that the spatial practice of outsourcing is creating globally dispersed nodes of production, it is also producing global centers of command, which are irrevocably linked to each other. The GooglePlex and Clarendon House, seen from this perspective, are both spatial products of one and the same spatio-financial practice. The two can be understood as equally important spatial manifestations intrinsically linked in the multinational corporation's efforts to reproduce capital, albeit with different roles to play in this pursuit.

The GooglePlex operates as the symbolic headquarters of Google. It represents a climax in the spatialization of the early twenty-first century model of production, one predicated on intellectual capital and the production of intangible services. Its formal aesthetics embodies the "turning inwards" of capital after the fall of the Berlin Wall and subsequent collapse of the Soviet Union.[15] This is evident in the triumph of the interior architect, Clive Wilkinson, in producing what is arguably the most significant corporate space today. Paradoxically, it is this intense focus on the "interior" that becomes Google's most

---

11. Description of the interior layout for the Clarendon house relies primarily on analysis of the drawings provided by OBMI, discussions with Fraser Butterworth, and a brief visit by the authors. We were not allowed to venture into the office, and CDP declined our interview requests.
12. The top floor of the Appleby offices was occupied solely by boardrooms and a kitchen, where invited chefs often provided meals for the meetings. Photography requests were declined.
13. Outside the boardrooms of Wakefield Quinn were installed speakers emitting white noise to provide further privacy.
14. One such office was that of Sovereign Asset Management within the offices of Wakefield Quinn.
15. Francis Fukuyama's 1992 book *The End of History and the Last Man* is a testament to the self-congratulatory nature of neoliberalism after its supposed triumph over socialism, or the territory "outside" of capitalist production. This "turning inward" is marked in architecture and urbanism by the burgeoning growth and symbolic significance of the interior as typified by gated communities, policed malls, and surveilled corporate atriums, all of which, in their defensiveness, nonetheless betray resonant concerns about the specter of the outside.

Googleplex interior: Photo from Clive Wilkinson Architects.

The Clarendon House: Home to thousands of corporate subsidiaries in Central Hamilton, Bermuda.

Atrium: connecting the south façade of the Clarendon House and the former Bank of Bermuda building.

The Wakefield Quinn vault: fireproof room contains mostly subsidiary filing papers and deeds.

symbolic and iconic representation towards the outside.

In contradistinction to its main headquarters, the Clarendon House is decidedly *not* iconic; it possesses no symbolic capital whatsoever. The Clarendon House, however, functions differently, but on an equally important level as the GooglePlex, sheltering the companies' foreign revenue from U.S. taxation. The less-savory financial maneuvers of Google are here displaced from the highly visible landscape of Silicon Valley, to the much more confidential space of Bermuda, drawing little attention from the public and leaving Google's public image unsullied. The Clarendon House is structured and organized in order to directly service these less-savory functions, materializing the legal structures that make tax havenry possible; it is an opportunistic architecture geared towards circumventing legal structures.

These two spaces, each a corporate utopia in its own right, are in fact sides of the same coin and must be examined as existentially linked spaces. As a utopian space designed exclusively for the circulation of capital, the tax haven is an archetypal space of capitalist globalization. And while the effects of outsourcing labor and production can be examined within the rubric of logistics and urbanism, so too must the practices of outsourcing of accounting and legal representation, for these practices have their own forms of urbanization and architectural development.

Architecture, as it is deployed in the logistical maneuver of the tax shelter, shares a structural affinity with other typologies predicated on the movement of goods and services. The tax shelter is the financial equivalent of the commodity transportation center, or the bulk retailer. If the windowless cinderblock expanse of Sam's Club is understood to be an iconic architectural representation for mass consumption, then the banal drop ceiling, beige cubicle, and wood-veneered boardroom of international finance is the perfect expression of instantaneous capital transaction. Neither wants to draw attention to their physical surroundings, focusing solely on cheap goods and expert service. Yet, even in these stripped-down, function-driven spaces, architects still have a hand in making this world possible, even though the image of Architecture, as it is commonly deployed, is an anathema to these spaces.

The specific logistical functioning of global finance might be outside of what is commonly understood as the traditional design narrative. But global financial networks, and their many valences and repercussions, are designed objects, much like the corporate headquarters from which they stem and the offshore financial centers at which they come to rest. And like all designed objects and spaces, architects and designers participate in their conception, implementation and legitimation.

Research for this project was funding by the William Kinne Fellows Traveling Prize, Columbia University Graduate School of Architecture, Planning and Preservation.

Jordan Carver is a writer, researcher, and educator. He is an Adjunct Assistant Professor of Architecture at Columbia GSAPP. His research is concerned with the spaces created where law, economics, and political rhetoric intersect.

Andy Vann is an architect, activist, and researcher based in New YorkCity. He is a co-founder of the collective Public Display of Affect and is an associate professor at the Columbia GSAPP.

PLUS ONE HUNDRED

Elijah Huge, Joyce Hsiang + Bimal Mendis

Island contouring: A gateway to the city of Busan and a new destination for global tourism, Gadeokdo Island introduces visitors to a new form of contour urbanism, where natural and constructed landscapes converge at Plus One Hundred.

As South Korea rapidly urbanizes, its coastline is radically and continually altered by infill, reclamation and extension. As a global center of maritime trade and activity, boasting the largest port in Korea and a continually expanding reclaimed coastline, Busan is literally a city built on water. In the inevitable future of a vast metropolitan region, the coastline of Busan faces extinction. Currently, coastal development expands horizontally at sea level, a relentless matte that isolates the dramatic terrain of the region's mountain peaks within a sea of built development.

Located off the coast of Busan, Gadeokdo Island is situated with views back towards the city's new harbour, the estuary of the Nakdong River, and the expanse of the Pacific Ocean. The proposed masterplan for this nearby island offers the potential for a new paradigm of development as an ecological city of the future.

Existing Coastal Growth Pattern: Reclamation

Conventional coastal development involves reclaiming land from the sea, creating new constructed coastlines while destroying the existing one. This ongoing process of redrawing the coastline continues to dramatically change the experience and ecologies of the Busan Metropolitan Area, making natural coastline an increasingly rare and valuable urban resource. Gadeokdo Island currently reflects, on a small scale, this development pattern: building is concentrated along the coastal zones and areas of low topographical slope thereby creating a strong hard edge between the city and the waterfront, ignoring the mountain peaks, and obliterating the natural coastline.

Rather than mimicking these patterns, *Plus One Hundred* preserves Gadeokdo's natural coastline by creating a new internal water's edge along which to concentrate development.

With a resulting length of developable waterfront that is nearly twice as long as the existing natural coastline, this new urban canal is both part of a larger water management plan and offers a broad variety of urban recreational resources to match the island's rich topography and natural resources.

New Datum

The proposed waterway establishes a new datum for re-territorializing development. Hovering between the mountains and the sea, an urban ring internalizes the coastline as an elevated canal city, circumscribing the island at +100 m, in the transitional zone between coastal and mountaintop eco-systems. This higher elevation of urbanism allows the scenic and environmentally valuable coastline and mountain peaks to remain undeveloped and preserved as future recreational and visual resources: a natural gateway to the international city of Busan. *Plus One Hundred* is both a city and a collection of cities interconnected as an urban ring. Concentrating urban development in an urban ring provides a shared armature for various forms of urban development and allows for the creation of a sustainable, pedestrian-friendly form of local growth.

Urban Ring

Together, the new datum line of development, the interior coastline, and a collection of landscape-based linkages form an urban ring where development, infrastructure, energy and ecology are organized into a dense and well-programmed system used to navigate topography, manage water, and provide infrastructural connections throughout the island. Unlike gridded platting, the ring allows for maximization of the ratio between public infrastructure and private development.

Along the ring, six different mini-cities assume their own identities, referencing universal urban typologies that are locally inflected to accommodate the multiple uses and the diverse local and international users. Multiple development and program possibilities emerge, while local and regional links are created. At the center of this ring, the life and activity of the canal is an analogy for the city itself: a new form of urbanism where natural and constructed landscapes complement each other in a symbiotic relationship.

Nature: from Isolation to Interconnection

If Gadeokdo were to be developed following the existing growth patterns of the larger Busan Metropolitan Area, the mountain peaks would be preserved as individual natural areas, engulfed and cut off from the coast by urban development like islands in a sea. Studies of wildlife habitats have consistently shown that isolated preservation areas suffer from this island effect and are substantially less effective than interconnected preservation areas of comparable size.

A collection of landscape terraces traverses the island's varied topography and provides landscape links between the mountain peak zones and the coastal zones, allowing for natural continuity between and accessibility to this range of habitats. These cultivated natural environments also operate as tools for water management as well as a broad range of recreational and productive land-uses, from parkland to phyto-remediating wetlands and small-scale agricultural plots.

Plus One Hundred uses the island's natural topography to full advantage, rather than treating it as an obstacle to overcome. The project creates a new ecological urban model for Gadeokdo through the preservation of the islands' natural coastline and mountain peaks, the active management of its valuable water resources, and the development of a site-specific urban model that creates both urban density and natural habitat continuity. As a result, the ecological footprint and environmental impact is reduced while the natural experience of the environment is heightened for visitors and residents. Just as the use of water is planned from coast to mountaintop, the terraces provide landscape links between the peak zones and the coastal zones, allowing for continuity and accessibility between varied habitats.

Project Credits: Joyce Hsiang, Elijah Huge & Bimal Mendis with Marc Cucco, Maria Derevencova, Martin Gallovsky, Gary Ku, and Mahdi Sabbagh.

Project Team: Marc Cucco, Mahdi Sabbagh, Gary Ku; Renderings: Maria Derevencova, Martin Gallovsky.

Joyce Hsiang is a founding principal of Plan B Architecture & Urbanism, an interdisciplinary research and design collaborative based in New Haven, CT. She is also a design critic at the Yale School of Architecture.

Elijah Huge is an architect and founder of the design firm Periphery. He is Associate Professor and Director of Studio Art at Wesleyan University where he leads the architecture studio track and the collaborative North Studio design group.

Bimal Mendis is the Assistant Dean, Director of Undergraduate Studies and Assistant Professor, Adjunct, at the Yale School of Architecture and leads studios in urbanism and design.

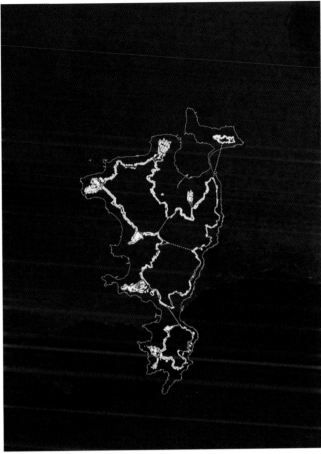

Concentration: Plus One Hundred is both a city and a collection of cities interconnected as an urban ring that circumscribes the island.

Interconnection: A collection of landscape terraces traverses the island's varied topography and provides landscape links between the mountain peak zones and the coastal zones.

Replication: Rather than build over and beyond the existing coastline of Gadeokdo, the proposal preserves the natural coastline and creates a new internal coastline along which to concentrate development.

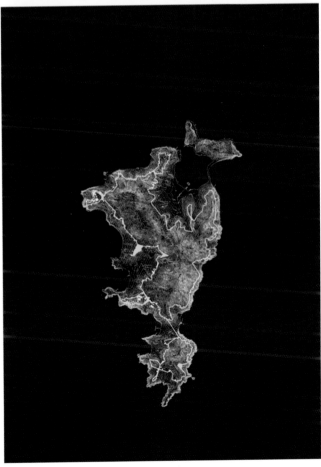

Elevated urbanism: A new internal coastline hovering between the mountains and the sea shore is simultaneously metropolitan and natural, a model for urban ecology.

Canal ring: Encircling the entire island, the canal is a piece of infrastructure that mediates between coastal and mountainous ecosystems, merging recreation, development, and landscape as a walkable linkage of island life.

OBSESSION AS A PROFESSIONAL TRAIT

Fabrizio Gallanti

Good architects should be obsessive, at least to some degree.

Architects' obsession is a psychological trait that is intertwined with the idealization of a role model, a quality almost analogous to the calm under stress that we expect from a surgeon, to the cunningness that we desire from our lawyer, to the endurance that a military has to display. The crystallization and emergence of obsession as one of the principal ingredients of the architect's identity seems to be located at the point of convergence between two historical trajectories: one following the history of architecture and the other tracking the emergence of the figure of the professional through modernity. The first trajectory addresses the prescriptive role of architectural design as it surged at the beginning of the Renaissance, after Leon Battista Alberti. Architects became intellectuals controlling the execution of buildings through abstract tools such as instructions and drawings, as opposed to the Middle Ages when they were builders on site—precision and control became fundamental for their role. The second is the result of the evolution of the social definition and perception of *obsession*; in the late 18th century it was considered as a limited pathology, but gradually came to be understood as a more diffused and sustainable condition.

In Mario Carpo's book, *The Alphabet and the Algorithm*, Alberti is highlighted as marking a fundamental moment of transition in the practice of architecture. In developing a complex set of notational tools, Alberti allows for the transformation of ideas into built matter by assigning sets of instructions to workers.[1] The architect became the central, controlling figure within an expanded field of expertise and knowledge—a field in which precision is paramount. The subsequent shift by Andrea Palladio, from stone cutting to drawing as the tool with which to control architecture, definitively modernized the role of the architect: less a craftsman and increasingly a fully articulated intellectual. In the western tradition of architecture, the project becomes a synthetic instrument that summarizes notions of economy, structural consistency, construction techniques, use of materials, functional program, symbolic expression, and reference to architecture's own historical development. Later, designs were charged with needing to conform to multiple external limitations determined by rules, regulations and consultants' input. All this seems to be an obvious, yet incomplete description of the tasks embedded in each project, from conception to the eventual final realization. If the tendency for precision and design control can be traced back to the Renaissance, it is after industrialization that architecture becomes a professional practice. The surging presence of organizational structures require of the architect not only "creativity", a generic attribute of artistic activities, but focus, precision, attention to detail, capacity for synthesis and a sense of authority.

Parallel to the emergence of new organizational protocols within professions and labor, since the end of the 18th century, the perception of obsession itself starts to change—oscillating between a desirable attribute, characterizing geniuses and good citizens, and its association with madness or other pathological conditions. In Europe and America, during the course of the 19th century, this duality is heightened, as precision, repetition, mechanization and standardization become increasingly valued by society. Contained obsession, which allows for the proper execution of tasks and activities, emerges as a much-needed quality. Since the 19th century, especially in the United States, the rise of a new meritocratic society, where delimitations of class are determined by skills and knowledge, and where the "professional" embodies a new rising social prototype, the thin border between commitment and obsession is constantly shifting.[2]

---

1. Mario Carpo, The Alphabet and the Algorithm (Cambridge, MA: MIT Press, 2011).

2. For an exhaustive history of the cultural and medical notions of obsession see Lennard J. Davis, *Obsession: A History* (Chicago: University of Chicago Press, 2008).

If architects, as professionals, embody within their own modus operandi and obsessive traits, this text explores the life and work of three architects, Livio Vacchini, Juan O'Gorman and Fernand Pouillon, where, in each case, obsession has approached an extreme. For these architects, the boundaries between life and work have collapsed; leaving instead a complex intertwining of ideology, culture, personal proclivities and professional achievements. In each case, the architect produced an autobiographical narrative that serves as the primary source documenting the extreme levels of obsession.

Livio Vacchini and the cult of the copy.

In 1999, Livio Vacchini, one of the main protagonists of the Scuola Ticinese (together with Aurelio Galfetti, Luigi Snozzi and Mario Botta) wrote a short contribution to the *2G* monograph dedicated to showcase 15 houses realized by Craig Ellwood in California in the '50s and '60s.[3] In that text Vacchini narrates how, in search of a suitable master to follow just after graduation, he shifted from Ludwig Mies van der Rohe to Ellwood. Vacchini writes of the epiphany he experienced when discovering Ellwood's work for the first time, inside a Swiss architectural magazine:

> One day a friend of mine put under my nose the second issue (1959) of *Werk: Bauen + Wohnen*. It was dedicated to a California house in Beverly Hills (CSH #16); the architects name was Craig Ellwood. Who was he? I carefully studied the plans. That man had been able to tame the beast! There was a parallelism with Mies' idea for the ground-floor house, but he was freer in opening and closing the perimeter walls, his construction systems were simpler, and he had solved with brilliant ease the practical problems I was also confronting.[4]

The practical problems that Vacchini was confronting were not just those inherent to the exercise of the architectural profession, just at the beginning of his career, but were more personal: in fact he was seeking for guidance in the design of his own house. In the same text Vacchini declares that the revelation generated by the magazine lead him to copy the Ellwood house as a model for his own. The house, built between 1968 and 1969 in Ascona, Switzerland, is described as a permanent laboratory, where, for almost 20 years, Vacchini experimented with continuous transformations and additions. Later in the essay, the author evokes a trip to Los Angeles, to visit the real house, which inspired his endeavor.

Interestingly, the Case Study house published in the issue of *Werk* is not the #16, as described by Vacchini, but the #18. A comparison of the actual plan of Vacchini's house with several of Ellwood's projects does not reveal any direct similarity between an eventual original prototype and the project realized in Switzerland.[5] Vacchini organized the interior plan of his house following a more rigid sequence of singular rooms, served by a longitudinal corridor. What is analogous are several individual features: the frosted façade to the exterior; the steel structure realized using square profiles, (rather than the then current I-beams); the integration of vertical partitions or screens that delimit outdoor and indoor spaces, and the light canopy, sustained by steel profiles that mediates between the interiors and the garden as in the Case Study #18.

The house in Ascona functioned throughout Vacchini's career as a dynamic exploration of expressive and technical questions, deployed through time, and strongly influenced by Ellwood's architectural language. It is a highly refined and intellectualized collage, but not the copy of an idealized original, as claimed by Vacchini. Nevertheless, in his own description of this relationship, Vacchini alters the real facts, thereby elevating his level of rigor and dedication towards recreating an exact copy to an almost mythical quality.

Juan O'Gorman and the ultimate design

The construction of his own image through autobiography was also crucial for the Mexican architect Juan O'Gorman. His progressive disenchantment with the possibility of architecture becoming an instrument of social and political advancement is at the core of his autobiography, published in 1973.[6] O'Gorman oscillated between frequent changes of mood and temper, changing his opinions and ideas over the course of his career. His architectural work during the '30s achieved a bare-boned purist and mechanistic language, essential in his mind, both for meeting the volume of construction needed to respond to the urgent needs of the Mexican proletarians, and for utilizing the building technologies

3. Livio Vacchini, "Craig Ellwood", *2G Craig Ellwood, 15 Casas*, (1999).

4. Livio Vacchini, "Craig Ellwood", *2G Craig Ellwood, 15 Casas*, 12 (1999).

5. Elizabeth Smith, *Case Study Houses* (Köln; New York: Taschen, 2002).

6. Juan O'Gorman, *Autobiografía*, Universidad Nacional Autónoma de México; DGE Equilibrista, 2007.

of the emerging national industries, especially cement.[7] After having realized a series of residential masterpieces, including the joint studio-houses of Diego de Rivera and Frida Kahlo (1931–1932), and realizing twenty-six elementary schools in Mexico City, while serving as director of the architectural office of the Ministry of Education, O'Gorman decided to abandon architecture in 1938, to devote his energies to painting. The escape from architecture was triggered by his perception that modernism was becoming merely a style, adopted by "mercenary" designers to serve greedy developers' needs for quick and cheap construction.

Through his painting and murals, O'Gorman was able to reintroduce a narrative and social notation into architecture. After having experimented with figurative stone mosaics, O' Gorman was asked to integrate his work into the design of the new facilities of the UNAM University in Mexico City in 1949. The large mosaic murals covering the blank facades of the central library, depicting crucial moments in Mexican history, represented the return to the profession.

In a series of conversations taped by the art critic Antonio Luna Arroyo between 1970 and 1972, O'Gorman describes moments of personal and professional crises. He identifies his constant quest for an ethical and political position for architects, almost inevitably thwarted by contextual conditions. The impossibility of bridging the gap between professional practice and his mission for advancing society proved insurmountable. The violent epilogue of O'Gorman's life is the result of a carefully crafted and often discussed project of suicide, where the attention to details and precision in planning, became one last project. On the 18th of January 1982, O'Gorman hanged himself with an electric cable hooked to a tree. While falling from the chair he shot himself in the mouth, and legend notes a bottle of poison ingested as part of a meticulous plan.

Fernand Pouillon and the project against disappearance

It is a declaration of failure that opens the *Mémoires d'un architecte* by French architect Fernand Pouillon.[8] On the night of September 8th, 1962 Pouillon was standing on a gutter outside the window of his room, just above the attic of a villa, used as a health facility. The rope that he braided himself was too short, because of the knots he made to reinforce it. He writes: "we think for a long time of every details, and at the very last moment, we discover that we forgot something elementary".[9] Pouillon was escaping from Ville d'Avray, a psychiatric clinic in Versailles. After jumping from the gutter, he had some time to quietly leave the premises as he had faked his silhouette in the bed putting some bolsters below the blankets and arranging his hair, cut the day before, so as to mimic a head resting on a pillow. He was almost free, after eighteen months of imprisonment, after a real estate scandal exploded in the spring of 1961 around a consortium of building companies and developers, the *Comptoir national du Logement*. Pouillon was fifty years old at the time of the escape. In his autobiography, Pouillon considers March 5th 1961, the day of his arrest and transfer to la Santé prison in Paris, as the end of his career, which started 26 years earlier, in 1935. The text, authored together with his wife Véra, was written in Fiesole, near Florence, where he found refuge after his escape. The text is instrumental in understanding how his previous life and achievements, as one of the most productive architects of post-war France, could have led to his fall. Pouillon was renowned for his classic inspired designs of the large housing complexes: *La Tourette* in Marseille (1949) and the notorious neighbourhood *Climat de France* in Algiers (1953). In many ways, Pouillon incarnated the original model of architect-builder, coming from a commitment to craft rather than an academic background. Acting in total opposition to the architectural language and building techniques of contemporary French architects, he was vehemently ostracized by his colleagues. He was a controversial figure; simultaneously engaging in the communist party and its fight for an independent Algeria while becoming immensely wealthy through cunning entrepreneurial enterprise.

Pouillon, who describes himself as a latter-day Savonarola, fighting for an architecture capable of returning to humanity an "agreeable" environment and therefore opposed to the self-referential game of modern architecture (Gropius, le Corbusier, Perret, Neutra and *L'Architecture d'Aujourd'hui* are among his frequent targets) failed because of his ambition.

---

7. The houses for de Rivera and Kahlo were directly inspired by the Ozenfant studio designed by Le Corbusier in 1923, while the use of bright coloured fields recalls the housing projects in Pessac or the Maison La Roche. The essential language adopted for the elementary schools achieved a level of simplification and tectonical austerity more radical than the European examples it was derived from and already acknowledged by international publications as Esther Born, Justino Fernández, Ernest Born, *The New Architecture in Mexico* (New York: Architectural Record, 1937).

8. Fernand Pouillon, *Mémoires d'un architecte* (Paris: éditions du Seuil, 1968)

9. ibid 9.

It is my ambition, what is often called my megalomania that caused my dishonor. Tiredness, excitation, then exasperation of being incapable of proving in a spectacular way, through multiple examples, that I was right, almost brought me at the border of madness.[10]

This candid admission of a psychiatric condition, follows an extremely precise narration of his life and professional activity. Part legal document and part memoir, the text exudes a fascinating attention for detail, where architecture is mixed with politics, economics, personal life, philosophical outbursts to fellow professionals, intimate wanderings of the mind and concerns for his family.

The book is the transcription of an obsession in restoring Pouillon's name and honor by demonstrating a succession of misjudgments on his part, stemming from his higher goal of providing homes to the people and the more mundane necessity of maintaining a vast system of architectural studios and collateral companies afloat. The tone of the long text includes moments of splendor, where the *grandeur* of Pouillon is almost blinding, and other moments of self-declared victimization; a vicious circle of self-references that drifts into a paranoid doubling of reality, marking a final transition from obsession as a controllable tool.[11]

As is often the case, autobiography, rather than revealing the truth, often uses the past to rearticulate a portrait where personal life, intellectual research and professional activity are fused to sustain an idealized profile. Traits of obsessive behavior often reveal an author's incessant quest for precision and control. The tone of such autobiographies are meant to amend or correct narratives eventually provided by others. For architects such as Pouillon, O'Gorman and Vacchini, the desire for control of their environment and practice is absolute, including the design of the stories of their own lives.

Fabrizio Gallanti has taught architecture in Chile and Italy. He contributes to numerous publications, and was the architecture editor at *Abitare*. He is currently the Associate Director Programs at the Canadian Centre for Architecture in Montreal.

---

10. Pouillon, *Mémoires d'un architecte*, 31.
11. The level of intoxication becomes such that Pouillon republishes in the book the picture of himself dressed in a white smoking with lace-cuffs protruding from his sleeves, that the Ministry of Information diffused on the eve of the arrest to undermine his reputation. In the picture, taken at one of Pouillon's daughters' birthdays, he is accompanied by the architect Gaston Castel, who harbours a visible facial deformation, due to an injury in the First World War. The thin, almost vampire Pouillon's figure and the monstrous head of Castel combine one of the uncanniest party's pictures ever. In the label of the picture, Castel is describes as *gueule cassée* (broken face). In Pouillon, *Mémoires d'un architecte*, 163.

EYES WIDE SHUT: ASTRONOMY IN THE ATACAMA DESERT[1]

Alessandra Ponte

Atop a high tower, as far as possible from Earth, there sits a human being who has altered his eyes through gigantic optical aids in such a way that they are capable of penetrating outer space as far as the most distant stars. In its environment, suns and planets circle at a solemn pace. Even swift-footed light takes millions of years to penetrate this environment space. And yet this whole environment is only a tiny excerpt from Nature, tailored to the capacities of the human subject.
— Jakob von Uexküll, *A Foray into the Worlds of Animals and Humans*, 1934.[2]

Chile, in particular its Atacama Desert's region, has been repeatedly labeled as astronomy's paradise.[3] According to a recent survey, the country currently hosts 42 percent of the world's astronomical observatories and, by 2018, it will be home to 70 percent of global astronomical infrastructure, or, following a different estimate, Chile will engender half of the world's astronomical images by 2025. This attractiveness is largely due to Chile's extraordinary and extreme geography. The Atacama Desert, which covers about 128,000 square kilometres (49,000 sq. mi) of Chile's territory, is the driest and possibly the oldest desert on earth, having experienced hyper-aridity for three million years. With the skies clear for 300 days per year, the average rainfall in the Atacama is a mere 15 mm per year with some of its weather stations never registering a single drop. Situated in the western Andes Mountains, the desert reaches unusual altitudes and does not experience major dust storms. Moreover, the region's widely dispersed settlements guarantee almost nonexistent levels of light pollution and radio interference. Such extreme aridity and minimal pollution create ideal conditions for astronomical observations and it is here that the international scientific community has heavily invested, particularly since the '90s when, with the return to democracy and the stabilization of the political climate, Chile emerged as one of the most secure and flourishing states in South America.[4]

In the words of a representative of the European Southern Observatory (ESO, a 15-nation intergovernmental research federation), economic and political stability are essential to the long-term, significant investments required to install the new generation of gigantic astronomical observatories. In a 2011 interview, ESO's spokesman focused on three schemes located in the Atacama Desert: the Very Large Telescope (VLT) fully operational since 2000; the European Extremely Large Telescope (E-ELT) on which construction begun June 2014; and the Atacama Large Millimeter/Submillimeter Array (ALMA), which at the time was in an advanced phase of development. However the construction of ALMA, the world's largest complex of radio telescopes, which has been working at full capacity since 2013 (even if the last of the antenna arrived in June 2014), required the combined forces of European, North American and East Asian scientific institutions together with the cooperation of the Republic of Chile.[5]

ALMA sits at 5000 metres above sea level, on a vast plateau of the Chilean Andes. The complex is serviced and manned by engineers, technicians, drivers, mechanics and controllers in charge of assuring the

1. The photographs presented here were taken during a fieldtrip and workshop organized by the AA School and titled Chile by Night. Directed by Pedro Ignacio Alonso (School of Architecture, Pontificia Universidad Católica de Chile, Santiago), the workshop took place in January 2013. Tutors and collaborators included: Thomas Weaver (AA School, London), Pilar Cereceda (geographer, Pontificia Universidad Católica de Chile), Francisco Förster and Elise Servajean (astronomers, Universidad de Chile, Santiago), Ignacio Garcia Partarrieu and Arturo Scheidegger (UMWELT architects, Santiago de Chile), and Alessandra Ponte (School of Architecture, Université de Montréal). Special thanks are due to Pedro Ignacio Alonso for gaining access to ALMA, and to Francisco Förster and Elise Servajean for introducing us to the

complexities of astronomy's extreme forms of imaging.
2. Jakob von Uexküll, A Foray into the Worlds of Animals and Humans with A Theory of Meaning, (Streifzüge durch die Umwelten von Tieren und Menschen, 1934), translated by Joseph D. O'Neil, introduction by Dorion Sagan, Afterword by Geoffrey Winthrop-Young, Minneapolis/London: University of Minnesota Press, 2010, p. 133.
3. See for example Why Chile is an astronomer's paradise, Gideon Long, BBC News, July 24, 2011, www.bbc.co.uk/news/world-latin-america-14205720
4. For a beautiful and poetic interpretation of the Atacama Desert as privileged space for astronomy but also as political space of repression and erasure of memory during the Augusto Pinochet's dictatorships, see Nostalgia for the Light (Nostalgia de la Luz), a documentary released in 2010 by Patricio Guzmán.
5. ALMA is funded in Europe by the European Southern Observatory (ESO), in North America by the U.S. National Science Foundation (NSF) in cooperation with the National Research Council of Canada (NRC) and the National Science Council of Taiwan (NSC) and in East Asia by the National Institutes of Natural Sciences (NINS) of Japan in cooperation with the Academia Sinica (AS) in Taiwan. ALMA construction and operations are led on behalf of Europe by ESO, on behalf of North America by the National Radio Astronomy Observatory (NRAO), which is managed by Associated Universities, Inc. (AUI) and on behalf of East Asia by the National Astronomical Observatory of Japan (NAOJ).

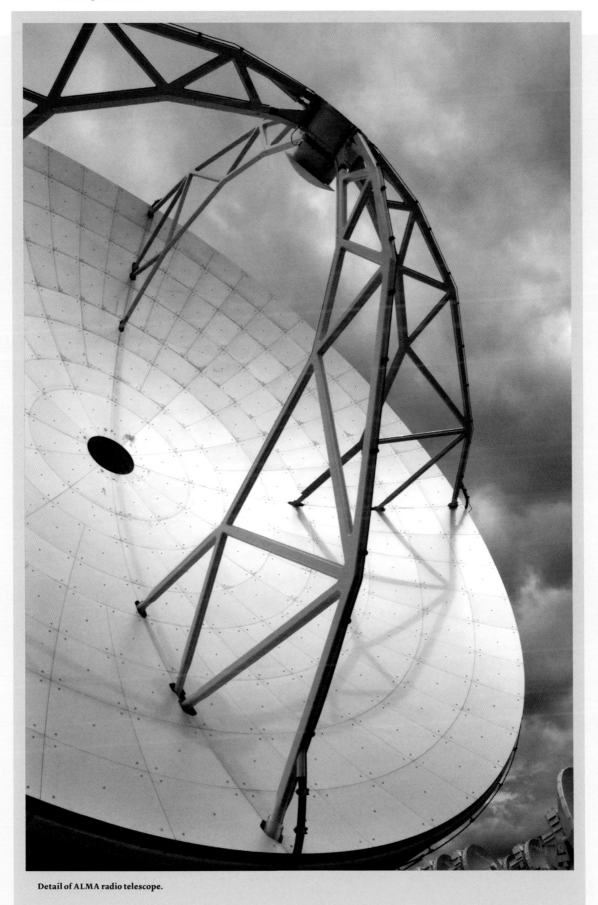

Detail of ALMA radio telescope.

Unobstructed view: The ALMA sits at 5000 metres above sea level on a vast plateau of the Chilean Andes.

smooth flow and processing of astounding amounts of data. While astronomers are able to physically occupy the research station with respiratory support on account of the altitude, they typically sit far away, in remote countries, in front of computer screens transcribing and interpreting information transmitted by ALMA's gigantic "hearing" aids.

Interestingly, astronomers seldom "listen" to the sounds from far-away stars and galaxies which are registered by the sixty-six dish-shaped 12-metre and 7-metre antennas slowly turning around in synchronic movement in an eerie mechanical ballet. Instead, astronomers prefer to look at the strings of numbers digitized by the sensitive receivers that amplify the radio signals collected by the antenna dishes. Astronomers, in collaboration with engineers and artists, then transform, enhance, filter and manipulate data which extremely powerful computers and apposite programs have already screened and altered. The final results are mesmerizing images and animations of cosmic objects and processes beyond any human perception.

ALMA has a resolution ten times bigger than the legendary Hubble Space Telescope, launched into Earth orbit by NASA in 1990. Nevertheless it will be surpassed by the Square Kilometre Array (SKA), projected to be completed by 2024 between South Africa and Australia. According to design, SKA will have 50 times the resolution of ALMA. Of course, much can be said about the severe conditions imposed on humans and machines by the extreme environments in which these

overwhelming and exponentially growing observation technologies are deployed, although even more astonishing is to reflect on how the data they collect is translated, interpreted, presented, and circulated. In fact, what such gigantic apparatuses produce are images, which are posted, almost daily, on the observatory's website, not to speak of innumerable scientific papers, reports, grant applications, research proposals, or works of vulgarization like picture books and calendars.

But what is the character of these images? Clearly they cannot be considered faithful copies, mechanical reproductions, or "objective" representations of cosmic objects and events so fundamentally beyond the grasp of human perception, no matter how technologically enhanced. Looking at these images will requires an even greater act of faith than the one suggested by Bruno Latour in his famous essay on iconophilia:

Iconophilia is respect not for the image itself but for the movement, the passage, the transition from one form of image to another. By contrast, idolatry would be defined by attention to the visual per se. Thus iconoclasm may be defined either as what attacks idolatry or as what destroys iconophilia, two very different goals. Because it seems so difficult to resist the temptation inherent in all images, that is to freeze-frame them, the iconoclast dreams of an unmediated access to truth, of a complete absence of images. But if we follow the path of iconophilia, we should, on the contrary, pay even more respect for the series of transformations for which each image is only

6. Bruno Latour, "How to be Iconophilic in Art, Science, and Religion", in Peter Galison and Caroline A. Jones (eds.), *Picturing Science; Producing Art*, (New York/ London: Routledge, 1998), 421.

Astounding processors: The complex is serviced and manned by engineers and controllers in charge of ensuring the smooth flow of data.

a provisional frame. In other words, we should be iconophilic in all domains at once, in art, in science, and in religion.[6]

Epistemologists Lorraine Daston and Peter Galison define, in the last section of *Objectivity*, a book that retraces the history of the notion of "objectivity" in science, the most recent generation of scientific images as *presentations* rather than *representations*. In their words, in the digital scientific atlases of today (including astronomical ones), images operate as tools, rather than evidences, and are used to make and change things, rather than serving as mere documentations. Digital images are, at least partially, interactive; they can be rotated, correlated, flied through, zoomed, coloured, and cut. Digital images present (rather than represent) in a triple sense: first, instead of portraying what already exists, they become "part of a coming-into-existence"; second, images are "produced to entice—scientifically and entrepreneurially," to promise things that exist only in incomplete or fictional form; and finally, liberated from the constraint of mechanical objectivity, they easily merge with artistic presentation.[7]

Daston and Galison's thesis is revisited, expanded and refined by Elizabeth Kessler in a recent analysis of the spectacular cosmic images "fabricated" with extremely sophisticated digital technologies employed to manipulate and interpret data sent to Earth by the Hubble Space Telescope. Tellingly titled *Picturing the Cosmo: Hubble Space Telescope Images and the Astronomical Sublime*, the study demonstrates how the compelling

images regularly circulated by the astronomic research institutions controlling Hubble operate as a "hybrid of science, art, and public relations." From fragmented signals that need to be carefully separated from noise, to black and white pictures of extremely hazy and distant celestial bodies, teams of engineers, artists, and astronomers produce seductive and colourful images that, as Kessler suggests, are uncannily similar in composition, palette, and visual contrast, to the celebrated "sublime" landscape paintings of the American West realized during the nineteenth century by artists such Albert Bierstadt and Thomas Moran.[8] Astronomers often refer to these sorts of representations as "pretty pictures," a formula implying a negative connotation. Nevertheless, they cannot deny the seductive powers of the images and the way they function beautifully, both within the scientific community but also at large, for the lay public, who almost inevitably responds to them as to "true" depictions of the universe.

7. Lorraine Daston, Peter Galison, *Objectivity,* (New York Zone Books, 2007), 383-4.

8. Elizabeth A. Kessler, *Picturing the Cosmos: Hubble Space Telescope Images and the Astronomical Sublime* (Minneapolis/London: University of Minnesota Press, 2012).

Mechanical ballet: ALMA's sixty-six antennas
rotate in a synchronic movement.

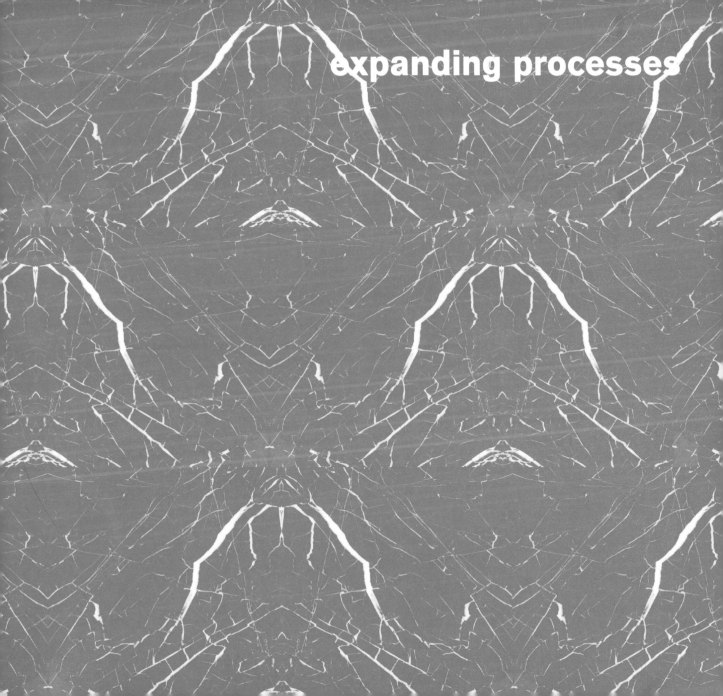

expanding processes

WORLDINDEXER

Joyce Hsiang + Bimal Mendis

The city of seven billion: An antidote to fragmentary analyses and arbitrary boundaries, WorldIndexer models global population and development as one unified urban entity without boundaries.

One World

Population growth that surpasses expectation has prevailed throughout history as a constant force of global development. From the rise of the industrial city and the modern metropolis to the proliferation of regional conurbations, megacities and suburban agglomerations, the built environment is a product of this unprecedented growth. As the world's population continues to increase, future development is positioned to critically overwhelm global resources. In an age of increasing connectivity, the instability of the future presents a collective dilemma.

WorldIndexer indexes our impact on the world. It confronts the exigencies of growth that reconfigure our global terrain. As an antidote to the fragmentation of global development, the installation erases divisions and differences, removing all boundaries of ownership, politics and responsibility. Rather than distinguishing between arbitrary and unstable dichotomies of rural and urban, developed and natural, land and water, *WorldIndexer* reflects our ambition to understand both the world, and our collective population, as one continuous entity, without boundaries.

Projection Systems

The project unfolds and reconstructs the entirety of the earth's surface to index global development. Projection systems for mapping the world are inevitably distorted, comprised of oppositional properties of area and shape, direction and bearing, distance and scale, agendas and biases. They are as much cartographic as they are deliberate cultural and political statements of intent. The *WorldIndexer's* system of projection builds upon the wealth of information and knowledge offered by satellite imagery and geographic information systems that have changed our global perspective and reconfigured our engagement with the world.

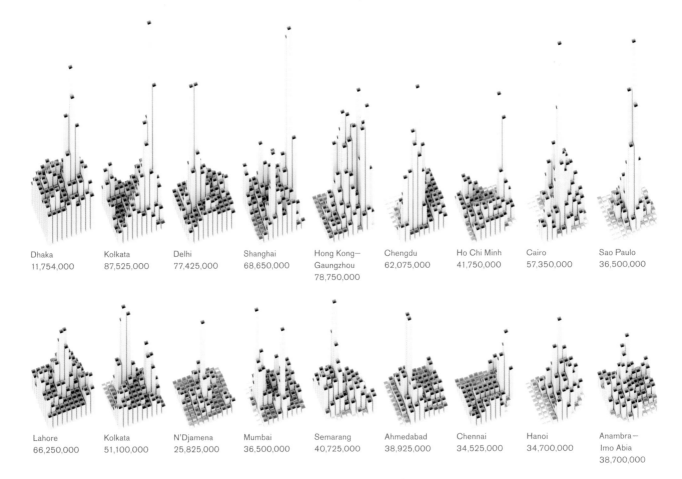

Dhaka	Kolkata	Delhi	Shanghai	Hong Kong—	Chengdu	Ho Chi Minh	Cairo	Sao Paulo
11,754,000	87,525,000	77,425,000	68,650,000	Gaungzhou	62,075,000	41,750,000	57,350,000	36,500,000
				78,750,000				

Lahore	Kolkata	N'Djamena	Mumbai	Semarang	Ahmedabad	Chennai	Hanoi	Anambra—
66,250,000	51,100,000	25,825,000	36,500,000	40,725,000	38,925,000	34,525,000	34,700,000	Imo Abia
								38,700,000

Urban epicenters: The extruded densities of population of known urban epicenters form a catalog of varied urbanization and development typologies. Built-up heights reflect the population for each 25km x 25km grid unit sampled across a swath of 250kmx250km land independent of prescribed boundaries. These urban forms offer new opportunities for classification, analysis and comparison across cities according to scale, breadth and pattern of densification.

Data Space

The project translates the abundance of information and urban indicators into the geographic domain, where spatial configurations and scenarios can be understood. The investigation bridges this divide, giving geographic and spatial significance to abstract numbers and values. By synthesizing development data with geographic space using evolving methodologies of mapping, this hybrid model offers a new three-dimensional cartography to assess the impact of global development.

A gridded projection system is used as a platform to integrate multiple systems of information on land use intensity and population density. The surface of the earth is unfolded, projected onto the interior walls of an inhabitable, inverted 3-metre cube at the scale of 1:2,500,000, and subdivided into 540,000 pixels. Each pixel represents a specific 25 km by 25 km plot. The grid is used as an anti-figural device that disregards the exactitudes of figures and boundaries and averages value across an objective field. While the grid is systemically disassociated from literal boundaries, the shape and figuration of conventional boundaries are still identifiable as a low-resolution pixilated figure.

The project locates and models data for each 25 km by 25 km parcel of land using a geographic 'spreadsheet.' The intensity of human use of land resources and the human impact to marine ecosystems is mapped and keyed for each plot of land and water. In addition, the number of people is modeled as a vertical extrusion—increasing height signifying the increasing density of population for each 25 km by 25 km pixel. The resulting topography constructs and physically indexes the fluctuating density of population, and intensity of land and water use. What emerges is a comprehensive map and model of the relative global concentrations of urbanization, spatializing the continuing crisis of growth.

A Continuous Urbanism

This method eschews the simplistic standard of totaling population for cities and urban areas, which are increasingly boundless and endlessly connected. Instead, this "built" formalization of population density offers a meaningful model with which to examine patterns of global development and land use. New typologies of development emerge, distinguished by their growth patterns, including contiguous mats of solid, fluctuating linear spines, incrementally buttressed peaks, or the adjacency of extreme and zero density.

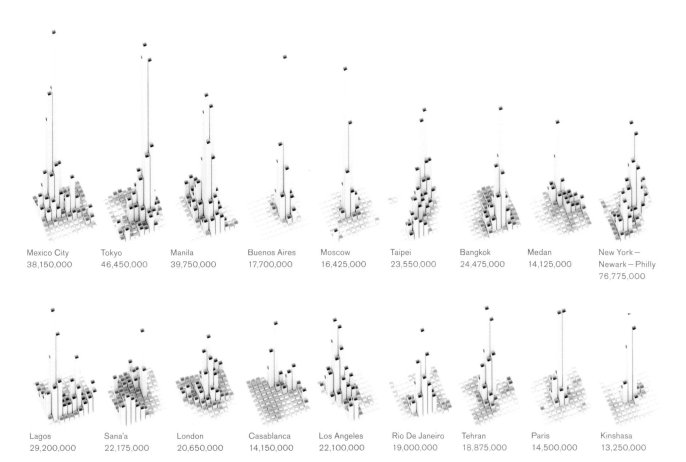

Mexico City
38,150,000

Tokyo
46,450,000

Manila
39,750,000

Buenos Aires
17,700,000

Moscow
16,425,000

Taipei
23,550,000

Bangkok
24,475,000

Medan
14,125,000

New York —
Newark — Philly
76,775,000

Lagos
29,200,000

Sana'a
22,175,000

London
20,650,000

Casablanca
14,150,000

Los Angeles
22,100,000

Rio De Janeiro
19,000,000

Tehran
18,875,000

Paris
14,500,000

Kinshasa
13,250,000

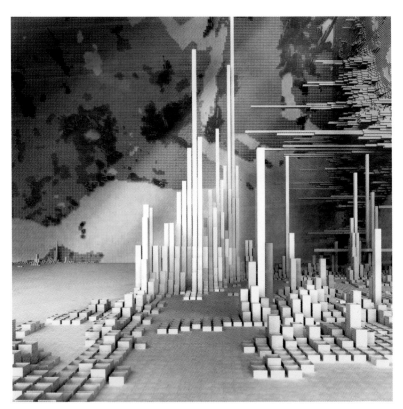

A new topography: This project indexes the fluctuating density of population, intensity of land and water use. By removing normative urban and administrative boundaries, distinct patterns of development emerge.

Global positioning: The inverted model of global development provides a uniquely immersive environment. The viewer is able to simultaneously position his local context within the larger phenomenon of global development. It juxtaposes individual experience with the collective impact of 7 billion inhabitants.

These newly formed cities and urban constellations of relative density provide opportunity for comparing, analyzing and speculating renewed organizational strategies for addressing global urbanization.

An Immersive Installation

By inverting the world and turning it inside out, the installation enables each viewer to stand at the center of the world, surrounded by a visualization of the unprecedented growth, complex linkages and competing demands placed on land and resources. An immersive and introspective spatial experience, the installation gives viewers the opportunity to contemplate their individual role and relationship to the world. Each viewer is able to locate his/her immediate community and understand a local context relative to a larger network of regional, national and global human impact. The collective contribution of human civilization to the physical realm is seen as being simultaneously fragile and sublime, ephemeral and substantive. An object of frightening and complex beauty, it is also a landscape of continual opportunity.

Project Credits: Joyce Hsiang & Bimal Mendis with Daniel Markiewicz, Ryan Welch, Christian Nakarado, Nicky Chang, Dana Wu, R.J. Tripodi and Jieming Yan.

Joyce Hsiang is a founding principal of Plan B Architecture & Urbanism, an interdisciplinary research and design collaborative based in New Haven, CT. She is also a design critic at the Yale School of Architecture.

Bimal Mendis is the Assistant Dean, Director of Undergraduate Studies and Assistant Professor, Adjunct, at the Yale School of Architecture and leads studios in urbanism and design.

MUDDY LOGICS

Lindsay Bremner

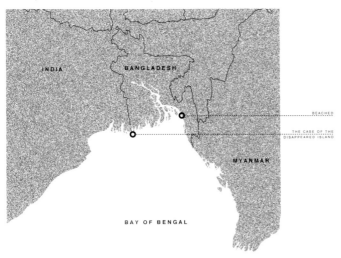
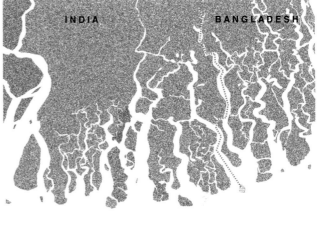

Muddy logics: Site Locations. The Ganges-Brahmaputra-Meghna Delta.

Spanning the delta islands of southern Bangladesh and West Bengal, the Sundarban region is a constantly mutating zone between land and sea, where the freshwater plumes of the Ganges, Brahmaputra and Meghna rivers deposit their silt and interact with the saline water of the Bay of Bengal. It has evolved over millennia through the natural deposition of upstream sediments and intertidal segregation, stabilized by the roots of the largest halophytic mangrove forest in the world.[1] Neither liquid nor solid, the organization of this fluid archipelago is anti-pattern: undifferentiated, oozy, squelchy, materializing and dematerializing in an ongoing process of deposition, accumulation, stabilization, erosion, ebb and flow. This very anti-pattern provides a sludgy, protective barrier to the intensely cultivated and populated lands of Kolkata, India's third largest metropolis, and Dhaka, Bangladesh's capital. Amphibious, disposable and expedient, its muddy logics offer strategies of both incorporation and resistance to forces of globalization.

This essay examines two sites in this liminal zone, the first marked by disappearance (The Case of the Disappeared Island), the second by entanglement (Beached). These are sites where ocean-based practices and protocols meet land-based ones and they figure both sea and land-based logics.

The essay examines their relations to, and consequences for international law and offers provisional thoughts about what they might mean for architecture and urbanism in today's hyper-articulated, globalised world.

The Case of the Disappeared Island

On March 24, 2010, the BBC reported that a tiny island, two kilometres south of the mouth of the Hariabhanga River, the border between India and Bangladesh, had sunk beneath the rising seas.[2] South Talpatti Island, as it was known in Bangladesh, or New Moore Island, as it was known in India, was a small uninhabited island that emerged in the Bay of Bengal in the aftermath of the Bhola cyclone in 1970.[3] In 1974 it was discovered by an American satellite, which showed it to have an area of twenty seven thousand square feet (approximately 150 x 150 feet). Over the years, due to the buildup of silt deposits and fluctuating currents, it expanded to an area about four times that size, including a number of ordinarily submerged shoals.[4] In March 2010 it vanished from sight.

The island's significance is that it lay at the center of a long-standing territorial dispute between India and Bangladesh.[5] India reportedly hoisted its flag on the island in 1981 and

1. Anuradha Banerjee, *Environment Population and Human Settlements of Sundarban Delta* (New Delhi: Concept Publishing, 1998).
2. "Disputed Bay of Bengal island 'vanishes' say scientists," *BBC.co.uk*, March 24, 2010, http://news.bbc.co.uk/2/hi/south_asia/8584665.stm [accessed March 25, 2010].
3. "The 10 deadliest storms in history," *Science on msnbc.com*, July 05, 2008,

http://www.msnbc.msn.com/id/24488385/ns/technology_and_science-science/ [accessed March 10, 2011]. This was the most severe and deadliest cyclone of all times, killing between 300,000 to 500,000 people.
4. "New Moore / South Talpatti," Wikipedia.org, last modified December 20, 2010, http://en.wikipedia.org/wiki/South_Talpatti_Island [accessed March 25, 2010].
5. Similar conflicting territorial claims and disputes

over navigation rights between Iran and Iraq in the Shat Al-Arab were among the main factors for the Iraq-Iran War of 1980 – 1988. See for instance T.D.P. Dugdale-Pointon, *Iran-Iraq War 1980-1988, Military History Encyclopedia on the Web*, September 09 2002, http://www.historyofwar.org/articles/wars_iraniraq.html [accessed March 30, 2010].

Rangabali Thana: Patuakhali district, South-western Bangladesh.

established a temporary border security base there, visiting regularly with naval gunships. Bangladesh laid similar territorial claim to the island on the basis of what is known as the thalweg principle.[6] This method of establishing a maritime border takes the line of greatest depth of a channel in a river, which corresponds to the line of the strongest current flow, as a territorial boundary. But flow is not fixed; it is dependent on all kinds of things such as the topography of the banks, surrounding vegetation, silting, and velocity. Each of these factors, in a region like the Ganges-Brahmaputra-Meghna Delta, is constantly in flux. While Bangladesh acknowledged that the main current of Hariabhanga River flowed east of South Talpatti Island, thus making it part of India, it claimed that this had not always been the case. This favorable flow was the result of India tampering with land-use upstream and altering the course of the river. As there is nothing in international law that states what should happen if a river changes its course or if natural dynamics produce or extinguish islands, the island could be India's one year and Bangladesh's the next. Bangladesh proposed that it be shared.[7]

What the disappearance of the island brings to light, if only because of its newly found uselessness in this regard, is a far reaching process of the territorialization of the world's oceans by the United Nation's Convention on the Law of the Sea (UNCLOS) since 1982.[8]

In 1494 when Christopher Columbus went on his first expedition to the Americas, Pope John Paul VI divided the seas between the then two major maritime powers: he declared that the North Atlantic belonged to Spain and the South Pacific and Indian oceans to Portugal. This established the principle of *Mare Clausum,* or closed seas. The principle was challenged in 1609 by Dutch jurist, Hugo Grotius, who proposed the principal of *Mare Liberum*, or the freedom of the seas. By the eighteenth century, it was widely accepted that beyond a three nautical mile limit (the distance a canon could shoot), *Mare Liberum* prevailed. There were a number of challenges to this, but it remained in place until after World War II, when President Truman unilaterally extended the United States' jurisdiction to the edge of its continental shelf, the submerged extent of the land mass of a continent. Other nations followed suit.[9] In 1967, in response to a chaotic and potentially conflictive situation, Malta called for "an effective international regime over the seabed and the ocean floor beyond a clearly defined national jurisdiction." [10] In 1973, the United Nations convened the Third United Nations Conference on the Law of the Sea.[11] Nine years later, the first constitution for the world's oceans, the United Nations Convention on the Law of the Sea (UNCLOS) was adopted, coming into force in 1994. One hundred and fifty eight nations have now ratified it.

6. Diganta, "How International are the International Laws?" *WordPress.com*, January 02, 2009, http://horizon-speaks.wordpress.com/2009/01/02/how-international-are-the-international-laws/ [accessed March 30, 2010].
7. Khondkar A. Saleque, "Energy Bangla Exclusive: Maritime Boundary Disputes: Bay of Bengal," *energybangla.com*, March 07, 2009, http://www.energybangla.com/index.php?mod=article&cat=SomethingtoSay&article=1909 [accessed March 30, 2010].
8. "United Nations Convention on the Law of the Sea,"

United Nations Division for Ocean Affairs and the Law of the Sea, http://www.un.org/Depts/los/convention_agreements/texts/unclos/unclos_e.pdf [accessed March 09, 2010].
9. "The United Nations Convention on the Law of the Sea (A Historical Perspective)," *United Nations Division for Ocean Affairs and the Law of the Sea*, http://www.un.org/Depts/los/convention_agreements/convention_historical_perspective.htm#Historical Perspective [accessed March 09, 2010].

10. "Third United Nations Conference on the Law of the Sea," *United Nations Division for Ocean Affairs and the Law of the Sea*, http://www.un.org/Depts/los/convention_agreements/convention_historical_perspective.htm#Third Conference [accessed March 09, 2010].

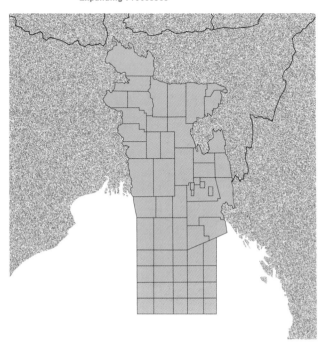

Bangladesh oil concession blocks.

This legislation demarcates the ocean into a number of territorial zones, beginning from a base line, which is the line of average low tide along a shore and, for all legal purposes, a state's legal boundary. From this line, a territorial sea, over which the littoral country has complete sovereignty, extends for twelve nautical miles. Then, for two hundred nautical miles from the baseline, or up to the end of the continental shelf (to a maximum of three hundred and fifty nautical miles) the ocean is considered an exclusive economic zone (EEZ), where the adjacent country has exclusive rights over all living and non-living resources. Beyond this lies the high seas, over which the United Nations and its agencies have jurisdiction.[12] This geometry of demarcation and its interpretation have been deployed by many nations to extend their territories and grab resources, particularly into oceans with rich petro-carbon or natural gas deposits. It has also produced unexpected new geographies; Australia, for instance, now lays claims to large chunks of Antarctica and France and South Africa are new neighbours in the southern Indian Ocean.

The Bay of Bengal has long been known as one of oil and natural gas's final untapped frontiers.[13] UNCLOS provided, for the first time, an instrument for parceling it out and transforming it from waves, winds currents and depths into exploitable territory. Because of the instability of the Ganges-Brahmaputra-Meghna delta however, defining a base line from which to measure which country could lay claim to what

eluded lawmakers. Where did land end and ocean begin in a fluctuating and constantly changing terrain? Bangladesh came up with a proposal that its base line should be drawn through eight imaginary points where the water is sixty feet deep.[14] India claimed that there was no precedence for this in international law, and used the principal of the furthest seaward extent of the low water line, hence its claim to the disappeared island. Bangladesh and Myanmar disputed the entitlement of St. Martins Island, an island belonging to Bangladesh lying off the coast of Myanmar, to a 12 km territorial sea. With India encroaching from the west and Myanmar from the east, Bangladesh was potentially left with a seriously eroded EEZ. In 2009, it made its case to The International Tribunal for the Law of the Sea (ITCLOS), one of the international juridical bodies for resolving such disputes. India consented to another process, arbitration under Annex VII of UNCLOS. In March 2012, the dispute between Bangladesh and Myanmar was resolved in a groundbreaking judgment by ITCLOS, its first maritime delimitation case.[15] The arbitration between India and Bangladesh continues.

Disputes aside, what is important here is not so much who has a right to what or who's territory overlaps with whose, but rather how international law has produced a new way of delimiting the ocean. The International Law of the Sea has transformed coastal waters into 'land-like, developable components of state territory'[16] and the Bay of Bengal into a

11. "United Nations Convention on the Law of the Sea," *Wikipedia.org*, last modified March 01, 2010, http://en.wikipedia.org/wiki/United_Nations_Convention_on_the_Law_of_the_Sea [accessed March 09, 2010]. The first conference (UNCLOS I) was held in 1956 and resulted in the conclusion of four treatises, the second (UNCLOS II) in 1960.
12. "United Nations Convention on the Law of the Sea," *United Nations Division for Ocean Affairs and the Law of the Sea*, http://www.un.org/Depts/los/convention_agreements/

texts/unclos/unclos_e.pdf [accessed March 09, 2010]
13. Ganpat Singh Roonwal, *The Indian Ocean: Exploitable Mineral and Petroleum Resources* (Berlin: Springer-Verlag, 1986).
14. "Why should equidistance be imposed on Bangladesh?" *thedailystar.net*, December 15, 2008, http://www.thedailystar.net/suppliments/2008/delimitation/index.htm [accessed March 30, 2010].
15. International Tribunal for the Law of the Sea, "Judgment in the Dispute Concerning Delimitation

of the Maritime Boundary between Bangladesh and Myanmar in the Bay of Bengal," March 14, 2012, http://www.itlos.org/fileadmin/itlos/documents/cases/case_no_16/1-C16_Judgment_14_02_2012.pdf [accessed July 28, 2012].

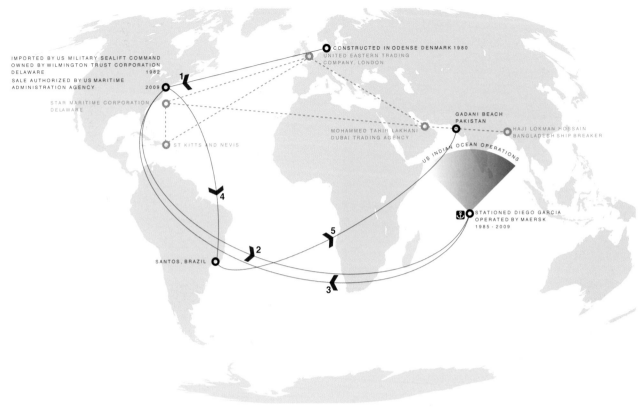

IMPORTED BY US MILITARY SEALIFT COMMAND
OWNED BY WILMINGTON TRUST CORPORATION
DELAWARE   1982
SALE AUTHORIZED BY US MARITIME
ADMINISTRATION AGENCY   2009

STAR MARITIME CORPORATION
DELAWARE

ST KITTS AND NEVIS

CONSTRUCTED IN ODENSE DENMARK 1980
UNITED EASTERN TRADING
COMPANY, LONDON

GADANI BEACH
PAKISTAN

HAJI LOKMAN HOSSAIN
BANGLADESH SHIP BREAKER

MOHAMMED TAHIR LAKHANI
DUBAI TRADING AGENCY

US INDIAN OCEAN OPERATIONS

STATIONED DIEGO GARCIA
OPERATED BY MAERSK
1985 - 2009

SANTOS, BRAZIL

SS voyages: Global movements of the SS Anders and SS Bony from building to breaking.

'potential giant gas-producing province'.[17] Whereas former cartographic practices sought to draw lines between land and sea as a way of defining territory, today's cartographic and juridical instruments recuperate sea as land. New maps of state territory flatten the distinctions between land and sea and the institutions that regulate them, portraying them as continuous topographies of abstract parcels of exploitable real estate to be tendered off to the highest bidder. The ocean has been striated and politicized in new ways and new resource driven territorial conflicts unleashed.[18]

Beached

In 1998, the Clinton Administration called for a moratorium on sending United States government ships to the South Asian shipbreaking yards after a report by the Baltimore Sun on conditions in Alang, India.[19] In August 2009, under Obama's watch, two ships, the SS Anders and the SS Bonny, left the United States, officially destined for Santos in Brazil. In January 2010, one of them surfaced in Pakistan,

raising suspicions that they had been sold as scrap, in violation not only of International Conventions, but also of United States law.[20, 21]

The two ships were built in 1980 as commercial cargo ships in Odense, Denmark.[22] Two years later they were imported by the United States, owned by the Wilmington Trust Corporation, of Delaware, and converted for use by the Military Sealift Command (MSC), which operates non-combatant, civilian crewed ships in support of the United States Military. They were stationed at Diego Garcia for twenty-four years, operated by the shipping company Maersk, in support of United States Military operations in the Indian Ocean, including Iraq.

From July 2009, the ships went through a succession of rapid ownership changes, and nationalities. Within a month, the boats had left the United States as empty cargo vessels destined for Santos, Brazil. If suspicions are confirmed, they have already surfaced in a South Asian scrapyard.[23]

16. Paul Steinberg, The Social Construction of the Ocean, p. 150 (Cambridge: Cambridge University Press, 2001)
17. GLG Expert Contributor, "Bay of Bengal: a potential giant gas producing province," glgroup.com, September 01, 2009, http://www.glgroup.com/News/Bay-of-Bengal-a-potential-giant-gas-producing-province-42897.html [accessed April 12, 2010]
18. Nabil Ahmed, "Entangled Earth," Third Text, Vol. 27, no. 1, pp. 44-53, 2013
19. Gary Cohn and Will Englund, Baltimore Sun, "The Shipbreakers," Pulitzer Prize for Investigative Reporting, 1998, http://www.pulitzer.org/

works/1998-Investigative-Reporting [accessed February 23, 2010].
20. Jacob Baynham, "Muddy Waters. Are US shipping companies still selling their clunkers to the toxic scrap yards of South Asia?" slate.com, September 18, 2009, http://www.slate.com/id/2228712/pagenum/all/ [accessed February 22, 2010] and Rajesh Joshi, "US Environmental protection Agency to let Anders sail," Basel Action Network, ban.org, August 28, 2009, http://www.ban.org/ban_news/2009/090828_usepa_to_let_anders_sail.html [accessed February 22, 2010].
21. The Jones Act (Merchant Marine Act of 1920, Section

27) forbids sale of United States government ships to foreign companies and the Toxic Substances Control Act (TSCA) forbids the export or the distribution in commerce of polychlorinated biphenyls (PCBs), which are highly toxic compounds of chlorine and benzene and were once widely used in ship construction.
22. "Obama's EPA allows toxic Navy ships to be dumped in Bangladesh," Basel Action Network, ban.org, August 27, 2009, http://www.ban.org/ban_news/2009/090827_toxic_navy_ships_to_be_dumped.html [accessed February 22, 2010]

Shipbreaking yard: Bhatiari, Sitakunda Upazila, Chittagong District, Bangladesh.

One of the slippery questions for the global shipping industry is how one defines and what one does with waste. Under the Basel Convention of 1992, it is illegal for developed countries to export hazardous waste to developing countries. End-of-life ships are considered hazardous waste because of the asbestos, oily wastes, polychlorinated biphenyls (PCB's) and toxic paints they contain. Selling ships to be broken without decontaminating them is a form of toxic dumping. What this has meant is that shipbreaking today is conducted via protocols of deception, back room deals, front companies, decoys and middlemen in networks that span the globe to avoid the cost of compliance with the principle of *polluter pays*.

Until the late '70s, shipbreaking was done in the dockyards of Europe, the United States and Japan. It was a highly mechanized operation. But as environmental standards and health and safety requirements increased, the costs of scrapping began to escalate. As a result, approximately 90 percent of the shipbreaking industry moved, firstly to Korea and Taiwan,[24] and then to India, Bangladesh, China, Pakistan and Turkey,[25] poor nations with seemingly endless supplies of exploitable labor and lax environmental and safety regulations.

The South East Asian industry began at Gadani Beach in Pakistan prior to that country's independence in 1947.[26] It was the largest shipbreaking site in the world until 1983, when it was surpassed by the yards at Alang in Gujarat, India, currently still the largest shipbreaking site in the world. In Bangladesh, the practice began by accident in 1965, when a twenty-thousand ton vessel was beached by a tidal wave at Bhatiari, just north of Chittagong on the Bay of Bengal. Today twenty ship breaking yards run by sixty-eight enterprises occupy a five-mile stretch of this beach.,[27, 28] It is the largest facility for large vessels in the world, scrapping some 52

23. A recent internet search for the ships drew a blank.
24. William Langewiesche, The Outlaw Sea (New York: North Point, 2004); Alfred Nijkirk, "Shipbreaking USA," *Recycling International*, March 2006, http://www.environmental- expert.com/Files/6496/articles/6415/Shipbreaking.pdf; "American Ship Breaking. It All Comes Apart at the Bottom of America," The Lay of the Land, Center for Land Use Interpretation, Spring 2010, http://www.clui.org/lotl/pdf/33_spring2010_color-200dpi.pdf; and "Annex 3 Dismantling Sites in Europe and the OECD," *sgmer.gouv.fr*, http://www.sgmer.gouv.fr/IMG/pdf/Annex_3_Dismantling_site_in_Europe_and_OECD.pdf [accessed March 10, 2011]. The United Kingdom, United States and the Netherlands were the major shipbreaking nations until after World War II. In the nineteen fifties,

shipbreaking yards opened in Belgium, followed by Spain, Greece, the former Yugoslavia, Mexico, Colombia, Japan and Taiwan. By the nineteen sixties, Taiwan was the leading shipbreaking country, with yards clustered around Kaohsiung. These closed in 1986, following a fatal explosion and the South Asian nations took over as the worlds primary ship breakers The United States still operates two ship breaking yards – at Chesapeake Virginia, and Brownsville Texas, where ships from the three federal Ghost Fleets (surplus ships built in the

1950's and held in reserve to be activated in times of war) are taken apart. In Europe, yards still operate in the ports of Gand in Belgium, Scheepssloperij in the Netherlands, Grenaa and Esburg in Denmark and Klaipeda in Lithuania.

25. http://www.greenpeace.org/india/campaigns/

toxics-free-future/ship-breaking [accessed April 09, 2012]. The world's major ship breaking yards today are at Gadani Beach in Pakistan, Alang in India, Aligia in Turkey, Bhatiary (just north of Chittagong) in Bangladesh and Panyu City, Guangdong, and Xiagang in the Yangtze delta in China.
26. http://en.wikipedia.org/wiki/Gadani_ship-breaking_yard#History [accessed April 09, 2010].
27. Ataur Rahman and A. Z. M. Tabarak Ullah, "Ship Breaking, A Background Paper," *International Labor Organization's Sectoral Activities Programme*, Dhaka 1999, http://ilo-mirror.library.cornell.edu/public/english/protection/safework/sectors/shipbrk/shpbreak.htm [accessed April 08, 2010].
28. This number has increased dramatically to 108, since the 2008 economic recession. In 2009, about 2.4

percent of all vessels above two hundred thousand dead-weight tons. The large tidal difference of twenty feet provides an ideal intertidal zone for beaching these large ships.[29]

By the time ships are rammed into a beach in a shipbreaking yard in South East Asia, they are not ships any longer, nor even waste. They are raw material, un-natural resources, to be mined, dismantled, sold, re-rolled and re-distributed, mostly for the construction industry. In Bangladesh, this provides 50 percent of the steel used in its construction industry, as well as the fittings, utensils, sanitary ware, linen etc. that furnish Bangladeshi homes and businesses.[30] And on the beach just north of Chittagong, a new, provisional post-urban assemblage has taken shape. This has transformed the coastline into a frictional zone where the murkiness of a sea-based economy meets an even more squelchy land-based one characterized by overlapping administrative jurisdictions, military and business collusions, nimble agents, middlemen, decoys and graft.

Bhatiari is described as the "hidden, green paradise of Chittagong,"[31] owing this reputation to its recreational lake in the forested hills above the Bay of Bengal. It lies in the Sitakunda Upazila, one of the oldest sites of human habitation in Bangladesh, known for its Islamic, Hindu and Buddhist shrines.[32] Local inhabitants have traditionally worked in agriculture and fishing and more recently in commerce and the service economy.[33] It also boasts the Bangladesh Military Academy, the Faujdarhat Cadet College, a military sponsored golf and country club, the Chittagong University Campus and a middle-income residential township laid by the Chittagong Housing Authority in the late 1980's.[34]

Between the hills and the sea, into this already charged landscape, ship breaking has injected a new anti-ecology. Tightly guarded, highly concealed tracks lead from the highway to the shipbreaking yards through fenced workers compounds, residual farmlands and stagnant water ponds. Goods stripped from ships (kitchen equipment, bathroom fittings, linen, machine parts) pile high for sale along roads; discarded lifeboats float in waterways; oil and other forms of hazardous waste seep into ground waters and pollute fishing grounds.

Here the more than one hundred thousand individuals who earn their livelihoods from the scrapping of vessels,[35] mostly recruited from the villages of northern Bangladesh,[36] crowd into makeshift shelters. In more than four hundred nearby steel mills, steel plate is smelted down, reformed, rerolled and resold. The highway is clogged with trucks, bicycles, taxis, tuk-tuks, motorbikes, cars and all kinds of makeshift vehicles transporting goods away.

All of this takes place on land which is state owned. Shipbreakers lease their land from the government, subject to an application procedure handled by the Bangladesh Mercantile Marine Department, administered by the Chittagong Port Authority; leases for adjacent inland areas are dealt with by the Bangladesh Inland Water Transport Authority (BIWTA); environmental matters associated with shipbreaking are under the jurisdiction of the Department of the Environment; import of vessels to Bangladesh for breaking is subjected to yet another governmental authorization procedure, this time from the Department of Commerce—all multiple, opaque jurisdictions that increase inscrutability and multiply opportunities for gain.[37]

The pattern of human settlement that has taken shape confounds accepted typologies or morphologies. It is both a productive landscape and a site of cultural transfer, weaving bits and pieces of ships into the cities, towns and villages of Bangladesh and beyond. It has reversed the direction of flow of the nineteenth century imperial formations (raw material from the colonies, production in the metropolitan center). Its model is not the nineteenth century factory town of the United Kingdom nor the plantations of the United States, but something very particular to the Indian Ocean itself, drawing on the deep archive of muddy logics through which people have put the ocean and its deposits to work for centuries.

Clues to this condition and the challenges it presents can be found in the architectures of software design, in particular those known as *Big Balls of Mud*.[38] These are software systems that survive precisely because of their lack of hierarchy or overall structure—"haphazardly structured, sprawling, sloppy, duct-tape and bailing wire, spaghetti code

million tons of iron were obtained from ships scrapped in Bangladesh, compared with 650,000 tons from 2007 to 2008 and 1.22 million tons in 2006. Opportunities are set to increase further as the European Union completes a phase-out of single-hull tankers operating in its waters. See Syed Tashfin Chowdhury, "Bangladesh shipbreakers survive headwinds," *Asian Times*, March 01, 2011, http://www.atimes.com/atimes/South_Asia/MC01Df02.html [accessed March 28, 2011].
29. Aage Bjorn Andersen, Erik Bjornbom and Terje Sverud, *Technical Report DNV RN 590, Decommissioning of Ships, Environmental Standards, Ship-breaking Practices / On-site Assessment, Bangladesh Chittagong Report No. 2000 3158, Revision No. 01* (Hovik, Norway: Det Norske Veritas, 2000).
30. 97 percent of the ships that are taken apart in Bangladesh are recycled.
31. Jennifer Ashraf, "Sunset Splendour at Bhatiary," *The Daily Star Home* 2, 49, June 14, 2005, http://www.thedailystar.net/lifestyle/2005/06/02/page02.htm [accessed April 09, 2010].
32. "Sitakunda Upzala," *Banglapedia.org*, 2006, http://

www.banglapedia.org/httpdocs/HT/S_0420.HTM [accessed April 10, 2010].
33. "Sitakunda Upzala," *Banglapedia.org*, 2006, http://www.banglapedia.org/httpdocs/HT/S_0420.htm [accessed April 10, 2010]. It has two hundred and eighty mosques, eight mazars, forty nine Hindu temples, four ashrams, and three Buddhist temples.
34. Group: 01(Warrior), "Report on the Impact of the Small Scale Real Estate Business on the Urbanization Patterns of Third World Cities: A Case Study on Chittagong Division," *scribd.com*, December 20, 2009 http://www.scribd.com/doc/24494329/The-Impact-of-the-Small-Scale-Real-Estate-Business-On [accessed April 10, 2010].
35. Aage Bjorn Andersen, Erik Bjornbom and Terje Sverud, *Technical Report DNV RN 590, Decommissioning of Ships, Environmental Standards, Ship-breaking Practices / On-site Assessment, Bangladesh Chittagong Report No. 2000 3158, Revision No. 01* (Hovik, Norway: Det Norske Veritas, 2000).
36. Greenpeace and International Federation for Human Rights in co-operation with Young Power for Social

Action, "End of Life Ships – The Human Cost of Breaking Ships," *fidh.org*, 2005, http://www.fidh.org/END-OF-LIFE-SHIPS-THE-HUMAN-COST-OF-BREAKING [accessed April 10, 2010]. Workers come from Nandail (north of Kishorganj), Saria Kandi (near Bogra) Chandan Baisha, Dac Bangla and Kolni Bari (south of Saria Kandi).
37. For details of the relations between the industry and government ministries and departments, and the structuring of the industry see Ataur Rahman and A. Z. M. Tabarak Ullah, "Ship Breaking, A Background Paper," *International Labor Organization's Sectoral Activities Programme*, Dhaka 1999, http://ilo-mirror.library.cornell.edu/public/english/protection/safework/sectors/shipbrk/shpbreak.htm [accessed April 08, 2010].
38. Brian Foote and Joseph Yoder, "Big Ball of Mud," *laputan.org*, August 28, 2001, http://www.laputan.org/mud/mud/html [accessed November 15, 2010].
39. Ibid.,2.

Scrapped lifeboats: Bhatiari, Sitakunda Upazila, Chittagong District, Bangladesh.

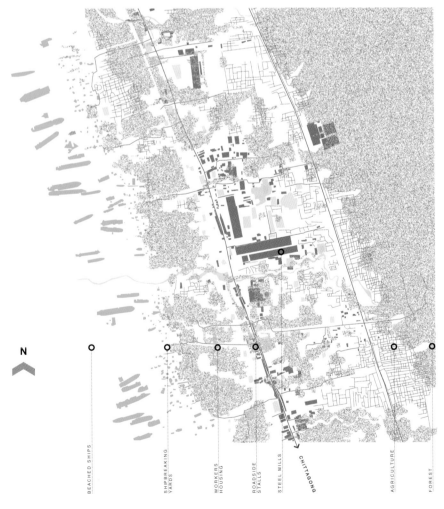

N

BEACHED SHIPS

SHIPBREAKING YARDS

WORKERS HOUSING

ROADSIDE STALLS

STEEL MILLS

CHITTAGONG

AGRICULTURE

FOREST

Shipbreaking map: Bhatiari, Sitakunda Upazila, Chittagong District, Bangladesh.

jungles."[39] They often emerge in the software design world from throw away codes, devised expediently in response to market demands or time constraints and never intended for permanent use, but which are then modified as conditions change. They evolve through patch after patch at the hands of multiple maintainers, each of whom tinker about, caring little about the consequences of what he or she is doing or how it might impact on the next. Over time, such processes become Big Balls of Mud—working systems without regulation, which have eroded and accreted unregulated growth and repeated, expedient repair.

It is precisely this lack of differentiation, hierarchy, structure or consequence that makes Big Balls of Mud work. They facilitate economies of speed and rapid change, protecting against market fluctuations and managing risk. Their lack or rather minimal reliance on overall infrastructure, co-ordination or capital investment means that they can nimbly adapt to change. They rely on homeostasis and retrospective feedback rather than prediction. They de-emphasize planning and upfront design for feedback and integration.

In the face of the agile inscrutability of such muddy logics, what might design do? Foote and Yoder argue that there are ways to improve the functionality and durability of such systems, given that their inbuilt stickiness tends to become a quagmire.[40] There are ways to cultivate them as they evolve. This is not through "rigid, totalitarian, top-down design,"[41] but through the kind of small, incremental transformations that produced the undifferentiated structure in the first place. In software design, this is known as *refactoring* or making tiny changes to a computer program's source code to improve its functionality. The cure for Big Balls of Mud is "flexible, adaptive feedback driven development"[42] that adapts internal and external forces to one another over time. There is no reason why these cannot incorporate demands for social and environmental justice as well as supply chains and markets. Key to this is a measure of enhanced scrutability to enable the identification of patterns, the establishment of frameworks, interfaces and protocols, the introduction of new components, and, in some cases, the isolation and complete refurbishment of irreparable parts of the system.[43]

These are the lessons learned from this excursion to the amphibious sites of South East Asia. Just as South Talpatti/ New More Island, appearing and disappearing according to the muddy logics of the Ganges, Brahmaputra Meghna delta threw into doubt the very possibility of transforming coastal waters into exploitable units of state territory, so on the beach at Bhatiari, a proto-urban assemblage has taken shape according to comparable, opaque logics. It makes no claims to being an industrial zone, a linear city, or anything at all really, despite housing 100,000 workers and producing half of Bangladesh's steel. It is a throwaway urbanism super-imposed on a dense, fragile ecosystem, devised expediently in response to market demands, time constraints and risk. If understood as a Big Ball of Mud, its multiple resources, multiple scales and multiple ecologies might be able to be refactored into a more resilient, equitable interface for today's contingent, open-ended, promiscuous world.

Lindsay Bremner is Director of Architectural Research at the University of Westminster. She is currently pursuing work on Geo-architecture, investigating relationships between architecture and geology, and Folded Ocean, examining sites in the Indian Ocean world.

40. Ibid.
41. Ibid, 9.
42. Ibid, 5.
43. Syed Tashfin Chowdhury, "Bangladesh shipbreakers survive headwinds," *Asian Times*, March 01, 2011, http:// www.atimes.com/atimes/South_Asia/MC01Df02.html [accessed March 28, 2011]. On February 17, 2011, shipbreaking was recognized as an industry by the Bangladesh government for the first time, partly in response to its staggering and projected growth since 2008. This formalizes its contribution to the Bangladeshi economy, increases scrutability and presents the possibly of new opportunities for its restructuring.

AWAROA LIGHTHOUSE

Nick Roberts, Henry Stephens + Jansen Aui

The presence of the lighthouse: The form gazes outward, protecting the endangered bird and plantlife, and the fragile landform of the Awaroa estuary.

The landscape: As the telemetric rods transition from the estuary out to sea, their change in density around the lighthouse indicates a performative shift from a surveying to protective state.

There are few things as fragile or vaunted as the rugged, otherworldly beauty of the New Zealand landscape. The siting of these two slender isles upon a contorted network of cracks and fault-lines has, in spite of its young history of human occupation, unearthed an archaic and unexpectedly singular terrain. Constant geological activity has meant this landscape bears the scars of generations of upheaval, ages before man—and yet it is now humankind who would prefer this fluctuating landmass held in stasis. Fundamental to the idealized imaginary of New Zealand is a vastly different skyline than the great metropolises of the world. Rather than promote an urbanised vision of architectural progress, it is instead the sea against the hills, the dramatic disjunction of the glacier carved into the high country, the barren Alps of the south that prove so attractive. An unspoken, yet pervasive anxiety over disrupting this natural silhouette is held nation-wide. In proposing a vertical structure designed to protect the landscape, we posited a fundamental architectural choice: would we disrupt an idyllic landscape with a built form, if by its presence we could protect that landscape for posterity? In this regard, we questioned the extremity of human intervention for the sake of preservation.

This project is located within New Zealand's Abel Tasman National Park, an environment that is susceptible to natural disaster. It is an estuary with a constantly shifting profile: tidal patterns, rain and erosion all contribute to a fragile site topography. Acknowledging this, the site also poetically

encompasses the conceptual thinking behind the project: there is anxiety over destroying a protected and plainly beautiful natural reserve bearing the very imagery we claim. Looking back at historical building archetypes, the lighthouse, so often pictured amidst precipitous coastline and shrouded by violent waters, embodies solidity and stability in its siting. This project seeks to rethink the architectural and iconographic typology of the lighthouse, in this respect. If the traditional lighthouse protected men-at-sea from the threatening, here the lighthouse is positioned as a man-made structure made for protecting the landscape from unpredictable, larger natural forces. By operating across boundaries of destruction, preservation and renewal, an integration between building and landscape is sought. Rather than building on land, or building in land, *Awaroa Lighthouse* proposes a system wherein the forces of architectural intervention and landscape are mutually dependent.

Functionally, the historical processes of the lighthouse as a navigational, directive, and organisational structure are re-imagined here as a symbol of foresight in the event of an earthquake or related natural disaster. The project expands the traditional lighthouse function by incorporating new monitoring roles; the Awaroa lighthouse records both immaterial data flows from satellite photography from a worldwide network of similarly earthquake-prone sites, and, more locally, seismic data from a network of telemetric rods at the tower's base. Both of these streams of data are consolidated

The lighthouse: Overwhelmed by the atmosphere of the landscape.

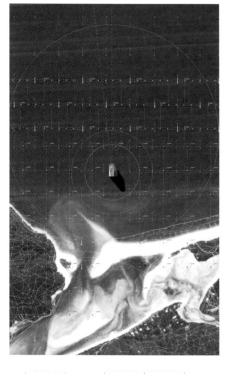
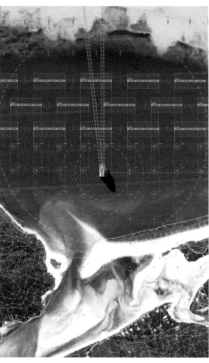
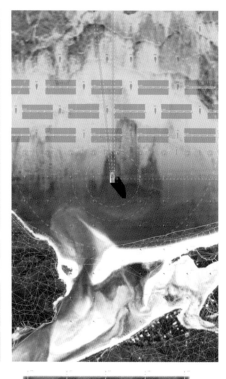

Sand wall defense system: During phases of environmental extremes, a network of staggered sand walls emerges to protect the contained landscape.

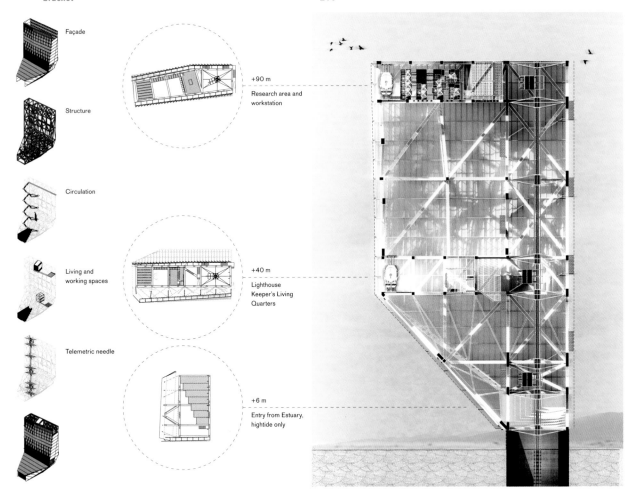

Façade

Structure

Circulation

Living and
working spaces

Telemetric needle

+90 m
Research area and
workstation

+40 m
Lighthouse
Keeper's Living
Quarters

+6 m
Entry from Estuary,
hightide only

Sublime routines: The external atmospheres of the
Awaroa estuary bleed into the cavernous internal volumes.

and interpreted by the lighthouse keeper who resides in the
tower. The rods, located at regular intervals across the site,
record the constantly shifting landforms of the estuary. A
constant feedback loop is created with the lighthouse while
a digital topography tracks the real site. When the keepers
forecast impending environmental extremes, the architectural
system shifts from its passive, 'recording' state to its active,
'protective' state. The rods beyond the lighthouse assume a
denser formation and a previously dormant system within the
telemetric rods distributes sand on site into a network
of staggered 'sand walls' between these outermost rods,
defending and preserving the landscape within. The project
actively transforms the sand that once made it vulnerable, in
order to defend itself.

Formally, the tower exposes a play of opposites. Its geometry is designed to look stable, but is in reality fragile. At once
austere and monolithic when confronted in one elevation,
another view reveals the mass as potentially fragile, susceptible to decay and weather. A play of anchors and cantilevers,
interrupted and dislodged views, and disproportionate scale
are purposeful absurdities aimed at experientially evoking anxiety. The project is interested in collective emotional notions
of architecture and landscape, and imposing a disruptive

order to this relationship—always teetering between fragility
and hardness.

Over the course of a day, the tower fluctuates between
functional and symbolic states. Illuminated from within at
night, the structural exoskeleton is revealed. Engaged in
both its physical and metaphysical contexts—the lighthouse
remains a beacon and symbol, but equally becomes an actor
in the landscape, where the endgame is mostly unwritten.

*Nick, Henry and Jansen would like to thank Athfield Architects for
access to their archives during the production of this project.*

Nick Roberts is an architect for UNStudio in Amsterdam, The
Netherlands, having studied at Victoria University of Wellington and
the University of California, Berkeley.

Jansen Aui is a practising Design Architect at Elenberg Fraser
in Melbourne, Australia having studied at Victoria University of
Wellington and the University of California, Berkeley.

Henry Stephens is an architect at Henning Larsen in Copenhagen,
Denmark having studied at The Royal Danish Academy of Fine Arts,
Victoria University of Wellington and the University of California,
Berkeley.

SACRED ANOMALIES

Samantha Lee

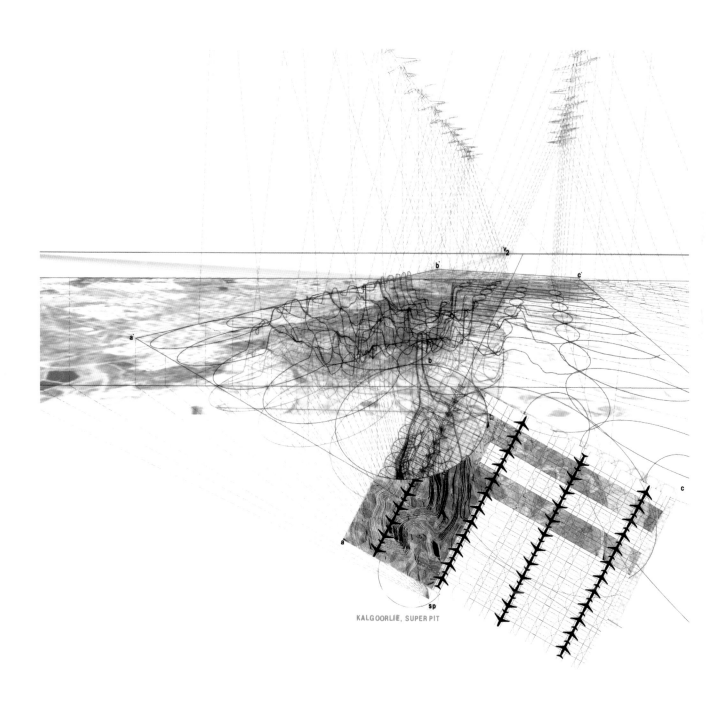

KALGOORLIE, SUPER PIT

Modes of viewing landscape: Drawing revealing the
mechanisms behind the technology of the LiDAR survey.

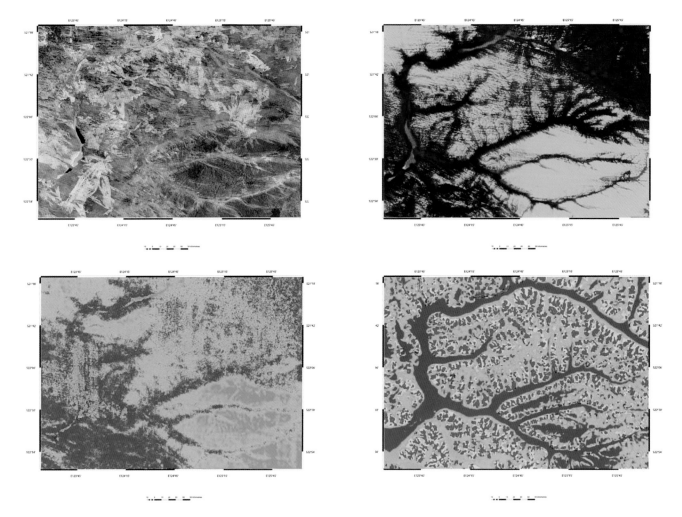

Atlas of Contested Terrain: A collection of survey maps and aboriginal paintings which document the same piece of land of the Martu territory around the Percival Lakes, WA. © Daniel Walbidi courtesy Short St Gallery Ilyara 2009, 74x149cm, acrylic on liner.

Sacred Anomalies: Infiltrating Landscape Surveys

The vast territories of the Australian Outback are highly contested landscapes, the value of which is assigned through the particular modes of viewing it through remote sensing technologies.

In the skies above, mining survey planes track back and forth, laser-scanning the earth, in search of topographic anomalies indicating pockets of undiscovered minerals. This spatial information is fed into computer models of floating ore bodies, represented as block models linked to stock market prices. Depending on the value of these ore blocks, the shape and size of the mine fluctuates as the software searches for optimum price efficiency. The physical terraforming of earth begins through its virtual construction.

On the ground, the ochre strokes of aboriginal landscape painters map the Songlines of their ancient Dreamtime stories, creation narratives embodied as an invisible network of sacred sites weaving across the country. These Songlines also acted as survival maps, revealing locations of waterholes in unforgiving expanses of land. Given there was no such vantage point from above, aboriginal painting could be seen as the first planimetric projection, where the journey of nomadic movement through landscape became one of map-making and remembering.

The technologies with which this ground is surveyed and recorded also become the political means through which groups claim ownership over it. In the continuous battle for "Native Title Rights", it is unique to Australia that aboriginal paintings are used as evidence to prove knowledge about country and traditional law. At the intersection of ancient culture and contemporary technology, aboriginal paintings come into direct conflict with mining exploration surveys. Painted narratives depicting the Rainbow Serpent that shaped the ancient riverbeds and filled the waterholes, sit next to the coloured pixels of hydrology surveys prospecting the underground paleodrainage channels and serpentine

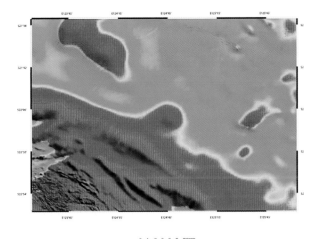
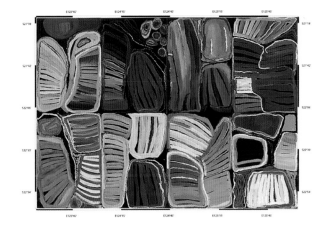

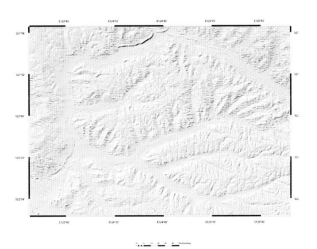
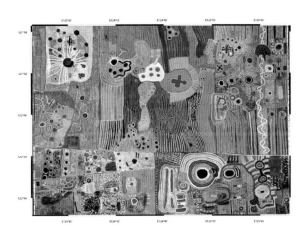

salt lakes. Through these creation stories and through the automated eyes of remote sensing, a seemingly vast and barren landscape is transformed into a complex and rich weaving of narratives and mineralogical value.

The project focuses on these mining landscape surveys as parallel architectural sites, where the primary design and intervention could only be experienced virtually. Defined as spaces of purely economic value, a series of strategies for subversion and distortion were developed to give these sites of Dreaming a presence within the datascapes of surveys. As a landscape drastically transformed by droughts caused by iron ore mining, these anomalies within the dataset become the digital ghosts of a lost network of aboriginal sacred waterholes.

The LiDAR Survey

Through the objective eyes of LiDAR [Light Detection and Ranging] planes, the landscape is mapped as a precise topographical cloud of points using large-scale terrestrial laser scanners fixed to aircrafts. The language of traditional aboriginal dot paintings presents a continuous field of densities much like a point cloud. Territories are fluid and imitate the flow of people's movement through the country and the tribal connections over space. Contemporary borders do not reflect the different tribal territories which are defined by nomadic lines across land rather than the fixed boundaries that enforce settlement. In practice 'Native Title' gives aboriginals the right to resources on the surface, such as sand, clay, water, while the underground is owned by the government (including any minerals, petroleum or gas) who also have the tools to view it from the air. The sacred sites are reduced to a thin surface, when, in fact, they are expressions of a large underground network of palaeodrainage channels which feed the system.

As a testing bed, a DIY 3D laser-scanner was built for the project, in order to recreate the principles of a LiDAR plane, scanning the landscape from above as a single moving viewpoint. This played the

Sectional Resources: The underground is owned by the government, reducing aboriginal sacred sites to thin surfaces.

role of both drawing tool and scaled aerial survey. Acting in a similar manner to visible light, laser wavelengths reflect, refract and absorb according to materiality and form. By using mirrored objects of varying curvatures, anomalies in the point cloud were designed to appear in cross section creating a 'deep scan' to be captured by the scanner and encoded as noise in the digital survey.

These new optical instruments stalk these territories as mysterious glistening beacons on the horizon, only to reveal a hidden ghost within the LiDAR survey. Pockets of unmappable space and point displacements generate virtual topographic anomalies laying claim to the invisible and subterranean realm.

The Magnetic Resonance Survey

In contrast to the traditional dot paintings, aboriginal artist and traditional healer, Jan Billycan represents landscape through x-ray vision. She charts the internal spaces of the human body in the same way she charts the land features of her birth country. As a result her paintings share a strange relationship to the magnetic resonance surveys searching for iron ore deposits. Surface topography is replaced by a field of energy and charge, where numerical peaks and valleys become a landscape of probable economic values.

At this larger scale of land claim, strategies for engineering artificial magnetic fields were explored, which might interfere with the existing mineral readings within the survey. A constellation of magnetic sources are proposed to orbit around aboriginal sacred sites in perpetual motion. When they meet, the magnetic field between them is amplified, large enough to create an anomalous reading. As they slowly move away from each other, they fade and disappear into the background energy field. Their slow orbital movements echo the seasonal migrations of aboriginal tribes previously traversing this country. They become a fluctuating phantom network, disturbing the terrain with false readings of promising mineralogical discovery.

The Ghost in the Data

Driving across the landscape, these new inhabitants mysteriously appear like floating navigational beacons, bending and warping on the horizon as you perceive them through the desert mirage. From the skies, they are a sea of numbers and points, perceived by the modern technologies that roam this ancient landscape. Their physical presence is a consequence of their virtual existence, where they lie out their lives haunting the economic mining surveys, interfering with the contemporary values of land use. This architecture of mirages exists at the threshold between the sky and the subterranean, between the physical and the virtual, to generate a ghostly constellation of sacred sites hidden within the dataset.

This project was developed as a Diploma thesis at the Architectural Association, London.

Samantha Lee is a London based designer and visual artist. She runs the Universal Assembly Unit, a cross disciplinary studio of digital storytellers and motion designers.

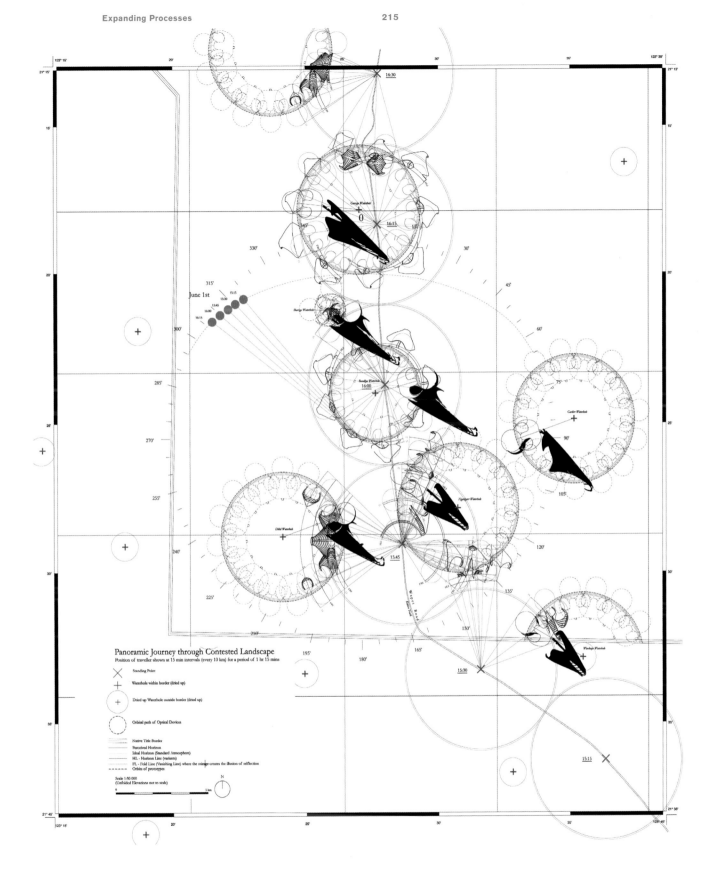

Panoramic Journey Unfolded: Shadows and optical
distortions at the 4 km horizon line of each sacred site.

NATIONAL
PURIST ROUTES

Gislunn Halfdanardottir + Mathias Kempton

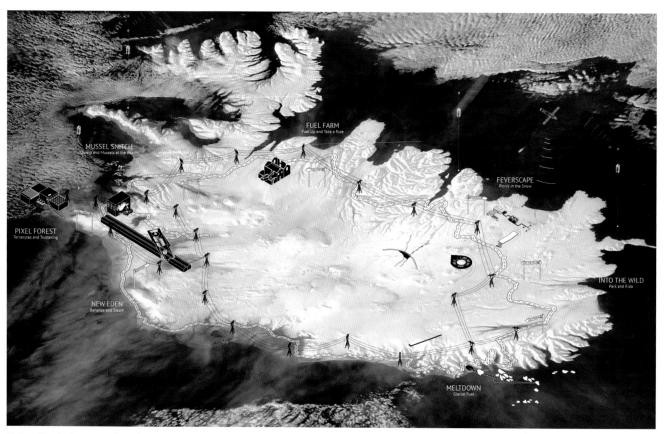

National Purist Routes: explores the intersecting
fields of hydro and thermal energy, tourism and
natural landscapes.

Following the 2008 financial meltdown, the International
Monetary Fund identified Iceland's key challenge as the ability
to "increase value retained from use of its hydro and geothermal resources". Seventy-four percent of Iceland's electricity
is consumed by the energy intensive production of aluminum.[1] The most recent project in this line of development is
the much contested "Karahnjukar project" which involves a
hydro-electric dam in the central highlands and an aluminium
smelter by the coast. The dam is situated in what used to be
one of Europe's largest areas of wilderness, yet the project
increased the electricity production of Iceland by 40 percent.

The debate in Iceland concerning nature and landscape
is highly emotional, the most extreme example of this being
Björk´s mother's well publicized hungerstrike against the
powerplant development. Iceland's landscape is literally and
metaphorically moving—shifting due to tectonic plate movement, transforming with the construction of these large-scale
dam infrastructure projects, and altering the public's perception and readings of Icelandic nature. Indeed, very few people
were even aware of Karahnjukar's existence at all before plans
for the dam were initiated; the actions of protesters, artists,
and writers produced identity for a rather unknown place.

This use of natural resources attracts much needed
foreign capital, but also brings up several questions: Who
and how many benefit from foreign capital? Should it be
part of a larger national project? Can the nation get more out
of the investments? And how does the harvesting of natural
resources change a nation's perception of landscape?

1. *Energy Statistics in Iceland.* (Reykjavik: The National
Energy Authority, 2009)

A conflict of interest?

Iceland's position across the Mid-Atlantic Ridge and its mountainous terrain provides an abundance of geothermal and hydro-electric energy resources. In the post-war era, energy politics aimed to replace imported coal with locally produced electricity and geothermal heating. Today the only remaining import of energy is fossil fuel for cars and fishing vessels. Since the '70s, policy has oriented itself towards attracting foreign investments through power-intensive industry. While Iceland already has the highest production of green energy per capita in the world, only forty percent of Iceland's hydro and thermal energy potential has been exploited thus far.[2] Both politicians and technocrats regard aluminium as an energy-export in solid state, since the island is not connected to a transnational power grid and cannot export energy as electricity. As Iceland seeks to attract foreign investments, and the global resource economy has its eyes on inexpensive green electricity, large new energy projects are planned.[3] The "Karahnjukar model", with power stations in the highlands and smelters by the coast, will most likely be repeated.

Simultaneously, the very same nature that holds such rich energy reserves (hot pools and magnificent waterfalls) is an object of desire for a global leisure economy. Tourism is the fastest growing sector in Iceland and the annual tourist population is almost twice the size of Iceland's permanent population.[4] In spite of this growth, the sector consists mainly of small actors and is insufficiently funded by the state. The main actor in the tourism industry is Icelandair. Public funding dropped to a bare minimum after the financial crisis in 2008, and in 2010 The Icelandic Tourism Board received only 40 million ISK (approx. 246,400 EUR) for project funding. As a comparison, the National Tourist Routes in Norway, which serves as an archetype for the Icelandic Tourist Board, receives fifty to sixty times more funds every year (15 million EUR in 2013). The result is a general lack of capital to develop tourism infrastructure such as viewing platforms, paths, and restrooms, creating a significant need for an alternative financial model.

As a result of the expanding energy sector, Icelandic authorities have, since 1997, been developing a master plan for the construction of power plants. The master plan evaluates the impact of the proposed plans on issues such as cultural heritage, tourism and biodiversity. These are largely qualitative subjects, but the master plan attempts to quantify the impact through numeric assessment. The Purist Scale is an example of how qualitative aspects are quantified and ordered within a ranking system and is applied to evaluate the effects that proposed power plants have on nature-tourism.

The scale is based on a legal definition of wilderness, established as a minimum area of 25 square km without any visible human interventions.[5]

Both industry and tourism capitalize on the unique nature found in Iceland, in what is regarded as a conflict of interest between "pure wilderness" and "the manmade." For instance, in Norway, a country that serves as a role model for Icelandic preservation practices, municipalities have tried to stop windmill projects in order to obtain status as host to a "National Tourist Route." Windmills, the very epitome of "pure green" is visually in conflict with the notion of an untouched landscape, overlooking, of course, the fact that a "National Tourist Route" is a road for automobiles.[6] Similar conflicts are seen around the presence of power lines near roads with a "Tourist Route" status.

National Purist Routes

As a polemic response, the *National Purist Routes* project explores the intersecting fields of hydro and thermal energy, tourism, and natural landscapes. It proposes a network of hydrogen filling stations for rental cars which can serve as destinations across Iceland, suggesting possible synergies between the expanding energy and tourism industries.

The title refers to: 1) Hydrogen as a pure fuel, 2) "The Purist Scale", as used in the work with Iceland's current master plan for power projects, 3) The "National Tourist Routes" of Norway.

Gasoline remains the only imported source of energy in Iceland. The project proposes to test hydrogen technology on the rental car fleet as a next step to fulfil Iceland's ambitions of becoming a hydrogen economy.[7] As a tourist commodity *National Purist Routes* explores IMF's challenge to increase value retained from the region's hydro and geothermal resources. It also suggests a possible model of funding for a much needed tourism infrastructure, as it proposes a cooperation between public institutions like the Icelandic Tourist Board and private partners like Hertz, Shell and the national energy company Landsvirkjun. The filling stations are developed as tourist destinations located along the Ring Road and the national electricity grid.

Test Lab Iceland

As the poles melt and the ice retreats, resources are exposed and shipping routes revealed. The Arctic regions have joined the global map of resources. In Greenland, melting glaciers form the basis of a repetition of the "Karahnjukar model", a project Alcoa and The Greenland Home Rule Government are studying. The discourse concerning these new frontiers

2. 20% of the geothermal and 40% of hydro-electric resources have been exploited so far. Source: Benedikt Steingrímsson,Sveinbjörn Björnsson,Hákon Adalsteinsson, *Master Plan for Geothermal and Hydropower Development in Iceland.* (Reykjavik: Iceland GeoSurvey, 2007)

3. To see a map of proposed energy projects, see http://www.umhverfisraduneyti.is/media/PDF_skrar/ Kort-ur-skyrslu.pdf (downloaded November 1st, 2011)

4. Icelandic Tourist Board 2011

5. The theory has been widely used in the planning of national parks, wilderness and other recreation areas in both North America and Scandinavia. The term originates from the '60s and was implemented in Norway and Sweden in the '80s.

6. Klepp Municipality tried to stop the windmill park at Friestad when it became clear that the National Tourist Routes board would cancel further development of Turistvei Jæren. *Stavanger Aftenblad* 05.30.2007.

7. In 1998, Iceland's prime minister announced an

ambition to make Iceland the world's first hydrogen economy,thereby becoming self-sufficient in energy. Hydrogen is produced by electrolysis of water and used in a fuel cell where it is converted into electricity. In practice, hydrogen cars are electric vehicles, but have the qualities of a petroleum driven car in terms of short filling time, long driving distances and a powerful engine.

Icelandic nature is always on the move: A sub-glacial
volcanic eruption washed away several km of Route 1
during July 2011.

Construction of the Karahnjukar dam, 2006: Photograph
by Asgegg, courtesy Wikimedia commons/Creative Commons

Road construction: the dam required several km of new roadwork into the Icelandic Highlands.

The Kárahnjúkar Hydropower Plant: the dam increased the electricity production of Iceland by 40 percent.

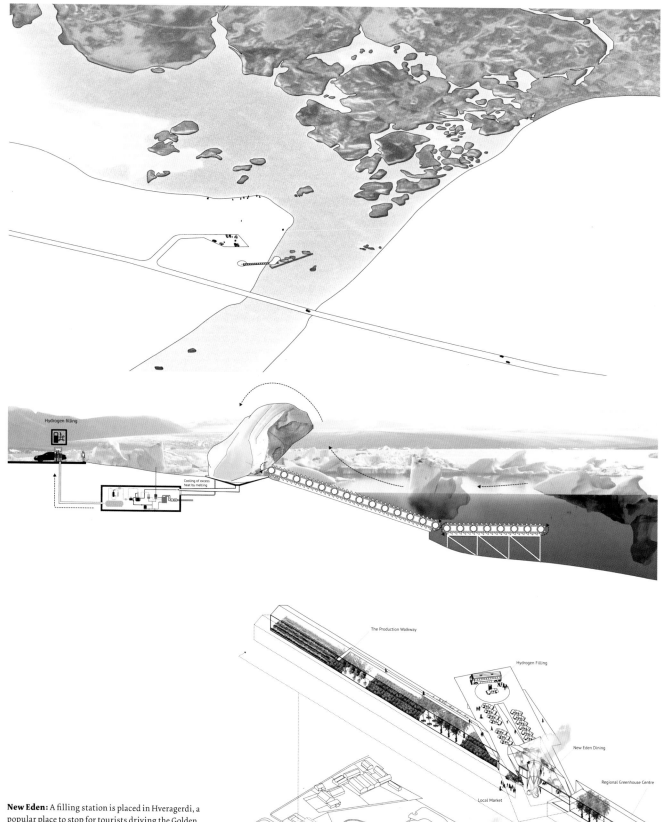

New Eden: A filling station is placed in Hveragerdi, a popular place to stop for tourists driving the Golden Circle. The station unites geothermal vegetable production with hungry tourists on the road.

Meltdown: Jökulsárlón, or "Glacier Lagoon" is located below the Vatnajökull glacier and is a well known site for tourists. Here the production of fuel becomes an attraction in itself, as melted ice runs down into the electrolyser and is turned into pure glacial hydrogen.

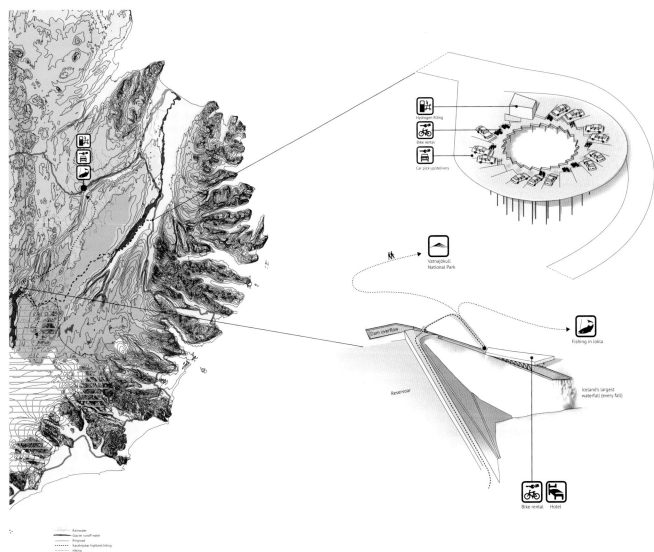

Rainwater
Glacier runoff water
Ringroad
Karahnjukar highland biking
Hiking
Vatnajökul National Park

10 km

Hydrogen filling

Bike rental

Car pick up/delivery

Vatnajökull
National Park

Fishing in Jokla

Dam overflow

Reservoar

Iceland's largest
waterfall (every fall)

Bike rental   Hotel

Into the Wild: New use is given to the roads developed
during the construction of the Kárahnjúkar dam. By
placing a combined filling station and bicycle rental
where the road starts, a new entry to the Vatnajökull
National Park is established. From the filling station you
can cycle through 70 km of wilderness on smooth tarmac
before reaching Kárahnjúkar. A hotel over Iceland's
highest waterfall, the overflow from the dam, gives
spectacular views. From here you can walk through the
National Park and pick up a new car at the Meltdown
filling station.

Feverscape: The next large energy project in line is at
Theistareykir, in the north of Iceland. Similar to the
Karahnjukar-project it is planned with a power plant
in the highlands and a smelter by the coast. Hot rivers
of excess heat are by-products of geothermal power
production. Instead of adding cooling towers, with the
sole purpose of cooling the water, we suggest a heated
landscape is proposed—a giant radiator that cools the
water and warms the tourists.

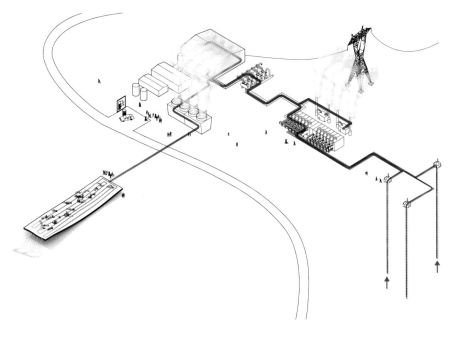

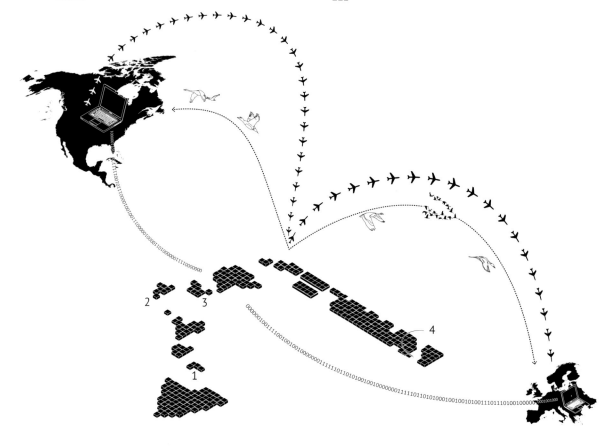

1: Heat and Sports

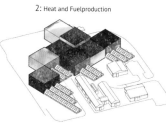

2: Heat and Fuelproduction

3: Heat and Cosmetic Herbs

4: Heat as Tourist Attraction

Pixel Forest: A former NATO-base becomes a forest of computers—and a place to fill up your car before returning it to Hertz at the airport. Excess heat from a large server park forms the basis of a new nature, where greenery and mild temperatures attract hungry migrating birds as well as curious tourists. At Pixel Forest, birds, people and computer signals cross paths on their journey across the North Atlantic.

of industrialization is increasingly being framed as a polarization of extraction versus preservation. Is there a third way? Echoing James Corner's call for a new landscape practice—could we view landscape as an active instrument to enrich culture, rather than a passive product of the culture?[8] Only two percent of the global geothermal energy potential has been utilized, and Iceland already regards knowledge and technology as export articles. National Purist Routes suggests Iceland acts as an Arctic testing ground where research is expanded beyond mere technical aspects, with an aim to include new cultural readings of the productive landscape as an asset for tourism and related industries.

Gislunn Halfdanardottir graduated from The Oslo School of Architecture and Design. She has worked for Fantastic Norway Architects and Conditions Magazine, and currently works at the Akershus County Council on a test-project for a regional hydrogen infrastructure.

Mathias Kempton has a degree from The Oslo School of Architecture and Design and is currently an architect at 4B Arkitekter. He has previously worked for Lateral Office, taught at the Universities of Waterloo and Toronto, and worked with the relocation of the arctic mining town Kiruna at Ghilardi+Hellsten Arkitekter.

8. Corner writes "While we ought to be thankful for the good work and increased visibility of both preservation and environmental groups, organized and funded at regional and national levels, the lack of any power or group aimed toward the cultivation of landscape as an innovative cultural agent is unfortunate; such forces are much needed" James Corner, *Recovering Landscape. Essays in Contemporary Landscape Architecture.* (New York: Princeton Architectural Press, 1999), 4.

TOWARDS ECOLOGICALLY INFORMED METHODS: DESIGN'S CONFRONTATION WITH COMPLEXITY

Maya Przybylski

As we understand an extreme as a position away from a balanced, predictable and familiar centre, it is reasonable to examine a condition of extreme as it relates to *complexity*. In particular, if complexity is understood as a characterization of the degree to which something is composed of many parts, the degree to which those parts are interrelated and, further, the sophistication of the processes that define these very relationships, it is possible to imagine moving towards an extreme complexity.

Acknowledging and managing increasingly higher levels of complexity within a design context is nothing new. Associative, or parametric, modeling is a well-established practice that places an interest in building complex, interrelated representations at the forefront. At one end of disciplinary activities, Building Information Modeling (BIM) combines physical and functional considerations of a design process by integrating spatial, material and performance-based representations in a single model. During the more exploratory phases of work, algorithmically generated forms and visualizations, whether through visual or procedural coding, have contributed to the creation of a variety of formal and organizational strategies. These, along with many others, have become reasonably accessible tools and techniques through which designers can confront complexity in their work.

Parallel to these developments focusing on the building scale, an effort within architecture, paired with the associated fields of landscape architecture and urban design, has also been interested in leveraging complexity, albeit at an entirely different scale. Specifically, these practitioners and researchers have become increasingly interested in developing *ecologically-informed* design strategies. These efforts are a revival and expansion of the inclusive design strategies originally outlined in such seminal texts as Ian McHarg's *Design with Nature*[1] and as such, these contemporary projects acknowledge the lessons acquired from ecological science, presenting natural systems as dynamic, interconnected, resilient, complex and indeterminate, and attempt to position strategies for design within this flux.

In particular, the discourse surrounding Landscape Urbanism, and its descendant discourse Ecological Urbanism, proposes that design should not set itself in opposition to natural processes, but instead be inclusive of and responsive to natural systems, operating on principles of synthesis and encouraging hybridity across natural and engineered systems.[2,3] In particular, Ecological Urbanism advocates a design practice wherein the

---

1. McHarg, Ian. 1969. *Design with Nature*. New York: The Natural History Press.
2. Waldheim, Charles. "On Landscape, Ecology and Other Modifiers to Urbanism." *Topos* 71 (2010): 20-24.
3. Thompson, Ian Hamilton. "Ten Tenets and Six Questions for Landscape Urbanism." *Landscape*

Research 37 (2012): 7 — 26.

project is seen to both affect and be affected by an inclusive set of environmental, social and economic factors.

Both in terms of how projects are identified and defined, and then how they are explored with an expanding set of tools, this discourse has contributed greatly to the first generation of tools that designers use to confront complexity. Seminal contributors are as follows: Keller Easterling pursues a description and analysis of environments generated more by systems of forces and flows—climatic, economic, social and political—than by willful formal acts.[4] Along similar lines, Alan Berger positions Systemic Design as a design framework which seeks to interact with environmental, economic and programmatic stresses across regional territories.[5] Berger claims that a systems-oriented relationship with design will lead to more intelligent project scenarios to address the most pressing challenges of our time. Although earlier in time, James Corner's pivotal landscape projects proposing the transformation of site through an ecologically informed methodology still stand strong as archetypes in this pursuit. The proposals, such as Fresh Kills Park and Downsview Park, are conceived as a result of intensive mappings of existing and proposed conditions and agents. These works are supported by Corner's writings on designing with process in time[6]: highlighting the proposed transformations as dynamic processes characterized by terms like fluidity, feedback, and non-linearity. By privileging these over such qualities as stability, predictability or rationality, Corner positions ecologically-informed concepts as essential to the designer.

Given the concerns of these and other projects, the appropriation of the term *ecology* is generally appropriate. Contemporary definitions of ecology foreground the importance of natural processes, defining the discipline as the study of "patterns and processes influencing the distribution of organisms, the interactions among organisms, and the interactions between organisms and the transformation and flux of energy, matter, and information."[7] In such a definition, ecology is not simply a synonym for the environment, nor does it necessarily suggest a 'green' agenda; instead it emphasizes a system-based holistic perspective of a given context. While this definition loosely supports the use of the term, the degree to which the principles of ecology are in fact pursued within a design practice and the opportunities found in its appropriation, are mostly left unarticulated.

Granted, such projects, some featured in this very volume, have advanced a generation of tools and techniques, such as spatial maps, timelines, organizational diagrams and other forms of visualizations to become potent drivers in the pursuit of presenting, synthesizing and mobilizing ecologically-informed design interventions. Yet, given the discussion surrounding complexity and extremes, it appears as though a limit is being approached. These drivers, for the most part, are presented as-is, with little explication of their validity, assumptions and limits. Consequently, they are, for the most part, bounded by the limits of metaphor; the authors assert the presence and agencies associated with Ecological Urbanism's suite of concerns while often stopping short of direct confrontation with the actual complexity represented.

That this relationship between design and ecology is based mostly on metaphor is not surprising, as metaphor is a likely point-of-entry for an appropriating discipline into the world of a specific science.[8] While metaphor is a useful communication tool across disciplines, as it can succinctly and accessibly summarize a mind frame, a general approach, a set of values, or a concept, it is critical to remember that there is a "rich, technical world" that stands behind each metaphor.[9] In seeking to apply principles of ecological science, moving beyond metaphor and confronting the details of the technical richness is critical, particularly in a pursuit related to confronting complexity in a more engaged way. This sense is

4. Easterling, Keller. 2005. *Enduring Innocence: Global Architecture and Its Political Masquerades.* Cambridge: The MIT Press.—. 1999. *Organizational Space.* Cambridge: MIT Press.

5. Berger, Alan. 2009. *Systemic Design Can Change the World.* Amsterdam: SUN Publishers.

6. Corner, James. 2006. "Terra Fluxus." In *The Landscape Urbanism Reader,* edited by Charles Waldheim, (New York: Princeton Architectural Press), 23-33.

6. Corner, James. 2006. "Terra Fluxus." In *The Landscape Urbanism Reader,* edited by Charles Waldheim, (New York: Princeton Architectural Press), 23–33.

7. Pickett, S.T.A., M.L. Cadenasso, and Brian McGrath. 2013. "Ecology of the City as a Bridge to Urban Design." In *Resilience in Ecology and Urban Design: Linking Theory and Practice for Sustainable Cities,* edited by S.T.A. Pickett, M.L. Cadenasso and

Brian McGrath, 7–26. Springer.

8. Ibid.

9. Ibid.

10. Reed, Chris. 2010. "The Agency of Ecology." In *Ecological Urbanism,* (Zurich: Lars Müller Publishers), 324-329.

11. Resnick, Mitchell. 1997. *Turtles, Termites, and Traffic Jams: Explorations in Massively Parallel Microworlds.* (Cambridge: MIT Press)

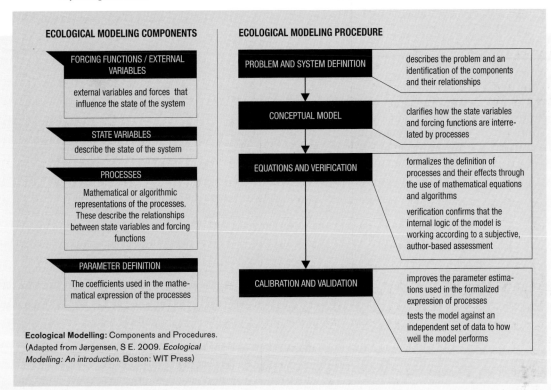

ECOLOGICAL MODELING COMPONENTS

FORCING FUNCTIONS / EXTERNAL VARIABLES

external variables and forces that influence the state of the system

STATE VARIABLES

describe the state of the system

PROCESSES

Mathematical or algorithmic representations of the processes. These describe the relationships between state variables and forcing functions

PARAMETER DEFINITION

The coefficients used in the mathematical expression of the processes

ECOLOGICAL MODELING PROCEDURE

PROBLEM AND SYSTEM DEFINITION — describes the problem and an identification of the components and their relationships

CONCEPTUAL MODEL — clarifies how the state variables and forcing functions are interrelated by processes

EQUATIONS AND VERIFICATION — formalizes the definition of processes and their effects through the use of mathematical equations and algorithms

verification confirms that the internal logic of the model is working according to a subjective, author-based assessment

CALIBRATION AND VALIDATION — improves the parameter estimations used in the formalized expression of processes

tests the model against an independent set of data to how well the model performs

Ecological Modelling: Components and Procedures. (Adapted from Jørgensen, S E. 2009. *Ecological Modelling: An introduction.* Boston: WIT Press)

even supported in the foundational text *Ecological Urbanism*, where, in his piece entitled "The Agency of Ecology", Chris Reed calls "for a fuller, more engaged approach to the ecological aspect of ecological urbanism."[10]

In search of a higher degree of engagement, a more complete unpacking of the tools and techniques utilized by the ecological sciences is necessary. The development of a robust modeling procedure, and the role of fieldwork and its recording, and the foregrounding of a process-oriented perspective, stand out as three mechanisms by which design can engage more directly with some of the 'rich technical world' of the ecological sciences.

Before examining each of these in more detail, it is worth pausing to consider that successfully appropriating these central concerns of the ecological sciences into a design context goes hand-in-hand with a more complete adaptation of computational tools and strategies.

To truly confront and mobilize the complexities of sites exposed by an inclusive, dynamic, systems-oriented design approach is deeply challenging. The territories exposed by an analysis focusing on dynamic processes dealing with forces, flows, interactions and feedback loops quickly grow in complexity, resulting in massively parallel micro-worlds.[11] Our human ability to manage these increasingly complex networks of causal relationships is limited, and complexity can become overwhelming and disabling for the designer. Abstraction can be used to make a problem more manageable through a process of reduction; but such filtering, efficacious as it may be, runs the risk, especially in an ecologically-oriented context, of losing the essence of the problem at hand. It is this liminal boundary that reinforces our dependence on metaphor and is resistant to designers' fuller embrace of complexity. Fortunately, the computational designer, in principle, is able to abstract the problem for initial action and then, relying on the machine as an automatic accountant, incrementally rebuild the lost complexity, thereby allowing the original richness of the problem space to be maintained. In the context of ecologically-informed design, the challenge for designers is not just how to develop these tools but how to expand their conception beyond formal concerns, to capture the process-oriented attributes of the problems they confront.

12. Soetaert, Karline, and Peter M.J. Herman. 2009. *A Practical Guide to Ecological Modelling: Using R as a Simulation Platform.* Springer.
13. Pickett, S.T.A., M.L. Cadenasso, and Brian McGrath.

2013. "Ecology of the City as a Bridge to Urban Design." In *Resilience in Ecology and Urban Design: Linking Theory and Practice for Sustainable Cities*, edited by S.T.A. Pickett, M.L. Cadenasso and Brian McGrath,

7–26. Springer.
14. Jørgensen, S E. 2009. *Ecological Modelling: An Introduction.* Boston: WIT Press.

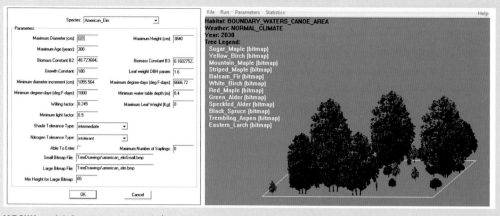

JABOWA model: Sample input and output. (Images courtesy of Daniel Botkin, www.danielbbotkin.com)

A Robust Modeling Framework

The need and general intentions of modeling are shared by both design and ecological sciences. A model is a simplified representation of a complex phenomenon. As mentioned above, abstraction through modeling highlights relevant aspects of a condition so as to support a focused action by the model's user. While models are used within both disciplines as a means of abstracting complex conditions, ecological modeling is a more mature practice with respect to addressing the inter-connections and dynamics associated with the subject complex phenomenon. Ecological modeling places emphasis on processes and playing out their dynamics in time and space by defining states of system components through the processes that affect them.[12] Contrarily, traditional design models propose and represent desired forms and the interactions that *should* be.[13]

Ecological modeling as a clear sub discipline of ecology appeared in the early '70s as a result of the development of models tackling increasingly sophisticated problems; a capacity closely linked to the emerging potentials and prevalence of computation. The maturity of the discipline was marked by the identification of a stepwise modeling procedure, which includes identifying the primary model components and considering not only the model's formation but also an evaluation of its usefulness.[14] Computational Ecology is an already established field examining these challenges directly. Developed in response to ecology's inherent interest in understanding complex systems, their transient qualities, and the challenges of creating replicable experiments under controlled conditions in the field, ecological modeling has become an increasingly powerful research tool to understand, and even predict, the dynamics of ecosystems.[15, 16]

Thus, ecological models are charged with additional essential attributes, which allow them to perform as the more precise instruments demanded by a systems-based perspective. Briefly, these expanded criteria require that authors of a model make explicit its purpose, its referenced collection of ideas and theoretical frameworks, its assumptions, its limits, and its behavior, as well as how its outputs can be used and interpreted.[17, 18] Key to all of this is the clarity by which the assumptions are outlined. In fact, some ecologists consider a model simply as an explicit set of assumptions working together to gain insights into the cause-and-effect of dynamic processes.[19]

One of these early models, with an updated version still in use today, is the JABOWA Forest dynamics model developed in 1970 by Daniel B. Botkin, James F. Janak and James R. Wallis, then of the IBM Thomas J. Watson Research Center. The JABOWA model was the first successful application of digital computer simulation to a complex natural ecosystem. It allows users to simulate forest growth by adjusting environmental inputs such as location,

15. Petrovskii, Sergei, and Natalia Petrovskaya. 2012. "Computational Ecology as an Emerging Science." *Interface Focus* 2 (2): 241-253.
16. Rykiel, Edward J. 1996. "Testing Ecological Models: The Meaning of Validation." *Ecological Modelling*

229-244.
17. Ibid.
18. Rykiel, Edward J. 1996. "Testing Ecological Models: The Meaning of Validation." *Ecological Modelling* 229-244.

19. Botkin, Daniel B. 1993. *Forest Synamics: An Ecological Model.* (Oxford University Press),8.

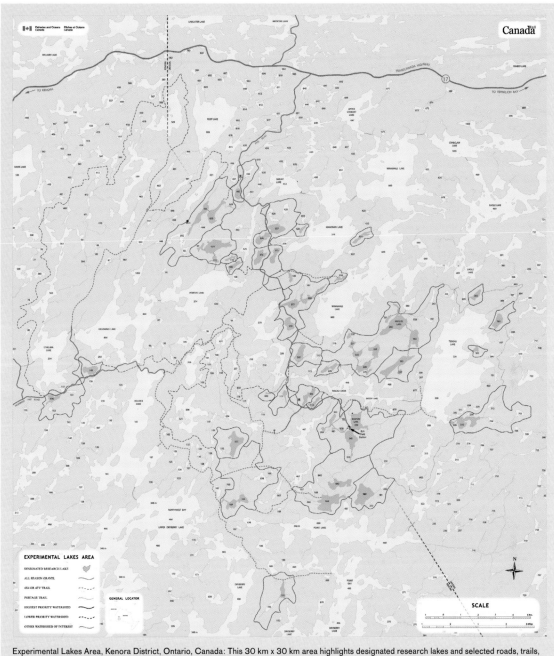

Experimental Lakes Area, Kenora District, Ontario, Canada: This 30 km x 30 km area highlights designated research lakes and selected roads, trails, and watersheds. (Image by: Fiseries and Oceans Canada / Pêches et Océans Canada)

elevation, soil, rainfall and external factors such as logging practices and climate change forces. The development of this model marked a switch from a time where concepts and ideas were not only expressed as static mathematical equations but were also mobilized into a research tool to simulate and investigate complex systems.[20] The development of this model follows closely the ecological modeling framework outlined above where the model is understood as a threefold assembly: the conceptual model, defining model context and philosophy; the technical definition, describing the equations and algorithms that drive the model; and the application, which describe the appropriate uses for the model.

20. Puettmann, Klaus J, David K Coates, and Christian C Messier. 2012. *A Critique of Silviculture: Managing for Complexity.* (Island Press), 84.

Although ecological science has committed to the development of a robust procedure for developing, using, and evaluating its models, it is still very much debated whether ecologists can explain the complexity of the systems with more sophisticated modeling techniques and increasing computer power, or, if the complexity of the subject systems is too complex to be simplified.[21] This ongoing debate has ensured that field-based experiments and collecting long-term background records remain active parts of ecology's work.

Fieldwork and Sharing Data

Ecological fieldwork can also be extreme. Canada's Experimental Lakes Area (ELA) is a network of lakes, located in remote Northern Ontario, dedicated to bold ecological manipulations since 1967. The area, remote enough to be pristine yet reasonably accessible only 300 kilometres east of Winnipeg, consists of 58 lakes in 17 watersheds spread over 1000 square kilometres. Through the over 50 massive experiments undertaken at the site throughout its history, the work at ELA ushered in an era of what researchers call "extreme science." [22] Because of the combination of location and scale, the projects carried out on site are among a shortlist in the world that can be considered as whole ecosystem experiments. During its 40 years of operation the experiments have manipulated food webs, examined effects of habitat destruction, and studied the impact of caged aquaculture just to name a few.[23] Among the more famous experiments conducted at the site confirmed phosphorous from detergents as the cause of algae blooms and provided compelling evidence of the harmful effects of acid rain.

The role that fieldwork plays in the context of ecologically-informed methods is twofold. On the one hand, the fieldwork provides base data from which to derive the numerically defined rules and standards that will drive the underlying logic of subsequent ecological models. On the other hand, fieldwork offers ecologists a mechanism by which to test and validate their modeling approaches. Conversely, modeling can contribute to fieldwork in its own right. By developing increasingly more reliable models, ecologists are effectively able to test and calibrate their experiments before going into the field. While not replacing the value of the fieldwork, the test simulations help researchers effectively design the experiments they plan to conduct thereby controlling costs and required resources. Thus, computer models can significantly enhance our ability to address the issues of cause-and-effect relations on temporal and spatial scales.[24] It's not surprising that many ecologists recognize that modeling and fieldwork have their respective strengths and weaknesses and that a productive relationship to the complex problems faced by the science requires a variety of coordinated approaches.

Process-Oriented Perspective

Ecologist Mary Cadenasso, has offered work presenting analytical fieldwork strategies that expand ecologically-informed design approaches. While not confronting the issues of ecologically-informed design modeling directly, Cadenasso does foreground a process-oriented, functional perspective of a context. Specifically, HERCULES (High Ecological Resolution Classification for Urban Landscapes and Environmental Systems), supports methods for recognizing, analyzing, representing and designing ecological heterogeneity.[25]

The system is presented as an alternative to existing methods used for documenting urban heterogeneity, which is typically accomplished through a functional classification system highlighting various land uses, such as residential, commercial, industrial, and so on. In this regard, the HERCULES system is focused on *land cover* rather than *land use*. Land use describes the socio-economic function of a landscape fragment and, from an ecological perspective, such classification is less useful as groups that exhibit similarities in land use may have entirely different ecological functioning. The example used by the authors of the system points to 'residential' as a common land use class and goes on to

21. Ibid.22. Stokstad, Erik. 2008. "Canada's Experimental Lakes." *Science*, November 28: 1316–1319.

22. Stokstad, Erik. 2008. "Canada's Experimental Lakes." *Science*, November 28: 1316–1319.

23. Ibid.

24. Botkin, Daniel B. 1993. *Forest Dynamics: An Ecological Model.* (Oxford University Press), 8.

25. Cadenasso, Mary L. 2013. "Designing Ecological Heterogeneity." In *Urban Design Ecologies (AD Reader)*,

by Brian (Ed) McGrath (London: John Wiley & Sons Ltd.), 272-281.

Extreme Science: A key experiment on ELA's Lake 226 shows the relationship between phosphorous-based fertilizer and the growth algae blooms. (1979, photographer unknown).

explain that "all residential land is not *structurally* the same due to the fine scale variation in building density, vegetation and the amount of impervious surfaces." [26] Such information, lost in the land use-centered approach, is considered potentially relevant in the understanding of ecological functioning. [27] Contrarily, a land cover approach foregrounds elements that influence ecological processes by referring to the physical pattern of biophysical structures present across a landscape.

The HERCULES system suggests a paradigm shift in how designers recognize, analyze and represent urban conditions. The tool foregrounds structural heterogeneity as key property in understanding urban conditions from an ecological perspective and keeps track of this property across a variety of scales. This shift demonstrates the potentials of transdisciplinary approaches to design. The tool, developed by an ecologist, recognizes the urban designer as being an influential agent in determining the spatial heterogeneity of urban systems and contributes an additional lens through which the designer understands site by biasing a reading of the site that foregrounds ecological functioning.

26. Ibid.
27. Ibid.

It is reasonable to assume that the availability of such a tool could support the expanding, inclusive set of interests identified by the ecologically-informed design approach. However, this classification system is still mostly about visualizing an existing or proposed condition. The functions and processes causing the changes in land cover are absent from this representation of the landscape.

Conclusion

Speculating on how this pairing of such analytical work could combine with modeling strategies in an ecologically-informed design context is seen as a worthwhile endeavor. Can an expansion of tools and approaches allow for a more integrated and committed relationship to the investigation of complex spatial/temporal systems in a design context? The challenge implied by this text is by no means trivial. Just as the advancement of ecological models marked a transition away from static mathematical equations towards dynamic research tools for investigating complex systems, the call here asks if such a switch is possible with respect to the current suite of approaches used in work associated with the Landscape Urbanism discourse.

In addition to acknowledging and appropriating the mechanisms described above, a collective effort is undoubtedly required as the sharing of existing knowledge and data is an essential. While early explorations will likely happen with over-simplified, over-abstracted systems, it should be hoped that as these dynamic tools are developed, they will incrementally grow in complexity.

A key element of ecology's computational modeling activity is the expanded set of reference materials and verified, by way of fieldwork, standards that are used by the community for specifying sub-components within increasingly complex models.[28] Within urban studies, efforts to create and expand such scientific, numerically-based standards for model components are appearing within an emerging discourse entitled the "science of the city".[29] This work will undoubtedly be useful for design in this context however, strategies for transferring and using the assembled knowledge in a design-focused domain remain a research frontier.

Thus, designers interested in building such ecologically-oriented approaches to design need a way to collectively build, share and validate the standards and data that will support the inner workings of the tools they develop. The ecological sciences has the ECOBAS project, an online database and system for documentation of mathematical descriptions of ecological processes. The system offers convenient access to information, complete and precise documentation of mathematical formulations and a standardization of documentation.

While the JABOWA Forestry model has inspired development of numerous new models for a variety of ecosystems around the world, it is motivating to note that, at its conception, it was driven by as much an interest in the computational potential of managing a complex system as it was in the specific ecological functioning of the forest in question.[30] It is in such spirit that this provocation to expand design-based modeling practices is considered. The goal in this early speculation is not to recreate the complexity right away but to begin speculating on how to develop a similarly rigorous procedure for ecologically-informed design modeling whereby designers are more prepared to venture into the extreme.

---

28. Jørgensen, S E. 2009. *Ecological modelling: An Introduction.* Boston: WIT Press.
29. Batty, Michael. 2013. *The New Science of Cities.* Cambridge: MIT Press.

30. Puettmann, Klaus J, David K Coates, and Christian C Messier. 2012. *A Critique of Silviculture: Managing for Complexity.* Island Press.

hacking ecologies

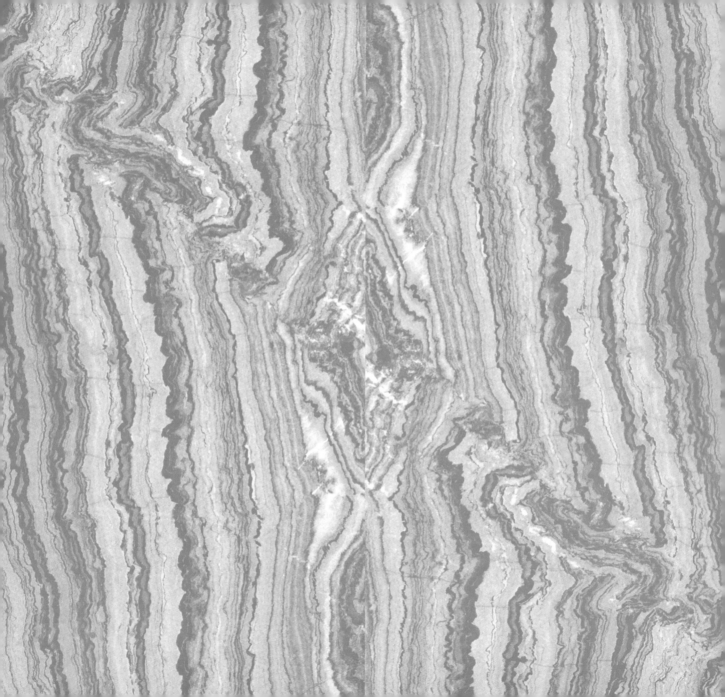

RAISING ISLANDS

Chris Knight

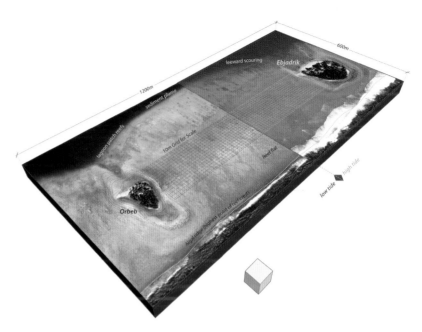

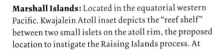

Marshall Islands: Located in the equatorial western Pacific. Kwajalein Atoll inset depicts the "reef shelf" between two small islets on the atoll rim, the proposed location to instigate the Raising Islands process. At

right, the contrast between high & low tide illustrates the highly variable nature of this edge condition.

To speak of an 'extreme environment' for human habitation is to bring to mind high mountains, scorching deserts or arctic expanses. The lushness of a tropical atoll is perhaps one of the last places we might imagine looking for such a landscape. Beginning with the descriptions of early explorers such as Cook and Wallace, the conventional image of the people of the Pacific islands has been overwhelmed with images of humankind in an undisturbed state of nature; a languid and carefree existence made possible by a benign and bountiful landscape which freely provides all the necessities of life. In fact, atolls are one of the most challenging environments ever colonized by mankind.

The islands are seldom more than two metres above sea level, and are composed entirely of sand derived from the living reefs which ring the atoll and grow in the lagoons. The sediment which make up these sand islands—or *motu*—is generated by the erosive power of waves crashing on the reefs, but also the significant biological erosion created by corallivorous fishes and invertibrates which feed on the living corals and excrete coralline sands into the water column. These sediments are driven by waves and currents up onto the flat reef shelf, and eventually into the lagoon. In effect, atolls are enormous natural sediment traps. There is no ground water; the porous bedrock beneath the sand, is saturated with salt-water. Rainfall, which soaks into the sand, percolates down until it reaches this saline layer, where—because of its lower density—it floats. Enough rainwater can build up in this way to form what is called a "Ghyben-Herzberg" lens, a body of freshwater soaked into the island sediment which presses down on the saline layer below it, forming the only tenuous source of drinking water.

There is no truly solid 'ground' in the atoll islands, in the sense that all of the land consists of a relatively thin layer of sand and rubble consolidated by a resilient scattering of plant species which are salt-tolerant enough to survive. The island environment is constantly in flux, periodically inundated by storm-driven tides, torn apart by cyclonic winds, or even completely washed away by cataclysmic waves which leave nothing behind but the bare coral shelf. Early settlers brought with them a whole host of resources (in the form of introduced plant and animal species), technologies (farming, forestry, hunting and fishing techniques) and cultural practices (such as land tenure, taboos, traditional laws, and the canoe-voyaging tradition) which enabled them to flourish. In contrast to the image of these

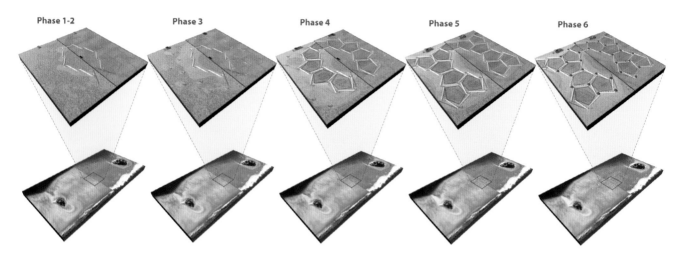

Phase 1-2   Phase 3   Phase 4   Phase 5   Phase 6

Overview of the Raising Islands process through its implementation over a 50 year time scale: Each diagram shows high & low tide. Beginning with completely submersible aquaculture infrastructure, the natural sedimentation process eventually makes seaweed and mangrove cultivation possible. In the final stages inhabitable islets have formed, anchored to the reef shelf with a mineral structure which encourages sedimentation and freshwater retention.

early settlers drawn by continental cultures, the people of the Pacific islands radically transformed their landscapes, modifying the flora and fauna to suit their needs and provide food and shelter.

In this era of dawning anthropogenic climate change, people of atoll nations face grievous threats to their future. Rising sea levels, a warming ocean, and changing weather patterns conspire with economic isolation, rapidly growing populations, and the loss of traditional livelihoods to perpetuate conditions of dependance and wardship which threaten the very existence of their island homes. *Raising Islands* examines an atoll nation of the equatorial Pacific, the Republic of the Marshall Islands (RMI). The RMI is a vast marine landscape consisting of twenty-nine atolls made up of thousands of kilometres of submerged reefs, azure lagoons, and many individual islets of sand bound together by a fragile mantle of vegetation. An outward appearance of pristine tropical paradise belies a tragic history of nuclear weapons and ballistic missile testing at the hands of the United States military, which has occupied the Marshall Islands since the Second World War. Despite the sustained efforts of Marshallese politicians and intellectuals—resulting in the establishment of the RMI as an independent sovereign state in 1986—the United States maintains a major military base on the largest atoll—Kwajalein. The upheavals caused by years of weapons testing have resulted in an extremely fragile situation on the tiny islet of Ebeye located adjacent to the military base. Known by the unfortunate epithet "the slum of the Pacific," Ebeye is a narrow strip of sand and concrete which is now home to some fifteen-thousand people, who are drawn by the promise of jobs on the military base or who have been evicted from their ancestral land to make way for the testing of missiles, which continues to this day.

This militarized landscape consists of a whole gamut of mechanisms which are imposed upon it to apprehend and maintain control by the prevailing regimes of power. These structures range from the abstract: cartographic manipulation; aesthetic, legalistic or scientific classification; and the descriptive appropriations of the landscape in a peoples' cultural imagination, to the physical walls, checkpoints, barriers and armed presence of the occupier on the land. *Raising Islands* proposes a design strategy which empowers local people to effectively occupy and reclaim their landscape by engaging with natural processes, albeit technologically enhanced. While islanders and the landscapes they inhabit have been consistently framed in a rhetoric stressing vulnerability and smallness, often to the advantage of distant powers maintaining explicit or *de facto* dominion from beyond the horizon, the independent, grassroots actions of local groups have achieved surprising and dramatic results in defiance of the policies and planners at the top.

The design concept utilizes *mineral accretion technology* (or MAT) to construct a marine infrastructure on the intertidal reef-flats of the atolls, in support of a variety of aquaculture enterprises. MAT is a process developed in the '70s by an architect/engineer named Wolf Hilbertz, further refined in the '80s with the input of an oceanographer, Thomas Goreau. Together, they developed a system whereby simple metal structures are submerged in seawater and undergo a process of mineral deposition

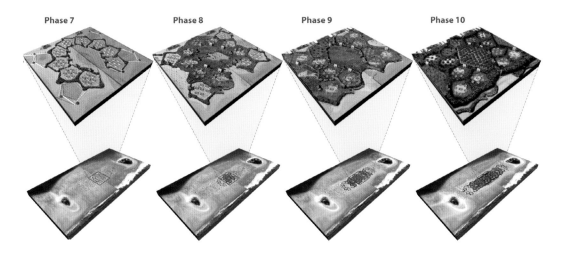

induced by the application of low-voltage electric current. Following the accretion process, living corals can be implanted on the frames, which form an ideal medium for coral growth. The system is a powerful tool for the rehabilitation and reinforcement of threatened coral habitats, and has been utilized to great success in more than twenty countries. This aquaculture infrastructure doubles as a framework to encourage the natural processes of sedimentation, acting as a transformative landscape generator. Over time this enables local people—acting in small, incremental ways, with cheap and lightweight components—to manipulate the marine and terrestrial environments in useful ways. The reef-flat infrastructures are paired with a number of activities which take place on adjacent islands and within the near-shore lagoon, including the installation of artificial reefs, the cultivation of sea-plants and mangroves, and the rehabilitation of the terrestrial landscapes with the reintroduction of traditional food-crops, and the introduction of new ones.

Making use of existing technologies—both traditional and contemporary, imported from success-ful examples abroad—the project argues that it is possible for the Marshallese to begin working immediately on the transformation of their land and sea-scapes to construct a new and unique system of inhabitation and livelihood production. The proposal focuses on incremental strategies, working with local groups, using cheap and easily implemented technologies, and the creativity, experience and innovativeness fostered by involvement in the production of a personal stake in ones' future, rather than the current dependance of large-scale, foreign influences.

Raising Islands builds on this idea, conceptualizing a mode of life in the atoll environment which recognizes that islanders have always 'raised' their islands out of nothing, and theorizes that this pro-cess might continue with the adoption and adaptation of new technologies and practices. The proposal also involves looking at environmental conditions in ways that are familiar to island people: rather than measuring in terms of land area and rainfall to determine the capacity of the terrestrial landscape, the proposal considers the marine landscape as an inseparable and essential component in the capacity of the atoll to support human endeavour. The process describes the possibility of quite literally 'rais-ing islands' from the reef shelf. The design does not propose a final condition, but suggests an array of systems, techniques, and livelihoods which, considered together, would empower local people to experiment and develop a format for inhabitation which is sustainable in the long-run.

Chris Knight is a graduate architect, designer and builder from Toronto. He received his Master's in Architecture from the University of Waterloo School of Architecture in 2012 and currently lives and works in Vancouver.

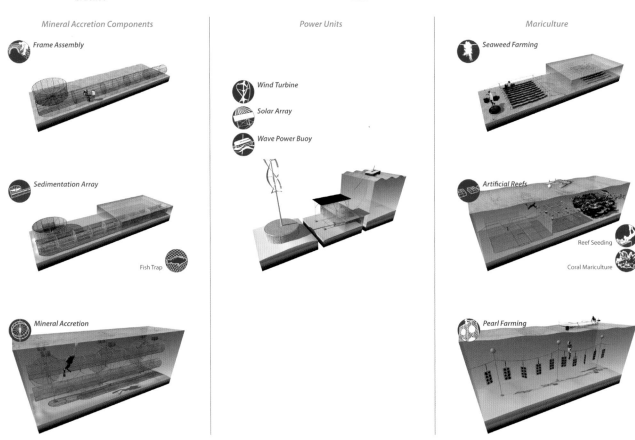

Mineral Accretion Components	Power Units	Mariculture
Frame Assembly		*Seaweed Farming*
Sedimentation Array	*Wind Turbine*	*Artificial Reefs*
Fish Trap	*Solar Array*	Reef Seeding
	Wave Power Buoy	Coral Mariculture
Mineral Accretion		*Pearl Farming*

Technologies & activities utilized in the Raising Islands process: The primary components in the sedimentation process are the "spars" & "pens" shown in the left-hand column; simple and lightweight, they can be manipulated by small groups of people to form large-scale structures which are then transformed by the mineral accretion process into permanent landscape elements.

Phase 5: The sedimentation array allows the culturing of seaplants in favourable conditions for growth while protecting them from grazers in "exclosures". The tide flows freely through - essential for the health of the crop - but slows its retreat, minimizing the time the plants exposed out of water. Over time the exclosures fill with sediment, forming a landscape suitable for mangrove cultivation.

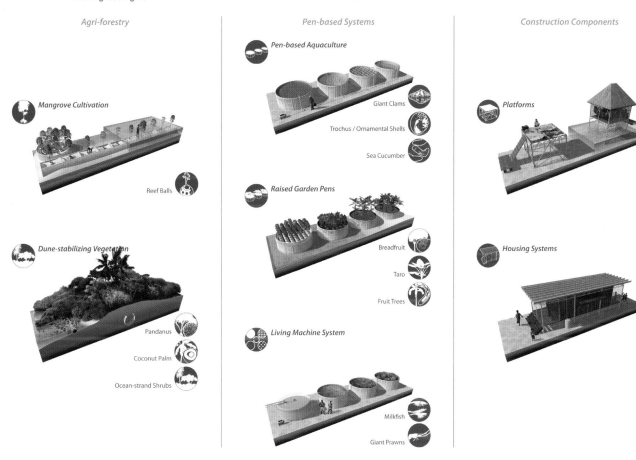

Agri-forestry

Mangrove Cultivation

Reef Balls

Dune-stabilizing Vegetation

Pandanus

Coconut Palm

Ocean-strand Shrubs

Pen-based Systems

Pen-based Aquaculture

Giant Clams

Trochus / Ornamental Shells

Sea Cucumber

Raised Garden Pens

Breadfruit

Taro

Fruit Trees

Living Machine System

Milkfish

Giant Prawns

Construction Components

Platforms

Housing Systems

Phase 8: A mangrove forest has vigorously colonized the sedimentation array. The mangroves continue the process catalyzed by the sedimentation array, stabilizing coralline sands driven up onto reef shelf. Sedimentation will eventually choke out the mangroves making it possible to clear the highest points of new islets for the planting of dune stabilizing vegetation.

Phase 10: The system is designed to advance horizontally; it is a process constantly in transition. Here, the inhabited sedimentation array stretches into the distance showing various stages of development. A fishtrap (phases 1-3) is visible in the foreground; beyond this seaweed exclosures give way to mangrove seedlings (phases 4–7). The section shows the new islet now firmly established above sea level.

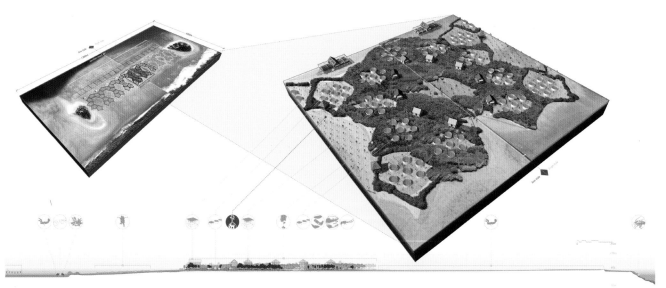

The emerging islets develop a broad base of livelihood activities: The enhanced environment is more responsive to sea-level change than natural motu, and much more resilient than urbanized atolls. A man-made reef is now a feature along the entire lagoon shore - providing fishing and hunting and producing sand which is washed up among the mangroves. Vegetation anchors the dunes, protecting landforms during storms. The people who settle here will also have to be resilient—prepared to take shelter on leeward islands in typhoon season, and willing to live in a challenging marine environment.

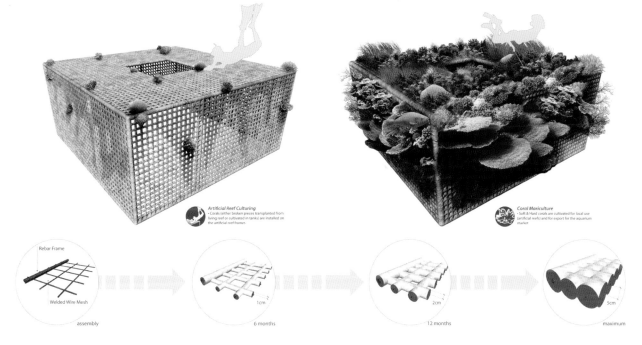

Man-made reefs: The sister component to the sedimentation array above water is the man-made reefs submerged in shallow lagoon waters. The array requires a source of sediment—all of the sand which makes up atoll islands is derived directly from the living reefs which surround them. The man-made reefs compliment existing reef ecosystems: used to spur the growth of existing reefs; repair damage caused by climate change, pollution or storm events; and to create new reef ecosystems in locations not naturally suitable for their growth.

TERRITORIES OF NOWHERE

Liz Lessig

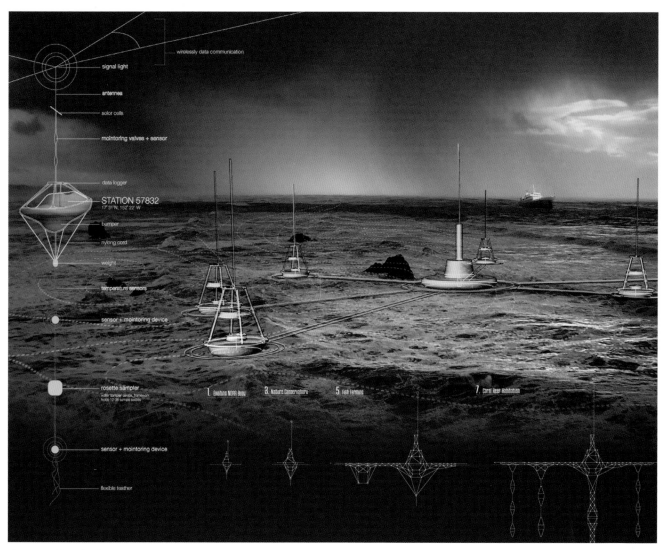

The new pacific archipelago: A network of programmed buoys.

Unless you plan to live in a space suit the rest of your life, you are going to have to engage relatively unprotected with the challenges of your surroundings. Architecture in collaboration with other disciplines, can invent new ways to design our future built environment, not as an isolation from the extreme, but as an exploit of adversity.
— *David Garcia*

Twenty-nine hours after reactor number four exploded at the Chernobyl plant in Ukraine, scientists in Sweden, located over one thousand kilometres away, were beginning to receive alarms of high levels of radiation. A moment of crisis,

this disaster had global ramifications beyond both political and geographic boundaries. The meltdown, the weather pattern, the scientists; they all represent the interdependencies of society and our ecological environment. Every day, we face environmental, political, and economic catastrophes which cross over the limits of the built environment. Whether that catastrophe is a nuclear meltdown or a severe weather condition, we are expanding our understanding of the environment as an increasingly complex web of interconnected networks, and their interrelated set of risks.

Risk Territories

Being at risk is the way of being and ruling in the world of
modernity; being at global risk is the human condition at the
beginning of the twenty-first century.

— Ulrich Beck, "Risk Society's Cosmopolitan Moment" [1]

The perception of risk is an expression of our fear of the
other, the alternative, the utopian, the future. Occupation no
longer operates in relation to boundaries, exclusions and
inclusions or controlled access, but relative to new geographies that transcend political and national borders. While
perception of risk often produces states of inequality and
destabilization, risk can also be a catalyst for the emergence
of new models of environmental conditions, landscapes,
and networks. Responding to both global and local forces,
these mutating territories are constantly shifting, crossing
national borders, creating new transnational geographies and
exposing new potential spatial orders. The qualities of these
territories are influenced by multiple forces including weather
patterns, air pollution, economic trends, and other intangible
forces. These form interior islands devoid of activity and
oversight, exterior to built form, power and activity.

Mapping Risk

Architecture's current representational techniques are not
capable of depicting the degrees of transformation evident
in today's built environment. Spanish theorist, Ignasi de
Sola-Morales suggested that "change in reality, in science, in
behavior, and in experience inevitably produce a permanent
strangeness." [2] Risk mapping offers a practice and a toolset,
to address the representational challenges that are confronting these nebulous zones.

   Many of these nebulous or risk territories are elusive,
yet retain a specificity and physicality. Atmosphere is an
invisible layer that is constantly in interaction with the built
environment we inhabit. Mark Wigley in "Architecture of
Atmosphere," writes that "atmosphere starts precisely where
the construction stops. It surrounds a building, clinging to the
material object." [3] David Gissen coins the term 'subnatures'
as elements of smoke, exhaust, dust, the heat of crowds, and
mud as "under-theorized, under-discussed, and under-visual-
ized in architecture." [4] He argues these are often "overlooked
in the more general discussion of what might be termed
natural architecture." [5] He describes subnatural as "the realm
in which we can barely exist in the state that we currently
conceive ourselves, both socially or biologically. It is that
zone that is most fearsome, because it describes the limits
in which contemporary life might be staged". [6]

   Six months after the accident at Fukushima, around the
clock news about the incident had ceased, but evidence of
scientific studies of radioactive material in the Pacific Ocean

became evident. As a result of the earthquake, a large amount
of urban artifacts, physical manifestations of the element, consisting of radioactive objects from the coast is moving along
the Pacific Ocean current towards the west coast of the United
States. Tracking and testing this data in the Pacific Ocean are
the monitoring stations and NOAA buoys (National Oceanic
and Atmospheric Administration). Territories of Nowhere
aims to provide methods for sensing, monitoring, testing,
and revealing the connection from the unpredictable aspect
of risk and the physical places we occupy. Data tracking is a
subversive, informal, bottom-up system designed to mark and
indicate where these risks conditions are.

Territory of Nowhere: The New Pacific Archipelago

Situated in the territory of the Pacific Ocean, the design
proposal entitled *The New Pacific Archipelago*, is tested
where fluctuating and ephemeral conditions of 'risk' explored
in the research are manifested. The site, seemingly void and
absent of activity, opens up possibilities. Though a hijacking of the existing buoy network in the Pacific Ocean, the
project proposes a new landscape—a re-rigging of the Pacific
through the phasing in of a new archipelagic typology—to
create a system of micro-islands and micro-economies. The
existing NOAA buoys, currently used to conduct oceanic and
geophysical observation, are augmented, repurposed and
hijacked to form an archipelago of technological islands that
are constantly mutating.

   The different morphologies or states enable the network
of island-buoys to grow and adopt other programmatic pieces.
For example, a nature conservatory, while still embedded
with the scientific data collection components, allows for an
expanded scaffolding system to provide shelter and substrate
for various marine life, fostering new ecologies for migrating seabird colonies. The stations become reconfigurable
offshore communities, mobile infrastructure, and aquatic
programmatic components. The phase change and growth of
these buoy also is dependent on economic factors that initiate
rapid growth as the program transitions into aspects such
as offshore banking and deep-sea aquaculture. At the large
scale, these configurations can cluster depending on oceanic
conditions, proximity to urban coastal areas, programmatic or
ecological opportunities. For instance, pairings begin to occur
between a nature conservatory and a casino overlapping,
merging ecosystems and human habitats.

   The project responds to environmental and political
conditions, subverting conventional ideas of building, land,
and architecture. The proposal looks at the forces, flows, and
energies that exist in the physical environment, and argues
that occupation is no longer operating in relation to defined
boundaries, but rather, relative to new geographies that transcend physical and political borders.

1. Ulrich Beck, "Risk Society's Cosmopolitan Moment"
(Lecture, Harvard University, Boston, MA, November
12, 2008).
2. Ignasi Solà-Morales, "Terrain Vague," in *Anyplace*, ed.

Cynthia Davidson (Cambridge: MIT Press, 1995), 118-23.
3. Mark Wigley, "The Architecture of Atmosphere,"
Daidalos, no. 68, (1998) 18
4. David Gissen, *Subnature: Architecture's Other*

Environments: Atmospheres, Matter, Life, (New York:
Princeton Architectural, 2009), 21.
5. Ibid, p.21
6. Ibid, p.23

PHASE 2: NATURE CONSERVATORY
STATION 84638
55° 0' 40", 171° 58' 50" W

PHASE 6: TIDAL HARVESTING + AQUACULTURE
STATION 84638
55° 0' 40", 171° 58' 50" W

VANCOUVER

PHASE 5: AQUACULTURE + RESEARCH
STATION 84638
55° 0' 40", 171° 58' 50" W

SAN FRANCISCO

LOS ANGELES

TOKYO

BEIJING

PHASE 6: TIDAL HARVESTING +
NATURE CONSERVATORY
STATION 84638
55° 0' 40", 171° 58' 50" W

PHASE 7: PRISON + GYRE BUSTER
STATION 57832
51° 9' 17" N, 179° 0' 2" E

PHASE 6: GYRE BUSTER
Station 57832
51° 9' 17" N, 179° 0' 2" E

HONG KONG

PHASE 8: TIDAL HARVESTING
STATION 84638
55° 0' 40", 171° 58' 50" W

MEXICO CITY

BANGKOK

PHASE 10: CASINO + CRUISE TERMINAL
STATION 22479
20° 56' 56" N, 132° 18' 49" E

PHASE 11: SOVEREIGN NATION
STATION 22479
20° 56' 56" N, 132° 18' 49" E

SINGAPORE

LIMA

PHASE 1: NOAA BUOY
STATION 55432
15° 4' 24" N, 145° 46' 11" E

PHASE 3: RESEARCH STATION
STATION 62845
55° 0' 40", 171° 58' 50" W

SYDNEY

VALPARAISO

Re-rigging the Pacific: Each node of buoys takes on
different clusters of programmatic functions.

Liz Lessig is a designer and urbanist, with an interest in urban
strategies in conjunction with data-driven methodologies. She is
currently a design strategist at MKThink, an architectural think tank
and recent MArch graduate from California College of the Arts.

ARCHIPELAGO MORPHOLOGIES

Existing NOAA Buoy [1]

Nature Conservatory [2]

Research Facility [3]

Aquaculture [4]

Tidal Harvesting [5]

TESTING

gps   anemometer   real time data   testing   research lab

ENVIRONMENTAL

sea birds   sealions   wetland vegetation   recycling   coral reef

INFRASTRUCTURE

aquaculture   tidal energy   production   transporation

OFFSHORE

prison   cruise liners   money sheltering   gambling   hotel   sovereignty

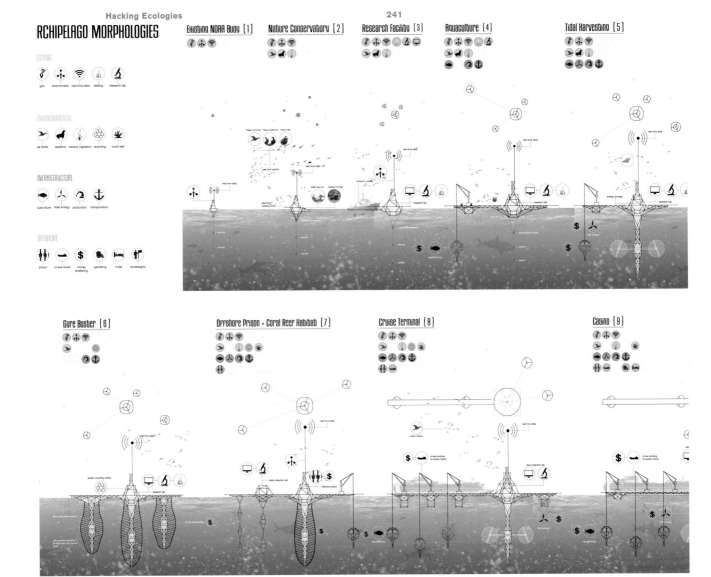

Gyre Buster [6]

Offshore Prison + Coral Reef Habitat [7]

Cruise Terminal [8]

Casino [9]

Tax Haven [10]

Sovereign Nation [11]

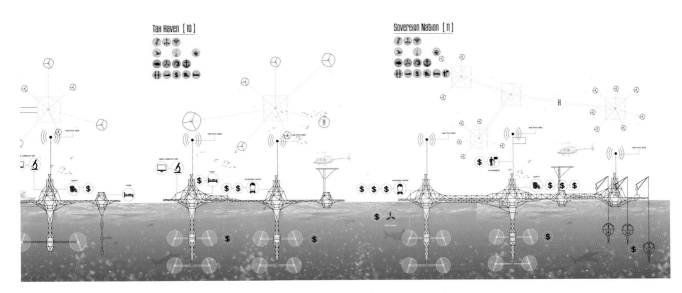

Archipelago morphologies: The proposal, a new pacific archipelago, are active landscapes that are constantly undergoing temporal mutations, represented in a series of morphologies. Each of these phase change has certain conditions it is responding to programmatically, representation through a notation system calling out four traits: testing, environmental, infrastructural, and offshore.

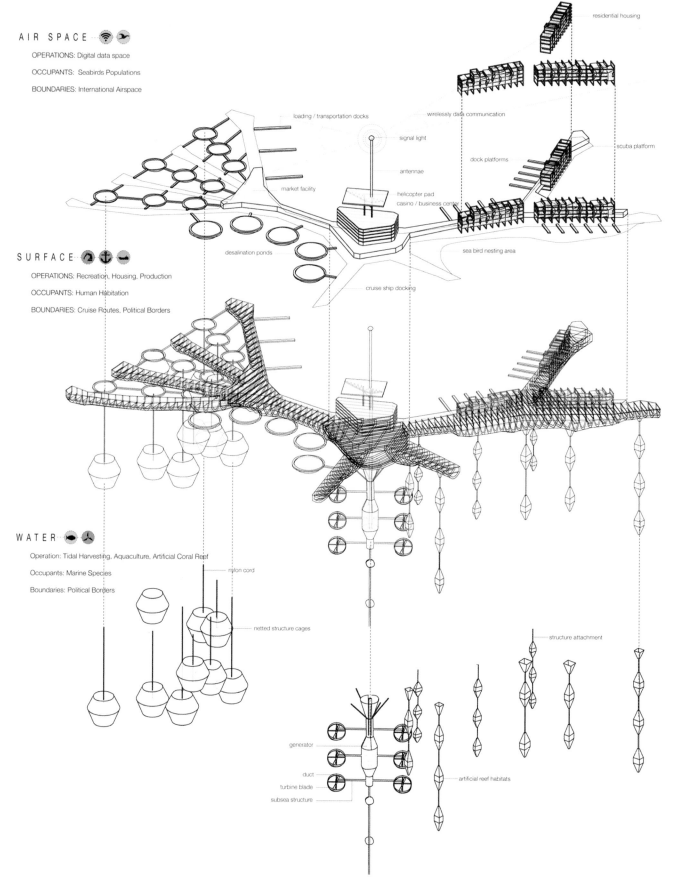

AIR SPACE

OPERATIONS: Digital data space

OCCUPANTS: Seabirds Populations

BOUNDARIES: International Airspace

residential housing

loading / transportation docks

wirelessly data communication

signal light

antennae

scuba platform

dock platforms

market facility

helicopter pad

casino / business center

SURFACE

OPERATIONS: Recreation, Housing, Production

OCCUPANTS: Human Habitation

BOUNDARIES: Cruise Routes, Political Borders

desalination ponds

sea bird nesting area

cruise ship docking

WATER

Operation: Tidal Harvesting, Aquaculture, Artificial Coral Reef

Occupants: Marine Species

Boundaries: Political Borders

nylon cord

netted structure cages

structure attachment

generator

duct

turbine blade

subsea structure

artificial reef habitats

Operations/Occupants/Boundaries: Embedded with programs that get around the rootedness of society. The urban network of data buoy stations provide an

opportunity to create overlapping narrative stories, where migrate bird populations meet prison, a new juxtaposition of ecologies.

Pacific Constellations: View seen from air at night
of this new territory—nebulous, every-changing,
used by many yet always elsewhere.

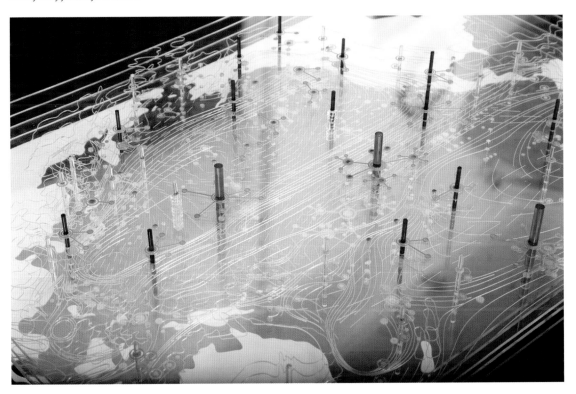

The new landscape of the pacific: a network of
micro-economies proposing new overlapping uses
and narratives, leveraging international shipping
routes, changing political border, and existing monitoring system.

HYBRID MIGRATIONS AND DESIGN OF DELUGE

Brett Milligan

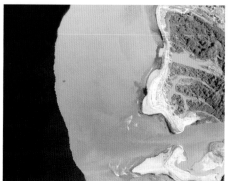

Sediment plume at the mouth of the Elwha River, 2012: These pulses of sediment are caused by the upstream removal of the Glines Canyon and Elwha Dams, releasing 84 years of the river's stored sediment load.

These entropic flows are expected to cause short term adverse effects to marine and freshwater organisms, followed by large scale ecosystem regeneration.
Photos: Tom Roorda, 2012; www.RoordaAerial.com

A dam is a structure that impounds or diverts water. By some estimates, there are up to 800,000 dams[1] in operation on at least 60 percent of the world's rivers.[2] Of these dams, 37,641 are registered as "large", meaning those that are at least fifteen metres in height, or with a minimum reservoir size of three million cubic metres.[3] Constructed of mass configurations of concrete, steel and earth, dams are typically designed for navigation (locks), water storage, flood control, and generating energy. Energy produced by hydropower reached a record 3,427 terawatt-hours, or about 16.1 percent of global electricity consumption as of the end of 2010.[4]

Rivers are loci of complexity, linear assemblies of convergence within terrestrial seams. Thus placing a massive wall of material in a river's path generates both intended and unintended effects. Mudslides and earthquakes can be induced by the weight of a reservoir's water column pressing down on faults and fissures in surrounding geology.[5] Dams tend to degrade water quality by increasing the amount of time water spends within a river, leading to elevated temperatures and

1. International Rivers, "Damming Statistics", 2011, www.internationalrivers.org/node/479.
2. GWSP Digital Water Atlas, 2011, www.gwsp.org/85.html.
3. International Commission on Large Dams, Registry of Dams, General Synthesis, www.icold-cigb.org/GB/World_register/general_synthesis.asp.
4. World Watch Institute, "Global Hydropower Installed Capacity and Use Increase, 2012, http://vitalsigns.worldwatch.org/vs-trend/global-hydropower-installed-capacity-and-use-increase.
5. Dams have produced earthquakes up to 6.3 (Richter) magnitudes. See McCully, Patrick, *Silenced Rivers: The Ecology and Politics of Large Dams* (London: Zed Books, 1996), 112-115.

diminished dissolved oxygen. Combined with the logistical challenges they present to the river's inhabitants, dams have had a decimating and costly effect on many freshwater and migratory fish. In total, dams and their reservoirs have inundated more than 400,000 square km of formerly terrestrial landscape, thereby displacing entire ecosystems and forty to eighty million people with their aqueous footprints.[6]

Data compilation on the global phenomena of large dams is a relatively new realm of investigation. The data tracked is equally nascent and investigators are challenged by the diversity and dynamism of the phenomena they pursue. Each dam is inherently unique, molding to the particularities of its surroundings and that surroundings' body politic. Yet emerging data provide tools with which to explore broader relationships, such as this:

> *"If the earth were left alone* [without human influence] *on the order of eight cubic kilometres (10.5 billion cubic yards) of the material of the continents would be swept away by rivers into the ocean every year…By some estimates, about a third of this natural volume is prevented from reaching the oceans as a result of being trapped behind dams and other* [hu] *man-made obstructions."[7]*

A dam's reservoir acts as a repository for sediments otherwise destined for downstream landforms or the river's terminus at the sea. As moving water hits these still pools, it decelerates and drops the sand, silts and gravel it carried. Most large dams trap and retain 98 percent of their river's sediment, thus holding a nearly complete material history of the system's work. And not only do reservoirs contain a river load, they also hold added sediment generated by increased rates of landscape erosion through mining, farming, deforestation and urbanization. Via these surface transformations, the rate at which soil slips from land to sea has exponentially increased. In the United States, 'geologic' erosion shears off only about 30 percent of total continental sediment, while 'accelerated' soil erosion from human influences accounts for the remaining 70 percent.[8] Dams are a curious place where this novel trajectory is inverted. Scientists have described dam reservoirs as a *"collision space of dispersed and opposing anthropogenic* forces" wherein we have *"simultaneously increased the sediment transport by global rivers through soil erosion, yet reduced the flux of sediment reaching the world's coasts because of retention within reservoirs.*[9] Each dam creates its own river delta, a material congealing of anthropogenic forces. In total, over 100 billion metric tons of sediment and one to three billion metric tons of carbon are estimated to now be inadvertently sequestered in reservoirs mostly constructed within the past 50 years.[10]

Approached as an aggregated collection of processes and megaforms, we encounter dam infrastructure as a tectonic body of sorts. The extremity of our co-intervention in the circulation of water and sediment is matched by the extremity of the notion that our agency could ever be fully removed from influencing the physical trajectories of these processes. Separation is futile, as we are geology.

What do we make of this ensemble of monumental blocks of concrete, stilled water, turbines, and masses of sediment held in suspended animation? We have yet to fully deploy a repertoire of language for such expansive and time-bending artifacts of the contemporary. Deleuze and Guattari provided us with the holism of the *assemblage.* Actor-network-theory followed suit with the *collective,* or the *crooked Daedalian labyrinths of machinery and Mechanizations[11].* Geology offers up the catch-all age of the Anthropocene. But perhaps most useful to what we are seeing here, is the notion of *hyperobjects.* As proposed by Timothy Morton, hyperobjects are things like global warming and plutonium 239 that defy local circumscription and bounded time. Like dams and their decelerated rivers, hyperobjects are "massively distributed in space-time."[12] They are *viscous, squishy,* and *uncanny[13]* things we cannot escape, outlive or distance ourselves from. They are, so to speak, *in the water,* intimately here with us beyond our desire or revulsion for them. Hyperobjects will be here when we leave, and their pervasive and indeterminate effects will need to be creatively encountered one way or another.

Massively (and Unevenly) Distributed in Space and Time

A world inventory of large dams reveals their global distribution to be lumpy, uneven, nationally distinct (political) and migratory. At the moment, China leads the world in dam construction—both in number and size. Relatedly, China also has one of the highest rates of continental erosion and is losing its soil at a rate fifty-seven times faster than it can be replaced.[14] Meshing this erosional trend with China's expanding reservoirs of anthropogenic *collision space* situates its ambitious dam building in a different light. Its landscapes of inundation —via engineered works like Three Gorges Dam—might be something more than an ecological catastrophe in the guise of modern progress, where 'peak soil' merges with massive and inadvertent hydroelectric catch basins. These dams are one of the few objects keeping China's soil on its continental surface rather than the floor of the Pacific Ocean.

Large dam infrastructure often emerges not only where harvestable rivers are located, but also where surges in economic and industrial development are occurring. In contrast to India and China, the United States is no longer building large dams. The U.S. era of big dam construction took hold around

6. International Commission on Dams, "Dams and Development: A New Framework For Decision Making" (UK: Earthscan Publications Ltd, 2000), www.internationalrivers.org/files/attached-files/world_commission_on_dams_final_report.pdf.
7. Welland, Michael, *Sand: The Never Ending Story* (Berkeley: University of California Press 2009), 84.
8. Northern Virginia Soil and Water Conservation

District, Conservation Currents, Jan 2003.
9. James P. M. Syvitski et al., "Impact of Humans on the Flux of Terrestrial Sediment to the Global Coastal Ocean", *Science Magazine*, 308 (2005), http://www.sciencemag.org/content/308/5720/376/rel-suppl/25ecc5c2efe282bb/suppl/DC1.
10. Ibid.
11. Latour, Bruno, *Pandora's Hope: Essays on the Reality of*

Science Studies (Boston: Harvard University Press,1999), 176.
12. Timothy Morton, "Zero Landscapes in the Time of Hyperobjects", *Graz Architectural Magazine* 7 (2011), 78–87
13. Ibid
14. The Land, "Experts Worry over Peak Soil", 2009, http://theland.farmonline.com.au/news/state/agribusiness-and-general/general/

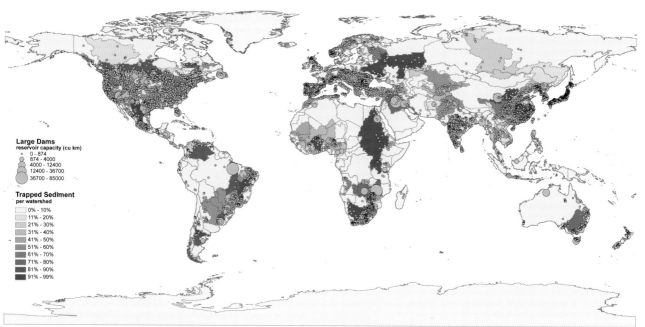

Large Dams
reservoir capacity (cu km)
- 0 - 874
- 874 - 4000
- 4000 - 12400
- 12400 - 36700
- 36700 - 85000

Trapped Sediment
per watershed
- 0% - 10%
- 11% - 20%
- 21% - 30%
- 31% - 40%
- 41% - 50%
- 51% - 60%
- 61% - 70%
- 71% - 80%
- 81% - 90%
- 91% - 99%

Sediment retained in global reservoirs: Map of the global distribution of large dams and their reservoirs, overlaid with percentages of sediment trapped within watersheds by dams or other obstructions. Data supplied by the Global Reservoir and Dam (GRanD) Database. Image by author, 2012; GIS data from the Global Reservoir and Dam (GRanD) Database

1940 and reached its peak in the early 1970s.[15] Funds for such projects are no longer politically available, and more poignantly, most prime locations for dams have already been utilized—a condition of "site depletion". The United States is a thoroughly *dammed* nation[16], wherein most of its high-flow rivers and opportune canyons are already occupied by strategic barricades of earth and concrete. Given its time to dwell amongst large dam infrastructure, the United States has had the opportunity to observe wider relationships and effects engendered by them. Here, dam infrastructure is changing more in qualitative ways rather than in distribution.

Coded Infrastructure

In the United States, all dams are regulated by state or federal agencies. Privately owned hydroelectric dams are regulated by the Federal Energy Regulatory Commission (FERC) through fifty-year licenses. Accordingly, every half century a dam must renegotiate its relationship to the river it spans. During relicensing the infrastructure is evaluated to determine if it meets current certification criteria, which has become more rigorous over time due to perceived short-comings of dams. A dam may pass as is, or if not, must be retrofitted to meet new standards or be deconstructed and erased from the landscape. The relicensing process thus creates a distinctive bifurcation in the infrastructure in which dams are further refined or meticulously removed. Both are

technical trajectories that further hybridize human agency within the workings of rivers.

In the Pacific Northwest of the United States (the states of Oregon, Idaho and Washington) nearly 70 percent of all energy is derived from hydropower.[17] Not surprisingly, one third of all Pacific Coast migratory salmon populations have disappeared from the region, and another third are considered threatened or protected under endangered species legislation.[18] These crisscrossed conditions—the endangering of fish and the proliferation of hydro-infrastructure—now encircle and co-create one another. Enter the fishway, defined by U.S. Congress, as "*any structure, facility, device, or structural or non-structural measure used for the safe and timely passage of all life stages of migratory or non-migratory fish, or both, either upstream or downstream, through, over, or around the project works of a hydroelectric power project.*"[19]

The eighty two metre tall *Round Butte Selective Water Withdrawal Tower* is a state-of-the-art example of fishway instrumentation. This submerged tower has been grafted onto Pacific Gas and Electric's 134-metre tall earth fill dam to perform multiple functions that enable fish to successfully migrate through the multiply dammed Deschutes River in Oregon. As a fishway, the Round Butte tower alters the flow of currents within the dam's reservoir, deliberately channeling ocean-bound migratory fish into its conveyance system. The entire volume of the river is screened as it passes through

experts-worry-over-peak-soil/1674679.aspx
15. United States Army Corps of Engineers, National Inventory of Dams. http://geo.usace.army.mil/pgis/f?p=397:5:3955553352875958::NO.
16. Ibid. The Army Corp of Engineers currently tracks 84,134 significant dams in its National Inventory.
17. Northwest Hydroelectric Association. "Resources: Northwest Hydro Generation",2008, http://www.

nwhydro.org/resources/northwest_hydro_generation.htm.
18. Richard Gustafson, "Pacific Salmon Extinctions: Quantifying Lost and Remaining Diversity". Conservation Biology, Aug (2007) 1009-20.
19. These fishways can include "(A) such structural measures as fish ladders, fish locks, lifts, elevators, fish bypass facilities and devices (such as screens) needed for

guiding fish unimpeded to an upstream or downstream passage facility, and breaches, notches, or other openings in a dam, (B) flows sufficient for guiding, attracting, or transporting fish and for operation of structural measures, and (C) such non-structural measures as periodic spill flows and gate openings.' U.S. Congress, "House Rule 3002, 1991, amending the Federal Power Act" http://thomas.loc.gov/cgi-bin/query/z?c102:H.R.3002:

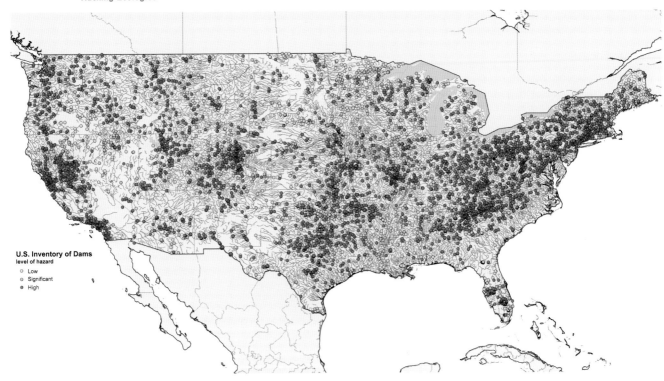

Dammed nation: Map of the distribution of U.S. dams, rated by hazard potential. Data recorded by the Army Corps of Engineers' National Inventory of Dams.

Image by author, 2012; GIS data from the USACE National Inventory of Dams

Round butte selective water withdrawal tower: Deschutes River, Oregon. Courtesy of Portland General Electric, 2011

Rendering of round butte: Selective Water Withdrawal Tower. Courtesy of Portland General Electric, Rendering by CH2M Hill, 2011

it, allowing only those fish deemed appropriate for passage. Once sieved, up to 15,000 migrating fish per day can be categorized, sorted and taxied overland beyond a series of three additional dams.[20] Without the Tower's diversions and industrial taxi services, fish would be forced to run through the gauntlet of the dams' power-generating turbines, which is akin to passing through an aquatic meat grinder. The Round Butte Tower also reduces elevated water temperatures in the dam's reservoir—a typical problem that leads to blooms of cyanobacteria and reduced dissolved oxygen. Large intakes at the tower's base circulate cool water from the bottom of the reservoir into warmer layers near the surface, improving reservoir and downstream water quality.

Fish ladders (staircases for fish that allow them to get over a dam), fish taxis, fish towers and other fishway gear extend the anthropogenic tooling of rivers. More materials and apparatuses are brought into the physical assembly of the system. With the Round Butte Tower, we see a rather simple reservoir becoming a more orchestrated choreography of pumps, chutes, screens, switchboards, sensors, architectural enclosures and designer water currents coaxing fish into swimming in desired directions.

Beyond the expanding technologies of fishways, fish themselves are mostly conceived in a dispersed network of fish hatcheries, which produce 80 percent of remaining Pacific Northwest migratory fish runs.[21] Hatcheries are where the technology of assisted migration reaches its hybridic climax. Since the 1960s the hatchery craft has proven quite productive. Yet the long-term effectiveness of making fish—an extraordinary process that should be observed in the flesh—is an evolutionary conundrum. Hatchery fish are a bit like inbreds in that they lack the diversity and spatio-genetic specificity of their wild counterparts. Hatchery-reared fish act differently, introduce new diseases, prey on and compete with wild stocks. If they successfully reproduce with their wild cousins, they tend to produce inferior and delicate offspring.[22] The hatchery process isn't cheap either. The annual cost of hatcheries in the Colombia Basin alone has been estimated at $350 million.[23] Yet hatchery conceived fish might be the only fish capable of adapting to conditions in the most hydrologically altered rivers.

Making Flux and Floods

In addition to building complicated fishways or other dam retrofits, engineers and fluvial morphologists are tinkering with new management regimes for releasing water. For example, in Arizona's Grand Canyon National Park, fish biologists and recreational campers noticed that the river's sand bars and beaches were disappearing. Sediments that used to nourish these backwater habitats are now held upstream, both in front of and behind the 220-metre tall Glen Canyon Dam. Since the dam was built and the river was regulated, the river bed no longer receives pulses of sediments through seasonal flooding. The U.S. Geological Survey and the Bureau of Reclamation began experimenting with opening the dam's floodgates to redistribute idled sediment downstream of the dam. The first intentional flood was performed in 1996, and again in 2004 and 2008, with each successive experiment providing recalibrated techniques for the next. At the 2008 event the former U.S. Secretary of The Interior ceremoniously opened the dam's jet tubes, boasting that water would be released into the Grand Canyon at a rate that would fill the empire state building within twenty minutes (41,500 cubic feet of water per second), transporting enough sediment to cover a football field one hundred feet deep with silt and sand.[24] It will likely take USGS scientists years to deduce what these floods actually do.

In the end these manufactured torrents might only add a little sand to a small portion of the Colorado River for a small amount of time. The flood events overshadow the fact that most of the sediment that the Grand Canyon and the rest of the Colorado River needs is resting behind Glen Canyon Dam in Lake Powell—the second largest reservoir in the U.S. Approximately one hundred million tons of sediment is deposited into Lake Powell annually and more than one-million acre feet of storage capacity has been lost within the lake due to sedimentation since the dam was completed in 1966.[25] How long the dam can remain operational before becoming too full of sediment is debatable and any hope of mechanically dredging the lake borders on the absurd and the Sisyphean. Situations like these remind us that we have yet to discover what the variable lifespans of our aging large dams will be, as well as what artifacts they will leave behind.

Entropy and Life Spans

Northwestern Lake was formed in 1913, when Condit Dam was constructed on the White Salmon River in southern Washington. The reservoir had a surface area of approximately ninety two acres, and in the ninety eight years of its existence, accumulated 1.8 million cubic metres of sediment.

Condit Dam reached the end of its hydroelectric lifespan in 2011. Under new relicensing requirements it would have cost its owner, PacifiCorp, far more than the dam was worth to graft contemporary fish ladders onto it. Through an arduous settlement agreement involving Indian tribes, environmental

20. The Round Butte Selective Water Tower was the "Project of the Year" recipient in the 2011 American Council of Engineering Companies Engineering Excellence Awards. See Sue Vorenburg, "ACEC Engineering Excellence Project of the Year: Round Butte Selective Water Withdrawal," Daily Journal of Commerce Oregon, 2011, http://djcoregon.com/news/2011/01/12/65476/

21. NOAA Northwest Fisheries Science Center. "Salmon Hatchery Questions and Answers" http://www.nwfsc.noaa.gov/resources/search_faq.cfm?faqmaincatid=3

22. National Ocean and Atmospheric Administration, "Hatcheries (Artificial Propagation)", 2012 www.nwr.noaa.gov/Salmon-Harvest-Hatcheries/Hatcheries/Index.cfm. See also Environment 360, "Hatch-22: The Problem with The Pacific Salmon Resurgence", 2010, http://e360.yale.edu/feature/hatch-22_the_problem_with_the_pacific_salmon_resurgence/2335/.

23. International Rivers, "Damming Statistics", 2007, www.internationalrivers.org/node/479.

24. United States Bureau of Reclamation, "Interior Secretary Kempthorne Launches Grand Canyon High Flow Experiment", 2008, www.usbr.gov/uc/feature/GC-hfe/index.html

25. The Glen Canyon Institute, "Sediment and Lake Powell", www.glencanyon.org/about/faq

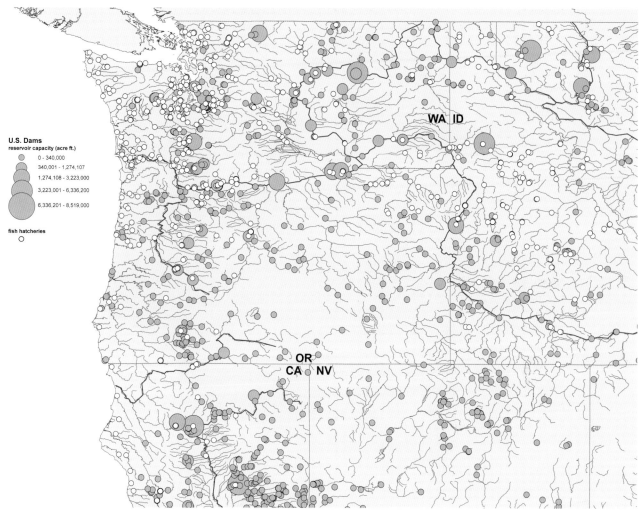

U.S. Dams
reservoir capacity (acre ft.)

- 0 - 340,000
- 340,001 - 1,274,107
- 1,274,108 - 3,223,000
- 3,223,001 - 6,336,200
- 6,336,201 - 8,519,000

fish hatcheries

Pacific Northwest dams and fish hatcheries:
Map of dams, reservoirs and fish hatcheries in the
Northwest region of the United States. Image by author,
2012; GIS data from the USACE National Inventory of
Dams and StreamNet Project, Pacific States Marine
Fisheries Commission

**Northwestern Lake, White Salmon River,
Washington, 2011:** Image was made just prior to the
breaching of Condit Dam. Courtesy of PacifiCorp, 2011

**Northwestern Lake, White Salmon River,
Washington, 2011:** Image was made one day after
the breaching of the reservoir's dam. Cameras in the
foreground are mounted to the crest of Condit Dam
to document patterns of water and sediment flows
through time lapse photography. Photo by author, 2011

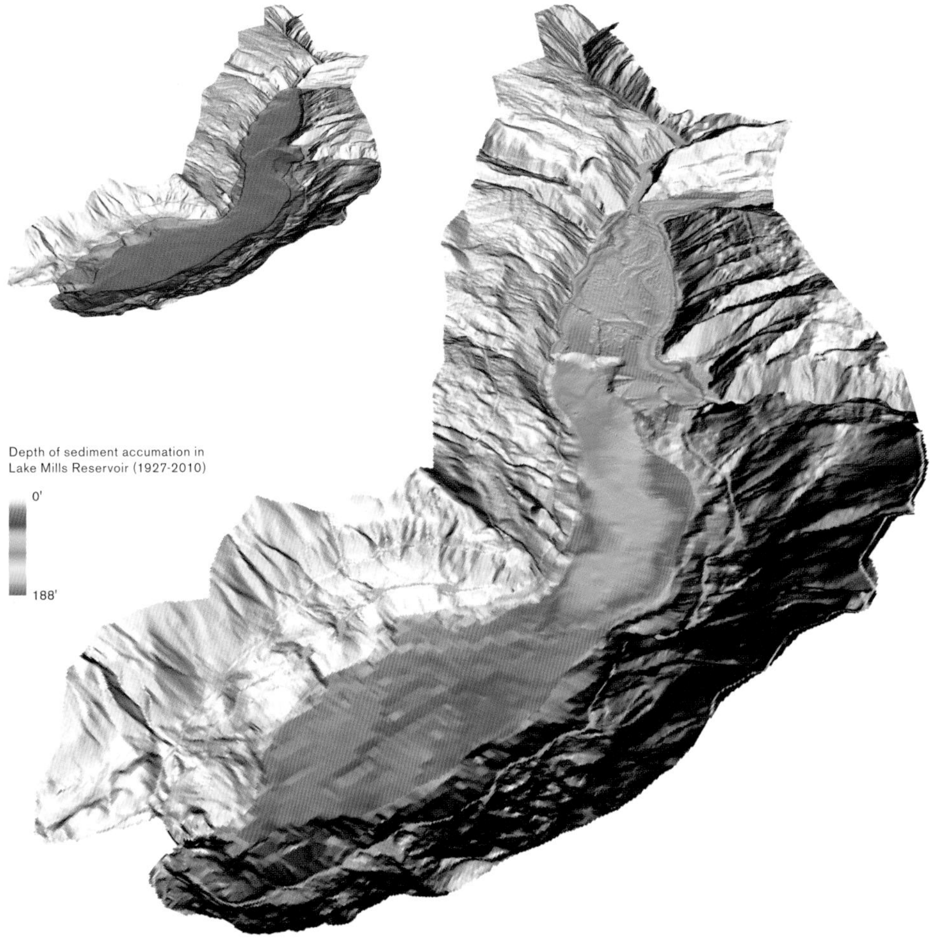

Depth of sediment accumation in
Lake Mills Reservoir (1927-2010)

0'

188'

Anthropogenic Delta of Lake Mills Reservoir, Elwha River, Washington: The inset model on the left shows the valley's topography as surveyed circa 1921 before the construction of Glines Canyon Dam. The model on the right (from the Bureau of Reclamation's 2010 LIDAR and Bathymetric surveys), indicates approximately thirty million cubic yards of sediment accumulated within the reservoir since the construction of Glines Canyon Dam in 1927. Image by author, 2012; all GIS data supplied by the U.S. Bureau of Reclamation

advocacy groups and government agencies, it was agreed that the dam be decommissioned.[26]

The approved and experimental method for breaching Condit Dam specified boring a tunnel through the base of the dam to within a few feet of its opposite side. The tunnel was then loaded with explosives and detonated. The drain tunnel would discharge water and sediment at a rate of about 10,000 cubic feet-per-second—approximately 25 percent of the peak discharge of the historic 1996 flood event on the White Salmon River. This flow would drain the reservoir and 1.6 million to 2.2-million cubic yards of sediment in approximately six hours.[27]

Theory was put into action on October 26th, 2011. The reservoir was emptied in just over one hour, rather than six. During the event, over half of the White Salmon River's centennial erosional work was mobilized downstream at one time. Long buried basalt canyon walls behind the dam were immediately uncovered, as were preserved tree stumps cut down

a century ago. Sediment concentrations downstream were higher than anticipated by the *Sediment Assessment, Stability and Management Plan*. After the breach, in-water turbidity measurements quickly exceeded the upper limits of detection of probes installed in the river (4,000 nephalometric units), and remained at those undetectable levels for two weeks.[28] In the ensuing hours and days after the breach, courser masses of sediment sloughed off their stone foundations in a cascade of landslides, mass wasting, rotational failures, tensional cracking and slumping. All of which was a mix of forecasting and the unknown.

Quasi-designed events like the flood experiments in the Grand Canyon and Condit's explosive demise reconfigure the collective otherness engendered by dams. What was held in compiled torpor for up to a century is suddenly jettisoned across landscapes like geological slurry. In a pulse of fluvial magma, destructive force is transmuted into a regenerative process. These large experiments go by the

---

26. The Condit Dam Settlement Agreement, as well as decommissioning plans and related documents, is available from PacifiCorp's website: www.pacificorp.com/condit.

27. Ibid. Condit Decommissioning Overview
28. Ibid. 90-day Post-Breach Preliminary Sediment Behavior Report.

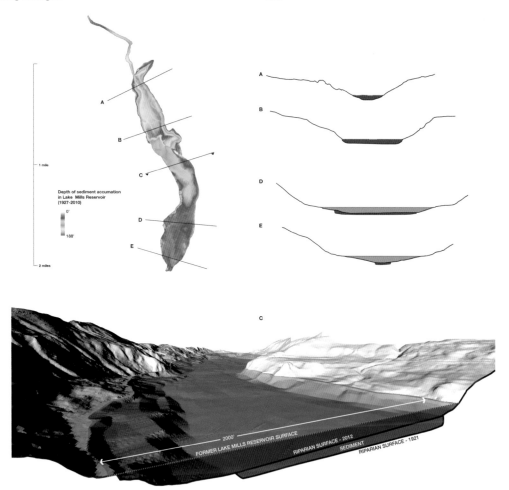

"Advancing" Mills Delta: The majority of sediment stored in Lake Mills is amassed within the delta at the upstream end of the Glines Canyon Dam's Reservoir. With the dam removed, the delta is now 'advancing' downstream in chaordic flows of sediment. Image by author, 2012; all GIS data supplied by the U.S. Bureau of Reclamation.

catchall designation of 'adaptive management'. We might also construe such endeavors as the delegation and recruitment of entropy, whereby dredging becomes co-collaborative land and river maker.

At Condit Dam the anthropogenic body within the reservoir appears to have been erased, but it persists in viscous motion. Where will the masses of liberated particles congeal and how will they be integrated and coopted by downstream entities?

Just over three miles downstream of Condit Dam, the White Salmon River merges with the much larger Columbia River. Here the gravitational onslaught of Condit's sediments met with the slack water from the Bonneville Dam's forty eight mile long, 537,000 acre ft. capacity reservoir. Here some of the mobilized sediments are forming a new migratory delta landscape.[29] On the day of the breach, USGS scientists attempted to measure the discharge at the confluence with the Columbia. Their plan was abandoned when it was determined that surface water was actually flowing *up* the White

Salmon River; a counterintuitive condition due to "*a powerful current flowing along the bed of the White Salmon River out into the Columbia River, consistent with a high bedload concentration and a density greater than that of clear water.*"[30] Seven days after the breach, buoys detected that the head of the sediment plume had arrived within the locks of the Bonneville Dam, reaching the limit of its journey and its new place of anthropogenic aggregation. The shifting particles had jumped from one reservoir to another. Bonneville Dam, a federal dam managed by the Army Corp of Engineers, generates power to places as distant as southern California and is not going anywhere any time soon.

Fresh Data Terrains and In-Situ Laboratories

Cameras shielded within metal housings were mounted on the crest of Condit Dam prior to its being cored through. These and other recording devices have been placed in the surrounding landscape and trained onto various shifting

---

29. Ibid. A photograph of this delta is provided on page 9.
30. Ibid, p.8.

Former Lake Aldwell: drained and rapidly eroding after
the removal of the Elwha Dam, 2012. Photos by author, 2012

terrains, like the drained reservoir and the dam itself. They
are part of multiple time-lapse documentation projects that
hope to provide archives of sediment dispersion patterns, the
erasure of the dam, and the assisted succession of riparian
and upland plant communities.[31] Combined with new light
detection and ranging flyovers, detailed in-the-field monitoring
and progress reports required by the FERC, rich new data
landscapes are being produced.

Techniques are emerging for how to de-engineer outmoded hydro-infrastructure. Dam removal projects larger and
more extensive than Condit are currently in process or under
consideration. The Elwha and Glines Canyon Dams on the
Elwha River in Washington State—the largest dam removal
project to date—are, at the time of writing, in the final stages
of being blasted apart. Their combined repository of sediment
dwarfs Condit's with a total of 34 million cubic yards being
creatively managed[32] as its redistributed. Here the Bureau of
Reclamation finds itself in a unique and somewhat cognitively
dissonant position, forced to learn how to re-reclaim that
which it reclaimed nearly a century ago.

Similarly, a bill currently sits in U.S. Congress[33] that would
precipitate the removal of four large dams on the Klamath
River, recovering 2,400 acres of submerged river and
upland landscape. Straddling the Oregon/California border,
the Klamath River used to harbor the third largest runs of
migratory salmon on the Pacific Coast, which have since
collapsed.[34] If dam removal is approved, an entirely new economy will be mobilized in this contested and divided region,
an economy based on de-engineering a huge assembly of
infrastructure and re-inscribing former landscape processes
in its place.

If the Klamath and other dam removals go forward,
they will be informed by the fluvial avant-garde experiments
preceding them. In these varied in-situ laboratories we
are re-associating with the peculiar assemblages we have
deliberately and inadvertently co-created; the dispersed
and time-warped bodies that we will continue to help mold.
Would such chaordic dealings in the theater of space seem
plausible and even regenerative just decades earlier when
ecology and ecosystem concepts were heavily premised
on cybernetic theories of balance, controllability and homeostasis?[35] That anodyne model has been superseded by one
where disturbance and environmental extremes are accepted
and embraced as stochastic norms indeterminately brought
about by humans, non-humans and their knotted entangle-
ments. In these new norms a sense of anthropogenic control
might still persist, but in more intimate terms and with unde-
fined edges. We are other, and the other gets more foreign
the closer we get to it.

Brett Milligan is an assistant professor of landscape architecture
and environmental design at the University of California, Davis. He
is the creator of Free Association Design and a founding member
of the Dredge Research Collaborative.

31. Ibid. Photographs and animated time lapse sequences
are provided under "decommissioning activities".
32. At the start of the Elwha dams decommissioning,
it was estimated that there were 24 million cubic yards
stored in the reservoirs. Halfway through the project,
that estimate was revised to 34 million cubic yards.
33. the Klamath Basin Economic Restoration Act, H.R.

3398, 2011, www.opencongress.org/bill/112-h3398/text
34. "Long-term declines in Klamath Basin fisheries have been
estimated at 92 to 96 percent for wild fall-run Chinook salmon,
98 percent for spring-run Chinook salmon, 67 percent for steel-
head trout (since 1960), 52 to 96 percent for Coho salmon, and
98 percent for Pacific Lamprey." Department of the Interior,
Secretarial Determination Draft Overview Report, 2012

p.23, http://klamathrestoration.gov/sites/klamathresto-
ration.gov/files/DDDD.SDOR.Full.1.24.12.pdf
35. See Adam Curtis' documentary "All Watched Over by
Machines of Loving Grace", Part II: "The Use and Abuse
of Vegetational Concepts", BBC 2011. Curtis provides an
overview of the origin of the ecosystem concept and the
various ways it has been deployed and coopted.

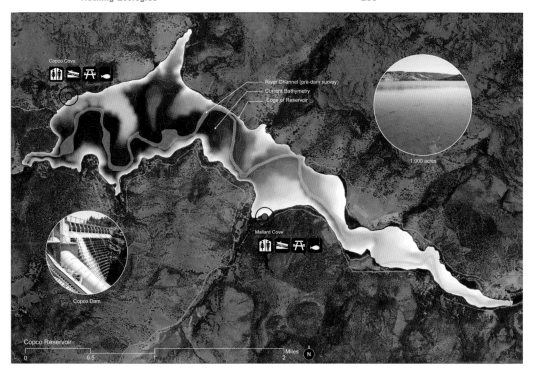

Copco Dam and Reservoir, Klamath River, California: Copco is one of four dams pending removal on the Klamath River. Image by author, 2012; from Migrating Infrastructures of the Klamath River: Past, Present and Speculative Futures, research funded in part by a grant from the Graham Foundation. Copco Reservoir data supplied by the U.S. Bureau of Reclamation

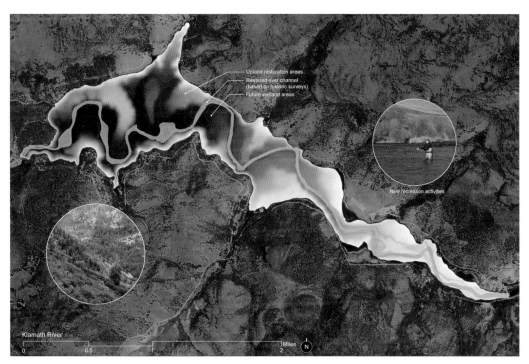

Potential Restoration of the Copco Reservoir: Copco reservoir currently inundates over 1000 acres of former riparian and upland habitats, which if drained, would instigate the deployment of revegetation schemes and shift how people recreate and use the landscape. Image by author, 2012; from Migrating Infrastructures of the Klamath River: Past, Present and Speculative Futures, research funded in part by a grant from the Graham Foundation. Copco Reservoir data supplied by the U.S. Bureau of Reclamation

DAM(NED)SCAPES

Patricia Joong

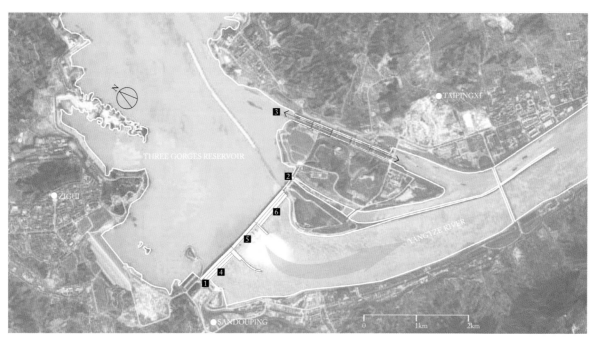

1. Three Gorges Dam   2. Ship Elevator   3. Five-Tier Shiplock   4. Power House #1   5. Spillway   6. Powerhouse #2

THREE GORGES DAM

THREE GORGES RESERVOIR
1045 sq.km.

The Three Gorges dam: The concrete gravity dam spans
2.3 km across the Yangtze River. With a height of 185 m
it supports a reservoir capable of holding 39.3 cubic kilometres of water and generating 22.5 GW across its
32 generators.

Notching occupation: The dam's uses are expanded to include human and ecological concerns.

At the turn of the twenty-first century, China's longest river would meet the world's largest dam — the steady flow of tradition truncated against the 'great wall' of progress. Together, river and dam define a complex, sometimes fatal boundary between nature and industry, between a government and its citizens. The point of intersection of these disparate linear entities has established a breeding ground for mounting ecological, social and political instability.

Dam(ned)scapes addresses these conditions, examining their effects on cultural landscapes within the context of the Three Gorges Dam. Once integral to shaping regional identity, new landscapes have emerged from China's industrialized age that persist as foreign territory. What opportunities arise at the physical and often conflicting convergence of civilization and nature? Can landscape resume its historical role as cultivator of culture and identity?

Hydrology has long defined the form and character of developing civilizations along the Yangtze. As China's longest river, the Yangtze forms a significant transportation and economic artery joining the nation's rugged Western frontier to its cosmopolitan extremity in the East. From its source elevation at 4,900 m, it winds through 6,300 km of diverse terrain, influencing the rich and varied composition of cultural landscapes along its path.

Over millennia, human inhabitants were drawn to the Yangtze's middle and lower reaches, with its vast, fertile plains giving rise to a prosperous agricultural heartland. Though it provided sustenance, the area was also prone to disastrous flooding, claiming countless lives and wreaking social and economic havoc. This volatile relationship with the natural world instilled, within those affected, a desire to manipulate nature, and encouraged the development of engineered landscapes. Dykes, embankments, and small reservoirs presented increasingly aggressive, hard separations between land and water. Lacking a functional understanding of fluvial ecosystems, the severity of flooding increased in several ways. Water diversion and impoundment structures, as well as heavy deforestation and wetland reclamation for agricultural uses effectively blocked off key components of the river's natural flood-control system, disturbing natural infiltration processes and diminishing its watershed drainage capacity.

In the early twentieth century, Dr. Sun Yatsen, the founding father of the Republic of China, pioneered the idea of damming the Yangtze as a means to mitigate flooding disasters, but also, to provide energy for a nation on the brink of major industrial development. Initial plans were developed in the

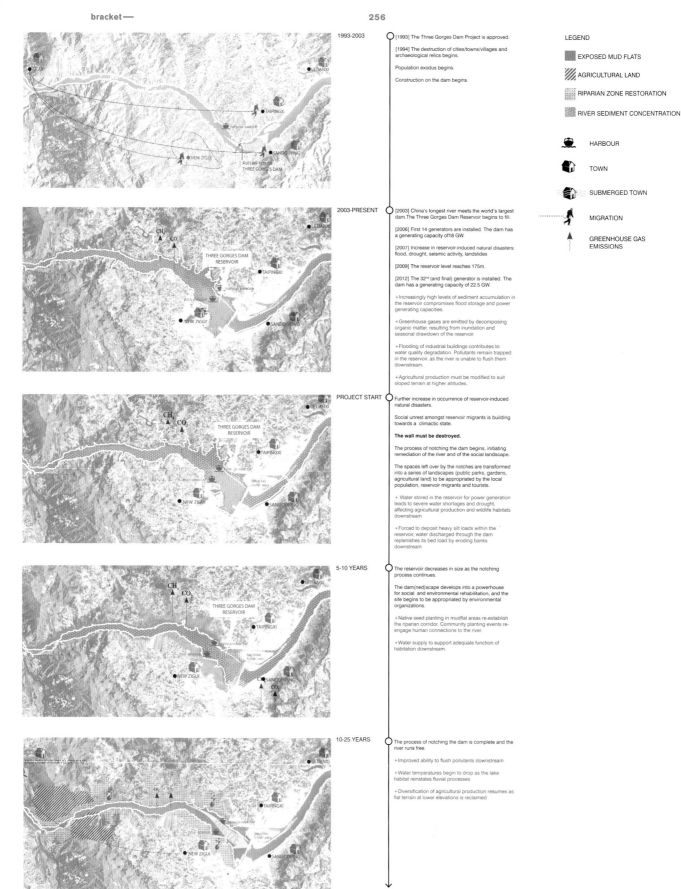

1993-2003

[1993] The Three Gorges Dam Project is approved.

[1994] The destruction of cities/towns/villages and archaeological relics begins.

Population exodus begins.

Construction on the dam begins.

2003-PRESENT

[2003] China's longest river meets the world's largest dam.The Three Gorges Dam Reservoir begins to fill.

[2006] First 14 generators are installed. The dam has a generating capacity of18 GW.

[2007] Increase in reservoir-induced natural disasters: flood, drought, seismic activity, landslides

[2009] The reservoir level reaches 175m.

[2012] The 32nd (and final) generator is installed. The dam has a generating capacity of 22.5 GW.

+Increasingly high levels of sediment accumulation in the reservoir compromises flood storage and power generating capacities.

+Greenhouse gases are emitted by decomposing organic matter, resulting from inundation and seasonal drawdown of the reservoir

+Flooding of industrial buildings contributes to water quality degradation. Pollutants remain trapped in the reservoir, as the river is unable to flush them downstream.

+Agricultural production must be modified to suit sloped terrain at higher altitudes.

PROJECT START

Further increase in occurrence of reservoir-induced natural disasters.

Social unrest amongst reservoir migrants is building towards a climactic state.

The wall must be destroyed.

The process of notching the dam begins, initiating remediation of the river and of the social landscape.

The spaces left over by the notches are transformed into a series of landscapes (public parks, gardens, agricultural land) to be appropriated by the local population, reservoir migrants and tourists.

+ Water stored in the reservoir for power generation leads to severe water shortages and drought, affecting agricultural production and wildlife habitats downstream

+Forced to deposit heavy silt loads within the reservoir, water discharged through the dam replenishes its bed load by eroding banks downstream

5-10 YEARS

The reservoir decreases in size as the notching process continues.

The dam(ned)scape develops into a powerhouse for social and environmental rehabilitation, and the site begins to be appropriated by environmental organizations.

+Native seed planting in mudflat areas re-establish the riparian corridor. Community planting events re-engage human connections to the river.

+Water supply to support adequate function of habitation downstream.

10-25 YEARS

The process of notching the dam is complete and the river runs free.

+Improved ability to flush pollutants downstream

+Water temperatures begin to drop as the lake habitat reinstates fluvial processes

+Diversification of agricultural production resumes as flat terrain at lower elevations is reclaimed

LEGEND

EXPOSED MUD FLATS

AGRICULTURAL LAND

RIPARIAN ZONE RESTORATION

RIVER SEDIMENT CONCENTRATION

HARBOUR

TOWN

SUBMERGED TOWN

MIGRATION

GREENHOUSE GAS EMISSIONS

Timeline of transformation of Three Georges Dam

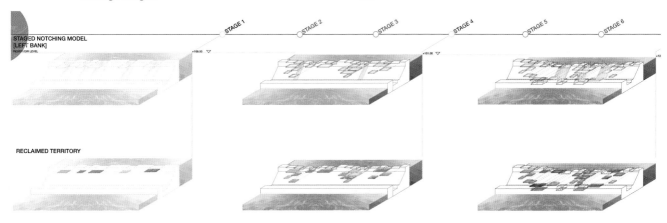

STAGED NOTCHING MODEL
[LEFT BANK]
RESERVOIR LEVEL

STAGE 1   STAGE 2   STAGE 3   STAGE 4   STAGE 5   STAGE 6

RECLAIMED TERRITORY

Reclamation through strategic notching.

mid-1940's in coordination with the U.S. Bureau of Reclamation, but the project lost momentum with the onset of the civil war and was halted by the Nationalist government. A major flood in 1954 encouraged the reconsideration of plans to dam the Yangtze and in the mid-1950's, the project was revived by the Communist Party.

Through the plethora of environmentally degrading projects realized during the Maoist era, large-scale infrastructural developments for hydrological control and electric power generation have proven to be the greatest source of cultural and ecological annihilation, inducing the forced relocation of approximately 7.8 million people in the '50s and '60s.[1] Of significant relevance is the socio-ecological disaster of the Sanmenxia Dam on the Yellow River, an important yet largely unstudied historical precedent to the Three Gorges Dam which induced the forced resettlement of 400,000 people, for which the government has taken little responsibility and suppressed public debate. Following its initial years of operation, the intensity of sediment build-up, predicted by many engineers, drastically reduced hydroelectric power production, leading to an increase in upstream flooding (attributed to its reservoir's reduced storage capacity). Though design amendments were made shortly after, its disadvantages have far outweighed its benefits and local residents continue to struggle with its resulting socio-environmental degradation. Further population resettlement in 1985 foreshadowed the issues that would arise in the Three Gorges Dam.

The (inevitable) *blitzkrieg* befell the Three Gorges Reservoir region in the '90s, when the Three Gorges Dam project was approved, despite intense debate, under Premier Li Peng's leadership. This unconventional exhibition of controversy within the Party exposed the severity of technical challenges involved in its construction. Citizens who openly opposed the project were silenced by censorship, and in certain cases jailed for dissent, activating an international brigade of environmental and human rights activists, archaeologists and engineers. Unlike the Sanmenxia Dam constructed during the Great Leap Forward, China was now opening its doors to the world, making the Three Gorges Dam difficult to slide under the international radar. Concerned by the abuse of human rights in its plans for population relocation, the project was denied funding by the World Bank. As issues continued to come to light through international media, it grew increasingly difficult to retain foreign support.

Simultaneously, Chinese inhabitants began the arduous process of forcefully stripping their physical history and identity. 13 cities, 140 towns and 1,352 villages crumbled at the mercy of 'progress' and initiated the largest resettlement scheme in history, comprising an exodus of roughly 1.4 million people from the reservoir region. 245 square kilometres of fertile land was inundated, which compromised the economic livelihood of the remaining population by creating land shortages and food security issues within an increasingly marginalized society.

In 2003, the rushing river was forced into a stagnant body, and its water levels slowly began to rise, spreading 600 km west from the site of the dam to the city of Chongqing. Further destruction ensued as the fluvial habitats of the region's silent citizens crumbled under newfound reservoir conditions, subject to alterations in water temperature, chemical composition and dissolved oxygen levels. The widening of navigable territory through the narrow gorges has increased both the nature and

---

1. Li, Heming, Paul Waley, and Phil Rees. "Reservoir Resettlement in China: Past Experience and the Thrree Gorges Dam." *The Geographical Journal*, 167.3 (2001): 197

New Occupations: one of the park's numerous public
recreational spaces.

frequency of shipping vessels, inhibiting migration of underwater species. An increased concentration of sewage and pollutants, emanating from the remnants of inundated factories and new industrial
development, can no longer be flushed out by free-flowing waters, despite a growing number of water
treatment plants along the river. These factors have exacerbated conditions for the Yangtze's endangered species.

Presently, human populations affected by the Three Gorges Dam continue to endure forced reloca-
tions due to landslides caused by the unnatural weight of this 39.3 cubic kilometre body of water and
fluctuating reservoir levels have eroded and contributed to the bank's geological instability. Theories
have been formulated which claim that the dam played a pivotal role in recent environmental disasters,
such as the 2010 regional drought (caused by an altered reservoir microclimate), and the 2008 earthquake (resulting from reservoir-induced seismicity) in nearby Sichuan Province.

Prediction

Dam(ned)scapes proposes its own set of predictions for the Three Gorges Dam. As the reservoir
continues to fill with sediment, it compromises its power-generating and flood-mitigating capacity.
Flood and drought cycles continue to ravage the region and unstable geological conditions cause further waves of resettlement. It becomes clear that the condition of instability caused by the site's artifici-
ality can no longer be ignored. Witnessing a critical decline in the quality of their natural environment,
protests surge across the nation, defining a new era in the democratic history of a politically repressed
nation—drawn together for the same cause: *The wall must be destroyed.*

Intervention

Post-resettlement patterns in China indicate that dam refugees, longing for the familiarity of the past,
often return to their place of origin. The occurrence of reverse-migration suggests the socio-cultural
importance of re-establishing a sense of place in the reservoir region. The dam is selected as the site
of intervention, as it remains the most potent physical link to a past left standing above water.

Following our prediction, the design proposes a strategy encompassing the partial removal of the
dam in an effort to rehabilitate the river. Over time, notches are sequentially cut into the wall, providing

temporary spillways for incremental draining of the reservoir. Recovery periods are scheduled between notches which allow water and wildlife downstream to adapt and stabilize to the stagnant reservoir's by-products.

It is here that the utilitarian process of restoring the river's flow is synthesized with an architectural agenda, where the spaces carved by the healing incisions become a series of landscapes appropriated by the public — generating an act of creation out of destruction. Initially, programming of the park responds to the socio-cultural issues plaguing the displaced population. The artificial landscape created by the dam's destruction provides the valley region with an unusually flat topographic condition, within which the reservoir migrants can begin to engage in traditional activities such as agricultural production, in order to rebuild social circles and alleviate food security issues through its community gardens. The landscape performs simply as a mnemonic device as it seeks to reclaim the values associated with the inundated land.

Following appropriation by reservoir migrants, the site continues to define itself in other ways, considering opportunities to incorporate the institutional activities of environmental organizations, and to explore revenue generation through tourism and recreation (the world's largest floating pool), establishing a site which engages and educates individuals, bridging technology, culture and nature. The act of community building and social rehabilitation, in symbiosis with ongoing river rehabilitation efforts, re-establishes the region's relationship to water.

The partial destruction of the dam revitalizes the region with an environment that memorializes the past in a performative and dynamic manner. With increased use and programming opportunities, the dam avoids the static and distant nature of the traditional monument. The dam(ned)scape becomes a curator of culture[2], where local traditions are rediscovered and re-interpreted within a post-industrial landscape.

Patricia Joong is a graduate of the McGill University School of Architecture, where she completed both her B.Sc (Arch) and M.Arch (Professional) degrees. She currently practices as a designer in Toronto.

2. Czerniak, Julia, ed. Case: Downsview Park Toronto.
New York: Prestel, 2001.

GROUND SWELL

Chris Holzwart

Grand Isle, Louisana.

The *Ground Swell* project speculates on land creation and development for Louisiana's most prominent barrier island, Grand Isle, over the course of the next 50 years. The project negotiates the volatile existence of coastal conditions in the Gulf of Mexico to consider emerging opportunities of occupation and land management in these continually changing ecologies. While this environment proves inappropriate for the finite qualities of conventional engineering, it is a culturally and economically lucrative borderland, which demands a flexible system to control its landscapes. To this end, the *Ground Swell* project envisions a future where the economic arena of Grand Isle's industries are integral in the morphological management of its coastal land masses.

It is widely documented that coastal Louisiana is deteriorating at an alarming rate, due to rising sea levels and the recurrence of devastating tropical storms.[1] Louisiana's land loss is a seemingly unstoppable reality, which requires an immense amount of human and natural resources to mitigate, if only temporarily, the stresses of erosion. Coastal degradation is not only caused naturally, but also by anthropogenic conditions created through the establishment of economies, industry, and various forms of island infrastructures.[2] Grand Isle is not a place that is truly "meant" to be occupied and yet, by virtue of its location, serves as a hub between the Gulf of Mexico, Barataria Bay, and mainland Louisiana. This productive condition does not exist without cost. In order for the island to maintain current operations, it must continually be adapted to battle the forces that contest its existence. Dredging, filling, damming, and other reparative and preventative operations instituted by the U.S. Army Corps

of Engineers, are necessary means deployed towards an unknown end.

As it stands today, the majority of the Grand Isle's perimeter consists of a stretch of lengthy beaches, Exxon Mobil oil facilities, the township of Grand Isle, marinas, portages, and a state park. The majority of the eastern and southern borders are subjected to the laminar sea-flows that move from east-to-west across the face of the island. Erosion-preventing stone revetments and dikes project seaward to mitigate the shifting of the soft landscape. These structures are implemented to inhibit the massive impact on the eastern side of the island, yet virtually close off the connection from land to ocean. Even though the flow of the tide is responsible for eroding the surface of the island, over the last few decades the eastern half has actually received a sizeable amount of growth. This growth is due to the fact that the plume of sediment-rich waters deposited from Mississippi River Delta, in partnership with tidal forces that push that sediment landward, have begun to accrete, or grow land naturally, on the eastern half of Grand Isle.[3] If capitalized upon, there exists an opportunity to harness deposited sediment as a means of landmass expansion. The *Ground Swell* system is derived from the phenomenal ability to create land.

Ground Swell leverages time as a physical factor in the process of design. The coastal conditions of Louisiana are finite and the notion of this temporality is embedded within the deployment of the engineered systems designed to control the conditions of the coast. Traditionally, levees are constructed to resist 25-, 50-, or even 100-year capacity levels, and are either grossly over-engineered which drastically

1. Mike Dunn and Bevil Knapp, *America's Wetland: Louisiana's Vanishing Coast* (Baton Rouge: Louisiana State University Press, 2005), 4.
2. Charles W. Finkl, *Saving America's Wetland: Strategies*

for Restoration of Louisiana's Coastal Wetlands and Barrier Islands (West Palm Beach: Coastal Education and Research Foundation CERF, 2005) 10.
3. NOAA "Barataria Bay and Approaches NOAA Office of

Response and Restoration" http://response.restoration.noaa.gov/dwh.php?entry_id=809

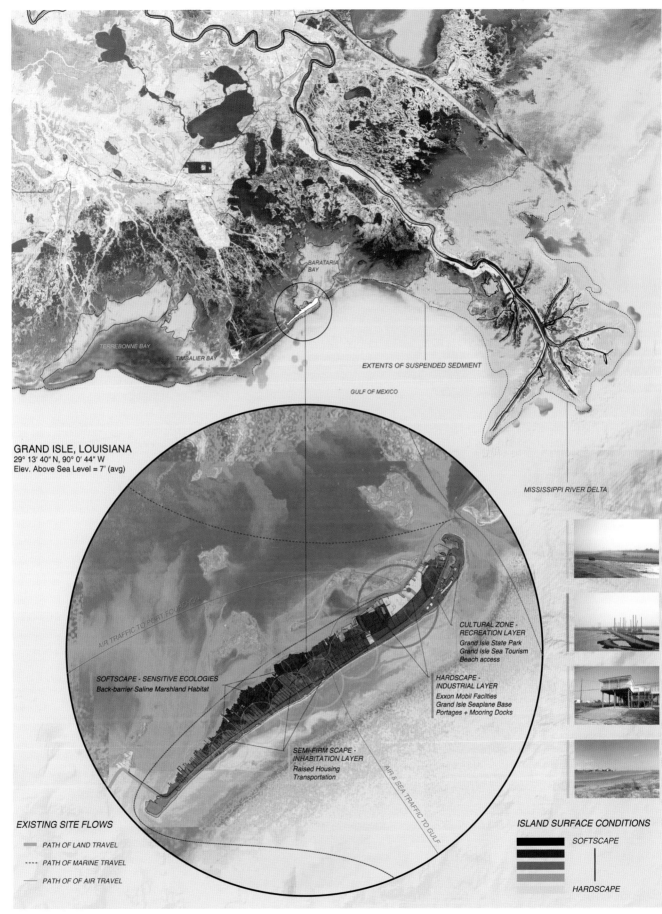

BARATARIA
BAY

EXTENTS OF SUSPENDED SEDMIENT

TERREBONNE BAY

TIMBALIER BAY

GULF OF MEXICO

GRAND ISLE, LOUISIANA
29° 13' 40" N, 90° 0' 44" W
Elev. Above Sea Level = 7' (avg)

MISSISSIPPI RIVER DELTA

AIR TRAFFIC TO PORT FOURCHON

CULTURAL ZONE -
RECREATION LAYER
Grand Isle State Park
Grand Isle Sea Tourism
Beach access

SOFTSCAPE - SENSITIVE ECOLOGIES
Back-barrier Saline Marshland Habitat

HARDSCAPE -
INDUSTRIAL LAYER
Exxon Mobil Facilities
Grand Isle Seaplane Base
Portages + Mooring Docks

SEMI-FIRM SCAPE -
INHABITATION LAYER
Raised Housing
Transportation

AIR & SEA TRAFFIC TO GULF

EXISTING SITE FLOWS

___ PATH OF LAND TRAVEL

---- PATH OF MARINE TRAVEL

— PATH OF OF AIR TRAVEL

ISLAND SURFACE CONDITIONS

SOFTSCAPE

HARDSCAPE

Grand Isle, Louisiana: Satellite Imagery of Grand Isle, LA.

Prototype Catalog for Surface Generation

Surface Components //

The surface generation consists of (2) primary input components, a Filled Cell and an Open Cell.

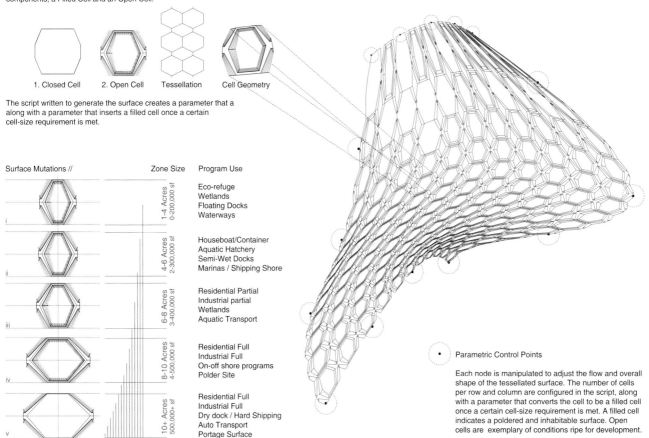

1. Closed Cell   2. Open Cell   Tessellation   Cell Geometry

The script written to generate the surface creates a parameter that a along with a parameter that inserts a filled cell once a certain cell-size requirement is met.

Surface Mutations //

	Zone Size	Program Use
i	1-4 Acres / 0-200,000 sf	Eco-refuge / Wetlands / Floating Docks / Waterways
ii	4-6 Acres / 2-300,000 sf	Houseboat/Container / Aquatic Hatchery / Semi-Wet Docks / Marinas / Shipping Shore
iii	6-8 Acres / 3-400,000 sf	Residential Partial / Industrial partial / Wetlands / Aquatic Transport
iv	8-10 Acres / 4-500,000 sf	Residential Full / Industrial Full / On-off shore programs / Polder Site
v	10+ Acres / 500,000+ sf	Residential Full / Industrial Full / Dry dock / Hard Shipping / Auto Transport / Portage Surface

• Parametric Control Points

Each node is manipulated to adjust the flow and overall shape of the tessellated surface. The number of cells per row and column are configured in the script, along with a parameter that converts the cell to be a filled cell once a certain cell-size requirement is met. A filled cell indicates a poldered and inhabitable surface. Open cells are exemplary of conditions ripe for development.

Cell prototype catalog: A cell-design prototype catalog derived through manipulations of parameter formulae.

inhibits the natural eco-aquatic order, or under-engineered and fail completely. Therein lies a need for an infrastructural architecture that is able to flexibly adapt to time and the current environmental conditions of the site. The project employs a coastal construction system which creates the opportunity for land to effectively be created through the hydrostatic inflation of geo-synthetic tubing used to accrete sediment in the sediment-rich water column of the Louisiana coast. Specific regions of the *Ground Swell* system are actuated for a determined amount of time, or deliver consistent pressure for extended periods to support projects of longer duration. The system, which can be distributed throughout the periphery of the island and beyond, serves as a method of facilitating the expansion of coastal life, extension of landmass, and protection for the native ecologies.

The long history of marine construction, oil platform construction, pipeline industry, and coastal engineering suggests multiple possible users of the Ground Swell system. Once planning for the use of the Ground Swel*l* system is complete, the massive coastal engineering process begins by

establishing nodal points on land and in water where hydraulic pumps or "hydro-nodes" will be strategically located. These pumps are vital to the *Ground Swell* system as they fuel the inflation of the geo-synthetic tubing. The geo-tubing is strung between the hydro-nodes, creating the armature for the cellular border of land to grow.

Ground Swell is a system which will create expansion onto the new waterfront; a critical shift from the restrictions borne from building on solid land to building flexible structures seaward, which rely on an entirely different set of logistics. Areas within the cellular land structures have the opportunity to become poldered, or artificially enclosed by virtue of a surrounding border; they can become a more solid layer to build upon, or designed to be left open to harbour wetlands, fisheries, or freshwater pools [4]

Grand Isle, is currently the only inhabited barrier island in Louisiana, and over the next half-century, may see a variety of outcomes in its economic and physiological morphology. The *Ground Swell* project envisions a future in which Grand Isle will eventually require adaptation due to changing

4. Koen Olthuis and David Keuning, *FLOAT! Building on Water To Combat Urban Congestion and Climate Change* (Amsterdam: FRAME publishers, 2010), 143.

a. OIL RIG NODES

b. DREDGING OPERATIONS

c. MARINA EMERGENCE

Grand Isle amidst growth: A. Marinas emerge as swell system is initially inflated, thus creating access to extensions of the landscape dredging operations. B. Build-out swell system and amplify land formation processes.

increased depths surrounding new ground allow sediment to flow further into the system, channelizing productive expansion. C. Abandoned oil rigs create nodes of offshore storage as well as become generators of aquatic

ecological habitats. this condition creates opportunities for further developing tourism and fishing economies already prevalent among island economies

economic conditions of its local economies in the oil and shipping sector, tourism, and ecological responsibilities. It is a region whose future cannot be masterplanned, rather, *Ground Swell* establishes permutations of the island's morphogenesis; intended to serve as possible outcomes for a variety of futures. If the current economic climate requires that the oil facilities expand to gain increased connectivity to their pipeline-to-oil rig infrastructure, they would employ the adaptive *Ground Swell* system, which will allow their growth to be a successive and impermanent process. If oil extraction in the Gulf dissipates and the landmass were no longer relevant in the overall composition of the island's ecosystem, the deflation of the Ground Swell cells will release the mass and the land will be carried tidally to be re-distributed in other proliferating cell systems on the island. *Ground Swell* proposes that the boundaries between industry, ecology, infrastructure, and site agents are erased. Adjacencies for such conventionally isolated networks are necessary in order to develop productive contingencies that allow entities to leverage one another and create a functioning physiological and economic environment that can operate as an ecology.

Project Advisors: Geoffrey Thün, Kathy Velikov.

Chris Holzwart is a graduate of the University of Michigan, Taubman College of Architecture and Urban Planning. His design interests seek to link technological, cultural, and ecological relationships between architectural environments and their users.

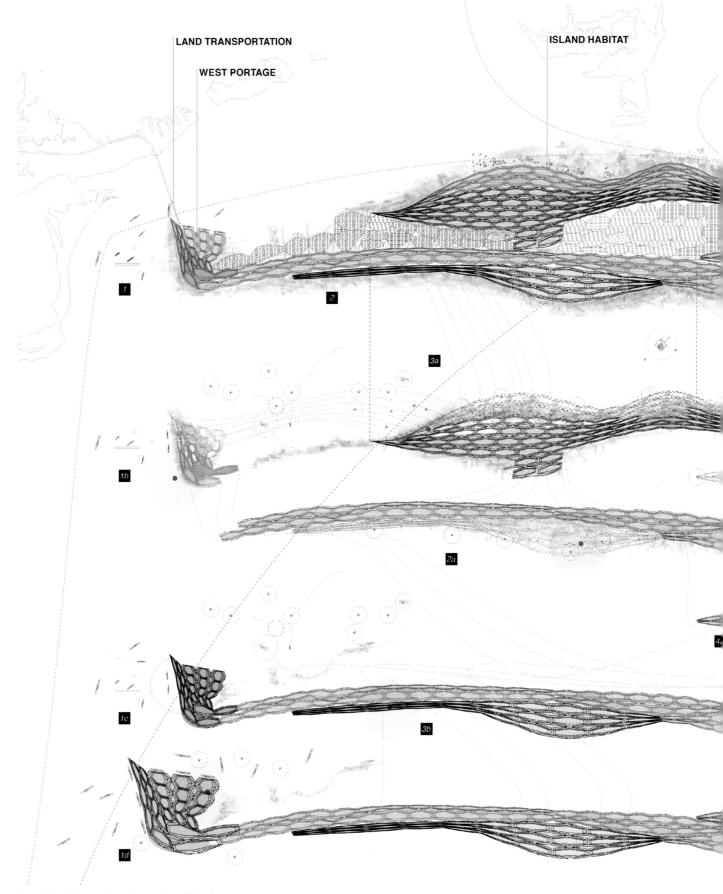

LAND TRANSPORTATION

WEST PORTAGE

ISLAND HABITAT

Ground Swell Permutations: Permutations of Grand
Isle's economic and physiological morphology.

AT EXTREMES

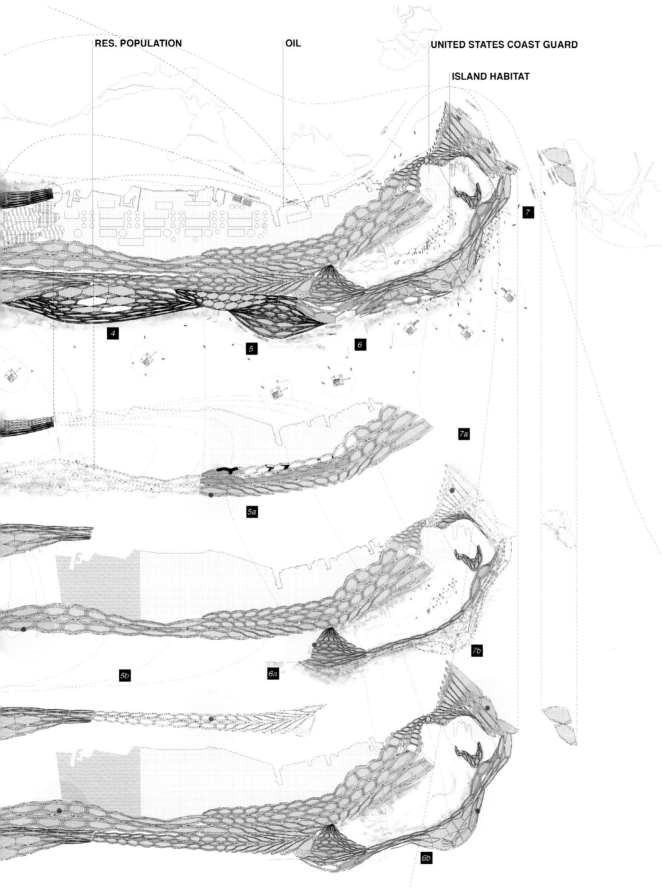

RES. POPULATION   OIL   UNITED STATES COAST GUARD

ISLAND HABITAT

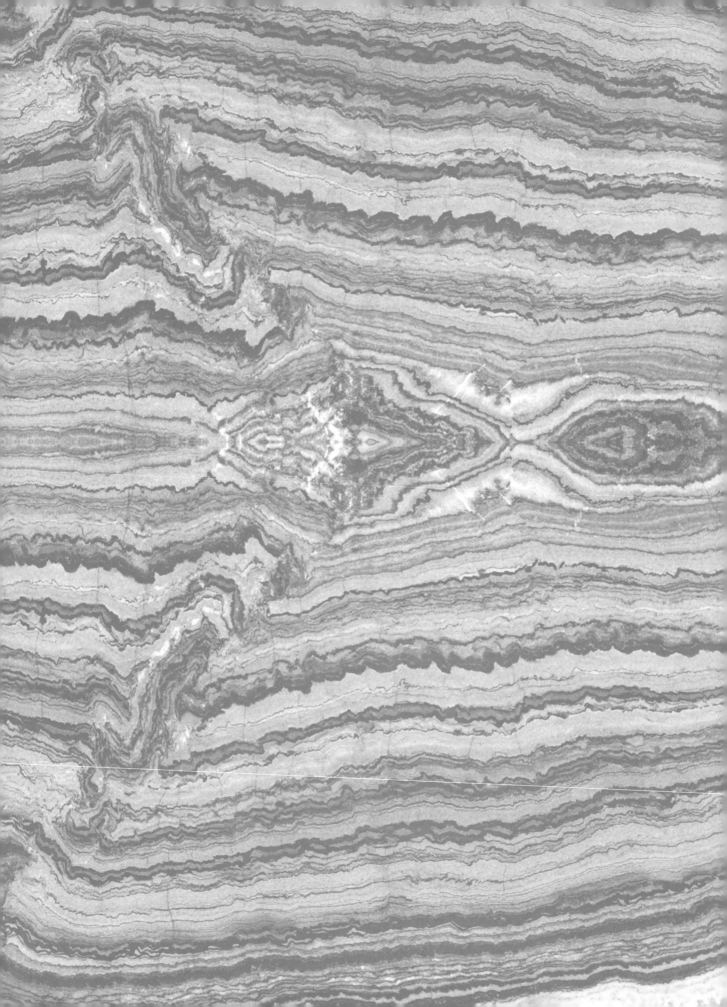

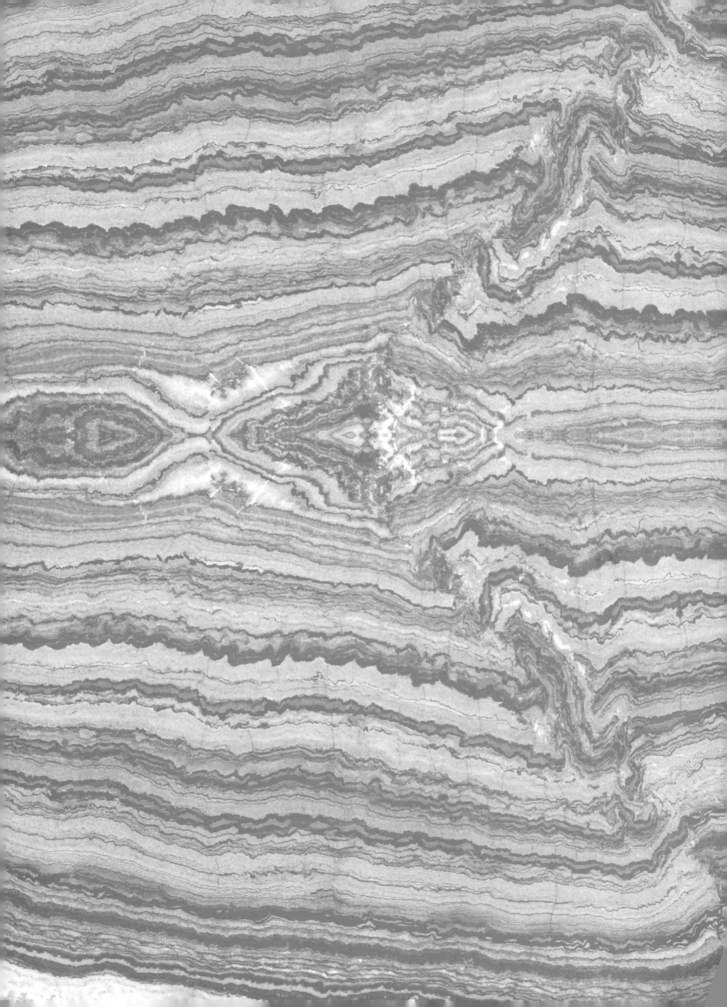

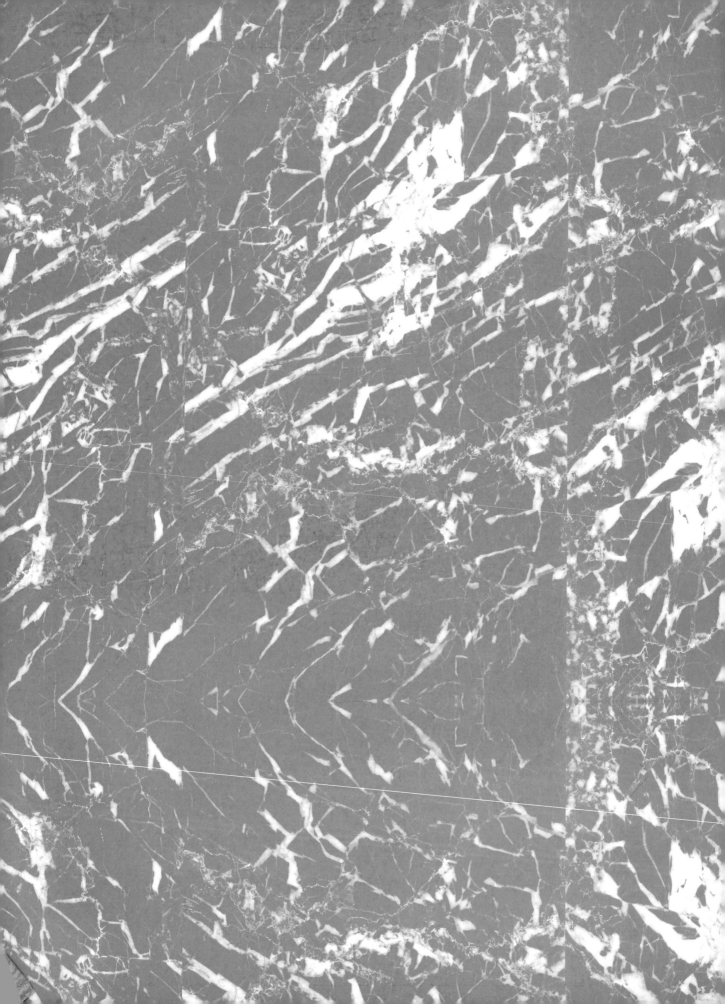